Arizona Legal Research Guide

Kathy Shimpock-Vieweg
Marianne Sidorski Alcorn

General Editor:
Kathy Shimpock-Vieweg
Contributing Authors:
Donna Larson-Bennett, John D. Leshy, Victoria K. Trotta

William S. Hein & Co., Inc.
Buffalo, New York
1992

Library of Congress Cataloging-in-Publication Data

Shimpock-Vieweg, Kathy.
Arizona Legal research guide / Kathy Shimpock-Vieweg, Marianne Sidorski Alcorn; general editor, Kathy Shimpock-Vieweg; contributing authors, Donna Larson-Bennett, John D. Leshy, Victoria K. Trotta.
p. cm.
Includes bibliographical references.
ISBN 0-89941-784-1

1. Legal research--Arizona. I. Alcorn, Marianne Sidorski.
II. Title.
KFA2475.S55 1992
340' .0720791--dc20 91-40052
CIP

Printed in the United States of America

This volume is printed on acid-free paper by
William S. Hein & Co., Inc.

To our children
Jessica and Jayme Vieweg
Geoff and Nicholas Alcorn

"...law was chaos with a full index."

T. Holland, *Essays Upon the Form of the Law.*

Contents

Preface and Acknowledgments

When Marianne Alcorn first spoke to me about the possibility of writing an *Arizona Legal Research Guide,* we both thought the project would be "quick and easy." Now, almost a year later, we've been surprised by the vast amount of information actually available. Much of this material has been ferreted out, for Arizona does not have many of the sources larger states may take for granted. There are, for example, no Arizona state legal encyclopedias and our state form books are yet to be completed. Practitioners rely mostly on state and county bar publications and analogize to California law when needed. An individual is more likely to hold the "key to knowledge" in this state than is a printed source. Arizona luckily has many skilled, knowledgeable and service-oriented public librarians willing to lend a hand to those researchers needing assistance. (See Appendix A for a listing of major Arizona Research Centers.)

This book, however, should not serve as a general guide to legal research. There are better sources available to assist with that task. For example, see Cohen, Berring, and Olson's *How to Find the Law*, and Jacobstein and Mersky's *Fundamentals of Legal Research.* The guide is intended instead for those already skilled in legal research, but needing assistance with Arizona materials. The researcher who does not understand what a digest is, or how to use a Shepard's citator, should first examine one of the previously mentioned sources.

And, finally, because this is the first legal research guide in this state, some less common sources may have been omitted. I am confident, however, that all the basic (and even some of the esoteric) sources are included. The text is presently current through 1991.

In conclusion, I would like to acknowledge the assistance of the many individuals and organizations who helped to make this book a reality: Marianne Alcorn for initiating this project, acting as coordinator of much administrative work and serving as joint author; John Leshy, Victoria Trotta and Donna Larson-Bennett for their erudite contributions (and especially to "Tory" for her editorial suggestions, good wishes and ever present humor); O'Connor, Cavanagh, Anderson, Westover, Killingsworth & Beshears for their "corporate" support of this project and individually to Larry L. Smith for his encouragement; Shirley Macias, Pam Wilkinson and Viki Lasher (special thanks are due to Shirley and Pam for their skillful and tenacious research); Arizona State University College of Law; Steptoe and Johnson (Phoenix office) for assistance with word processing; Joe Bedgood, Gail Marion, Dorothy Molstad (and staff) at West Publishing Co. for their ever extraordinary service; Mark Scott, Karla Ekblaw and Carol J. Glaser-Atkins at Mead Data Central; Nicholas J. Wallwork, Glenn Feldman, Lucy A. Trujillo, Sierra Russell and Jonathan Rose for their comments and suggestions on specific chapters; Carol S. Mulford for her *invaluable* and sacrificial effort to input numerous drafts of my text; Cheryle Woods for the final word processing, clean-up and editing; the William S. Hein & Co., Inc. for their interest and backing of this project through numerous delays; and lastly, to all those unnamed family and friends who stuck by me through the insanity of writing a book.

KSV

Author Biographies

Kathy Shimpock-Vieweg is the Director of Library Services for the law firm of O'Connor, Cavanagh, Anderson, Westover, Killingsworth & Beshears in Phoenix, Arizona. She holds a B.A. from Colorado College, a J.D. from the University of Wyoming and an M.L.L. from the University of Denver. Ms. Shimpock-Vieweg is the author of several articles with topics ranging from marketing law libraries to bibliographies on international antitrust law and bankruptcy. She is a member of the State Bar of Arizona. She has also worked at the University of Bridgeport College of Law as Assistant Professor of Law and Law Librarian, and at Stanford University College of Law as Assistant Librarian. In addition, she has consulted with law firms for over ten years.

Marianne Alcorn has been a Reference Librarian at Arizona State University, College of Law Library since 1980. Prior to this position she was a Reference and Circulation Librarian at the University of Washington Law Library. She has taught legal research annually through the Arizona State University, Center for Executive Development paralegal program. She holds a B.A. from the University of Washington and an M.L.S. from the University of Southern California.

Victoria K. Trotta is the Law Librarian for the law firm of Lewis and Roca in Phoenix, Arizona. She holds a B.A. from Occidental College, an M.L.S. from the University of California, Los Angeles, and a J.D. from the University of Southern California. She has previously worked as the Associate Law Librarian at the University of Southern California College of Law. She is a frequent participant in educational programs of the American Association of Law Librarians, upcoming Chair of its Private Law Libraries Section, and has written in the area of Law Librarianship.

John D. Leshy is Professor of Law at Arizona State University College of Law where he teaches among other topics Arizona Constitutional Law, Constitutional Law and Natural Resources Law. He has an A.B. and J.D. from Harvard University. He is author of *The Mining Law: A Study in Perpetual Motion* and comparative law topics. His forthcoming book to be published by Greenwood Press in 1992 is *The Arizona State Constitution: A Reference Guide.*

Donna Larson-Bennett is Government Documents Librarian at Arizona State University, College of Law Library. She is the author of *Guide to U.S. Government Directories, 1970-80* and *Guide to U.S. Government Directories, Volume 2: 1980-84*. She is a past president of the Phoenix Area Association of Law Libraries. She holds an A.B. in Russian Language and Literature and an M.A.L.S., both from the University of Michigan.

Chapter 1

The Arizona Constitution

John D. Leshy

A. Introduction

Admitted to the Union as the forty-eighth state on February 14, 1912, Arizona is still operating under its original constitution. The charter was drafted in the fall of 1910, a little more than a year before statehood. It is saturated with provisions reflecting the dominance of labor and Progressive movement interests at the constitutional convention. It includes initiative, referendum, and recall processes, a constitutional commission to regulate corporations, and a number of other features relatively radical for its time.

The constitution has been amended slightly more than one hundred times since statehood, but has not undergone fundamental revision. Although most changes have been relatively minor, the charter has not escaped modern constitutional trends. For example, Article VI, dealing with the judiciary, was overhauled in 1960, and a merit selection process for judges was added in 1974. More recently, major amendments have been made to Article IX, dealing with public debt, revenue, and taxation, in an effort to place fiscal limitations on state and local government. These have added substantially to the constitution's length.

Forthcoming in 1992 from Greenwood Press (an imprint of the Greenwood Publishing Group, Inc., Westport, Connecticut) is Professor John D. Leshy's *The Arizona State Constitution: A Reference Guide.* The book will contain an essay on the state's constitutional history, the current text of the constitution with a section-by-section commentary, a bibliographic essay, table of cases, and a comprehensive index.[1] It should prove a welcome addition to the literature, because to date relatively little commentary has been published on the formation, evolution, and interpretation of the Arizona Constitution. This brief essay highlights the available sources for the reader wishing to inquire further.

The Arizona constitution is located in volumes 1 and 1A of the *Arizona Revised Statutes Annotated* published by the West Publishing Company. It has case annotations, historical notes, references to some law review articles and to West key numbers. (See Illustration A, p.12.) It is updated annually by pocket supplements. Volume 1A contains an index to the Constitution. The General Index can also be used. More current developments can be followed through the *Arizona Legislative Service* and the *Interim Annotation Service,* both published by West. Very recent amendments to the Constitution can be obtained from the Secretary of State's Office.

The Michie Company also publishes an edition of the *Arizona Revised Statutes,* which is not annotated. (See Illustration B, p.13.) The Arizona constitution is located in volume 4. It does not have a separate index so the general index must be used. It is a soft-bound set which is replaced each year with a new edition. A paperbound supplement to the *Arizona Revised Statutes* is also issued annually containing legislation from any special sessions of the Legislature.

B. Territorial Antecedents

The best territorial history, which covers Colorado, New Mexico and Utah, as well as Arizona, is Howard Roberts Lamar's *The Far Southwest 1846-1912* (New Haven: Yale U. Press, 1966). It contains an excellent bibliographic essay. Robert W. Larson's *New Mexico's Quest for Statehood 1846-1912* (Albuquerque: University of New Mexico Press, 1968), also addresses Arizona's fight for statehood, which was intertwined with New Mexico's, in considerable detail.

Another highly informative work is Jay J. Wagoner's *Arizona Territory: 1863-1912* (Tucson: University of Arizona Press, 1970). Subtitled "A Political History," it also contains a useful bibliography. The other major source on the territorial period is *Legislative History: Arizona 1864-1912* (Phoenix: Manufacturing Stationers, 1926). Assembled by the State Historian, George H. Kelly, it contains summaries of each territorial legislative session, a biographical section and a miscellany of other information, including an article on the struggle for statehood by Marcus Smith, formerly a territorial delegate to Congress.

1 This chapter has been drawn from material prepared for Professor Leshy's book, and is included here with the kind permission of Greenwood Press. The author appreciates the helpful comments of Professor Emeritus Bruce B. Mason, Arizona State University, on a draft of this chapter.

William F. Swindler's compilation, *Sources and Documents of United States Constitutions* (Dobbs Ferry, NY: Oceana Pubs., 1973) 1: 234-316, contains relevant territorial documents, the draft constitution of 1891 (a manifestation of an earlier effort to gain statehood), the 1910 enabling act and constitution, and the statehood resolutions, President Taft's veto message, and the proclamation of statehood.

C. The Constitutional Convention of 1910

The most comprehensive work is J. Leshy, "The Making of the Arizona Constitution," *Arizona State Law Journal* 20 (1988): 1-113. It references other available sources. A shorter treatment is Gordon M. Bakken, "The Arizona Constitutional Convention of 1910," *Arizona State Law Journal* 1978 (1978): 1-30. An earlier, out-of-print work focusing on the statehood process and the constitutional convention is J. Morris Richards' slim *The Birth of Arizona: The Baby State* (Phoenix: no publisher given, 1940).

Gordon M. Bakken's *Rocky Mountain Constitution Making 1850-1912* (New York: Greenwood Press, 1987) usefully examines, in comparative fashion, some fundamental issues involved in the drafting of the original constitutions of the states of Colorado, Idaho, Montana, Nevada, New Mexico, Utah and Wyoming, as well as Arizona.

1. *Researching the Deliberations of the Arizona Constitutional Convention of 1910*

The convention process typically worked this way: A proposed piece of constitutional text, as broad as an entire multi-section article or as narrow as a single sentence, would be introduced by a delegate or, in a few cases, by a number of delegates. These were called propositions, and they were referred to the appropriate convention committee upon introduction. The convention created twenty-one standing committees to address particular subjects. They ranged in size from three to thirteen delegates.

The committee to which a specific proposition was assigned could ignore it or recommend that the full convention adopt it, either as introduced or as modified in committee. Committee proposals were debated on the floor of the convention, sometimes cursorily and sometimes extensively. Occasionally the full convention sent proposals back to the committees, where they might be buried or reworked and reported back to the convention.

The following sets out the information that is available on the convention's workings.

a. The Propositions

The convention kept no formal record of the substance of the propositions that were introduced, but several convention delegates later donated their sets of the propositions to the state library. There were 153 propositions in all.

b. Committee Deliberations

There was apparently never any effort to keep minutes or other records of committee deliberations. Moreover, committee recommendations to the floor were rarely accompanied by any narrative explanation or report other than a "do pass" recommendation. Contemporary newspaper accounts provide little insight into committee meetings, although they were apparently open to the press.

c. Floor Proceedings

Early on the delegates contentiously debated whether to keep any report of the floor proceedings. Ultimately they decided, by a narrow margin, to maintain such records, which were called "journals" and furnished to convention delegates. The journals kept proved not very satisfactory. This may have been due to the lack of competent stenographers (remarks were apparently initially transcribed by hand), to delegates' concern about expense or how posterity would view their remarks, and to the fact that delegates sometimes spoke simultaneously in the debates.

Near the end of the convention proceedings, the delegates addressed the question of whether and how to prepare the so-called "verbatim report" for publication. A key issue in the debate was the accuracy of the stenographic account in the journals. They omitted some delegates' speeches entirely, and a number of delegates alleged inaccurate transcriptions in other places. Almost no one appeared satisfied with leaving the journals alone, and after considering whether to destroy them or to correct, edit, and publish them, the majority favored the latter. To this end the convention authorized President Hunt to create a small bipartisan committee of two delegates to prepare the report for publication.

This task was apparently never completed. Several copies of the journals survive. Many of them contain handwritten notes, but it is not clear whether these notes were made by delegates, nor when they were made. In 1925 the State Librarian, Con P. Cronin, compiled a clean copy of the journals. This Journal, as it styled itself, omits handwritten notes, yet is no more complete than the journals from which it was derived. Some three hundred separate delegate speeches (ranging from a paragraph to as many as two or three type-written pages) are omitted.

Another record of proceedings is the so-called "verbatim report." This was apparently kept by the convention clerks for their own use. It has the advantage of containing most, though not all, of the longer speeches made on the convention floor that are omitted from the journals. Only two copies of the original, mostly-typed verbatim report survive. One was Convention President Hunt's copy, which he donated to the University of Arizona library. The other was kept for many years on open file at the State Library in Phoenix.

Perhaps the revision committee appointed by Convention President Hunt did try to carry out its assignment, because both extant copies show extensive passages crossed out by hand, without explanation and other passages with numerous longhand alterations. There is, however, no way to ascertain the source or reliability of these changes. Also, some parts are missing from both surviving copies, although they are not the same parts. In short, the verbatim report is a mess, although it is not without utility.

The convention kept minutes which were published almost immediately. *Minutes of the Constitutional Convention of the Territory of Arizona* (Phoenix:

Phoenix Printing Co., 1910). For the most part they merely record dry details such as the opening and closing times of each session, attendance of the delegates, and the results of voting on formal motions and numbered propositions. These details are not, however, available from any of the other sources. The minutes do contain a very brief, general subject index.

The floor deliberations of the convention were open to the press, and contemporary newspaper accounts occasionally provide somewhat more information than the official accounts derived from the propositions, minutes, journal, and verbatim report, although it should be noted that delegates sometimes voiced complaints about inaccurate press coverage.

Given the unsatisfactory state of records or accounts of convention proceedings, researchers of the Arizona Constitutional Convention confront considerable challenges. Neither the propositions nor the journal nor the verbatim report is indexed. The only way to locate discussions of a particular topic has been, first, to read through the propositions to identify the one(s) addressing the topic, then to use the index to the minutes to identify the days on which those propositions were considered on the convention floor, and then to search the journal, the verbatim report, and contemporary newspapers to find accounts of the relevant discussion(s) on the identified days.

Because neither the minutes nor the journal nor the verbatim report sets out the specific language of the propositions (either as originally offered by a delegate or as reported by a committee), constant cross-referencing is required. In some cases, in fact, the specific language being proposed by a committee to the floor does not exist in any of these sources, and can only be inferred from the debates.

The researcher's task has been substantially simplified with the publication of *The Records of the Arizona Constitutional Convention of 1910* by the State Bar of Arizona for the Arizona Supreme Court in 1991. This work is the product of Professor John Goff of Phoenix College who has painstakingly assembled all the available information on the convention from all the sources described above and provided a general index. This book will not, however, contain how the delegates voted on individual propositions, but that information is available in the published minutes.

D. Researching the Amendments to the Arizona Constitution

The office of the Secretary of State in the State Capitol has publicity pamphlets for most of the amendment propositions that have appeared on the ballot. A few are missing, however, particularly from the early years. Contemporary newspaper accounts during the campaigns may also contain useful information. The Secretary of State of Arizona has published the *Arizona Blue Book 1986* (with periodic supplements), that contains voting statistics on all proposed constitutional amendments that have been submitted to the voters since statehood.

Like most states, there is very little official information kept regarding the passage of bills in the legislature, including bills that propose constitutional amendments.

Brief discussions of some of the amendments are found in some of the histories cited in the next section.

E. Arizona Constitutional Evolution and Interpretation

1. *General Works*

A general overview is provided in the college-level text, *Constitutional Government in Arizona* (Tempe, AZ: Cleber Publishing Co., 7th ed. 1982), by Professors Bruce B. Mason and Heinz R. Hink. Mason, John P. White, and Russell B. Roush have published *A Guide to the Arizona Constitution* (Scottsdale, AZ: Cross Plains Publishers, 1982), a section-by-section commentary.

An earlier secondary school/college text is *Constitutional Development of Arizona* (Phoenix, AZ: no publisher given, 1933), written by then Professor, later Congressman, John R. Murdock. Donald R. Van Petten's *The Constitution and Government of Arizona* (Phoenix, AZ: Sun Country Inc., 1956) is another general, college-text treatment of the subject.

General Arizona histories typically spend a few pages discussing the constitutional framework and background. An early work was James H. McClintock's three-volume *Arizona* (Chicago, IL: S.J. Clarke Publishing Co., 1916). See especially vol. 2, pp. 361-83. The third volume contains biographical sketches. Another similar work is Richard E. Sloan and Ward R. Adams, *History of Arizona,* 4 vols. (Phoenix, AZ: Record Publishing Co., 1930). See especially vol. 2, pp. 208-225. Volumes 3 and 4 contain biographical sketches. Frank Lockwood's *Pioneer Days in Arizona: From the Spanish Occupation to Statehood* (New York, NY: The Macmillan Co., 1932) contains some material on the constitution, as does R.K. Wyllys in his *Arizona: The History of a Frontier State* (Phoenix, AZ: Hobson & Herr, 1950), and Edward H. Peplow, Jr. in his three-volume *History of Arizona* (New York, NY: Lewis Historical Publishing Co., 1958). See especially vol. 2, pp. 1-30. Volume two also has an extensive bibliography at pp. 549-65. (The third volume contains histories of prominent Arizona families).

The University of Arizona published *Arizona: Its People and Resources* (James L. Cross, Elizabeth H. Shaw, and Kathleen Scheifele, eds., 1960), on its 75th anniversary. This volume has a modestly useful, though of course somewhat outdated, discussion of the Arizona constitution and government. Gerald Hansen's *Arizona: Its Constitution and Government* (Washington, D.C.: University Press of America, 1979), is not useful.

Professor John S. Goff's *Arizona Civilization* (Cave Creek, AZ: Black Mountain Press, 2d ed. 1970) contains some information on the constitution and its evolution, arranged by topics. Goff also published a biography of the influential convention president and seven-time governor, *George W.P. Hunt and His Arizona* (Pasadena, CA: Socio Technical Publications, 1973); a useful *Arizona Biographical Dictionary* (Cave Creek, AZ: Black Mountain Press, 1983); and, with Myles E. Hill, *Arizona Past and Present* (Cave Creek, AZ: Black Mountain Press, 1970), a college-level text on state history and government.

James M. Murphy's *Law, Courts, and Lawyers* (Tucson, AZ: University of Arizona Press, 1970) contains some materials on the evolution of the judicial system under the constitution. Roy D. Morey's *Politics and Legislation: The Office of the Governor in Arizona* (Tucson, AZ: University of Arizona Press, 1965) focuses on the governor and the legislative process and its evolution since statehood. James Byrkit's *Forging the Copper Collar* (Tucson, AZ: University of Arizona Press, 1982) examines labor politics in early Arizona, and devotes considerable discussion to labor's influence on the constitutional convention.

In 1949, the state legislature created a special legislative committee on state operations that contracted with a private consulting firm, Griffenhagen & Associates, to produce a comprehensive report on, and recommendations for improving, the structure and organization of state government. This so-called "Griffenhagen Report," along with some supporting materials, was published as a supplement to the Journal of the Senate in the first special session of the Nineteenth Legislature in 1950. It contains useful information on the evolution of state government since statehood, in the process addressing a number of constitutional issues. A number of its recommendations, such as for limits on the size of the legislature and longer terms for state executive offices, were eventually adopted as constitutional amendments.

The Arizona Academy, a private nonprofit institution formed in 1962, semiannually holds Town Halls at which invited community leaders address various issues facing the state. The Academy usually commissions research reports on the topic, which it then publishes along with the report of the Town Hall discussion. Several Town Halls have dealt with constitutional issues, including one in 1964 on the subject of revising or replacing the constitution. See Arizona Academy, *Fifth Town Hall on Revision of Arizona's Constitution* (Tempe, AZ: Arizona State University, 1964). The background study for this convocation was prepared by Professors Bruce B. Mason and Heinz R. Hink, entitled *Revision of Arizona's Constitution* (Phoenix, AZ: Arizona Academy, 1964). Earlier works on the same subject are Mason and Hink's "Revision of the Arizona Constitution: A Commentary" (Tempe, AZ: Arizona State University, Bureau of Governmental Research, Research Study No. 4, 1961); and Mason's "A Model Constitution for Arizona?" *Public Affairs Bulletin* (Tempe, AZ: Arizona State University, Bureau of Governmental Research, vol. 1, no. 4, 1961).

Monographs and articles in political science, public administration, and historical journals have occasionally addressed Arizona constitutional issues. Helpful ones include Neal D. Houghton, "Arizona Experience with the Initiative and Referendum", *New Mexico Historical Review* vol. XXIX, no. 3 (July 1954) :183-209; David A. Bingham, *Constitutional Municipal Home Rule in Arizona* (Tucson, AZ: Bureau of Business and Public Research, University of Arizona, November 1960); and David A. Bingham, "Legislative Apportionment: The Arizona Experience," *Arizona Review of Business and Public Administration* (Tucson, AZ: Bureau of Business and Public Research, University of Arizona, vol. 11, no. 10, October 1962).

2. *Law Journal Articles*

Compared to many other states, there is relatively little legal commentary on Arizona constitutional topics. An assortment of articles on Arizona constitutional issues have appeared in the law journals published four times each year by the law schools at the University of Arizona (since 1959, as the *Arizona Law Review*) and Arizona State University (from 1969-73 as *Law and the Social Order,* and since 1974 as the *Arizona State University Law Journal*).

A good place to start is a special symposium issue in volume 20 of the *Arizona State Law Journal,* published in 1988. Since the publication of this symposium, the pace of law journal commentary has quickened.

From 1968 until 1984, the *Arizona Law Review* annually published compendia of student analyses of significant appellate court decisions in Arizona. (Until 1973, the review covered Arizona Supreme Court decisions only; thereafter, it covered court of appeals decisions as well.) Some of these decisions addressed Arizona constitutional issues. These compendia are found at *Arizona Law Review* 10 (1968):148; 11 (1969):61; 12 (1970):89; 13 (1971):315; 14 (1972):409; 15 (1973):593; 16 (1974):489; 17 (1975):640; 18 (1976):585; 19 (1977):485; 20 (1978):985; 21 (1979):136; 22 (1980):1055; 23 (1981):371; 23 (1981):1298; 24 (1982):105; 25 (1983):491.

Law review articles addressing the Arizona constitution in general or broad topics under it include:

- John D. Leshy, "The Making of the Arizona Constitution," *Arizona State Law Journal* 20 (1988):1-113.
- Gordon M. Bakken, "The Arizona Constitutional Convention of 1910", *Arizona State Law Journal* (1978):1-30.
- Stanley G. Feldman and David L. Abney, "The Double Security of Federalism: Protecting Individual Liberty under the Arizona Constitution," *Arizona State Law Journal* 20 (1988):115-150.
- Steven J. Twist and Len L. Munsil, "The Double Threat of Judicial Activism: Inventing New 'Rights' in State Constitutions," *Arizona State Law Journal* 21 (1989):1005-1065.
- Donald W. Jansen, "Arizona's Constitutional Restraints on the Legislative Powers to Tax and Spend," *Arizona State Law Journal* 20 (1988):181-208.
- Paul Marcus, "State Constitutional Protection for Defendants in Criminal Prosecutions," *Arizona State Law Journal* 20 (1988):151-179.
- John M. Roll, "Merit Selection: The Arizona Experience," *Arizona State Law Journal* 22 (1990):837-894.
- Heinz R. Hink, "Judicial Reform in Arizona," *Arizona Law Review* 6 (1964):13-26.

Other articles that address more specific topics arising under the Arizona constitution include:

- Noel Fidel, "Preeminently a Political Institution: The Right of Arizona Juries to Nullify the Law of Contributory Negligence," *Arizona State Law Journal* 23 (1991):1.
- Thomas W. Bade, "Safe Yield Versus Maximum Return: The Constitutionality of the Arizona Groundwater Code as Applied to State Trust Land," *Arizona State Law Journal* 22 (1990):261.
- Bill Eggleston, "The Preferred Right to Lease State Trust Land," *Arizona State Law Journal* 21 (1989):793.
- James Weinstein, "The Language of Impeachment," *Arizona State Law Journal* 20 (1988):209.
- Kathleen Coughenour, "The Right to Recover Damages: Tort Reform and the Arizona Constitution," *Arizona State Law Journal, 20 (1988):227.*
- Deborah Scott Engelby, "The Corporation Commission: Preserving its Independence," *Arizona State Law Journal* 20 (1988):241.
- Douglas C. Erickson, "Undermining the Arizona Constitution: Recent Developments in Dramshop Law," *Arizona State Law Journal* 20 (1988):263.
- Tom Quigley, "Do Silver Platters Have a Place in State-Federal Relations? Using Illegally Obtained Evidence in Criminal Prosecutions," *Arizona State Law Journal* 20 (1988):285.
- David Smith, "Economic Substantive Due Process in Arizona: A Survey," *Arizona State Law Journal* 20 (1988):327.
- Barbara Callaway, "The Right to Die Under the Arizona Constitution," *Arizona State Law Journal* 20 (1988):345.
- M. Maureen Anders, "Gubernatorial Constitutional Power - Executive Oversight of Rulemaking in Arizona," Arizona State Law Journal (1986):243.
- Barbara L. Borden, "Legislative Review of Agency Rules in Arizona: A Constitutional Analysis," *Arizona State Law Journal* (1985):493.
- David L. Abney, "Nunchakus and the Right to Bear Arms in Arizona," *Arizona Law Review* 24 (1982):134.
- Roberta H. Schulte, "Inherent Judicial Power and Regulation of the Practice of Law," *Arizona Law Review* 23 (1981):1313.
- David Edward Borcher, "Fair Trial and Free Press: Preliminary Hearing, Gateway to Prejudice," *Law and the Social Order* (1973):903.

The indices to the two journals, or the standard *Index of Legal Periodicals,* may be consulted for others. A recent publication, *Constitutions of the States:*

A State by State Guide and Bibliography to Current Scholarly Research. Bernard D. Reams, Jr., and Stuart D. Yoak, eds. (Dobbs Ferry, NY: Oceana, 1988), 10-25, is not very helpful because it simply lists, without discrimination, journal articles that discuss Arizona constitutional issues with those that do not.

3. Court Decisions

Most of the court decisions and attorney general's opinions that interpret specific constitutional provisions can be located in the "annotations" (brief summaries with legal citations) found in the first two volumes of the *Arizona Revised Statutes Annotated* published (with annual updates in pocket parts in the back of each volume) by the West Publishing Company of St. Paul, Minnesota. A *caveat* to their use: The annotations are both under-inclusive (sometimes failing to capture all of the decisions that discuss the Arizona constitution) and over-inclusive (sometimes listing cases where the court focused exclusively on the federal rather than the state constitution). Thus, these annotations should only be used as a starting point.

Shepard's Arizona Citations (Statute Edition) (Colorado Springs, CO: Shepard's McGraw-Hill, 3d ed. 1985, at pp. 49-65) (with periodic supplements), lists citations to the Arizona constitution in reported decisions of Arizona and federal courts, in articles in numerous legal periodicals, in several legal texts, in annotations and in laws of Arizona.

Modern computer databases may also be used to locate constitutional decisions. Both WESTLAW and LEXIS can act as a citator to find relevant Arizona cases. (See Chapter 10 for further information.) The annotated Arizona constitution is available only on WESTLAW.

4. Unpublished Materials

The Arizona Room and the collection of the Arizona Historical Foundation in Hayden Library at Arizona State University include unpublished material that bear on the Arizona Constitution, such as the papers of George W.P. Hunt. The University of Arizona Library in Tucson and the State Capitol Library also have some relevant materials. Finally, some unpublished theses have addressed Arizona constitutional issues, and are cited in the various bibliographies noted above, and in Leshy, "The Making of the Arizona Constitution," *Arizona State Law Journal* 20 (1988): 1-113. Some of these works are the most helpful sources for particular constitutional issues, and are listed below, in chronological order.

Tru A. McGinnis, "The Influence of Organized Labor on the Making of the Arizona Constitution" (Tucson, AZ: University of Arizona, 1930, unpublished M.A. thesis).

Charles F. Todd, "The Initiative and Referendum in Arizona" (Tucson, AZ: University of Arizona, 1931, unpublished M.A. thesis).

Y. LaCagnina, "The Role of the Recall of Judges Issue in the Struggle for Arizona Statehood" (Tucson, AZ: University of Arizona, 1951, unpublished M.A. thesis).

Calvin N. Brice, "The Constitutional Convention of Arizona" (Tempe, AZ: Arizona State University, 1953, unpublished M.A. thesis).

J. Patrick White, "Progressivism and the Judiciary: A Study of the Movement for Judicial Reform 1901-1917" (Ann Arbor, MI: University of Michigan, 1957, unpublished Ph.D. thesis) (while dealing with the subject on a national basis, this work devotes considerable attention to Arizona because of its central role in the movement).

David R. Barney, "Arizona and Public Utility Control: A Problem in Constitutional Law and Politics" (Tempe, AZ: Arizona State University, 1961, unpublished M.A. thesis).

A.V. Johnson, "Governor G.W.P. Hunt and Organized Labor" (Tucson, AZ: University of Arizona, 1964, unpublished M.A. thesis).

M.H. Wilson, "The Gubernatorial Career of George W.P. Hunt of Arizona" (Tempe, AZ: Arizona State University, 1973, unpublished Ph.D. thesis).

Illustration A

Art. 4 Pt. 2 § 13 CONSTITUTION OF ARIZONA

§ 13. Subject and title of bills

Section 13. Every Act shall embrace but one subject and matters properly connected therewith, which subject shall be expressed in the title; but if any subject shall be embraced in an Act which shall not be expressed in the title, such Act shall be void only as to so much thereof as shall not be embraced in the title.

Cross References

Appropriation bills limited to one subject, see Const. Art. 4, Pt. 2, § 20.

Library References

Statutes ⚷64(2), 107(1).
C.J.S. Statutes §§ 92 et seq., 217, 218.

Notes of Decisions

In general 1
Amendments, scope of title 6
Animals 13
Appropriations 11
Banks and banking 12
Burden of proof 31
Certification of title 9
Civil service 14
Contracts 15
Corporations 16
Crimes and offenses 17, 18
  In general 17
  Severability 18
Gambling 19
Garnishment 20
Highways 21
Index to legislation, scope of title 5
Industrial development 22
Juries 23
Liberal construction 3
Power districts 24
Public improvements 25
Public lands 26
Public officers and employees 27
Purpose 2
Railroads 28
Repeals, scope of title 7
Review 32
Scope of title 4–7
  In general 4
  Amendments 6
  Index to legislation 5
  Repeals 7
Severability
  In general 10
  Crimes and offenses 18
Sufficiency of title 8
Taxes 29
Traffic rules and regulations 30

1. In general

In determining the extent and operation of an act, the court must consider not only the law itself but also its title. In re Twenty-One Slot Machines (1951) 72 Ariz. 408, 236 P.2d 733; Maricopa County v. Douglas (1949) 69 Ariz. 35, 208 P.2d 646; Valley Nat. Bank of Phœnix v. Gloyer (1945) 62 Ariz. 538, 159 P.2d 292.

When the body of an act is ambiguous in its meaning, the court may take the title into consideration. Garrison v. Luke (1938) 52 Ariz. 50, 78 P.2d 1120.

This section does not apply to constitutional amendments proposed by initiative petition. Barth v. White (1932) 40 Ariz. 548, 14 P.2d 743.

Though legislation must fall within terms of its title, context of bill is controlling as respects its purpose. Rowland v. McBride (1929) 35 Ariz. 511, 281 P. 207.

This section refers only to titles of acts as enacted by the legislature and has no application to section headings used in the completed code. Op.Atty.Gen. No. 66–25–L.

2. Purpose

Requirement of this section that every act embrace but one subject and matters properly connected therewith which shall be expressed in the title is designed to enable legislators and the public, upon reading the title, to know what to expect in the body of the act so that no one would be surprised as to the subjects dealt with by the act. State v. Sutton (1976) 27 Ariz.App. 134, 551 P.2d 583, affirmed in part, reversed in part, on

496

Illustration B

Section 24. The enacting clause of every bill enacted by the Legislature shall be as follows: "Be it enacted by the Legislature of the State of Arizona," or when the Initiative is used: "Be it enacted by the People of the State of Arizona."

§ 25. Continuity of governmental operations in emergency

Section 25. The legislature, in order to insure continuity of State and local governmental operations in periods of emergency resulting from disasters caused by enemy attack, shall have the power and the immediate duty to:

1. Provide for prompt and temporary succession to the powers and duties of public offices, of whatever nature and whether filled by election or appointment, the incumbents of which may become unavailable for carrying on the powers and duties of such offices.
2. Adopt such other measures as may be necessary and proper for insuring the continuity of governmental operations.

In the exercise of the powers hereby conferred, the Legislature shall in all respects conform to the requirements of this Constitution except to the extent that in the judgment of the Legislature so to do would be impracticable or would admit of undue delay.
1962

ARTICLE V. EXECUTIVE DEPARTMENT

§ 1. Executive department; state officers; terms; election; residence and office at seat of government; duties

Section 1. A. The executive department shall consist of the governor, secretary of state, state treasurer, attorney general, and superintendent of public instruction, each of whom shall hold office for four years beginning on the first Monday of January, 1971 next after the regular general election in 1970.

B. The person having a majority of the votes cast for the office voted for shall be elected. If no person receives a majority of the votes cast for the office, a second election shall be held as prescribed by law between the persons receiving the highest and second highest number of votes cast for the office. The person receiving the highest number of votes at the second election for the office is elected, but if the two persons have an equal number of votes for the office, the two houses of the legislature at its next regular session shall elect forthwith, by joint ballot, one of such persons for said office.

C. The officers of the executive department during their terms of office shall reside at the seat of government where they shall keep their offices and the public records, books, and papers. They shall perform such duties as are prescribed by the constitution and as may be provided by law.
1989

§ 2. Eligibility to state offices

Section 2. No person shall be eligible to any of the offices mentioned in section 1 of this article except a person of the age of not less than twenty-five years, who shall have been for ten years next preceding his election a citizen of the United States, and for five years next preceding his election a citizen of Arizona.
1989

§ 3. Governor, commander-in-chief of military forces

Section 3. The Governor shall be commander-in-chief of the military forces of the State, except when such forces shall be called into the service of the United States.

§ 4. Governor; powers and duties; special sessions of legislature; message and recommendations

Section 4. The Governor shall transact all executive business with the officers of the Government, civil and military, and may require information in writing from the officers in the Executive Department upon any subject relating to the duties of their respective offices. He shall take care that the laws be faithfully executed. He may convene the Legislature in extraordinary session. He shall communicate, by message, to the Legislature at every session the condition of the State, and recommend such matters as he shall deem expedient.

§ 5. Reprieves, commutations and pardons

Section 5. The Governor shall have power to grant reprieves, commutation, and pardons, after convictions, for all offenses except treason and cases of impeachment, upon such conditions and with such restrictions and limitations as may be provided by law.

§ 6. Death, resignation, removal or disability of governor; succession to office; impeachment, absence from state or temporary disability

Section 6. In the event of the death of the Governor, or his resignation, removal from office, or permanent disability to discharge the duties of the office, the Secretary of State, if holding by election, shall succeed to the office of Governor until his successor shall be elected and shall qualify. If the Secretary of State be holding otherwise than by election, or shall fail to qualify as Governor, the Attorney General, the State Treasurer, or the Superintendent of Public Instruction, if holding by election, shall, in the order named, succeed to the office of Governor. The taking of the oath of office as Governor by any person specified in this section shall constitute resignation from the office by virtue of the holding of which he qualifies as Governor. Any successor to the office shall become Governor in fact and entitled to all of the emoluments, powers and duties of Governor upon taking the oath of office.

In the event of the impeachment of the Governor, his absence from the State, or other temporary disability to discharge the duties of the office, the powers and duties of the office of Governor shall devolve upon the same person as in case of vacancy, but only until the disability ceases.
1968

Chapter 2

Arizona Statutory Research

Kathy Shimpock-Vieweg

A. Introduction

Finding applicable statutory law is essential to most legal questions and should, therefore, be the first step taken when researching the law. State legislation can be broadly construed to include the constitution, statutes and session laws, and municipal and interstate compacts. The strategy for state statutory research is similar to that found in the federal model.[1]

Arizona's statutory law is a maze of session laws and numerous compilations - some authorized and some unauthorized by the legislature. Many of the earlier versions were printed in small numbers and are often difficult to locate. Not until 1956 did Arizona have an adequately indexed code.

1 Morris L. Cohen, Robert C. Berring, and Kent C. Olsen, *How to Find the Law,* 9th ed. (St. Paul, MN: West Publishing Co., 1989), 144.

Arizona's law itself is an amalgamation of Spanish, Mexican, and American legal traditions.[2] Arizona was luckily able to synthesize this law to comprise a unique legal system. The first statutory compilation, the *Howell Code,* incorporated both Mexican mining laws and Spanish community property and water laws. Prior to statehood the *New Mexico Code* was the law of Arizona. The "Organic Act" for the Arizona Territory stated that this law would hold until an Arizona code was promulgated.

B. Historical/Superseded Statutes

A bibliographic listing of Arizona's historical statutory compilations is as follows:

1. ***The Howell Code.*** **Prescott, AZ: Office of the Arizona Miner, 1865. 511 p.**

This code was adopted by the first Legislative Assembly of the Arizona Territory. It contains the Bill of Rights, U.S. Constitution, various treaties with Mexico, and 61 consecutively numbered chapters. No index was published. Only 250 paper covered copies were printed. Few libraries presently hold this edition, but a copy can be found in the Arizona State Archives and Public Records Library (in Phoenix), and the University of Arizona College of Law Library (in Tucson).[3]

2. **Coles Bashford, comp. *Compiled Laws of the Territory of Arizona: Including the Howell Code and the Session Laws from 1864 to 1871 Inclusive.* Albany, NY: Weed, Parsons & Co., 1871. 627 p.**

This unofficial compilation includes the U.S. Constitution, Organic Acts of Arizona and New Mexico, the U.S. Mining Law and the Bill of Rights. Ninety-five chapters were included with an index.

3. **John P. Hoyt, comp. *Compiled Laws of the Territory of Arizona: 1864-1877.* Detroit, MI: Richmond, Backus & Co., 1877. 693 p.**

These compiled laws continued to follow the Howell arrangement, although now with 88 chapters. A topical index was included.

4. **Cameron H. King, Ben Goodrich and E.W. Wells, comps. *Revised Statutes of Arizona.* Prescott, AZ: Prescott Courier Print, 1887. 907 p.**

This revision separated the penal code from the civil code for the first time. The statutory offenses of the new penal code were largely expanded. "Chapters" were now designated as "titles".

2 Arizona was initially influenced by California and New York law. For more information on Arizona's statutory heritage, *see* James M. Murphy, *Laws, Courts and Lawyers: Through the Years in Arizona* (Tucson, AZ: University of Arizona Press, 1970), 73; and James M. Murphy, *The Spanish Legal Heritage in Arizona* (Tucson, AZ: Arizona Pioneers' Historical Society, 1966).

3 Murphy, *Law Courts and Lawyers,* 74.

Separate indices were provided for both copies as well as for the Arizona Constitution, Organic Act and the Appendix. The Appendix included appropriations, private acts, and other matters.

5. C.W. Wright, J.C. Herndon, L.H. Chalmers, and R.E. Sloan, comps. *Revised Statutes of Arizona Territory*. Columbia, MO: E.W. Stephens, 1901. 1516 p.

The 1901 code was liberally amended prior to its adoption by the legislature.[4] These revised statutes marked the introduction of margin notes. The appendix included private laws and appropriation legislation.

6. Samuel L. Pattee, comp. *Revised Statutes of Arizona: Civil Code*. Phoenix, AZ: The McNeil Co., 1913. 3 v.

This was the first code to be published after Arizona achieved statehood. It also was the first to publish separately the civil and penal codes. Printed margin notes indicated a section's source (providing even out-of-state references) and some case law. Statute arrangement followed the 1901 format, except that all titles relating to civil proceedings were now consolidated.

7. Samuel L. Pattee, comp. *Revised Statutes of Arizona: Penal Code*. Phoenix, AZ: The McNeil Co., 1913. 1 v.

Arizona's Penal Code of 1887 was initially drafted to conform with California's legislation. This compilation, however, omits some provisions of the California Code due to differences in physical conditions. Other changes resulted from the passage of acts prior to statehood or from later revisions. Margin notes referred to the Penal Code of Arizona 1901, and the Penal Code of California, giving the source for each section.

Chapter 64, Laws of 1913, Third Special Session of the First Legislature, authorized the code's inclusion of annotations to the decisions of the Supreme Court of Arizona and the Circuit Court of Appeals for the Ninth Circuit.

8. F.C. Struckmeyer, comp. *The Revised Code of Arizona: 1928*. Phoenix, AZ: The Manufacturing Stationers, 1930. 1360 p.

The prior code of 1913 contained 7,057 sections while 4,499 sections had been enacted since this compilation. Therefore, Chapter 35, Laws of 1925 directed the Code Commissioner to "revise and codify the laws of the state... harmonize where necessary, reduce in language and remove inconsistencies where the same found to exist." With this charge in mind, Struckmeyer reduced the code to 5,349 sections. Brief annotations to the statutes were included providing cites to case law and to the *A.L.R.* and *Cal. Jur.* The statutes are arranged by chapter, article and section number.

a. Harold B. Clark, comp. *Statutory Tables: Added to Revised Code*. San Francisco, CA: Bancroft-Whitney Co., 1930. 60 p.

These tables were often located in the back of the bound code for 1928. They contained a "Table of Parallel Sections, Revised Statutes 1913 - Revised Code

4 *Ibid.*, 79.

1928," a "Table of Parallel Sections, Revised Statutes 1901 - Revised Code 1928," and a "Table showing the Disposition of Session Laws" (from the Regular Session of 1912 through the 4th Special Session of 1927).

b. William H. Courtright, comp. *Supplement to the Revised Code of Arizona Annotated 1934.* Denver, CO: W.H. Courtright Publishing Co., 1934. 543 p.

This supplement was printed as a deluxe limited edition with only 500 copies issued. The purpose was to provide Arizona lawyers with an adequate index (although no cross references were actually given in this publication).

The supplement contained all laws of a general nature passed from the 1928 Special Session through the 1935 Regular Session. Included also was an appendix of all unpublished laws passed at the 1933 and 1935 Regular and Special Sessions not contained in the supplement.

At the beginning of each chapter there was an analysis of the chapter's contents with article or section headings. Annotations to all Arizona and Federal decisions decided since the enactment of the 1928 code were also included.

c. William H. Courtright, comp. *Supplement to the Revised Code of Arizona Annotated 1936,* 2d ed., Denver, CO: W.H. Courtright Publishing Co., 1936. 717 p.

This supplement contained all laws of a general nature passed from the 1928 Special Session to the 1935 Regular Session. An appendix was also included containing all laws passed at these sessions not found within the supplement. The supplement was annotated with Arizona and Federal court cases decided after 1928.

It should be noted that Courtright gave special attention to the index in an attempt to make it usable for both attorneys and the general public. Most cross references were eliminated. Comparative tables showed where each session law section appeared in the supplement. This was a deluxe edition of only 500 copies.

9. Henry D. Ross, Alfred C. Lockwood, and Archibauld G. McAlister, comps. *Revised Code 1939.* Indianapolis, IN: Bobbs-Merrill Co., 1940. 6 v.

The 1939 official compilation was Arizona's first multi-volume code to provide pocket parts for future supplementation. The code was divided into five major sections: the Political Code, Civil Procedure, Probate Law and Procedure, Penal Code and Procedure, and an alphabetical arrangement of General Laws. There was a general index volume containing various tables, and a separate index found within each volume. An index was also located after the U.S. Constitution in Volume 1.

Historical notes provided legislative changes through amendments or repeals. A listing of out-of-state comparative legislation and cross references were included. An extensive "Notes to Decisions" section was found after the historical notes. This section annotated the code with applicable Arizona cases. It also listed collateral references to *A.L.R.* and *Cal. Jur.* cites. In addition, the Arizona Rules of Civil Procedure and the Rules of Criminal Procedure included the prior superseded statutes in the notes section for reference.

a. ***Cumulative Pocket Supplement: Arizona Code 1939.*** **Indianapolis, IN: Bobbs-Merrill Co., 1949. vol. 2.**

This supplement included laws enacted since the year 1939 to the 1949 Regular Session. Annotations were contained through volume 203, *Pacific Reporter* second series.

b. ***Cumulative Pocket Supplement: Arizona Code 1939.*** **Indianapolis, IN: Bobbs-Merrill Co., 1951. vol. 2.**

This supplement compiled amendments and new legislation passed from 1939 to the 1951 First Special Session. Additional annotations completed the code's coverage through volume 223, *Pacific Reporter* second series.

c. ***Cumulative Supplement: Arizona Code 1939.*** **Indianapolis, IN: Bobbs-Merrill Co., 1952. 3168 p.**

Annotations were provided to bring the *Arizona Code 1939* current through volume 238 *Pacific Reporter* second series. Amendments and new legislation enacted from 1939 were compiled through the 1952 Regular Session. Parallel Reference Tables and a combined General Index were also included.

d. ***Supplement: Arizona Code 1939.*** **Indianapolis, IN: Bobbs-Merrill Co., 1953. 386 p.**

This supplement contained annotations from Volume 239 *Pacific Reporter* second series to volume 256 *Pacific Reporter* second series. Amendments to acts and new legislation enacted during the 1953 Regular Session were also included.

e. ***Supplement: Arizona Code 1939.*** **Indianapolis, IN: Bobbs-Merrill Co., 1954. 1017 p.**

This supplement updated the 1952 cumulative supplement to the *Arizona Code 1939*. Annotation coverage was from volume 239, *Pacific Reporter* second series to volume 269 *Pacific Reporter* second series. New legislation enacted during the 1953 and 1954 sessions was also included.

f. ***Supplement: Arizona Code 1939.*** **Indianapolis, IN: Bobbs-Merrill Co., 1955. 245 p.**

Updating the 1952 and 1954 supplements, this volume included annotations to the *Arizona Code 1939* from volume 270 *Pacific Reporter* second series to volume 281 *Pacific Reporter* second series. Amendments and new legislation enacted at the 1955 session were also included.

10. Arizona Superseded Statutes and Codes.

The William S. Hein & Co. has issued superseded *A.R.S.* on microfiche from 1939 to date. These will be updated annually by filming volumes of the *Arizona Revised Statutes Annotated* that have been replaced. The company has plans to film the code prior to 1939 in the future.

C. Current Compilation of Laws

The Arizona statutes mandate the House and Senate to prepare copies of all laws and resolutions passed or adopted.[5] The Director of the Arizona Legislative Council edits and prepares this legislation and its annotations for publication.[6] The Secretary of State is then responsible for publishing the slip laws and for the distribution of statutes and journals to state officials.[7] However, either the Speaker of the House or the President of the Senate may jointly or singly contract for legislative printing.[8]

Arizona presently has two versions of its revised statutes. The *Arizona Revised Statutes Annotated* is a 43 volume hard bound compilation published by the West Publishing Company. The Michie Company also issues a four volume unannotated paperback version. The intricacies of these sets are set forth below.

1. *Arizona Revised Statutes Annotated.* St. Paul, MN: West Publishing Co., 1956- 43 v.

In 1956, the Arizona legislature authorized the publication of the *Arizona Revised Statutes Annotated.*[9] Originally only 20 volumes, this revision became the official law for Arizona and provided a system for further updating with annual pocket parts or bound revisions.

a. Arrangement

The *Arizona Revised Statutes* are a subject compilation of all laws of a "general, public and permanent nature."[10] The statutes are arranged alphabetically into 49 separate titles; with the exception of Title 1, "General Provisions", and Title 28, "Transportation."

The titles are divided into chapters and the chapters, articles. Legislation may be further divided into sections, subsections, paragraphs, subdivisions and items.

A hyphenated numbering system organizes the legislation, (e.g., § 1-101). The first number represents the title while the digits to the right of the hyphen indicate the section number. The first section of each title is numbered 101. If additional section numbers are needed decimal places to the hundredth place are given.

The following 49 titles are presently found within the *Arizona Revised Statutes.* Volume numbers and dates of bound volume publications are also given:

Title No.	Subject Area	Vol. #	Date of Publication
1	General Provisions	2	1989
2	Aeronautics	2	1989
3	Agriculture and Dairying	2	1989
4	Alcoholic Beverages	2	1989

5 Ariz. Rev. Stat. Ann. § 41-1177.02(A)(B)(1985).
6 Ariz. Rev. Stat. Ann. § 41-1304.01 (West Supp. 1990).
7 Ariz. Rev. Stat. Ann. § 41-121, 41-123 (1985).
8 Ariz. Rev. Stat. Ann. § 41-1171 (1985).
9 1956 Ariz. Sess. Laws 129.
10 Ariz. Rev. Stat. Ann. § 1-102 (1989).

Title No.	Subject Area	Vol. #	Date of Publication
5	Amusements and Sports	2	1989
6	Banks & Financial Institutions	2A	1989
7	Bonds	2A	1989
8	Children	2A	1989
9	Cities and Towns	3	1990
10	Corporations and Associations	3	1990
11	Counties	3A	1990
12	Courts and Civil Proceedings	4, 4A	1982
13	Criminal Code	5, 5A, 5B	1989
14	Decedents' Estates, Guardianship, Protective Proceedings and Trusts	6	1975
15	Education	6A (Part 1 & 2)	1991
16	Elections and Electors	6B	1984
17	Game and Fish	6B	1984
18	Highways and Bridges	7	1990
19	Initiative, Referendum, and Recall	7	1990
20	Insurance	7, 7A	1990
21	Juries	7A	1990
22	Justices of the Peace and Other Courts Not of Record	7A	1990
23	Labor	8, 8A	1983
24	Livestock and Animals	8A	1983
25	Martial and Domestic Relations	9	1991
26	Military Affairs and Emergency Services	9	1991
27	Minerals, Oil and Gas	9	1991
28	Transportation	9A, 9B	1989
29	Partnership (Vol. includes an Index/Appendix)	9B	1989
30	Power	10	1986
31	Prisons and Prisoners	10, 10A	1986
32	Professions and Occupations	10	1986
33	Property	11	1990
34	Public Buildings and Improvements	11	1990
35	Public Finances	11	1990
36	Public Health and Safety	11A, 11B	1986
37	Public Lands	11B	1986
38	Public Officers and Employees	12	1985
39	Public Records, Printing & Notices	12	1985
40	Public Utilities and Notices Carriers	12	1985
41	State Government	12A	1985
42	Taxation	13	1991
43	Taxation of Income (Vol. includes Appendix and Prior Laws)	13A	1980
44	Trade and Commerce	14	1987
45	Waters	14	1987
46	Welfare	15	1988

Title No.	Subject Area	Vol. #	Date of Publication
47	Uniform Commercial Code	15	1988
48	Special Taxing Districts	15A, 15B	1988
49	Environment	15B	1988
Constitution	Articles 1 to 5	1	1984
Constitution	Articles 6 to End	1A	1984

The following constitutes bound volume replacements for *Arizona Revised Statutes Annotated.* This is an updated listing based on the checklists of Meira Pimsleur in *Checklists of Basic American Legal Publications,* (Littleton, CO: Fred Rothman & Co., 1988). This is reprinted with the permission of the American Association of Law Libraries.

Volume Number	Replacement Year
14	1967
8	1971
17	1973
17A	1973
16	1973
2	1974
11	1974
11A	1974
12	1974
6	1975
6A	1975
7	1975
9	1976
9A	1976
10	1976
3	1977
Index Cumulative Supplement	1977
5	1978
5A	1978
13	1980
13A	1980
4	1982
4A	1982
Index; v 19-21	1982
8	1983
8A	1983
1 (Constitution)	1984
1A	1984
6A	1984
6B	1984
12	1985
12A	1985
11A	1986
11B	1986

Volume Number	Replacement Year
10	1986
10A	1986
14	1987
16	1987
17	1987
15	1988
15A	1988
15B	1988
17A	1988
17B	1988
9A	1989
9B	1989
2	1989
2A	1989
5	1989
5A	1989
5B	1989
11	1990
3	1990
3A	1990
7	1990
7A	1990
Index	1991
13	1991
6A (Part 1 & 2)	1991
9	1991

b. Authority as Law

The *Arizona Revised Statutes* were reenacted as positive law (i.e., "the authoritative, binding text of the laws, and the determinative version if questions arise from textual variations in subsequent printed versions.")[11] The Laws of 1955, 3rd Special Session, Chapter 3 proclaim "Be it Enacted by the Legislature of the State of Arizona: The Arizona Revised Statutes are hereby adopted and enacted into law as follows." This "enacting clause" has alone been held sufficient in many states to expressly repeal earlier compilations.[12] Arizona law, however, also expressly repeals all prior session laws, revisions and compilations.[13]

Amendments to the statutes are cited by title and section and prefaced with a statement "Amended by Laws." The laws contained in the most current pocket parts or supplements constitute "prima facie" evidence of the Revised Statutes if they represent a reproduction of subsequently enacted laws.[14] These supplements are authenticated with a facsimile signature of the Secretary of State

11 Cohen, *How to Find the Law,* 145.

12 Miles O. Price, Harry Bitner, and Shirley Raissi Bysiewicz, *Effective Legal Research*, 4th ed. (Boston, MA: Little, Brown and Co., 1979), 133. For Arizona, see Ariz. Rev. Stat. Ann. § 1-101 (1989).

13 Ariz. Rev. Stat. Ann. §§ 1-102, 1-245 (1989).

14 Ariz. Rev. Stat. Ann. § 1-106 (1989).

and a reproduction of the Great Seal. The certificates are also printed in each *A.R.S.* volume and indicate that the text in each volume is a correct copy of the *A.R.S.* on the date given.

c. Content

As stated previously, the *Arizona Revised Statutes* include all statutes of a "general, public and permanent nature." Therefore, obsolete legislation, private acts and appropriation legislation is not included. However, the *A.R.S.* does contain the following additional materials: The Arizona Constitution; the U.S. Constitution; the Declaration of Independence; Treaty of Guadalupe Hidalgo; Gadsden Treaty; the Enabling Act; Election Ordinance No. 2, Constitutional Convention; Admission of the State of Arizona; Proclamation of Admission; the State Anthems; the Rules of Civil Procedures; Rules of Evidence; Supreme Court Rules; Civil Appeal Procedure Rules; and various other court and administrative board rules. Index and tables volumes can also be found within the set.

d. Editorial Matter

West Publishing Co. includes a wide range of helpful information in their annotated codes. All editorial matter should be examined as a quick source for additional research. It should be noted, however, that headings to sections, source notes, reviser's notes and cross references are not part of the law but are provided only for reference.[15]

The beginning of each title contains an outline of the statutory materials. Sample WESTLAW search queries can also be found to assist in updating statutory or case references. Each chapter provides a separate table of contents by article and section, "Constitutional Provisions" relating to the specific article covered, and "Cross References" of relevant constitutional and legislative citations. The "Library References" section includes citations to West's Digest topic and key numbers, WESTLAW topic numbers, and pertinent sections in *Corpus Juris Secundum.* (See Illustration A, p.44.)

After each statute there are "Historical Notes". These are essential for compiling an Arizona legislative history. This section provides information on the source of the provision and explains any legislative changes in the "Reviser's Note." These notes often include the partial text of prior legislative versions. "Constitutional Provisions" and "Cross References" are also provided. In addition, there is a listing of "Law Review Commentaries" with references to pertinent articles found in Arizona legal journals, and information on "WESTLAW Electronic Research."

The "Notes of Decisions" section provides annotations of Arizona and Federal cases and Attorney General opinions. West's references to these decisions are similar in format to the head notes found in their reporters. A listing of the topical headings used to arrange the annotations can be found at the section's beginning. (See Illustration B, p.45.)

15 Ariz. Rev. Stat. Ann. § 1-212 (1989).

e. Index

The *A.R.S. Annotated* has a three volume paperback index. The present volumes cover the laws enacted through the end of the Fortieth Legislature First Regular Session and First and Second Special Sessions. The index contains references to the Arizona Constitution. In addition, there is a Legislative Highlights Index of important legislation passed during the most recent session and a Popular Name Table. The index is replaced annually. In addition, separate indices can be found with the Arizona and U.S. Constitutions; Titles 9, 10, 11, 13, and 28; the Rules of Civil Procedure; Rules of Criminal Procedure; Rules of Evidence; Rules of Supreme Court; and Rules of Civil Appellate Procedure.

West states their general index includes topical, descriptive, conceptual and colloquial headings. Cross references and "see, also" headings are also provided. (See Illustration C, p.46.)

It may be necessary to examine earlier index volumes when researching prior topical law. In general, it is necessary to start with the current index and work backwards until the correct entry is located.

f. Tables

The *Arizona Revised Statutes Annotated* contains one volume of tables. Parallel conversion tables are included providing citations from one compilation or revision of statutes to another. The following tables each show the distribution of prior Arizona law into the *A.R.S.: Arizona Code Annotated 1939* (and supplement), *Revised Code of 1928, Revised Statutes of 1913, Penal Code of 1913, Revised Statutes of 1901,* and the *Penal Code of 1901.* (See Illustration D, p.47.)

Parallel conversion tables from the session laws (1864 to 1956) to the *A.R.S.* are also included. (See Illustration E, p.48.) These tables allow a researcher to trace provisions found in a session law or earlier compilation into the *Arizona Revised Statutes.* They also indicate the provision's disposition; whether the legislation is still in force or whether it has been amended, repealed, or is omitted.

In addition, each repealed or renumbered section number is included within a chapter's text. The "Historical Note" contains information on a section's status and the location of any internal disposition table. Disposition and Derivation tables are generally located at the beginning of the applicable title. Disposition tables indicate where repealed, transferred or renumbered sections of law are covered in a revision. Derivation tables show where revised sections were located in earlier versions. This information is essential to easily locating a statute. In rapidly changing areas of law two or more internal disposition tables may be consulted. (See Illustration F, p.49.)

Helpful but extraneous materials are also provided in the bound tables volumes (e.g., mortality tables, annuity tables, actuaries tables, interest tables, Stern's U.S. Calendar and Stafford's office calendar). However, the interest table is the only one updated within the paper supplement.

g. Updating

The West annotated code is updated with several publications. First, pocket parts and supplements are published annually. These materials directly supplement and annotate the individual volumes of the *A.R.S.*

The company also issues "Interim Annotation Service Pamphlets" to supplement the annual pocket parts with judicial decisions from Arizona and Federal Courts. The pamphlets contain the text of sections affected by laws passed since the pocket parts were issued. Updates to various court rules are also included. (See Illustration G, p.50.)

The *Arizona Legislative Service,* however, provides the most currently published unofficial version of Arizona Session Laws. This service issues pamphlets containing recent laws enacted throughout the legislative session. The text is printed to highlight statutory changes. Deletions in a previous section's language are indicated by strikeouts while additions are indicated by underlining. (See Illustration H, p.51.)

These acts are arranged in a numerical chapter order. Each session law has an official chapter number, bill number and ultimate *A.R.S.* citation. (See Illustration I, p.52.) The pamphlets also reprint proposed constitutional amendments, executive orders, veto messages, memorials, resolutions, initiative measures, declarations of emergency, proclamations, election results and court rule amendments. There is an alphabetical listing of all items.

Cumulative Tables include the following: Arizona Constitution and *Arizona Revised Statutes* affected by proposed amendments, Uncodified Session Laws affected by current Session Laws, Status of Bills, Resolutions and Memorials, Executive Orders, Proclamations Including Declarations of Emergency, and Court Rules changes. A separate section describes the effective dates of laws. In addition, each pamphlet contains an index.

2. ***Arizona Revised Statutes.*** Charlottesville, VA: The Michie Co., 1988- 4 v.

Market driven to produce a new version of the revised statutes by the increasing costs associated with maintaining the annotated set, Michie began publishing their four volume code in 1988. This desktop unofficial version is unannotated and paperback. Each new edition completely replaces the prior version. An updated edition is published soon after the legislative session ends.

The Michie set is composed of four volumes. The titles are divided as follows: Volume 1, Titles 1-17; Volume 2, Titles 18-32; Volume 3, Titles 33-44; and Volume 4, Titles 45-49; the Arizona State Constitution and the Index. A table of contents is found at the beginning of each volume and also prior to each title and chapter.

After the text of a section, a year number is printed which indicates the date the section was last affected. As 1955 was the year the Revised Statutes were enacted, it should be the earliest year listed after any section. In addition, any italicized text printed following a section's headings provides special information which may relate to the section's effective dates, applicability, validity or codification. The editors warn the researcher to look for alternate versions of a section when this occurs. (See Illustration J, p.53.)

The General Index covers both the Constitution and the Revised Statutes and is arranged by topical headings. The headings are derived from common legal terminology and language found in the *A.R.S.* Cross references are included. The editors suggest the following guidelines when using their index: "1) Gain familiarity with the contents of the *Arizona Revised Statutes* and the index, 2) Consult the principal subject and not the secondary subject, 3) Look for the noun and not the adjective, 4) Consult the most pertinent subject, 5) Consult allied headings, and 6) Use cross references."[16] (See Illustration K, p.54.) Popular names of acts are included within the index alphabetically.

There are no parallel conversion tables included within this set. A serious problem occurs, however, when a title or chapter has been repealed or re-numbered. The Michie set provides no reference to the location of a section from one year to the next. It is then necessary for the researcher to either use the West's tables volume or the title's disposition table also found within the annotated code. (See Illustrations L-1, L-2, pp.55-56.)

The Michie set is updated with a small supplement containing legislation passed during any Special Sessions. It follows the same format as the paperback set.

3. Subject Compilations

Subject compilations of Arizona statutes are published in several areas. Many of these, however, are issued irregularly by various state agencies. Because the updating may be infrequent, these state compilations are not the best source for current law. The following, however, is a listing of the more common subject compilations:

a. ***West's Arizona Criminal Law and Rules.*** St. Paul, MN: West Publishing Co., 1987- annual. paperback.

This paperback edition provides Arizona Criminal Law including Article II of the Constitution of the State of Arizona; and applicable sections from Titles 4, 5, 8, 13, 21, 22, 28, 31, and 36 of the *Arizona Revised Statutes.*

b. ***West's Arizona Education Code.*** St. Paul, MN: West Publishing Co., 1987- annual. paperback.

West reprints an unannotated version of Title 15, the Education Code of the *Arizona Revised Statutes.*

c. ***Real Estate and Commissioner's Rules.*** Phoenix, AZ: Arizona Department of Real Estate, 1989-90. biennial.

Includes applicable sections from Titles 32, 33, and 44 of the *Arizona Revised Statutes.* Purchase from the Arizona Department of Real Estate Licensing Division.

16 "Foreword to the Index" in *Arizona Revised Statutes,* (Charlottesville, VA: The Michie Co., 1989).

d. **Victor H. Verity, *Laws and Regulations Governing Mineral Rights in Arizona.* 8th ed. Phoenix, AZ: Arizona Department of Mineral Resources, 1979. 1988 supplement, irregular.**

Purchase from the Arizona Department of Mineral Resources.

e. ***A.R.S. Title 20: Corporations and Associations.* Phoenix, AZ: Arizona Corporation Commission, 1990. irregular.**

Purchase from the Arizona Corporation Commission.

f. ***Arizona Hotel and Motel Laws.* Phoenix, AZ: Arizona Hotel and Motel Association, 1987. looseleaf.**

D. Session Laws

In addition to the updating services provided in the annotated and unannotated codes, the State of Arizona also publishes slip laws and session laws. Once a bill is passed and either signed by the Governor or allowed to become law without a signature, it becomes an "enacted law." These individual laws can be purchased from the Secretary of State.

The *Session Laws of Arizona* compile these slip laws. They are published annually and can be purchased from either the Chief Clerk of the House or the Secretary of the Senate. The official version, however, is normally issued much later than the *Arizona Legislative Service.* The acts of the legislature are arranged by chapter and section number. Each new act represents a chapter. The bill number is also given. (See Illustration M, p.57.)

1. Historical Listing of Session Laws[17]

a. Territory of Arizona: Legislative Assembly (1899-1911)

Title	Year	Assembly	Comments
Arizona Acts, Resolutions and Memorials of the Legislative Assembly of the Territory of Arizona. Prescott, Phoenix, AZ: (1864-1909)	1864	1st Ass'y	
	1865	2nd Ass'y	
	1866	3rd Ass'y	
	1867	4th Ass'y	
	1868	5th Ass'y	(2 versions: one a photostat)
	1871	6th Ass'y	(2 versions: one a reprint R.A. Ogg 1935)
	1873	7th Ass'y	
	1875	8th Ass'y	
	1877	9th Ass'y	
	1879	10th Ass'y	(161 p.)
	1879	10th Ass'y	(171 p.)

17 Compiled and updated from Meira Pimsleur, *Checklists of Basic American Legal Publications* (Littleton, CO: Fred Rothman & Co., 1988). Reprinted with permission from the American Association of Law Libraries.

Title	Year	Assembly	Comments
Arizona Acts, Resolutions and Memorials of the Legislative Assembly of the Territory of Arizona. (continued)	1881	11th Ass'y	(221 p.)
	1881	11th Ass'y	(211 p.)
	1883	12th Ass'y	
	1885	13th Ass'y	
	1887	14th Ass'y	(Also found in *Revised Statutes* 1887)
	1889	15th Ass'y	(119 p.)
	1889	15th Ass'y	(25 p.)
	1891	16th Ass'y	
	1893	17th Ass'y	
	1895	18th Ass'y	
	1897	19th Ass'y	(145 p.)
	1897	19th Ass'y	(161 p.)
Acts of the Legislative Assembly of Arizona	1889	15th Ass'y)	
	1891	16th Ass'y)	(In one volume,
	1893	17th Ass'y)	reprinted by
	1895	18th Ass'y)	State)
	1897	19th Ass'y)	
Arizona Acts, Resolutions and Memorials	1899	20th Ass'y	
	1901	21st Ass'y	(In *Revised Statutes 1901*)
	1903	22nd Ass'y	
	1905	23rd Ass'y	
	1907	24th Ass'y	
	1909	25th Ass'y	(332 p.)
	1909	25th Ass'y	(261 p.)

b. Arizona State Legislature Session Laws (1912-)

Title	Year	Session	Comments
Session Laws, State of Arizona (Phoenix, AZ: 1912-)	1912	1st Reg. Sess.,)	(In one
	1912	1st Spec. Sess.)	volume)
	1913	2nd Spec. Sess.	(In *Revised Statutes 1913*)
	1913	3rd Spec. Sess.	(In *Revised Statutes 1913*)
	1913	2nd Spec. Sess.,)	(In one
	1913	3rd Spec. Sess.)	volume)
	1915	2nd Reg. Sess.,)	
	1915	1st Spec. Sess.,)	(In one
	1915	2nd Spec. Sess.)	volume)
	1917	3rd Reg. Sess.	
	1918	1st Spec. Sess.	
	1919	4th Reg. Sess.	
	1920	4th Spec. Sess.,)	(In one
	1921	5th Reg. Sess.)	volume)
	1922	5th Spec. Sess.	
	1923	6th Reg. Sess.	
	1925	7th Reg. Sess.	

Title	Year	Assembly	Comments
Session Laws, State of Arizona (Phoenix, AZ: (1912-) (continued)	1927 1927 1927	8th Reg. Sess.,) 1st Spec. Sess.,) 8th Leg.,) 2nd Spec. Sess.,) 8th Leg.)	(In one volume)
	1927 1927	3rd Spec. Sess.,) 8th Leg.,) 4th Spec. Sess.,) 8th Leg.)	(In one volume)
	1928 1928	5th Spec. Sess.,) 8th Leg.,) 6th Spec. Sess.,) 8th Leg.)	(In one volume)
	1929	9th Reg. Sess.	
	1931	10th Reg. Sess.	
	1931	1st Spec. Sess., 10th Leg.	
	1933	11th Reg. Sess.	
	1933	1st Spec. Sess., 11th Leg.	
	1933	2nd Spec. Sess., 11th Leg.	
	1934	3rd Spec. Sess., 11th Leg.	
	1935	12th Reg. Sess.	
	1936	1st Spec. Sess., 12th Leg.	
	1937 1937 1937 1937	13th Reg. Sess.,) 1st Reg. Sess.,) 13th Leg.,) 2nd Spec. Sess.,) 13th Leg.,) 3rd Spec. Sess.,) 13th Leg.)	(In one volume)
	1938 1939	4th Spec. Sess.,) 13th Leg.,) 14th Reg. Sess.)	(In one volume)
	1940 1941	1st Spec. Sess.,) 14th Leg.,) 15th Reg. Sess.)	(In one volume)
	1942 1943	1st Spec. Sess.,) 15th Leg.,) 16th Reg. Sess.)	(In one volume)

Title	Year	Assembly	Comments
Session Laws, State of Arizona (Phoenix, AZ: 1912-) (continued)	1944	1st Spec. Sess., 16th Leg.,)	
	1944	2nd Spec. Sess., 16th Leg.,)	(In one volume)
	1945	17th Reg. Sess.)	
	1945	1st Spec. Sess., 17th Leg.,)	
	1946	2nd Spec. Sess., 17th Leg.,)	(In one volume)
	1946	3rd Spec. Sess., 17th Leg.,)	
	1947	18th Reg. Sess.)	
	1947	1st Spec. Sess., 18th Leg.,)	
	1947	2nd Spec. Sess., 18th Leg.,)	
	1948	3rd Spec. Sess., 18th Leg.,)	
	1948	4th Spec. Sess., 18th Leg.,)	(In one volume)
	1948	5th Spec. Sess., 18th Leg.,)	
	1948	6th Spec. Sess., 18th Leg.,)	
	1948	7th Spec. Sess., 18th Leg.,)	
	1949	19th Reg. Sess.)	
	1950	1st Spec. Sess., 19th Leg.,)	
	1950	2nd Spec. Sess., 19th Leg.,)	(In one volume)
	1951	1st Reg. Sess., 20th Leg.)	
	1951	1st Spec. Sess., 20th Leg.,)	(In one volume)
	1952	2nd Reg. Sess., 20th Leg.)	
	1952	2nd Spec. Sess., 20th Leg.,)	(In one volume)
	1953	1st Reg. Sess., 21st Leg.)	
	1953	1st Spec. Sess., 21st Leg.,)	(In one volume)
	1954	2nd Reg. Sess., 21st Leg.)	

Title	Year	Assembly	Comments
Session Laws, State of Arizona (Phoenix, AZ: 1912-) (continued)	1955	1st Reg. Sess.,) 22nd Leg.,)	
	1955	1st Spec. Sess.,) 22nd Leg.,)	
	1955	2nd Spec. Sess.,) 22nd Leg.,)	(In one volume)
	1955	3rd Spec. Sess.,) 22nd Leg.,)	
	1956	2nd Reg. Sess.,) 22nd Leg.)	
	1957	1st Reg. Sess., 23rd Leg.	
	1958	2nd Reg. Sess.,) 23rd Leg.,)	
	1958	1st Spec. Sess.,) 23rd Leg.)	(In one volume)
	1959	1st Reg. Sess., 24th Leg.	
	1960	2nd Reg. Sess., 24th Leg.	
	1961	1st Reg. Sess., 25th Leg.	
	1961	1st Spec. Sess.,) 25th Leg.,)	
	1962	2nd Reg. Sess.,) 25th Leg.)	(In one volume)
	1963	1st Reg. Sess.,) 26th Leg.,)	
	1963	1st Spec.Sess.,) 26th Leg.,)	(In one volume)
	1963	2nd Spec.Sess.,) 26th Leg.)	
	1964	2nd Reg. Sess., 26th Leg.	
	1965	1st Reg. Sess.,) 27th Leg.,)	
	1965	1st Spec. Sess.,) 27th Leg.,)	(In one volume)
	1965	2nd Spec. Sess.,) 27th Leg.,)	
	1965	3rd Spec. Sess.,) 27th Leg.)	
	1966	2nd Reg. Sess.,) 27th Leg.,)	
	1966	4th Spec. Sess.,) 27th Leg.)	(In one volume)

Title	Year	Assembly	Comments
Sessions Laws, State of Arizona (Phoenix, AZ: 1912-) (continued)	1967	1st Reg. Sess.,) 28th Leg.,)	
	1967	1st Spec. Sess.,) 28th Leg.)	(In one volume)
	1967	2nd Spec. Sess.,) 28th Leg.,)	
	1967	3rd Spec. Sess.,) 28th Leg.,)	(In one
	1968	2nd Reg. Sess.,) 28th Leg.,)	volume)
	1968	4th Spec. Sess.,) 28th Leg.)	
	1969	1st Reg. Sess., 29th Leg.	
	1970	1st Spec. Sess.,) 29th Leg.,)	
	1970	2nd Reg. Sess.,) 29th Leg.)	(In one volume)
	1971	1st Reg. Sess., 30th Leg.	
	1971	1st Spec. Sess.,) 30th Leg.,)	
	1972	2nd Reg. Sess.,) 30th Leg.)	(In one volume)
	1973	1st Reg. Sess.,) 31st Leg.)	(In two volumes)
	1974	2nd Reg. Sess.,) 31st Leg.,)	
	1974	1st Spec. Sess.,) 31st Leg.,)	(In two volumes)
	1974	2nd Spec. Sess.,) 31st Leg.)	
	1975	1st Reg. Sess., 32nd Leg.	
	1976	2nd Reg. Sess.,) 32nd Leg.,)	
	1976	1st Spec. Sess.,) 32 Leg.)	(In one volume)
	1977	1st Reg. Sess., 33rd Leg.	
	1978	2nd Reg. Sess.,) 33rd Leg.,)	
	1978	1st Spec. Sess.,) 33rd Leg.,)	(In one
	1978	2nd Spec. Sess.,) 33rd Leg.)	volume)

Title	Year	Assembly	Comments
Session Laws, State of Arizona (Phoenix, AZ: 1912-) (continued)	1979	1st Reg. Sess., 34th Leg.,	
	1979	1st Spec. Sess., 34th Leg.	(In one volume)
	1979	2nd Spec. Sess., 34th Leg.	
	1980	2nd Reg. Sess., 34th Leg.,	
	1980	2nd Spec. Sess., 34th Leg.,	
	1980	3rd Spec. Sess., 34th Leg.,	(In one volume)
	1980	4th Spec. Sess., 34th Leg.,	
	1980	5th Spec. Sess., 34th Leg.	
	1981	1st Reg. Sess., 35th Leg.,	
	1981	1st Spec. Sess., 35th Leg.,	
	1981	2nd Spec. Sess., 35th Leg.,	
	1981	3rd Spec. Sess., 35th Leg.,	
	1981	4th Spec. Sess., 35th Leg.,	(In one volume)
	1981	5th Spec. Sess., 35th Leg.,	
	1981	6th Spec. Sess., 35th Leg.,	
	1981	7th Spec. Sess., 35th Leg.	
	1982	2nd Reg. Sess., 35th Leg.,	
	1982	5th Spec. Sess., 35th Leg.,	(In one volume)
	1982	6th Spec. Sess., 35th Leg.	
	1983	1st Reg. Sess., 36th Leg.	
	1984	2nd Reg. Sess., 36th Leg.,	
	1983-84	1st Spec. Sess., 36th Leg.,	
	1984	2nd Spec. Sess., 36th Leg.,	(In one volume)
	1984	3rd Spec. Sess., 36th Leg.	
	1985	1st Reg. Sess., 37th Leg.	
	1986	2nd Reg. Sess., 37th Leg.	

Title	Year	Assembly	Comments
Session Laws, State of Arizona (Phoenix, AZ: 1912-) (continued)	1987	1st Reg. Sess., 38th Leg.,	(In one volume)
	1987	1st Spec. Sess., 38th Leg.,	
	1987	2nd Spec. Sess., 38th Leg.,	
	1987	3rd Spec. Sess., 38th Leg.	
	1988	2nd Reg. Sess., 38th Leg.	
	1989	1st Reg. Sess., 39th Leg.,	(In one volume)
	1989	1st Spec. Sess., 39th Leg.,	
	1989	2nd Spec. Sess., 39th Leg.	
	1990	2nd Reg. Sess., 39th Leg.	
	1990	2nd Spec. Sess., 39th Leg.,	(In one volume)
	1990	3rd Spec. Sess., 39th Leg.,	
	1990	4th Spec. Sess., 39th Leg.,	
	1990	5th Spec Sess., 39th Leg.	

a. Arrangement

The trick to using old session laws is to question the information printed on the spine. The spine labels are not an accurate source for volume contents. For example, the *Session Laws of 1921* includes acts from the Special Session of the Fourth Legislature and the Regular Session of the Fifth Legislature. The spine states that the session laws contain the "Special Session Fourth Legislature 1920." In addition, many of these older volumes do not have a comprehensive table of contents, nor are there section dividers. Special Session laws are often located after the Regular Session index. Therefore, when the legislation enacted during a session is little, it often becomes difficult to locate.

b. Content

In addition to the acts of the legislature, the official session laws also contain memorials and resolutions; and often the governor's legislative message or address, the governor's veto messages, election proclamations, proposed constitutional amendments and initiative petitions.

There are tables listing the "Order of Acts" arranged by bill number, and parallel conversion tables from "Chapter to Bill" and from "Bill to Chapter." The volumes also include a limited index to the acts. The index in recent years has been arranged by statute titles and further subdivided by a brief subject description. (See Illustration N, p.58.) Earlier versions are indexed by broad subject headings.

Many volumes also contain a listing of elected Arizona State and U.S. officials and members of the Arizona Senate and House of Representatives.

E. Online Resources

Both WESTLAW and LEXIS have Arizona statutes online. WESTLAW has the annotated and unannotated statutes from 1988. The AZ-ST-ANN database includes annotated Arizona statutes and court rules, while the AZ-ST database contains the unannotated version. WESTLAW also includes an online index. The AZ-ST-IDX database has documents from the *Arizona Revised Statutes Annotated* General Index volume. In addition, the AZIN-ST database contains only Insurance statutes from Title 20 and other applicable titles.

The *Arizona Legislative Service* is also available on WESTLAW from 1988. The AZ-LEGIS database includes primarily legislation passed by the Arizona Legislature, but also contains resolutions, constitutional amendments, propositions, executive orders, governor's veto messages, proclamations, declarations of emergency, or initiative measures. Slip laws may be included into the database prior to receiving their full editorial enhancements.

The LEXIS Arizona Library (ARIZ) contains only the current year of the unannotated Arizona statutes (file name: CODE). There is, however, a separate file containing the Arizona Constitution (CONST) and one for the Arizona Advance Legislative Service (ALS). The AZCODE file combines the Arizona Code, Constitution and Advance Legislative Service files. There is no online index.

F. Statutory Citators

Shepard's Arizona Citations-Statutes provides citation to the Arizona Constitution, codes, laws not yet codified, court rules, jury instructions, and municipal charters and ordinances as cited in Arizona and federal courts, legal periodicals, treatises, annotations, and Arizona laws. References are also given to Arizona court decisions and Arizona laws citing the U.S. Constitution or federal law.

Shepard's provides a mini legislative history of a statutory provision, listing amendments, repeals, etc. A letter abbreviation indicates the legislation's status, (e.g., RS1971C94 translates into Repealed and Superseded by the Arizona Legislature in an act found in Chapter 94 of the 1971 Arizona Session Laws). Shepard's also provides citations to state and federal court decisions which determine a section's validity or constitutionality. This is indicated by a preceding letter abbreviation. (See Illustration O, p.59.)

A table of Arizona Acts referred to by popular names or short titles is also provided. Each act listed contains its *A.R.S.* or Arizona Session Law's citation. (See Illustration P, p.60.)

Shepard's statutes volume can now be updated with *Shepard's Express Citations.* This monthly publication provides citations to recent Arizona slip opinions as published in various sources including *Arizona Advance Reports* and the "Arizona Business Gazette."

Additional references to case law can be located in the "Table of Statutes Construed," "Statutes," or "Cumulative Statutes" tables found in the bound volumes of Reporter Advance Sheets (e.g., *Arizona Advance Reports, Arizona Reports, Pacific Reporter* or various federal reporters). In addition, WESTLAW and LEXIS can always be used as a citator to find the most recent citations. (See Chapter 10 for further information.)

G. Uniform Laws and Model Codes

Most Uniform Acts and codes are drafted by the National Conference of Commissioners on Uniform State Laws. Their goal is to encourage "uniformity in state laws where uniformity is deemed desirable and practicable."[18] The conference names an act "uniform" when its passage is likely by many jurisdictions. "Model Acts" are those drafted in less popular subjects areas.

Locating Uniform Acts in Arizona is a multi-phase process. One complication is that organizations other than the National Conference entitle their legislation "uniform" or "model" acts. To ascertain whether a specific uniform law has been enacted in this state, it may be necessary to examine the following sources: 1) the *A.R.S.* Index volume under the heading "Uniform Laws"; 2) the *Uniform Laws Annotated*,[19] "Directory of Uniform Acts and Codes, Tables - Index" volume; and 3) the *Handbook of the National Conference of Commissioners on Uniform State Laws*.[20] Unfortunately, no one source listed all applicable acts.

The following uniform and model laws are presently in force in Arizona:

Title	**A.R.S.Citation**	**Date Enacted**
Acknowledgement Act	§§33-511 to 33-513	1971
Act Regulating Traffic on Highways (Promulgated by the National Conference on Street and Highway Safety)	§§28-601 to 28-1080	1950
Act to Secure Attendance of Witness from Without a State in Criminal Proceedings	§§13-4091 to 13-4096	1937
Anatomical Gift Act	§§36-841 to 36-849	1970

18 National Conference of Commissioners on Uniform State Laws, *Handbook of the National Conference of Commissioners on Uniform State Laws and Proceedings of the Annual Conference Meeting in its Ninety-Fourth Year* (Buffalo, NY: William S. Hein, 1989), 555.

19 *Uniform Laws Annotated* (St. Paul, MN: West Publishing Co., 1990). 23 vols.

20 National Conference of Commissioners on Uniform State Laws, *Handbook,* 691 p.

Title	A.R.S.Citation	Date Enacted
Arbitration Act	§§12-1501 to 12-1518	1962
Business Records as Evidence Act	§12-2262	1951
Certification of Questions of Law Act	§§12-1861 to 12-1867	1984
Child Custody Jurisdiction Act	§§8-401 to 8-424	1978
Commercial Code	§§47-1101 to 47-11107	1967
Article 9 Revision	§§47-9101 to 47-9501	1984
Common Trust Fund Act	§§6-871 to 6-874	1971
Condominium Act	§§33-1201 to 33-1270	1985
Conservation Easement Act	§§33-271 to 33-276	1985
Contribution Among Tortfeasors Act	§§12-2501 to 12-2509	1984
Controlled Substances Act	§§36-2501 to 36-2553	1979
Criminal Extradition Act	§§13-3841 to 13-3869	1937
Declaratory Judgments	§§12-1831 to 12-1846	1927
Division of Income for Tax Purposes Act	§§43-1131 to 43-1150	1983
Durable Power of Attorney Act	§§14-5501 to 14-5502	1973
Enforcement of Foreign Judgments Act (1964)	§§12-1701 to 12-1708	1971
Federal Lien Registration Act	§§33-1031 to 33-1035	1990
Fiduciaries Act	§§14-7501 to 14-7512	1951
Fraudulent Transfer Act	§§44-1001 to 44-1010	1990
Guardianship and Protective Proceedings Act	§§14-5201 to 14-5212	1973
Insurers Liquidation Act	§§20-611 to 20-648	1954
Limited Partnership Act	§§29-301 to 29-366	1982
Mandatory Disposition of Detainers Act	ARIZ. R. CRIM. P. 8.3(b)	1958

Title	A.R.S.Citation	Date Enacted
Marriage and Divorce Act	§§25-311 to 25-339	1973
Minor Student Capacity to Borrow Act (Model)	§§44-140 to 44-140.01	1971
Model Business Corporation Act (promulgated by the ABA Section of Corporation Banking and Business Law and the American Bar Foundation)	§§10-002 to 10-149	1975
Model Rules of Professional Conduct (promulgated by the American Bar Foundation)	Sup. Ct. R., R. Professional Conduct 42, 46-73	1983
Motor Vehicle Safety Responsibility Act	§§28-1101 to 28-1262	1951
Nonprofit Business Corporation Act (Model)	§§l0-1002 to 10-1127	1979
Partnership Act	§§29-201 to 29-244	1954
Principal and Income Act	§§14-7401 to 14-7413	1984
Probate Code	§§14-1101 to 14-7307	1973
Reciprocal Enforcement of Support Act	§§12-1651 to 12-1691	1970
Recognition of Acknowledgments Act	§§33-501 to 33-508	1971
Residential Landlord and Tenant Act	§§33-1301 to 33-1381	1973
Rules of Evidence (1974)	Ariz. R. Evid. 101 to 1107	1977
Simplification of Fiduciaries Security Transfers	§§14-7601 to 14-7610	1961
Simultaneous Death Act	§§14-2804 to 14-2810	1984
Single Publication Act	§12-651	1953
State Administrative Procedure Act (1981) (Model) (1961) (Model)	§§41-1001 to 41-1066	1981, 1961

Title	A.R.S.Citation	Date Enacted
State Antitrust Act	§§44-1401 to 44-1413	1974
Testamentary Additions to Trust Act	§14-2511	1973
Trade Secrets	§§44-401 to 44-407	1990
Transfers to Minors Act	§§14-7651 to 14-7671	1988
Trustees' Powers Act	§§14-7231 to 14-7237	1984
Unclaimed Property Act	§§44-301 to 44-340	1983

Annotations to these "uniform" and "model" acts can be located after each *A.R.S. Annotated* section, in the *Uniform Laws Annotated* and in the Arizona Shepard's statutory citator.

H. Interstate Compacts

Interstate compacts are authorized by Article 1, Section 10 of the *U.S. Constitution* which reads "No State shall, without the Consent of Congress..., enter into any Agreement or Compact, with another State, or with a Foreign Power." Therefore, once a compact is approved by each party state, it must be returned to Congress for authorization. Most compacts will appear in both the *U.S. Statutes at Large* and in the session laws of each party state. It is only when the interstate activity does not touch on the federal sphere that prior Congressional approval is unnecessary.[21]

After adoption a state is forbidden from impairing its contractual obligations or from a unilateral renouncement except as previously agreed.[22] An interstate compact, as a contract, takes precedence over any conflicting state laws.[23]

Interstate compacts are employed when a permanent contractual agreement is needed among states. They have often been used in an attempt to solve broad social problems: those beyond a single state's legislation (e.g., nuclear energy, transportation, or natural resources). Interstate compacts have also established intergovernmental agencies which provide a new legal channel among the participating states.

The Council of State Governments publishes the *Interstate Compacts & Agencies Report*,[24] which describes the various interstate compacts, lists party states, and indexes "defunct or dormant" compacts. Between revisions, this volume is updated by the Council's *Book of the States* (published biennially).[25] Another

21 *Cuyler v. Adams,* 449 U.S. 433, 440 (1981).

22 *Texas v. New Mexico,* 462 U.S. 554, 563 (1983).

23 Ariz. Rev. Stat. Ann. § 1-104(A)(8), (1989).

24 *Interstate Compacts & Agencies* (Lexington, KY: Council of State Governments, 1983).

25 *The Book of the States,* 1990-91 ed. (Lexington, KY: Council of the State Governments, 1990), 636 p.

source for locating these agreements is the *A.R.S.* Index under the heading "Interstate Compacts," or "Compacts."

Arizona is presently a party to the following interstate compacts:

Title	A.R.S.Citation	Date Enacted
Agreement on Detainers (nationwide)	§§31-481 to 31-482	1970
Arizona-California Boundary Compact	§41-522, note 2 (Laws 1963, Ch. 77)	1963
Arizona-Nevada Boundary Compact	§41-523 Historical note. (Laws 1960, Chapter 69)	1960
Civil Defense and Disaster Compact (nationwide)	§26-309 Historical note. (Executive Order 76-2)	1976
Colorado River Compact Ratification (AZ, CA, CO, NV, NM, UT, WY)	§45-1311	1944
Compact for Education (nationwide)	§15-1901	1981
Driver License Compact (nationwide)	§§28-1601 to 28-1605	1963
Interstate Compact for Jurisdiction on the Colorado River	§37-620.11	1985
Interstate Compact for the Supervision of Parolees and Probationers (nationwide)	§§31-461 to 31-466	1973
Interstate Compact on Juveniles (nationwide)	§§8-361 to 8-367	1961
Interstate Compact on Placement of Children (United States and Canadian provinces)	§§8-548 to 8-548.06	1976
Interstate Corrections Compact (nationwide)	§§31-491 to 31-492	1972
Interstate Oil and Gas Compact (only oil and gas producing states eligible)	§§27-601 to 27-603	1935

Title	A.R.S.Citation	Date Enacted
Multistate Highway Transportation Agreement (Western States)	§§28-2301 to 28-2303	1982
Southwestern Low-Level Radioactive Waste Disposal Compact	§§30-721 to 30-722	1988
Upper Colorado River Basin Compact (AZ, CO, NM, UT, WY).	§45-1321	1949
Vehicle Equipment Safety Compact (nationwide)	§§28-1611 to 28-1618	1964
Western Interstate Corrections Compact (nationwide)	§§31-471 to 31-475	1970
Western Interstate Nuclear Compact (AZ, CA, CO, ID, MT, NV, NM, OR, UT, WA, WY)	§§30-701 to 30-705	1969
Western Regional Cooperation in Higher Education Compact (AZ, CA, CO, HI, ID, MT, NV, NM, OR, UT, WA, WY)	§§15-1741 to 15-1746	1981
Wildlife Violator Compact	§§17-501 to 17-503	1990

Annotations to these interstate compacts can be located after each *A.R.S. Annotated* section, and in the Arizona Shepard's Statutory Citator.

I. Legislative Citation Form

In Arizona the bibliographic format for citing Arizona legislation varies depending upon whether the *Uniform System of Citation*[26] or the *A.R.S.* format is used.

The *Uniform System of Citation* suggests the following abbreviated format:

Arizona Revised Statutes Annotated:
Ariz. Rev. Stat. Ann. § x (19xx)

Arizona Session Laws:
19xx Ariz. Sess. Laws xxx

26 *The Bluebook: A Uniform System of Citation,* 15th ed. (Cambridge, MA: The Harvard Law Review Association, 1991), 343 p.

(West) Arizona Legislative Service:
19xx Ariz. Legis. Serv. xxx (West)

Arizona State Constitution:
Ariz. Const. art. x, § x.

However, although the "Blue Book" format is the standard, the statutes themselves state that the *Arizona Revised Statutes* may be cited as "A.R.S." followed by the number of the title and section, separated by a dash (e.g., *A.R.S.* §2-101).[27] Alternative citation forms can be found in the front of the West annotated code volumes.

27 Ariz. Rev. Stat. Ann. §1-101 (1989).

Illustration A

CHAPTER 1

ARIZONA REVISED STATUTES

ARTICLE 1. IN GENERAL

Constitutional Provisions

Article 4, pt. 1, § 1, vests legislative authority in the legislature with a reservation to the people of initiative and referendum powers.

Cross References

Appropriation bills, see Const. Art. 4, pt. 2, § 20.
Approval or veto of legislative acts, see § 41-1181 et seq.
Commission on uniform laws, see §§ 41-1306, 41-1307.
Distribution of copies of revision of laws, see § 41-123.
Law library, library division, see § 41-1337.
Legislation by reference prohibited, see Const. Art. 4, pt. 2, § 14.
Local and special laws prohibited, see Const. Art. 4, pt. 2, § 19.
Printing of laws, see § 41-121.
Statutes to embrace single subject expressed in title, see Const. Art. 4, pt. 2, § 13.
Tax statutes authorized, see Const. Art. 9, § 3.
Tax statutes to specify object, see Const. Art. 9, § 9.
Veto of legislation, see Const. Art. 5, § 7.

ARTICLE 1. IN GENERAL

Library References

Statutes ⇐105 et seq., 129 et seq., 151 et seq., 248 et seq.
WESTLAW Topic No. 361.
C.J.S. Statutes §§ 150, 212, 243, 282, 399, 402.

§ 1-101. Designation and citation

The Arizona Revised Statutes adopted and enacted into law by this Act, and as hereafter amended and supplemented and printed and published pursuant to § 1-106, shall be known as Arizona Revised Statutes and may be cited as "A.R.S." followed by the number of the Title and the number of the Section in the Title, separated by a dash. Example: This section may be cited: "A.R.S. § 1-101".

Cross References

Citation of Rules of Civil Procedure, see Rules Civ.Proc., Rule 85.

2

Illustration B

insurance department or departments, or as a full-time staff member of a public accounting or actuarial firm regularly employed to conduct examinations for a state insurance department.
Amended by Laws 1985, Ch. 343, § 2.

Historical and Statutory Notes

Source:
Laws 1954, Ch. 64, Art. 2, § 7.
Code 1939, Supp. 1954, § 61-1407.

Reviser's Note:
Laws 1954, Ch. 157, § 1 amended Laws 1949, Ch. 116, § 5 (61-301b, C. '39, Supp. '52) by providing that the director of insurance might appoint a chief examiner. The section is omitted as superseded by Laws 1954, Ch. 64, Art. 2, § 7.

§ 20–148. Deputies and other employees; special services

A. The director shall appoint such other deputies, assistants and clerks, as necessary properly to discharge the duties imposed upon the director under this title.

B. The director may from time to time contract for and procure, on a fee or part time basis, or both, such actuarial, technical and other professional services as he may require for the operation of his office.

C. The compensation of each deputy, actuary, assistant and clerk shall be as determined pursuant to § 38–611.
Amended by Laws 1970, Ch. 204, § 47.

Historical and Statutory Notes

Source:
Laws 1954, Ch. 64, Art. 2, § 7.
Code 1939, Supp. 1954, § 61-1407.

Cross References

Filed rates, compliance, independent contractor examiners, see § 20–400.05.
Insurance examiners revolving fund, compensation, see § 20–159.

Notes of Decisions

Employees 1

1. Employees

Insurance examiner hired to examine one insurer, given letter of introduction and authorization to conduct examination and present claims for customary charges, given general guidelines, and required only to render report of examination without guarantee of reemployment is not an "employee" within the Social Security Act, 42 U.S.C.A. § 410(j)(2), and is not covered by agreement entered into between federal security administrator and state. Op. Atty.Gen. No. 67-17-L.

Insurance examiners engaged under this section and paid pursuant to § 20–159 are not "employees" of state within definition of Social Security Act, 42 U.S.C.A. § 410(j)(2) and are not covered by agreement entered into by federal security administrator and state. Id.

§ 20–149. Prohibition on certain activities by employees; conflict of interest

A. The director, or any deputy, examiner, assistant or employee of the director shall not be financially interested, directly or indirectly, in any

Illustration C

INSURANCE

207

Illustration D

TABLE I

ARIZONA CODE ANNOTATED 1939 AND SUPPLEMENTS

Showing the distribution in Arizona Revised Statutes or other disposition of sections appearing in Arizona Code Annotated 1939 and Supplements of 1952, 1954, 1955.

ABBREVIATIONS

Am	Amended
Appn	Appropriation
A.R.S.	Arizona Revised Statutes
Civ	Rules of Civil Procedure
Cov	Covered by other legislation
Crim	Rules of Criminal Procedure
Eff	Effective date
Emerg	Emergency clause
Expired	Expired or obsolete legislation
Init Meas	Initiative Measure
Omtd	Sections relating to practice and procedure omitted by Supreme Court or sections omitted by Code Commission
Omtd '28	Omitted from Revised Code 1928
R	Repealed
Repealer	Repealing clause or section
RN	Reviser's Note under cited section of Arizona Revised Statutes explaining diposition
SCR	Rules of Supreme Court
Special	Special or local legislation
Sup	Superseded or impliedly repealed
Temp	Expired by legislative limitation
Uncon	Unconstitutional

Code 1939 and Supp.	A.R.S.
1-101	1-211
	1-244
1-102	1-243
1-102a	1-242
1-102b	1-242
1-103	1-211
	1-213
	1-214
	1-215
	1-216
	1-217
	14-101
1-104	1-245
1-105	1-252
1-106	1-201
1-107	1-251
1-108	1-250
1-109	1-249
1-110	1-248
1-111	1-202
	44-121
1-112	1-241
2-101	41-1101
2-102	41-1102
2-103	41-1102
2-104	41-1102

18 Ariz.Rev.St.Anno.—1 1

Illustration E

1955 TABLE VII—SESSION LAWS

LAWS 1955, 2ND SPECIAL SESSION—Cont'd

Ch.	Sec.	A.R.S.
1	28	42-1423
	29	42-1425
2	1	42-1321
	2	RN 42-1321

LAWS 1955, 3RD SPECIAL SESSION

Ch.	Sec.	A.R.S.
1	1-4	Appn
	5	Emerg
2	1	41-1103
	2	41-1134
	3	Temp
	4	Emerg
3	1	Enactment of A.R.S.
	2	Emerg

LAWS 1956

Ch.	Sec.	A.R.S.
1	1	45-313
	2	Emerg
2	—	Appn
3	—	Temp
4	—	Appn
5	—	Appn
6	1	41-581.01 to 41-581.10
	2	Temp
	3	Emerg
7	1	13-1721
8	1	12-1225
9	1	13-1673
10	1	1-301
11	1	41-144
12	—	Appn
13	—	Appn
14	—	Appn
15	1	46-311
16	1	42-276
17	1	36-1062
	2	Emerg
18	1	9-101
19	—	Appn
20	—	Appn
21	—	Appn
22	—	Appn
23	—	Appn

LAWS 1956—Cont'd

Ch.	Sec.	A.R.S.
24	—	Appn
25	—	Appn
26	1	28-798
	2	Emerg
27	1	24-292
28	1	9-497
29	1	11-261
30	1	1-215
31	—	Appn
32	1	36-1671 to 36-1674 36-1681 to 36-1685 36-1691 to 36-1698
	2	Eff
33	—	Appn
34	1	27-121
	2	27-122
	3	27-141
35	1	18-107
36	—	Appn
37	1	42-1507
38	1	32-1334
	2	Emerg
39	1	32-1305
40	—	Appn
41	—	Appn
42	—	Appn
43	—	Appn
44	—	Appn
45	—	Appn
46	1	12-612
	2	12-613
47	—	Appn
48	—	Appn
49	1	15-444.02
50	1	17-261.01
51	1	23-982
52	—	Appn
53	1	15-1248
	2	Emerg
54	1	41-332
55	1	Repealer
	2	3-231 to 3-242

496

Illustration F

CHAPTER 1

STATE HIGHWAYS [REPEALED]

Chapter 1, consisting of Article 1, §§ 18–101 to 18–118, Article 2, §§ 18–131 to 18–140, Article 2.1, §§ 18–141 to 18–150.03, Article 3, §§ 18–151 to 18–163, Article 4, §§ 18–181 to 18–185, and Article 5, § 18–191, was repealed by Laws 1973, Ch. 146 § 85, effective July 1, 1974.

DISPOSITION TABLE

Showing where the subject matter of sections repealed by Laws 1973, Ch. 146, § 85, effective July 1, 1974, was covered by new sections:

Repealed Sections	New Sections
18–101	28–1801
18–102	28–104, 28–104.01, 28–105
18–103	None
18–104	28–105
18–105	None
18–106	28–106, 28–1803
18–107	18–1802
18–108	28–1803
18–109	28–1803
18–110	28–1803
18–111	28–1802
18–112	None
18–113	28–1804
18–114	28–109
18–115	None
18–116	28–1805
18–117	28–1806
18–118	28–1807
18–131	28–1821
18–132	28–1822
18–133	28–1823
18–134	28–1824
18–135	28–1825
18–136	28–1826
18–137	28–1827
18–138	28–1828
18–138.01	28–1829
18–139	28–1830
18–139.01	28–1831
18–140	28–1832
18–141	28–1841
18–142	28–1842
18–143	28–1843
18–144	28–1844
18–145	28–1845
18–146	28–1846
18–147	28–1847
18–148	28–1848
18–149	28–1849
18–150	28–1850
18–150.01	28–1851
18–150.02	28–1852
18–150.03	28–1853
18–151	28–1861
18–152	28–1862
18–153	28–1863
18–154	28–1864
18–155	28–1865
18–155.01	28–1865.01
18–156	28–1866
18–157	28–1867
18–158	28–1868
18–159	28–1869
18–160	28–1870
18–160.01	28–1871
18–161	28–1872
18–162	28–1873
18–163	28–1874
18–181	28–1881
18–182	28–1882
18–183	None
18–184	28–1883
18–185	28–1884
18–191	28–1891
18–501	28–1901
18–502	28–1902
18–503	28–1903
18–504	28–1904
18–505	28–1905
18–506	28–1906
18–507	28–1907
18–508	28–1908
18–601	28–2001
18–602	28–2002

2

Illustration G

TITLE 12

COURTS AND CIVIL PROCEEDINGS

CHAPTER 3.—FEES AND COSTS

ARTICLE 5. RECOVERY OF COSTS

§ 12–341. Recovery of costs

Notes of Decisions

Comparative negligence, successful parties 4.5

---

4. Successful parties—In general

In cases involving various competing claims, counterclaims, and setoffs all tried together, the "successful party" for purposes of recovery of costs is the net winner. Ayala v. Olaiz (App. 1989) 161 Ariz. 129, 776 P.2d 807.

4.5. —— Comparative negligence, successful parties

Plaintiff in a comparative negligence personal injury case involving no counterclaim was the "successful party" entitled to receive all of her taxable costs even though the jury determined that she was 65% at fault. Ayala v. Olaiz (App. 1989) 161 Ariz. 129, 776 P.2d 807.

5. —— Partially successful parties

Party who recovers judgment for only a part of a demand or claim is entitled to all taxable costs in the absence of a statute providing for apportionment or some other rule. Ayala v. Olaiz (App.1989) 161 Ariz. 129, 776 P.2d 807.

§ 12–341.01. Recovery of attorney's fees

United States Supreme Court

Attorney fees, prevailing party in civil rights litigation, significant issue test, see Texas State Teachers Association v. Garland Independent School District, 1989, 109 S.Ct. 1486, 103 L.Ed.2d 866, on remand 874 F.2d 242.

Notes of Decisions

5. Successful parties

Fund Manager of Public Safety Personnel Retirement System was entitled to attorney fees as prevailing party in contested action arising out of contract for prevailing in action brought by state Attorney General challenging constitutionality of subsec. L of A.R.S. § 38–848 exempting contracts for goods and services approved by Fund Manager retroactively from requirements of Procurement Code, A.R.S. §§ 41–2501 to 41–2652. The Fund Manager v. Corbin (App. 1988) 161 Ariz. 348, 778 P.2d 1244, opin. aff'd in pt, appeal dismissed in pt 161 Ariz. 364, 778 P.2d 1260.

Homeowners could recover attorney fees as "successful parties" on appeal which resulted in reversal of trial court's grant of summary judgment on their claim against contractor's surety for bad faith. Dodge v. Fidelity and Deposit Co. of Maryland (1989) 161 Ariz. 344, 778 P.2d 1240.

26. Settlement and compromise

Award of attorneys' fees to defendant as a consequence of plaintiff's breach of settlement agreement was proper. Hays v. Fischer (App. 1989) 161 Ariz. 159, 777 P.2d 222.

§ 12–348. Award of fees and other expenses against the state or a city, town or county; reduction or denial of award; application; basis for amount of award; source of award; definitions

Notes of Decisions

7. Political subdivisions

Where class of indigent chronically mentally ill persons prevailed in special action to compel state and county to provide mental health services, county could properly be held responsible for one third of attorney fee award under "private attorney general doctrine." Arnold v. Arizona Dept. of Health Services (1989) 160 Ariz. 593, 775 P.2d 521.

14

Illustration H

SECOND REGULAR SESSION—1990 Ch. 190

3. "Certified laboratory" means a laboratory certified by the United States department of health and human services.

~~1.~~ 4. "Clinical laboratory" or "laboratory" means any facility, agency, institution, medical office, health care institution, building, or place which provides through its ownership or operation facilities for the ~~employment of methods and instruments of precision for the examination of secretions, body fluids and excretions of the human body and its functions to aid in the diagnosis of disease, follow the course of disease, or aid in the treatment of such disease, or which purports to offer such examinations, except as provided in section 36-461.~~ microbiological, serological, chemical, immunohematological, hematological, cytologic, histologic, radiobioassay, cytogenetic, histocompatibility, pathological, toxicological or other examination of materials derived from the human body for the purpose of providing information for the diagnosis, prevention and treatment of a disease or an impairment or the assessment of human health conditions or to determine the presence, absence or concentration of various substances in the body. Clinical laboratory does not include law enforcement crime laboratories.

~~2.~~ 5. "Department" means the department of health services.

~~3.~~ 6. "Director" means the director of the department of health services.

~~4. "Director of a clinical laboratory" means a person who administers the technical and scientific operation of a medical clinical laboratory, including the reporting of the findings of clinical laboratory tests. The director of a clinical laboratory may not merely be nominal, but shall participate actively in its operation to such extent as may be necessary to assure compliance with the objects and purposes of article 2 of this chapter.~~

7. "Federally licensed laboratory" means a laboratory licensed pursuant to the United States Clinical Laboratory Improvement Amendments of 1988 (P.L. 100-518).

8. "Governing authority" means the individual, agency, group or corporation that is appointed, elected or otherwise designated and that has the ultimate responsibility and authority for the conduct of the health care institution.

9. "Health care institution" has the same meaning as prescribed in section 36-401.

10. "License" means a regular license, renewal license or provisional license issued by the department pursuant to this chapter.

~~5.~~ 11. "Person" means any individual, firm, partnership, association~~,~~ or corporation, whether or not organized for profit, or any other form of business enterprise.

Sec. 2. Section 36-461, Arizona Revised Statutes, is amended to read:

§ 36-461. Exceptions to this article

The provisions of this article ~~shall~~ apply to all clinical laboratories and directors of clinical laboratories~~, except~~ but do not apply to the following:

1. Clinical laboratories operated, licensed or certified by the United States government.

~~2. A person licensed under chapter 13 or chapter 17 of title 32, whose operation of a laboratory is limited to laboratory analyses performed for his own patients and within the scope of his license.~~

~~3. Personnel employed in clinical laboratories other than the director of the clinical laboratory.~~

~~4. Hospitals licensed by the state, except that said hospitals shall be required to maintain the same level of practice in their clinical laboratories as required of any other clinical laboratory licensed under the provisions of this chapter.~~

Additions are indicated by underline; deletions by ~~strikeouts~~— 627

5 Ariz.Leg.Serv. '90—3

Illustration I

Ch. 186 — 39th LEGISLATURE

MOTOR VEHICLES—WEIGHT FEE EXEMPTION FOR NONPROFIT SCHOOLS—CONDITIONS

CHAPTER 186

H.B. 2283

AN ACT RELATING TO TRANSPORTATION; PRESCRIBING AN EXEMPTION FROM WEIGHT FEE FOR MOTOR VEHICLES, TRAILERS AND SEMITRAILERS OPERATED BY CERTAIN NONPROFIT SCHOOLS UPON CERTAIN CONDITIONS, AND AMENDING SECTION 28-207, ARIZONA REVISED STATUTES.

Be it enacted by the Legislature of the State of Arizona:

Section 1. Section 28–207, Arizona Revised Statutes, is amended to read:

§ 28–207. Exemption from payment of weight fees; religious institutions; nonprofit schools; disaster assistance organizations; government entities; pupil transportation

A. Motor vehicles, trailers or semitrailers owned and operated by religious institutions and used exclusively for the transportation of property produced and distributed for charitable purposes without compensation are exempt from the weight fee provided by section 28–206.

B. For the purposes of subsection A of this section, "religious institution" means a recognized organization having an established place of meeting for religious worship which holds regular meetings for that purpose at least once each week in not less than five cities or towns in the state.

C. Motor vehicles, trailers and semitrailers owned and operated by nonprofit schools which are recognized as being tax exempt by the federal or state government, are exempt from the weight fee provided by section 28–206 if ~~and~~ used exclusively for any of the following:

1. The transportation of pupils in connection with the school curriculum ~~are exempt from the weight fee provided by section 28–206~~.

2. The training of pupils.

3. The transportation of property for charitable purposes without compensation.

D. Motor vehicles, trailers and semitrailers owned by any nonprofit organization in this state which presents to the motor vehicle division a form approved by the director of the division of emergency services pursuant to section 26–318 are exempt from the weight fee provided by section 28–206.

E. A vehicle owned and operated by a foreign government, a consul or other official representative of a foreign government, by the United States, by a state or political subdivision of a state or by an Indian tribal government is exempt from the weight fees provided by section 28–206.

F. A motor vehicle which is privately owned and operated exclusively as a school bus pursuant to a contract with a school district is exempt from the weight fee prescribed by section 28–206, subsection A. If a privately owned and operated school bus is temporarily operated for purposes other than those prescribed by section 28–101, paragraph 52, the registering officer shall assess and collect a monthly weight fee equal to one-tenth of the annual weight fee

620 **Additions are indicated by underline; deletions by ~~strikeouts~~**

Illustration J

peace courts, and municipal courts and shall submit a report to the legislature and to the governor by December 31, 1989 detailing actual costs incurred by the courts in processing each individual type of action and recommending appropriate fees for each type of action. 1989

12-116. Time payment fee

Repealed effective January 1, 1996

A. In addition to any other assessment authorized by law, a fee of eight dollars shall be assessed on each person who pays a court ordered penalty, fine, or sanction on a time payment basis. A time payment basis shall be any penalty, fine, or sanction not paid in full the date the court imposed the fine, penalty or sanction. Notwithstanding any other law, the time payment fee shall be collected first. A judge may not waive or suspend a time payment fee.

B. Three dollars of this fee shall be deposited in the judicial collection enhancement fund established in section 12-113. Two dollars of this fee shall be allocated to the county public defender training fund established in section 12-117. The remainder shall be kept by the court imposing the fee to be utilized by the court to improve, maintain and enhance the ability to collect and manage monies assessed or received by the courts, to improve court automation and to improve case processing or the administration of justice. The court shall submit a plan to the supreme court which must be approved by the supreme court prior to the court expending such monies. 1989

12-117. County public defender training fund; appropriation

Repealed effective January 1, 1996

A. The county public defender training fund is established consisting of monies allocated to the fund pursuant to section 12-116. The supreme court shall administer the fund.

B. On the first day of each month the state treasurer shall deposit in the fund the monies collected for the fund. All monies deposited in the fund are continuously apppropriated to the supreme court for distribution to each county public defender as provided in subsection C of this section.

C. The allocation of monies collected shall be made to each county public defender office in proportion to the number of felony cases assigned to that office in the last fiscal year.

D. Monies received shall be used exclusively for the purpose of county public defender training. Each county public defender office receiving training fund monies shall submit to the supreme court an annual report of all financial receipts and expenditures from the training fund. 1989

ARTICLE 1.1. COURT OF APPEALS

12-120. Creation of court of appeals; court of record; composition; sessions

Text of section effective July 1, 1989

A. There is created a court of appeals which shall constitute a single court and such court shall be a court of record.

B. The court of appeals shall be divided into two divisions which shall be designated as division 1 and division 2. Division 1 shall have fifteen judges, separated into five departments of three judges each, denominated, respectively, department A, department B, department C, department D and department E. Division 2 shall have six judges, separated into two departments of three judges each, denominated, respectively, department A and department B.

C. Division 1 shall consist of the counties of Maricopa, Yuma, La Paz, Mohave, Coconino, Yavapai, Navajo and Apache.

D. Division 2 shall consist of the counties of Pima, Pinal, Cochise, Santa Cruz, Greenlee, Graham and Gila.

E. The sessions of divisions 1 and 2 shall be held in Phoenix and Tucson, respectively. Sessions may be held at places other than Phoenix or Tucson when in the opinion of a majority of the judges of a division or department the public interest so requires. The judges of the respective divisions and departments may hold sessions in either division and shall do so when directed by the chief justice of the supreme court. Each judge of the court of appeals may participate in matters pending before a different division or department.

F. No more than three judges of the court of appeals, including superior court judges and retired judges sitting with the court, shall hear and determine a matter and render a decision, and a majority of two of the three judges shall be sufficient to render a decision. 1988

12-120.01. Qualifications of judges; terms; ballots; vacancies

Text of section effective July 1, 1989

A. A judge of the court of appeals shall be:

1. Not less than thirty years of age.
2. Of good moral character.
3. A qualified elector of the county of his residence, and a resident of such county for not less than three years next preceding taking office.
4. A resident of the division in which he is elected.
5. Admitted to the practice of law in the state of Arizona for not less than five years next preceding taking office.
6. A resident of Arizona for not less than five years next preceding taking office.

B. Except for the initial term, each judge shall hold office for a term of six years to commence on the first Monday in January following his election and until his successor is elected and qualified. The three additional judges necessary to increase division 1 to fifteen judges under the provisions of section 12-120 shall be appointed by the governor pursuant to article VI, section 37, Constitution of Arizona. Of the additional judges two shall be residents of Maricopa county and otherwise qualified for such positions, and one shall be a resident of one of the counties in division 1 other than Maricopa county and otherwise qualified. The additional judges shall serve an initial term pursuant to article VI, section 37, Constitution of Arizona. Thereafter such additional judges shall be elected to six year terms in the same manner as is operative for the existing division 1 judgeships. 1988

12-120.02. Election of judges.

Text of section effective July 1, 1989

A. In division 1, ten of the judges shall be residents of and elected from Maricopa county and five of the judges shall be residents of the remaining counties in the division and shall be elected by the voters of the counties in division 1, excluding Maricopa county

Illustration K

Illustration L-1

§§ 18-131 to 18-140 HIGHWAYS AND BRIDGES
Repealed Title 18

ARTICLE 2. STATE HIGHWAY FUND AND BUDGET [REPEALED]

§§ 18-131 to 18-140. Repealed by Laws 1973, Ch. 146, § 85, eff. July 1, 1974

Historical and Statutory Notes

The repealed sections, relating to the State highway fund and budget, were derived from:

Laws 1927, 4th S.S., Ch. 2, subch. 4, §§ 1, 3, 6, 8 to 13, 16 to 19.
Laws 1927, 4th S.S., Ch. 13, § 1.
Rev.Code 1928, §§ 1575 to 1581, 1584 to 1586.
Laws 1931, Ch. 100, § 8.
Laws 1933, Ch. 27, § 1.
Code 1939, §§ 59-303, 59-310.
Laws 1945, 1st S.S., Ch. 10, §§ 1 to 8.
Laws 1947, Ch. 102, § 1.
Laws 1947, 2nd S.S., Ch. 35, §§ 1, 2.
Code 1939, Supp.1952, §§ 59-301, 59-302, 59-304 to 59-308, 59-311, 59-312.
Laws 1968, Ch. 89, § 15.
Laws 1970, Ch. 120, § 1.

Prior to repeal, § 18-138.01 was added by Laws 1968, Ch. 89, § 1, and § 18-139.01 was added by Laws 1970, Ch. 120, § 1, and the following sections were amended:

§ 18-132 .....Laws 1966, Ch. 117, § 1
§ 18-135 .....Laws 1970, Ch. 190, § 25
Laws 1971, Ch. 155, § 2
§ 18-137 .....Laws 1970, Ch. 190, § 26
Laws 1971, Ch. 132, § 1
§ 18-138 .....Laws 1968, Ch. 89, § 14
Laws 1972, Ch. 141, § 13
§ 18-138.01 ..Laws 1972, Ch. 141, § 14
§ 18-139 .....Laws 1965, Ch. 14, § 1
Laws 1968, Ch. 89, § 16
Laws 1972, Ch. 141, § 15
§ 18-140 .....Laws 1968, Ch. 89, § 17
Laws 1972, Ch. 141, § 16

For disposition of the subject matter of repealed sections, see Disposition Table preceding § 18-101.

ARTICLE 2.1. RELOCATION ASSISTANCE AND REAL PROPERTY ACQUISITION POLICIES [REPEALED]

§§ 18-141 to 18-150.03. Repealed by Laws 1973, Ch. 146, § 85, eff. July 1, 1974

Historical and Statutory Notes

The repealed sections, relating to relocation assistance and real property acquisition policies, were derived from Laws 1969, Ch. 50, § 1, and Laws 1971, Ch. 85, § 9.

Prior to repeal, the following sections were amended:

§ 18-141 .....Laws 1969, Ch. 50, § 1
Laws 1971, Ch. 85, § 2
§ 18-142 .....Laws 1969, Ch. 50, § 1
Laws 1971, Ch. 85, § 3
§ 18-143 .....Laws 1969, Ch. 50, § 1
Laws 1971, Ch. 85, § 4
§ 18-144 .....Laws 1969, Ch. 50, § 1
Laws 1971, Ch. 85, § 5
§ 18-145 .....Laws 1969, Ch. 50, § 1
Laws 1971, Ch. 85, § 6
§ 18-146 .....Laws 1969, Ch. 50, § 1
Laws 1971, Ch. 85, § 7
§ 18-147 .....Laws 1969, Ch. 50, § 1
§ 18-148 .....Laws 1969, Ch. 50, § 1
Laws 1971, Ch. 85, § 8
§ 18-149 .....Laws 1969, Ch. 50, § 1
§ 18-150 .....Laws 1969, Ch. 50, § 1

For disposition of the subject matter of repealed sections, see Disposition Table preceding § 18-101.

Illustration L-2

TITLE 18

HIGHWAYS AND BRIDGES

CHAPTER 2

COUNTY HIGHWAYS

ARTICLE 1. CONSTRUCTION, MAINTENANCE AND ABANDONMENT

ARTICLE 2. COUNTY HIGHWAY BONDS AND COUNTY HIGHWAY COMMISSION

ARTICLE 1. CONSTRUCTION, MAINTENANCE AND ABANDONMENT

18-201. Establishing, altering or abandoning local highways

The board of supervisors may establish, alter or abandon highways in the county and other legal subdivisions, and acquire real property for such purposes by purchase, donation, dedication, condemnation or other lawful means. Such highways may be established or altered by presentation of a petition signed by ten or more resident taxpayers of the county to the board of supervisors, or upon petition to the board by the governing body of a legal subdivision, praying that a highway be established or altered and giving its beginning, terminus and its general course and direction. The board may either reject the petition or act thereon as prescribed by this article. The board may abandon or vacate such highways by resolution as provided in title 28, chapter 14, article 1. 1976

18-202. Survey of proposed highway; notice of hearing

A. Upon filing the petition, the board shall direct the county engineer to make a survey of the proposed highway and file with the board a report of the proposed highway, together with a map as surveyed, showing thereon the legal subdivision of the lands traversed by the survey. If a survey and maps have already been made for any purpose, such data and maps may be used instead.

B. The board shall thereupon set a date for a public hearing on the petition. The board shall give notice to the public by advertising once a week for two consecutive weeks in a newspaper in the county. The notice shall state the purpose and the date of the ensuing hearing, and shall direct all persons desiring to object to the action prayed for in the petition to file with the board a statement in writing setting forth their objection or opposition, and to show cause why the petition should not be granted. 1961

18-203. Hearing

A. At the hearing provided for in § 18-202 the board shall consider the feasibility, advantages and necessity of the highway sought to be established, and, if in the opinion of the board the proposed highway is a public necessity, the board may approve the establishment thereof by resolution, and may accept any right of way or property donated to the state or the county.

B. A landowner or party affected may make and execute a written waiver or release of all compensation or any part thereof, or may grant an easement or other conveyance of property for such purposes. 1961

18-206. Exercise of eminent domain by county to obtain right of way for federal-county highway

A. When a board of supervisors enters into an agreement with the United States acting through its duly authorized officers or agents, pursuant to an act of Congress for acquiring a right of way for a highway in a county, and the United States has constructed a part of the highway described in the agreement, but the board of supervisors has been unable under the provisions of §§ 18-201 and 18-202 to acquire a right of way necessary for completion of the highway, it is the duty of the county attorney of the county upon demand by the agent of the United States having charge of the work to be done by the United States under the agreement, and upon resolution by the board of supervisors directing him so to do, to file in the superior court of the county in which the land is located, proceedings for condemnation as provided in § 12-1116 in the name of the county.

Illustration M

FIRST REGULAR SESSION—1989 Ch. 207

COURTS AND CIVIL PROCEEDINGS—SUBPOENA DUCES TECUM—HEALTH CARE PROVIDERS

CHAPTER 207

SENATE BILL 1170

AN ACT

RELATING TO COURTS AND CIVIL PROCEEDINGS; PRESCRIBING DEFINITIONS; PRESCRIBING COMPLIANCE BY HEALTH CARE PROVIDERS WITH A SUBPOENA DUCES TECUM; PRESCRIBING REQUIREMENTS FOR SERVICE OF THE SUBPOENA; PRESCRIBING NOTICE TO THE PATIENT; PRESCRIBING EXCEPTIONS; PRESCRIBING OBJECTION BY PATIENT; PRESCRIBING OBJECTION BY HEALTH CARE PROVIDER; PRESCRIBING CONTENTS OF AFFIDAVIT ACCOMPANYING RECORDS; PRESCRIBING PRODUCTION OF RECORDS UPON CERTAIN COURT ORDER; PRESCRIBING LIMITATION ON LIABILITY; MAKING TECHNICAL AND CONFORMING CHANGES; AMENDING SECTIONS 12-2281, 12-2282 AND 12-2283, ARIZONA REVISED STATUTES; REPEALING SECTION 12-2285, ARIZONA REVISED STATUTES, AND AMENDING TITLE 12, CHAPTER 13, ARTICLE 7, ARIZONA REVISED STATUTES, BY ADDING A NEW SECTION 12-2285 AND SECTION 12-2287.

Be it enacted by the Legislature of the State of Arizona:

Section 1. Section 12-2281, Arizona Revised Statutes, is amended to read:

12-2281. Definitions

In this article, unless the context otherwise requires:

1. "Health care ~~institution~~ PROVIDER" means:

(a) A health care institution as defined in section 36-401~~, and includes~~ OR a health care services organization holding a certificate of authority pursuant to section 20-1054.

(b) A PERSON LICENSED UNDER TITLE 32 TO PROVIDE HEALTH CARE, MEDICAL SERVICES, NURSING SERVICES OR OTHER HEALTH RELATED SERVICES, OR A CORPORATION AUTHORIZED TO PROVIDE SUCH SERVICES UNDER SECTION 10-901.

2. "Records" means the records of OR HELD BY a health care ~~institution~~ PROVIDER in this state relating to the medical care or treatment of a patient in OR BY such health care ~~institution~~ PROVIDER.

Sec. 2. Section 12-2282, Arizona Revised Statutes, is amended to read:

12-2282. Compliance with subpoena duces tecum for health care provider records; issuance of subpoena; notice; exception

A. A SUBPOENA SEEKING RECORDS SHALL BE SERVED ON THE HEALTH CARE PROVIDER, THE PATIENT OR THE PATIENT'S ATTORNEY AND ANY PARTY TO THE PROCEEDINGS AT LEAST TEN DAYS BEFORE THE PRODUCTION DATE ON THE SUBPOENA. PROOF THAT SERVICE WAS MADE AT LEAST TEN DAYS BEFORE THE PRODUCTION DATE ON THE SUBPOENA SHALL ACCOMPANY EACH SUBPOENA SERVED.

B. NOTICE TO THE PATIENT SHALL ACCOMPANY THE SUBPOENA SERVED UNDER SUBSECTION A OF THIS SECTION STATING THAT THE SUBPOENA SEEKS PRODUCTION OF THE PATIENT'S RECORDS MAINTAINED BY A HEALTH CARE PROVIDER WHICH MAY BE PRIVILEGED UNDER STATE OR FEDERAL LAW, THAT THE PATIENT MAY FILE AN OBJECTION WITH THE PARTY SEEKING THE RECORDS AND WITH THE HEALTH CARE PROVIDER NO LATER THAN FIVE DAYS BEFORE THE PRODUCTION DATE ON THE SUBPOENA AND THAT THE PATIENT MAY WISH TO CONSULT AN ATTORNEY REGARDING THE SUBPOENA.

C. PROOF OF SERVICE AND NOTICE TO THE PATIENT IS NOT REQUIRED IF, AFTER REASONABLE INQUIRY, THE PERSON SEEKING THE RECORDS CANNOT DETERMINE

deletions by ~~strikeouts~~

Reprinted from 1989 *Session Laws of Arizona.*

Illustration N

INDEX TO ACTS

(includes cross-indexing by subject)

THIRTY-NINTH LEGISLATURE	FIRST REGULAR SESSION		
Statute Titles	Bill No.	Ch.	Page
CORRECTIVE LEGISLATION (not otherwise listed)			
1989 corrections bill	2259	283	1301
AGRICULTURE AND DAIRYING (Title 3)			
agricultural use: definition and criteria	1366	61	246
citrus, fruit & vegetable regulation	2255	66	253
milk and dairy products regulation	2042	99	336
Arizona iceberg lettuce promotion council	1164	146	556
Arizona iceberg lettuce research council	1165	147	561
Arizona department of agriculture	2090	162	620
coliseum executive director duties	1022	187	731
water quality; agricultural BMP's	1323	263	1132
Arizona native plant act	1086	294	1426
ALCOHOLIC BEVERAGES (Title 4)			
bingo regulation	1010	106	358
classified driver's license	2303	220	850
liquor laws; amendments	1144	234	1001
AMUSEMENTS AND SPORTS (Title 5)			
fishing tournament permits	2098	41	195
physical therapists; licensure: exception	2036	63	249
bingo regulation	1010	106	358
off-highway vehicles; permanent decals	1280	193	743
economic development	1397	203	787
horse and harness racing; percentage to state	2074	243	1064
sales tax exemption; hayrides; stables	2491	244	1071
ticket scalping	2276	245	1074
lottery; special games; economic development	2632	260	1121
sales tax exemption; cactus league	1404	299	1461
BANKS AND FINANCIAL INSTITUTIONS (Title 6)			
banks; investment of fiduciary funds	1083	131	468
county fiscal procedures	2656	180	699
BONDS (Title 7)			
school bond election canvass	2067	9	108
special district impact statement	2232	44	199
municipal bonds; mini-bonds	2219	52	228
highway bonding; limits	2011	62	248
appearance bond; forfeiture	2501	76	279
mortgage revenue bonds	1347	155	595
bonds; freeway mitigation	1408	157	613
building and fire safety	2236	164	630
securities sales; registration by qualification	2277	174	668
state highway bonding authorization	1217	184	707
municipal bonds; negotiated sale	2218	214	832
telephone solicitations; registration	2458	221	892
CHILDREN (Title 8)			
probate; conservators; protective proceedings	1046	38	182
child support central registry	2416	56	241
surrogate parentage contracts	2360	114	393
fingerprinting school personnel; teachers	2368	115	395
child support; order for assignment	2448	119	406
welfare; services; rent subsidies	2620	121	424

1645

Reprinted from 1989 *Session Laws of Arizona.*

Illustration O

ARIZONA REVISED STATUTES, (AS AMENDED BY REPLACEMENT VOLUMES TO 1983) AND SUPPLEMENT, 1983-1984 § 33-1105

535P2d33
550P2d230
574P2d57
642P2d882
655P2d800
661P2d1151
676P2d645
25BRW332
Subd. A
90Az139
93Az238
131Az537
134Az260
135Az451
367P2d196
379P2d908
642P2d882
655P2d800
661P2d1152
676P2d644
14AzL629
Subd. B
135Az451
661P2d1152
676P2d646
Subd. C
110Az188
516P2d324
§ 33-965
A1964C92
§ 33-981
et seq.
91Az177
94Az331
105Az99
105Az583
113Az572
123Az31
124Az323
132Az382
135Az159
26AzA477
370P2d661
385P2d211
459P2d724
469P2d68
549P2d257
558P2d917
597P2d184
604P2d252
646P2d267
659P2d1304
275FS873
C379FS997
381FS713
412FS670
420FS704
§§ 33-981 to
33-1006
135Az156
137Az442
659P2d1301
671P2d420
§§ 33-981 to
33-1001
13AzA348
476P2d869
2AzL222
§ 33-981
A1973C140
A1979C202
80Az169
81Az148
89Az235
89Az307
91Az177

94Az331
96Az70
101Az297
102Az258
103Az305
105Az99
122Az84
124Az323
127Az84
130Az92
130Az577
135Az159
137Az439
2AzA321
3AzA495
4AzA484
12AzA90
12AzA137
13AzA348
20AzA214
24AzA566
27AzA771
294P2d661
302P2d534
360P2d481
361P2d734
370P2d661
385P2d211
391P2d925
408P2d841
415P2d893
419P2d81
421P2d917
428P2d115
441P2d65
459P2d724
467P2d930
468P2d404
476P2d869
511P2d658
540P2d185
558P2d966
593P2d307
597P2d184
604P2d252
618P2d254
634P2d19
637P2d1080
659P2d1304
671P2d417
389FS1322
420FS704
Subd. A
89Az307
104Az103
105Az99
120Az79
123Az31
127Az84
135Az159
12AzA90
27AzA771
361P2d734
449P2d31
459P2d724
467P2d930
558P2d966
584P2d60
597P2d184
618P2d254
659P2d1304
Subd. B
91Az177
105Az99
123Az31
13AzA348

370P2d661
459P2d724
476P2d869
597P2d184
Subd. C
117Az30
570P2d801
Subd. D
135Az160
659P2d1305
§ 33-983
A1960C20
A1963C99
103Az23
126Az328
130Az93
20AzA214
436P2d479
511P2d658
614P2d870
634P2d20
Subd. A
126Az328
614P2d870
§ 33-987
130Az92
20AzA214
511P2d658
634P2d19
§ 33-988
A1973C172
§ 33-989
127Az84
618P2d254
Subd. A
127Az84
618P2d254
Subd. B
¶ 1
127Az84
618P2d254
§ 33-990
A1978C201
130Az579
637P2d1082
§ 33-991
A1959C5
130Az89
12AzA90
20AzA214
467P2d930
511P2d658
634P2d16
275FS873
Subd. A
104Az103
7AzA466
440P2d1006
449P2d31
Subd. B
104Az103
126Az328
20AzA214
449P2d31
511P2d658
614P2d870
§ 33-992
106Az381
122Az84
130Az87
137Az418
137Az439
2AzA321
12AzA90
21AzA217
408P2d841

467P2d930
476P2d836
517P2d1110
593P2d307
634P2d14
671P2d396
671P2d417
§ 33-992.01
Ad1979C202
A1983C143
135Az156
659P2d1301
Subd. B
135Az160
659P2d1305
Subd. C
135Az160
659P2d1305
§ 33-992.02
Ad1979C202
§ 33-993
A1966C63
A1973C140
A1979C202
A1983C143
81Az148
89Az307
104Az103
114Az426
119Az377
125Az523
127Az86
130Az87
130Az150
137Az417
137Az438
2AzA321
12AzA90
12AzA137
13AzA318
13AzA348
21AzA217
24AzA80
302P2d534
361P2d734
408P2d841
449P2d31
467P2d930
468P2d404
476P2d524
476P2d869
517P2d1110
535P2d1311
561P2d750
580P2d1231
611P2d106
618P2d256
634P2d14
634P2d962
671P2d416
671P2d695
678P2d454
275FS873
389FS1322
420FS704
425FS654
20BRW387
Subd. A
114Az426
119Az265
119Az482
561P2d750
580P2d726
581P2d1132
678P2d454

¶ 1
114Az426
119Az377
126Az328
130Az151
20AzA214
21AzA217
511P2d658
517P2d1110
561P2d750
580P2d1231
614P2d870
634P2d963
¶ 2
114Az426
119Az377
13AzA348
476P2d869
561P2d750
580P2d1231
¶ 4
126Az328
614P2d870
Subd. B
114Az426
119Az482
130Az90
561P2d750
581P2d1132
634P2d17
678P2d455
¶ 1
678P2d456
¶ 2
678P2d454
¶ 3
678P2d456
¶ 4
678P2d456
¶ 5
678P2d456
§ 33-994
89Az307
11AzA336
361P2d734
464P2d656
§ 33-995
A1966C63
84Az308
327P2d994
§ 33-996
125Az523
611P2d106
§ 33-997
389FS1322
§ 33-998
A1966C63
137Az417
137Az438
4AzA134
13AzA348
24AzA566
418P2d129
476P2d869
540P2d185
671P2d395
671P2d416
275FS873
389FS1322
420FS704
20BRW387

§ 33-999
13AzA348
476P2d869
§ 33-1000
A1966C63
106Az381
476P2d836
§ 33-1001
94Az331
385P2d211
§§ 33-1002 to
33-1005
Ad1973C140
§ 33-1002
A1976C176
A1979C202
126Az168
613P2d630
Subd. A
126Az168
613P2d631
¶ 1
126Az168
613P2d631
Subd. B
126Az168
613P2d630
§ 33-1003
A1976C162
A1982C125
130Az577
637P2d1080
§ 33-1004
389FS1322
425FS654
§ 33-1006
Ad1974C68
A1979C202
137Az419
137Az439
671P2d397
671P2d417
§ 33-1011
529P2d255
§ 33-1021
et seq.
134Az140
22AzA482
528P2d868
654P2d288
§ 33-1021
A1970C103
22AzA482
528P2d868
9AzL282
§ 33-1022
10AzA7
21AzA30
22AzA482
455P2d294
515P2d57
528P2d868
Subd. B
119Az466
122Az599
132Az586
21AzA30
22AzA482
515P2d57
528P2d868
581P2d700
596P2d737
647P2d1184
677P2d278
Subd. C
22AzA482

528P2d868
9AzL283
§ 33-1022.01
Ad1978C139
§ 33-1023
A1978C139
A1979
(2dSpC9
A1983C98
127Az349
135Az234
621P2d36
660P2d485
Subd. C
1960C127§55
§ 33-1101
et seq.
C22AzA195
C526P2d402
20BRW666
§§ 33-1101 to
33-1107
118Az161
129Az30
135Az449
443P2d921
575P2d360
628P2d67
661P2d1150
676P2d645
1AzL38
8AzL106
§§ 33-1101 to
33-1103
676P2d644
§ 33-1101
Rs1971C94
A1977C106
A1982C123
A1983C237
84Az204
130Az319
131Az117
135Az449
2AzA228
18AzA336
C22AzA195
325P2d881
407P2d417
501P2d964
C526P2d402
636P2d97
638P2d1363
661P2d1150
307F2d380
378FS961
5BRW324
6BRW728
13BRW816
14BRW834
25BRW332
1983AzS13
62Geo805
Subd. A
135Az449
661P2d1150
1978LF796
¶ 1
13BRW816
Subd. C
5BRW325
14BRW833
27BRW31

§ 33-1102
Rs1971C94
A1983C237
129Az30
131Az117
135Az451
2AzA228
407P2d417
628P2d67
638P2d1363
661P2d1152
676P2d644
676P2d646
307F2d380
Subd. A
307F2d380
Subd. B
5BRW325
14BRW833
§ 33-1103
A1959C14
A1971C136
A1971C94
A1983C237
135Az451
C22AzA195
C526P2d402
661P2d1152
333F2d278
63CaL1469
62Geo849
Subd. A
130Az319
636P2d97
307F2d380
62Geo803
¶ 1
135Az452
661P2d1153
307F2d380
62Geo848
¶ 2
135Az453
661P2d1154
307F2d380
Subd. B
307F2d380
§ 33-1104
A1973C172
A1983C237
84Az204
129Az30
325P2d881
628P2d67
Subd. A
62Geo805
§ 33-1105
A1971C94
R1983C237§5
135Az448
661P2d1149
676P2d645
Subd. A
135Az450
661P2d1151
Subd. B
135Az450
661P2d1151
Subd. C
135Az450
661P2d1151
62Geo800
Subd. D
135Az450

Continued

309

Illustration P

A

Accessory After the Fact Act
Az. Rev. Stat., §§13-2510 to 13-2512

Accounts Receivable Act (Assignment)
Az. Laws 1952, Ch. 132

Acknowledgment Act
Az. Rev. Stat., §33-501 et seq.

Acknowledgments Recognition Act
Az. Rev. Stat., §33-501 et seq.

Administrative Procedure Act
Az. Rev. Stat., §41-1001 et seq.

Administrative Review Act
Az. Rev. Stat., §12-901 et seq.

Adoption Act
Az. Rev. Stat., §8-101 et seq.

Adult Protective Services Act
Az. Rev. Stat., §§46-451, 46-452

Aeronautics Act
Az. Rev. Stat., §2-101 et seq.

Agreement on Detainers Act
Az. Rev. Stat., §§31-481, 31-482

Agricultural Administration Act
Az. Rev. Stat., §3-101 et seq.

Agricultural Employment Relations Act
Az. Rev. Stat., §23-1381 et seq.

Agricultural Improvement District Act
Az. Rev. Stat., §45-901 et seq.

Agricultural Minerals Act of 1947
Az. Laws 1947, Ch. 136

Agricultural Nuisance Protection Act
Az. Rev. Stat., §3-1051, §3-1061

Agricultural Prorate Act
Az. Rev. Stat., §3-401 et seq.

Air Pollution Control Act
Az. Rev. Stat., §36-770 et seq.

Airspace Act
Az. Rev. Stat., §2-111 et seq.

Alcoholic Beverages Act
Az. Rev. Stat., §4-101 et seq.

Alibi Act
Az. Rules of Criminal Procedure 1973, Rule 15.2

Alien Land Law
Az. Rev. Stat., §33-1201 et seq.

Anatomical Gift Act
Az. Rev. Stat., §36-841 et seq.

Annexation Act (Cities and Towns)
Az. Rev. Stat., §9-471

Anti-Blacklisting Law
Az. Constitution 1910, Art. 18 §9

Anti-Discrimination Act (Public Employment)
Az. Rev. Stat., §41-1461

Anti-Featherbedding Act (Railroad)
Az. Rev. Stat., §§40-881, 40-886.01, 40-886.02

Anti-Injunction Act
Az. Rev. Stat., §12-1808

Anti-Nepotism Act
Az. Rev. Stat., §38-481

Anti-Picketing Act
Az. Rev. Stat., §23-1321 et seq.

Antitrust Act
Az. Rev. Stat., §44-1401 et seq.

Anti-Yellow-Dog Contract Act
Az. Rev. Stat., §23-1341

Appeal Act,
Az. Rev. Stat., §12-2101 et seq.

Arbitration Act
Az. Rev. Stat., §12-1501 et seq.

Arizona Agricultural Prorate Act of 1939
Az. Rev. Stat., §3-401 et seq.

Arizona Board of Regents Revenue Bond Act of 1974
Az. Rev. Stat., §15-782 et seq.

Arizona Business Corporation Act
Az. Rev. Stat., §10-001 et seq.

Arizona-California Boundary Compact
Az. Laws 1963, Ch. 77

Arizona Citrus Fruit Standardization Act
Az. Rev. Stat., §3-441 et seq.

Arizona Communist Control Act of 1961
Az. Rev. Stat., §§16-805, 16-806, 38-231, 38-233

Arizona Egg and Egg Products Act of 1952
Az. Rev. Stat., §3-701 et seq.

Arizona Estate Tax Act of 1937
Az. Laws 1937, Ch. 27

Arizona Fertilizer Materials Act of 1956
Az. Rev. Stat., §3-261 et seq.

Arizona Fruit and Vegetable Standardization Act
Az. Rev. Stat., §3-481 et seq.

439

Chapter 3

Finding Arizona Legislative History

Victoria K. Trotta

A. Introduction

Because the Arizona appellate courts are frequently in the business of interpreting statutes, the study of statutory construction and interpretation count as a perennial and persistent challenge to all legal researchers. The *Arizona Revised Statutes* §§1-211 through 218 lay out the general rules of statutory construction. The general purpose of statutory construction is to determine what the intent of the legislature really is, so that courts can solve legal disputes before them in accordance with the legislature's wishes.

These statutory provisions are a beginning, but the courts have developed their own priorities for examining and construing Arizona statutes involved in the legal matters before them. In Arizona, "the cardinal rule of statutory construction is to ascertain the meaning of a statute and the intent of the legislature at the time the legislature enacted it. To arrive at legislative intent, this Court first looks to the words of the statute..." *Kriz v. Buckeye Petroleum Company* 145 Ariz. 374 (1985).

In many instances, the plain language of the statute is insufficient to clarify its meaning. The Arizona courts then must consider "the context of the statute, the language used, the subject matter, the historical background, the effects and consequences, and the spirit and purpose of the law." *Arizona Newspapers Association v. Superior Court,* 143 Ariz. 560 (1985).

A search of the Arizona case file in the WESTLAW database reveals 1,145 opinions that mention some aspect of legislative history or intent included in their legal analysis and subsequent decision. Consequently, investigating statutory history is frequently an important part of an Arizona legal researcher's routine. Unlike the United States Congress, where tomes of background material on contemplated, proposed and pending legislation are recorded for posterity, state legislatures typically provide little in the way of historical record for the legislation they enact. Arizona is no exception, and it suffers from a frustrating lack of this important background material. The trail left by the Arizona legislature in its law-making duties is sparse, and the process of determining legislative intent remains a particular challenge for the legal researcher.

After the researcher has collected all the clues of legislative intent that the legislature has recorded, the daunting prospect still remains of fashioning those clues into a convincing legal argument. This process is an art and puts the advocate's skills to the supreme test. It is also beyond the scope of this chapter, but the reader is directed to any number of substantive articles on the subject.[1]

This chapter will outline the Arizona legislative process and guide researchers to potential sources of historical material. It will not cover the sources of history for constitutional provisions, which are covered in Chapter 1.

B. The Arizona Legislature

1. Legislative Session

Ariz. Rev. Stat. Ann. §§41-1101 through 1134 set out the general organization, duties, and legislative services provided by the Arizona legislature. The regulations and parliamentary processes of legislative enactment are to be found in the *Rules of the House of Representatives* and the *Rules of the Senate.* Specific areas of coverage in the rules include duties and responsibilities of the officers, the order of business, the committees and their reporting responsibilities, voting, debate, motions, order of business, agendas and notice of meetings, and codes

1 A search of the Legal Periodicals Index in the Westlaw database produces 487 articles on some aspect of legislative history. Three recent, thought-provoking and sprightly articles written by law librarians include Schanck, Peter C. "The only game in town: an introduction to interpretive theory, statutory construction, and legislative histories." 82 *Law Library Journal* 419 (Summer 1990); Jacobstein, J. Myron and Roy M. Mersky. " Congressional intent and legislative histories: analysis or psychoanalysis?" 82 *Law Library Journal* 297 (Spring 1990); Schanck, Peter C. "The uses and values of legislative histories: a reply." 82 *Law Library Journal* 303 (Summer 1990).

of ethics. Rules of both houses are adopted and published biennially before each legislative session commences.

Before 1950, the Arizona Legislature convened in one regular session every two years. Since 1951, each legislative session covers a two year period. The first year of the session is considered the first regular session; the second year of the session is considered the second regular session. The rules of each chamber of the legislature decree that each legislative session is to be approximately 100 days in length. The President of the Senate or the Speaker of the House of Representatives may extend the session for an additional seven days. After that, a majority of the House and the Senate must vote to extend the session any further. With today's complex legislative agendas, sessions of 120 to 160 days are no longer uncommon. Additional special sessions may be called by gubernatorial proclamation, and must be called for a specific purpose. These special sessions are usually very short, sometimes lasting only a single day.

2. *Committees*

Several joint committees are required by statute. These are the Legislative Council (Ariz. Rev. Stat. Ann. § 41-1301), the Joint Legislative Budget Committee (Ariz. Rev. Stat. Ann. § 41-1271), the Joint Legislative Tax Committee (Ariz. Rev. Stat. Ann. § 41-1321), the Joint Committee on Capital Review (Ariz. Rev. Stat. Ann. § 41-1251), and the Joint Legislative Oversight Committee (Ariz. Rev. Stat. Ann. § 41-2353).

The Standing Committees of the House of Representatives include Appropriations; Banking and Insurance; Commerce, Counties and Municipalities; Education; Environment; Government Operations; Health, Human Resources and Aging; Judiciary; Natural Resources and Agriculture; Public Institutions and Rural Development; Rules; Tourism, Professions and Occupations; Transportation; and Ways and Means. The Standing Committees of the Arizona Senate include Appropriations; Commerce, Labor, Insurance, and Banking; Education; Finance; Government; Health, Welfare, Aging, and Environment; Judiciary; Natural Resources and Agriculture; Rules; and Transportation. These committees constitute the heart of the Arizona legislative process. They meet routinely during the regular sessions of the legislative session and consider proposed pieces of legislation.

Both the House and the Senate may appoint Special, Select, or Interim Committees to study particular subjects. These committees may meet concurrently during the regular sessions of the legislature, or they may meet during the intersession period after the legislature has adjourned.

Proposed legislation can result from the hearings and studies conducted during these Special, Select or Interim Committees.

3. *How a Bill Becomes Law*

A bill becomes law in Arizona in much the same way it does in other states. A bill may be introduced by a member or members, or by a Standing Committee of either the House or the Senate. By House and Senate rule, bills must be introduced during the first 29 days of a regular session, or during the first ten days of a special session. After that period has passed, new bills may be introduced only with the consent of the Rules Committee. Under certain circumstances, bills may also be pre-filed, before the beginning of a legislative term. After the bill is filed, and after its first reading, it is referred to the appropriate Standing Committee and is ordered to be printed.

Every bill referred to a Standing Committee must be reported. If no action is taken on a bill, that fact must be reported at the last committee meeting of the session. Each committee must publish an advance agenda of the bills it is considering, and only those bills that appear on a published agenda may be considered. The Senate rules decree that their Committees must hear all bills introduced before the Saturday of the week of the 60th day from the beginning of the session. Transferred House bills are to be considered by the appropriate Senate committee before the Saturday of the week of the 90th day of the regular session. The House of Representatives has a similar rule. After those dates have passed, the President of the Senate or the Speaker of the House must approve further Committee consideration of any bills.

While certain standing committees are considering the merits of a proposed bill, the Rules Committee is examining the bill to ensure that the measure comports with constitutional requirements. After considering the bill, the Committees are ready to report their recommendations to their entire chamber. At this point, the bill is placed on the legislative chamber's active calendar for the bill's second reading and consideration by the Committee of the Whole (COW). The Committee of the Whole is a session of the entire House or Senate membership which offers debate, amendments and recommendations of passage. The roll call vote follows the third, and final reading of the bill. If the bill passes, it is transferred to the opposite chamber of the Legislature, where the entire process is repeated. If the bill is passed and returned to the originating chamber in the identical language, the bill then goes to the Governor for signature. If the bill returns to the originating chamber passed but amended, the amended bill may be accepted and sent on to the Governor, or rejected and sent to a Conference Committee.

Conference Committees are "simple" or "free." A Simple Conference Committee is limited to points of disagreement between the House and the Senate and the committee may not consider unrelated or new material in its deliberations. A Free Conference Committee may recommend broader amendments including inserting new matter. After compromise is reached, a Conference Report is sent back to each chamber for approval.

After final passage by both chambers, the bill is sent to the Governor for signature. If the Governor signs the bill, or does nothing for five days (or ten days after adjournment), the bill becomes law. If the Governor vetoes the bill, the Governor must notify the legislature in writing of the reasons why the bill was vetoed. The House and the Senate may then override the veto if two-thirds vote to do so.

A bill that is passed is assigned a chapter number, and is transferred to the Legislative Council for publication and for codification into the *Arizona Revised Statutes.*

4. *Amendments*

Both chambers of the Arizona legislature have a number of rules governing when and how amendments may be made to a proposed bill. Amendments may be proposed and adopted within the Standing Committee, the Committee of the Whole and during Conference Committee consideration. Amendments can be as short or as long as the legislators deem necessary, up to and including the entire bill.

The ability to substitute one completely new bill for another is referred to in the Rules as a "strike everything after the enacting clause" amendment. Legislators refer to this technique as an "amendment to strike," a "strike everything amendment," a "strike-out" or simply as a "striker." As an example, a recent Senate bill was originally introduced with the short title "economic development contributions." After a strike-out amendment, the bill that ultimately passed concerned "parental consent for abortion." Legislators use this device to circumvent the time limit on introduction of new legislation or in the compromise process that is a part of any legislative activity. It presents some special challenges for the legal researcher, since such amendments may lower the probability any written record of committee deliberations exists to support the history behind these amendments.

5. *The Legislative Council*

The composition and the responsibilities of the Legislative Council are enumerated in Ariz. Rev. Stat. Ann. §§ 41-1301 through 1310. The Council is comprised of the Senate President, the House Speaker and a rotating membership of six members of Senators and Representatives. The Council is served by a full time administrative and professional staff whose primary duties include legislative research support, bill drafting and code revision.

The Legislative Council provides research to the members of the Arizona Legislature and drafts bills on request. The Council also provides analyses as well as pros and cons of any provisions put forward for statewide general election as part of the publicity pamphlet sent to registered voters in advance of the election.

In addition to providing research and proposed legislation to the legislature at the members' request, the Council is also responsible for Arizona's code revision and annotation development. The Council is statutorily required to report to the legislature on defects in the Arizona Constitution and laws. This process frequently produces draft bills and resolutions that carry out the recommendations in their reports.

Ariz. Rev. Stat. Ann. § 41-1304.01 *et seq.* outlines the Legislative Council's authority for codification of new Arizona session laws. No temporary and emergency laws are to be codified, and "all purpose, validity and construction clauses" are to be omitted "unless it may be necessary to retain some of them to preserve the full meaning and intent of the law." Where a particular section of the Arizona statutes is added or amended by two or more chapters from the same legislative session, the Director of the Legislative Council has discretion to "combine them into a single section, as long as no substantive change is effected."

Note that application of the statute is largely a matter of discretion for the Legislative Council, and careful researchers have discovered that portions of enacted session laws are never codified into the Arizona Revised Statutes. Tax statutes, and health services entitlement programs with statutory time limits included are particularly susceptible to non-codification and remain session law. Session laws have the full force of law, regardless of whether every part of that session law is codified; the careful researcher will always look for portions that may not have survived the codification process and made their way into the statutes.

It should be noted that the reports and recommendations of the Legislative Council are not systematically disseminated to the Arizona State Library or other public facility. The Arizona State Library, Research Division, the library that supports the Arizona Legislature, does receive a number of the Council's reports, but their holdings are sporadic.

C. Sources of Legislative History

Although researchers should be forewarned that there is usually little evidence of substantive legislative intent to be found, there is a systematic approach to finding what is there. What follows is an annotated list of sources that the researcher must consult in order to conduct a thorough legislative history of an Arizona statutory provision.

1. *The Codes*

Arizona Revised Statutes Annotated: Published under legislative authority, Laws 1956, Chapter 129. -- St. Paul, MN. : West Publishing Co. Fully Annotated. Available on WESTLAW. (See Illustration A, p.44.)

Arizona Revised Statutes. -- Charlottesville, VA.: Michie Publishing Co. 4 volume set. Annual. Unannotated desk set. Available on LEXIS.

Arizona Code, Annotated, 1939. -- Indianapolis, IN. : Bobbs Merrill Co., 1940. Supplemented in 1952, 1953, 1954, 1955.

Revised Code of Arizona, 1928. -- Phoenix, AZ. : Manufacturing Stationers, Inc., 1930. Supplemented in 1934, 1936.

Revised Statutes of Arizona, 1913 - Civil Code. -- Phoenix, AZ.: McNeil Co., 1913.

Revised Statutes of Arizona, 1913 - Penal Code. -- Phoenix, AZ.: McNeil Co., 1913.

Revised Statutes of Arizona Territory, 1901. -- Columbia, MO: E.W. Stephens. 1901.

Revised Statutes of Arizona, 1881. -- Prescott, AZ.: Prescott Courier Print, 1887.

Compiled Laws of the Territory of Arizona, 1864-1877. -- Detroit, MI.: Richmond, Backus & Co., 1877.

Compiled Laws of the Territory of Arizona, 1864-1871. -- Albany, NY.: Weed, Parsons & Co., 1871.

Howell Code : Adopted by the First Legislative Assembly of the Territory of Arizona. -- Prescott, AZ. : Arizona Miner, 1865.

Begin with the particular code section(s) you wish to research. Each section will contain a source note that will indicate the chapter number assigned to the session law, the year the section was originally adopted, and any chapters that subsequently amended the section. The historical note immediately following the source note will frequently point out which exact parts of the section were amended and when. Make note of all full chapter citations that apply to the sections under study.

The present edition of the *Arizona Revised Statutes* was enacted in 1956. If your history note indicates that the section(s) you are researching were part of an earlier codification, you will have to extend your research into the sources that cover those earlier codifications.

2. *The Session Laws*

Acts, Resolutions and Memorials of the [th] Legislative Assembly of the Territory of Arizona. -- Prescott, AZ. 1864-1909 (See Illustration M, p.57.)

Session Laws, State of Arizona: [th] Legislature.. -- Phoenix, AZ. 1912- Annual. Available from the Clerk of the House of Representatives or from the Secretary of the Senate.

Arizona Legislative Service, [th] Legislature.. -- St. Paul, MN.: West Publishing Co. Published throughout the current session. Available on WESTLAW. (See Illustration I, p.52.)

Slip Laws from the current legislative session are available from the Secretary of State. The status of current bills can be discovered by contacting the Senate Secretary or the House Chief Clerk. Single copies of current bills are available at the Legislative Information Desk at the Capitol Building.

Arizona State Senate Legislative Summary : [th] Legislature. Phoenix, AZ. : The Senate. Annual. A digest of bills drafted and enacted.

Summary of Appropriations and Legislation of the [th] Arizona Legislature.-- Phoenix, AZ. : The House of Representatives. Annual. Digest of legislation enacted into law, legislation passed and vetoed, and digest of memorials and resolutions passed.

Legislative Report / The Arizona News Service. Published daily only when the Legislature is in session. Includes daily legislative activities and amendments. This is a commercially published service, and is very expensive ($395/mo.). Monitoring information can be accessed electronically through LOLA (Legislation On Line Arizona), also owned by the Arizona News Service. LOLA provides bill summaries, histories, indexes by code section, key word, and bill number. The publishers indicate that full texts of proposed bills may be added to LOLA in 1992.

Locate the session law or laws that serve as the basis of the code section(s) under review. Note the chapter number, the sponsor, the bill number and the date of passage. This will be important later. Because portions of the session law may not be codified, it is important to compare the language of the session law with its codified form.

3. *The Journals and Rules*

Journals of the [th] Legislative Assembly of the Territory of Arizona. -- Prescott, AZ. 1864-1909.

Journal of the Senate, [th] Legislature. -- Phoenix, AZ.: Bowne of Phoenix, Inc. Annual. Available from the Secretary of the Senate.

Journal of the House of Representatives, [th] Legislature. -- Phoenix, AZ. : Publisher varies. Annual. Available from the Clerk of the House of Representatives.

Rules of the Arizona House of Representatives, [th] Legislature -- Phoenix, AZ. : The House. Published before each two year legislative session. Available from the Chief Clerk of the House of Representatives.

Senate Rules [th] Legislature, State of Arizona. -- Phoenix, AZ. : The Senate. Published before each two year legislative session. Available from the Secretary of the Senate.

The annually published *Journals* record the proceedings of the Senate and th House of Representatives. (See Illustration A, p.77.) There will be an entry for each of a bill's three readings, along with a notation of any action taken. Debates are not recorded, although a notation that a debate occurred will be included. By House and Senate rule, the members of the House and Senate may request to have an individual, short statement included in the appropriate *Journal.* In practice this rarely happens. Roll call votes are also recorded. The *Journals* since statehood in 1912 are virtually useless for any substantive clues as to legislative intent. The *Journals* from the territorial period (1864-1912) in some cases have a few sentences of discussion concerning their passage, although even these entries are relatively rare.

The *Journals* include a number of lists that are useful. These lists include rosters of standing and interim committees, executive appointments and confirmations, governor's messages, lists of bills not reported, lists of bills passed, lists of strike-outs, and indexes to the entire legislative output. For the researcher, the single most valuable portion of the House and Senate *Journals* are indisputably the chronological bill histories. (See Illustration B, p.78.).

The bill histories include a chronological record of a bill's path through the legislature. Be sure to check your bill number in the history section of both the House and the Senate journals because both chambers will have considered the bill in committee, and each will have contributed a bill history. The bill's caption will note if it has been affected by a "strike-out" amendment.

Take note of the committees that considered the bill as well as the dates the bill was considered. This information will help you locate pertinent portions of committee files. You will find references to the Rules Committee in the chronology. This committee is required to check the bill for constitutional appropriateness, and since it proposes no substantive changes, its reports contain no information relevant to legislative intent. Therefore, you will not need to consult the Rules Committee file when developing a legislative history.

If the legislation under review was enacted during one of the legislature's special sessions, there will be a gubernatorial proclamation, which may include historical information about the intent of the legislation. This proclamation will also appear in the *Session Laws* volume for the year in which the measure was passed. Chronological bill histories from Special Sessions are separately collected in the *Journals.*

As mentioned earlier, the Rules of the House and the Senate set out the procedures and protocols by which legislation is introduced, debated, and passed into law. They are mentioned here as a miscellaneous source of background information about the workings of the Arizona Legislature.

4. The Committee Files

The Chief Clerk of the House of Representatives and the Secretary of the Senate maintain two sets of files, one on each of the standing committees and one on each bill that becomes a law. For each session law that you research, you will need to examine the file for each committee that considered it as well as its bill file.

The committee files are most likely to contain the best information about the history and the intent behind the legislation you are researching. The typical contents of a committee file include: agendas and minutes of every committee meeting, a list of speakers present, and a list of bills discussed, with a summary of each bill. The file also contains any proposed amendments, a roster of those observers in attendance, and any roll call votes taken.

The minutes are the most likely source of any real clues as to the intent of the legislature. Because you know from the analyzing the chronological bill history what time period the legislation was considered, you can narrow the search through the committee file to that same time period.

The committee minutes are brief digests of the deliberations that take place during each of the committee meetings. There will frequently be notations of the purposes behind the legislation at hand.

If you are very fortunate, the minutes will contain a reference to a report that has been prepared either by the Legislative Council or by an interim committee that has been formed to study a particular problem that the proposed legislation addresses. Typically, but inexplicably, a copy of the report is not appended to the committee file. If you find such a notation in the minutes of the committee, check immediately with the Clerk of the House of Representatives or the Secretary of the Senate to see if they have maintained a copy of the report. If the report is a product of a standing, interim or special committee that is listed in the House or the Senate *Journal,* it is probable that a copy of the report is on file in one of these offices. Older reports of interim, special and select committees in the House of Representatives are in storage and are not indexed; they are literally housed in a single covered records box. The Clerk of the House of Representatives will retrieve the container holding those reports, and will usually allow the researcher to search through the box.

If the Chief Clerk of the House or the Secretary of the Senate does not have a copy of the cited Legislative Council study or the committee report, researchers should check the holdings of the Arizona State Library, conveniently located in the same complex as the Arizona Legislature. Check the card catalog for possible Legislative Council reports or for reports from the standing, special or interim committees that originated the legislation. Although neither the Legislative Council nor the various legislative committees routinely send copies of their reports to the library, a good number of them manage to find their way into that collection. While the library's collection of Legislative Council and committee reports is far from comprehensive, it is surprisingly large.

As a last resort, researchers may check with the Office of the Legislative Council for a copy of a referenced report. As the research arm of the Arizona Legislature, the Council is not truly a public agency and is therefore not technically open to the public, although they will usually respond to specific questions and requests. Therefore, while researchers should not rely on them routinely for assistance, the Council's administrative and professional staff is approachable and helpful if all other avenues have been exhausted.[2]

5. *The Bill Files*

The Chief Clerk of the House of Representatives and the Secretary of the Senate maintain files of all bills ultimately passed into law. The contents of the so-called bill file will include the bill as originally introduced, along with all amendments that have been proposed and adopted. Note that there is no ongoing integration of the amendments with the original text.

Researchers can sometimes extrapolate legislative intent from the progression of amendments that are proposed and adopted, although arguments based on this technique are rarely successful with Arizona courts. What counts with them is the plain language of the statute that was ultimately adopted.

Since both the House and the Senate must independently consider each proposed bill, the researcher must remember to check with both the House and the Senate offices to inspect the committee and the bill files for those bills under review.

Researchers should call the Chief Clerk of the House or the Secretary of the Senate before in-person visits are scheduled so that the appropriate files can be located and retrieved. Many of them are in storage areas. Many very old committee and bill files no longer exist.

2 The Legislative Council administrative staff as well as the Staffs of both the House and Senate administrative offices are under tremendous time pressures during legislative sessions. Researchers will find both groups extraordinarily helpful during the intersession periods. Researchers should be sensitive to this pressure when visiting any of these offices during a legislative session.

6. *Statutes Created through Initiative and Referendum*

Arizona publicity pamphlet: propositions to be submitted to the qualified electors of the State of Arizona at the General Election [date]. -- Arizona Secretary of State. Includes the complete text of each proposed measure, a legislative council analysis, arguments for and against, and the effect of a "yes" or "no" vote.

Occasionally, the source and history notes of a statutory provision indicate that it originated from a vote of the Arizona electorate. The Arizona Secretary of State may have an archival copy of the publicity pamphlets it has produced. The *Publicity pamphlet* is the best source for historical information about proposed measures of this type.

7. *Secondary Sources of Information*

Arizona Attorney. -- State Bar of Arizona. This bar journal sometimes highlights major new legislation, and sometimes legislative intent is included in the discussion. Citations to journal articles that cover statutes will be noted in the annotations to the *Arizona Revised Statutes.*

Arizona Business Gazette. -- Weekly business newspaper which includes a section on Law and the Courts. Available through Vu/Text, Business Dateline and Datatimes from 1986- .

Arizona Capitol Times. -- Arizona News Service. This weekly newsletter monitors the actions of the Arizona Legislature. Unfortunately, the publication is not available electronically.

Arizona Republic . -- The major daily newspaper. Good ongoing source of political information. Available through Vu/Text, Datatimes, Business Dateline, NEXIS from 1986.

The Arizona State Library maintained a card index file on the *Arizona Republic* before the publication became available electronically. Subject access is broadly based, but can be a useful tool for historical investigations.

Arizona Law Review (University of Arizona) and *Arizona State Law Journal* (Arizona State University). These local law reviews sometimes contain articles that examine various Arizona statutes. Relevant citations will be noted in the annotations to the *Arizona Revised Statutes.*

8. *Miscellaneous*

The State Library also houses a small, special microfilm collection of legislative histories. This collection covers Senate bills from 1969 to 1978 and House bills from 1971 to 1975. There are no plans to enlarge this collection. The microfilm includes copies of bills and their amendments from Committee or from the legislative chamber, an enumeration of the vote and occasionally an analysis provided by the Legislative Council. There is no index to the compilation, and researchers can expect to spend a good deal of time browsing through the microfilm in search of anything useful. The scope of the collections as well as the impediments inherent in accessing them make them of limited usefulness.

9. *The Territorial Period, 1864-1912*

The thrust of this Chapter has focused on locating legislative history of enactments since statehood. While the process for tracking histories of territorial legislation is the same, the researcher must be prepared for the probability that most traces of legislative decision-making have vanished.

Researchers are directed primarily to the *Journals* and the *Session Laws* of the Arizona territory (see page 68, supra). Recall that occasionally the territorial journals will contain a statement about the intent of the statute.

Researchers may also consult Kelly, George H. *Legislative History: Arizona, 1864 - 1912.* Phoenix, AZ.: Manufacturing Stationers, Inc. 1926. This slim volume contains a listing of the legislation enacted during each year of the territory's existence along with an excerpt from the Governor's message.

APPENDIX A

Sources for Further Reading and Research

Arizona Bill: How "Bill" becomes law. -- Phoenix, AZ. : Arizona House of Representatives, 1977. The legislative process in chart form, in folksy language. Includes useful glossary of terminology connected with the legislative process.

Fisher, Mary L. *Guide to State legislative and administrative materials/* 4th ed. -- Littleton, CO. : Fred B. Rothman & Co., 1988. (AALL Publication Series, no. 15). Excellent source of current information for all states.

Hellebust, Lynn. *State Legislative Sourcebook, 1991 : a resource guide to information in the fifty states* --Topeka, KA. : Government Research Service, c1990. 1 v. (looseleaf).

Legislative process / sponsored by the State Bar of Arizona. -- Phoenix, AZ. : Continuing Legal Education of the State Bar of Arizona, 1980. Very useful compilation of articles about the Legislature and its staff.

State Documents Bibliography: Arizona . -- Chicago, IL. : American Association of Law Libraries, 1986. (AALL Occasional Papers).

APPENDIX B

Sources of Legislative Offices, Government Agencies and Commercial Publishers

Arizona Business Gazette
400 E. Van Buren Street
Phoenix, Arizona 85004
(602) 271-7300

Arizona Legislature
State Capitol
1700 W. Washington Street
Phoenix, Arizona 85007

Chief Clerk, House of Representatives
Room 111
(602) 542-3032

Secretary of the Senate
Second Floor
(602) 542-4231

Information Desk
(602) 542-3559

Arizona Legislative Council
State Capitol
1700 W. Washington Street
Phoenix, Arizona 85007
(602) 542-4236

Arizona Department of Library, Archives and Public Records
Reference Division
State Capitol, 3rd floor
1700 W. Washington
Phoenix, Arizona 85007
(602) 542-3701

Arizona News Service
14. N. 18th Avenue
Phoenix, Arizona 85007
(602) 258-7026

Arizona Republic
Phoenix Newspapers
120 East Van Buren Street
Phoenix, Arizona 85004
(602) 271-8000

Arizona Secretary of State
State Capitol, West Wing
1700 W. Washington
Phoenix, Arizona 85007
(602) 642-4285

Arizona State University
School of Law
Tempe, Arizona 85027
(602) 965-6287

University of Arizona
School of Law
Tucson, Arizona 85721
(602) 621-1373

Illustration A

24 JOURNAL OF THE SENATE

Tuesday, January 10, 1989

Second Day

The Senate convened at 11:00 a.m.

Dr. Hugh Shelby Lee, Minister Emeritus, First Congregational Church, Sun City, offered prayer.

Pledge of Allegiance to the Flag was led by Senator Arzberger.

The following Senators answered on roll call:

Alston, Arzberger, Bartlett, Brewer, Corbet, Corpstein, De Long, Denny, Gabaldon, Gillespie, Gutierrez, Hardt, Hays, Henderson, Higuera, Hill, Mawhinney, Osborn, Patterson, Pearce, Pena, Rios, Sossaman, Steiner, Stephens, Stump, Todd, Walker, Wright, President Usdane

JOURNAL

The President announced that without objection reading of the Journal of Monday, January 9, 1989 was dispensed with and approved as recorded by the Secretary.

INTRODUCTION AND FIRST READING OF BILLS

The following bills were introduced, read the first time by number and short title and placed under second reading of bills:

Senate Bill 1006: An Act relating to taxation; providing for exemption from transaction privilege tax for contracts with the United States government; amending section 42-1310.17, ARS, as added by Laws 1988, chapter 161, section 4; repealing section 42-1310.17, ARS, as amended by Laws 1988, chapter 161, section 7, and repealing Laws 1988, chapter 161, section 17.

Senate Bill 1007: An Act relating to crimes; prescribing the delivery to the county sheriff of unclaimed, stolen or embezzled property that is not claimed by the owner, and amending section 13-3942, ARS.

SECOND READING AND REFERENCE OF BILLS

The following bills were read the second time by number and short title and referred to committees:

Senate Bill 1001: to Finance
Senate Bill 1002: to Finance
Senate Bill 1003: to Commerce, Labor, Insurance and Banking
Senate Bill 1004: to Transportation
Senate Bill 1005: to Government
Senate Concurrent Resolution 1001: to Transportation

Reprinted from *Journal of the Senate, 39th Legislature,* 1989.

Illustration B

1194 HISTORY OF HOUSE BILLS

HOUSE BILL 2613, by Representatives Johnson, Miller: Barnes, Burns B, Burns R, Evans, Hermon, Killian, McCarroll, Meredith, Mills, Mundell, Skelly, Steffey -- children; sexual exploitation; obscene devices, see HB 2611

2-8	First Reading--referred to Rules, Jud	157
2-9	Second Reading	170
2-27	Jud--dpa (corrected)	214
3-7	Rules--c&p	257
3-9	Committee of Whole--dpa	266
3-14	Third Reading--passed amended, 57-0-3	284
	Held in Senate	

SENATE ACTION:

3-15 Introduction and First Reading
3-17 Second Reading--referred to Jud
Held in Committees

HOUSE BILL 2614, by Representatives Wessel: Gerard -- public attorneys; pro bono activities, similar to SB 1467

2-8	First Reading--referred to Rules, GovOp, Jud	157
2-9	Second Reading	170
	Held in Committees	

HOUSE BILL 2615, by Representatives Wessel, Kenney: Gerard, Hink -- defensive driving schools (now: civil traffic violations; schools; defensive driving)

2-8	First Reading--referred to Rules, Trans, GovOp	157
2-9	Second Reading	170
2-21	Trans--dpa	201
3-7	GovOp--dpa	256
3-20	Rules--c&p	342
3-21	Committee of Whole--dpa	358
3-28	Third Reading--passed amended, 58-0-0-2 exc (Mundell, Wilcox)	402
6-12	Senate passed amended, 29-0-1	716
6-13	House concurred--Final Passage, 52-3-4-1 exc (Mundell)	728
6-28	Governor signed	794
	CHAPTER 307 - Emergency	

HOUSE BILL 2616, by Representatives Wessel: Burns B, Burns R, Hindman, Hink, Senators Alston, Brewer, Denny, Stump, Wright -- city underground utility facilities; authority

2-8	First Reading--referred to Rules, Com, CM	157
2-9	Second Reading	170
2-13	Com--dp	178
3-7	CM--dpa	252
	Held in Rules	

Reprinted from *Journal of the House, 39th Legislature,* 1989.

Chapter 4

Arizona Judicial System

Marianne Sidorski Alcorn

A. History

The Mexican influence is visible throughout Arizona; it was a significant influence in the structure and temperament of the common law courts created by the territorial legislature.[1] The Organic Act signed by Abraham Lincoln in 1863 achieved separate territorial status for Arizona from New Mexico.[2] The act established a Supreme Court consisting of three members, one of whom was the chief justice, and allowed for "inferior courts."[3] (See Illustration A, p.89). In 1891 a fourth judge was added,[4] and in 1905 a fifth and final judge was added to the Supreme Court.[5]

1 Murphy, James M. *The Spanish Legal Heritage in Arizona* (Tucson:Arizona Pioneers' Historical Society, 1966), p.11.

2 Goff, John S. *Arizona Territorial Officials, volume 1; The Supreme Court Justices 1863-1912* (Cave Creek, Arizona:Black Mountain Press, 1975), p.10.

3 Organic Act of 1863, 12 Stat. 664,665 (1863)

4 Ch. 131, 26 United States Statutes at Large 747(1891).

5 Ch. 1429, 33 United States Statutes at Large 998 (1905).

After Arizona became a territory, three levels of courts were established; the supreme court, the district and probate courts, and the justice of the peace courts. The justice courts had jurisdiction for minor criminal and civil cases. The District courts tried the majority of cases, both civil and criminal, while the probate court handled estates and maintained titles for real estate.[6] The three district courts were located at Tucson (Chief Justice William Turner), La Paz (Judge Henry T. Backus) and Prescott (Judge Harley H. Cartter).[7]

The three supreme court justices were each the judge of one of the district courts. Each year they met and formed the Arizona Supreme Court. The first meeting occurred on December 26, 1865 in Prescott. If a litigant was in front of Judge Cartter in Prescott at the district court level and felt there had been an appealable error, the case would be sent to the Arizona Supreme Court. At its annual meeting the litigant would find himself arguing his case in front of Justices Turner, Backus and ironically, Cartter again. This seemingly unfair practice was ended in 1891 by the U.S. Congress: "The supreme court of the Territory of Arizona shall consist of a chief justice and three associate justices, any three of who shall constitute a quorum; but no justice shall act as a member of the supreme court in any action or proceeding brought to such court by writ of error, bill of exception or appeal from a decision, judgment, or decree rendered by him as judge of a district court, unless one of the other justices is disqualified to sit in such action."[8] (See Illustration B, p.90) This same act divided the territory into four judicial districts with each of the supreme court justices being a judge for one of the districts.

Generally every decade or two there was a push for restructuring of the courts. In 1973 there was the 22nd Arizona Town Hall entitled, *The Adequacy of Arizona's Court System.* The Town Hall membership's report stated, "The desirability of modernizing Arizona's court system is recognized by the Bench, the Bar and a substantial segment of the lay public. A single integrated court system will, it is believed, improve both the quality and quantity of justice. The change proposed would bring the police courts, the city magistrates, and the justices of the peace into the existing single system now consisting of the Superior Court."[9] (See Illustration C, p.91)

In 1990 the goal of the Arizona Supreme Court's Court Reform Plan was: "To provide the citizens of Arizona with a court system that is accessible, that is managed effectively and that is an economical organization. The Arizona Court System will be a three-tier structure:

The Supreme Court

The Court of Appeals

A Unified Trial Court"

(See Illustration D)

6 Murphy, James M. *Laws, Courts, and Lawyers* (Tucson:University of Arizona Press, 1970), 17.

7 Id. at 20.

8 Ch.131, 26 U.S. Stat. at Large 747(1891).

9 Arizona Academy. *Twenty-second Arizona Town Hall on The Adequacy of Arizona's Court System* (Phoenix: Arizona Academy, 1973).

The Arizona Court system has been the subject of study for many years. Sandra Day O'Connor spoke at Arizona State University College of Law at the Conference on Lower Court Improvement on November 27, 1981. She commented, "Arizona has studied the problem long enough. The study efforts in Arizona which began in 1958 have all resulted in recommendations for some unification of our courts of limited jurisdiction and for improved court management. Surely, after 23 years of study, this state is ready to buckle down and finish the job it has begun with our court system." It is interesting to follow the various studies and conferences and note that some of the same recommendations surface decade after decade.

The Arizona Town Hall of 1973 strongly recommended changes in the existent system of judicial selection. Under the Town Hall's recommendations, which now reflect the current manner of judicial selection, judges are appointed rather than elected. Previously, candidates for the bench were required to appear on the ballot in the general election without party designation.

Under the current method of judicial selection, potential candidates for the bench are first screened by a bipartisan committee composed of lawyers and laypersons. This endorsing committee then recommends three candidates to the governor, and the governor appoints one of these candidates to the bench. At the end of each term (four years), the appointed judge is required to stand for re-election on his or her record of performance. The general public then is given an opportunity to vote on the question, "Should Judge Smith be retained in office?" Significantly, the incumbent judge is not required to face an opposition candidate. This has resulted in an extraordinarily high rate of retention. In four elections since 1984 the bar has either taken no position or opposed only eleven judges and all were retained by the voters.[10]

The Town Hall of 1973 also recommended that the superior court commissioner system be expanded in authority and jurisdiction to handle more complex matters.[11]

In an article in the *Arizona Attorney* in 1990 another recommendation was made: "Another step that could easily be instituted is to increase the utilization of Court Commissioners as Judge Pro Tems to hear all civil motions except those seeking a judgment or dismissal of a case."[12] The American Bar Association has stated that the use of judges pro tempore should be on an emergency basis and that in no event should judges pro tempore be used because of a continuing permanent lack of judicial resources.[13]

10 "Panel Splits on Evaluating State Judges," *Phoenix Gazette,* 29 April 1991, sec. B.

11 Arizona Academy. *Twenty-second Arizona Town Hall on the Adequacy of Arizona's Court System* (Phoenix: Arizona Academy, 1973), summary of recommendations X.

12 Levine, Jack, "Improving Judicial Decision Making," *Arizona Attorney* (March, 1990):p.8.

13 *Standards Relating to Court Organization,* 1990 edition, American Bar Association, Judicial Administration Division (Chicago:ABA, 1990), section 1.26.5.

B. Courts Today

The structure of the Arizona court system of today is shown in Illustration E, p.92.

The following descriptions of the structure and jurisdiction of the Arizona courts are taken from the *Arizona Annual Judicial Report,* Fiscal Year 1990.[14]

Structure

Five Justices sit on the Arizona Supreme Court. The Chief and Vice Chief Justice are elected by their peers. The Chief Justice serves a five year term and may have consecutive terms. The Vice Chief Justice serves a term determined by the entire court. Historically, the Vice Justice has usually been elected by his peers to succeed the Chief Justice at the expiration of his term.

Arizona Supreme Court

Jurisdiction

The jurisdiction of the Supreme Court, as provided in Article VI, Section 5 of the Arizona Constitution, includes appellate jurisdiction, the issuance of extraordinary writs and the power to make rules relative to any procedural matter in any court. The Supreme Court may review a decision of the intermediate appellate court when someone files a "petition for review." Death penalty cases are appealed directly to the Supreme Court. Legislation passed in 1989 gave the Court of Appeals direct jurisdiction when a life sentence is imposed. The decisions of the Court of Appeals in life sentence cases are subject to the filing of a petition for review in the Supreme Court.

The Supreme Court exercises its rule making authority by the "Rule 28" process, the rule of procedure that permits any person, association or agency to petition for adoption, amendment or repeal of rules or procedures for the Arizona courts.

The Supreme Court regulates the State Bar of Arizona, the admission of new attorneys to the practice of law and decides attorney-discipline cases filed in the Court. The Court also serves as the final decision-making body on judicial disciplinary recommendations filed by the Commission on Judicial Conduct.

Court of Appeals

Structure & Jurisdiction

The Arizona Court of Appeals is a single court with two divisions and is exclusively a court of review having no original jurisdiction. The Court has jurisdiction in all proceedings appealable from the Superior Court with the

14 Arizona Supreme Court, *Arizona Annual Judicial Report.* (Phoenix:Arizona Supreme Court, Administrative Office of the Courts, 1990).

exception of criminal death penalty cases which by law must be appealed directly to the Supreme Court.

Division One of the Court of Appeals is located in Phoenix and consists of five departments with three judges assigned to each department. Appeals from Apache, Coconino, La Paz, Maricopa, Mohave, Navajo, Yavapai and Yuma counties are filed in Division One. Division One has statewide jurisdiction for all Writs of Certiorari concerning awards by the Industrial Commission, appeals from the Unemployment Insurance Appeals Board and all appeals from the Arizona Tax Court.

Division Two of the Court of Appeals serves the counties of Cochise, Gila, Graham, Greenlee, Pima, Pinal and Santa Cruz. It is located in Tucson and consists of two departments with three judges sitting in each department.

Superior Court

Structure & Jurisdiction

The Superior Court is the court of general jurisdiction for Arizona. There are 116 Superior Court judges located throughout the 15 counties of Arizona. The Superior Court acts as the appellate court to the Justice of Peace and Municipal Courts and its original jurisdiction extends into all case types except small claims, minor offenses and violations of city codes and ordinances. The Superior Court also oversees those adults and juveniles placed on probation. In some counties, the Superior Court has separate adult and juvenile probation departments.

As part of the Superior Court, the Arizona Tax Court exists to hear tax related issues exclusively. Created by legislative action in 1988, the Tax Court is physically located in and is administered by the Superior Court in Maricopa County.

Since the 1970's, Arizona has been engaged in the general adjudication of most of the surface and groundwater rights in the state. These are being conducted under the authority of A.R.S. §§ 45-251 to 260. One case involving the water rights of the Gila River Basin, has been assigned to the Superior Court in Maricopa County. The case involves more than 60,000 water rights claims and an estimated 25,000 parties. A second case, concerning the water rights of the Little Colorado River Basin, is assigned to the Superior Court in Greenlee County. This case consists of 11,000 claims and 3,000 parties.

The Supreme Court has appointed a Special Master to hear contested cases arising from these adjudications. The Master's compensation and expenses are fixed by the Court and paid by claimants in these two cases.

Justice of the Peace Courts

Structure & Jurisdiction

Justice of the Peace Courts are established according to precinct boundaries as determined by each County Board of Supervisors. Traffic related cases make up the majority of the cases heard in Justice Courts.

In FY 90, civil filings within the Justice Courts included exclusive jurisdiction in cases filed under $500, small claims filings (up to $1000), civil filings between $500 and $2500 (concurrent jurisdiction with Superior Court), and forcible entry and detainer (where rental value does not exceed $750 per month and damages do not exceed $2500).

[Article 6 §32 of the Arizona Constitution was amended November, 1990 and increased the jurisdiction of Justice of the Peace Courts and Courts inferior to the Superior Courts in civil cases from the current limit of $2,500 to a maximum of $10,000 excluding interest and costs. The passage of Senate Bill 1083 by the Thirty-ninth legislature, Second Regular Session, 1990 increased the civil jurisdiction of the Justice Court to $5,000 (A.R.S. § 22-201B); raised the small claims jurisdiction from $1000 to $1,500 (A.R.S. § 503A); and increased jurisdiction in forcible entry and detainer cases where the rental value of the property does not exceed $1,000 per month and where damages are $5,000 or less (A.R.S. § 201C).][15]

Petitions for Order of Protection in domestic violence cases and Petitions for Injunction Against Harassment are also heard in Justice Courts.

Justice Courts handle non-traffic misdemeanor cases, failure to appear cases in traffic and misdemeanor criminal cases, and hold felony preliminary hearings.

Municipal Courts

Structure & Jurisdiction

Also known as magistrate or police courts, municipal courts are required by statute to be established by charter provision or municipal ordinance in all incorporated cities and towns. There were 83 municipal courts in Arizona at the end of FY 90.

Municipal courts have concurrent jurisdiction with Justice of the Peace Courts on all traffic-related cases occurring within the city or town limits. Municipal courts also handle violations of city or town ordinances, Petitions for Order of Protection in Domestic Violence cases and Petitions for Injunction Against Harassment.

Traffic cases (civil and criminal) represent the greatest amount of court activity in municipal courts, with non-traffic criminal misdemeanor cases a smaller proportion of the cases filed.

Municipal courts have no civil jurisdiction except in domestic violence cases.

15 Thanks to Bob Wininger, Director, Court Services Division for providing this information.

C. Future Proposals

In 1989 The Commission on the Courts issued 50 recommendations to improve the courts. The Committee on Court Reform will be implementing these. The following are the approved recommendations from the Commission on the Courts.

The Arizona Supreme Court's Court Reform Plan

In Response to the Commission on the Courts Recommendations

GOAL: *To provide the citizens of Arizona with a court system that is accessible, that is managed effectively and that is an economical organization.*

The Arizona Court System will be a three-tier structure:

- The Supreme Court
- The Court of Appeals
- A Unified Trial Court

MANAGEMENT AND STAFFING

- Management of the Arizona Courts should be the responsibility of the Chief Justice working through the Administrative Director of the Courts at the state level, the Presiding Judge and Court Administrator at the local level.*
- Future judicial vacancies should be filled by merit selection process.*
- A judicial performance review program should be developed.*
- Judicial qualifications should be increased reflecting the responsibilities of the position.
- Professionalism at all levels of the court structure should be enhanced.

COURT OPERATIONS—RESOLVING DISPUTES

- Innovative alternative dispute resolution programs should be developed.
- Effectiveness of court-annexed arbitration should be enhanced.
- An Office of Public Dispute Resolution should be established to provide assistance in resolving disputes utilizing all forms of dispute resolution.

ENHANCING PRODUCTIVITY

- Court case processing standards should be adopted.
- Case flow management techniques should be adopted.
- Court control and management of all case-related activities should be in place.
- Pilot projects and studies should be undertaken to determine the effectiveness of available technology for courts at all levels.
- Pro-bono work by lawyers should be encouraged.
- On-line data bases for Supreme and Appellate Court decisions should be established.

ISSUES – CRIMINAL JUSTICE SYSTEM/ LEGAL NEEDS OF CHILDREN AND FAMILIES

- The Arizona Rules of Criminal Procedure should be modified to streamline pretrial proceedings.
- A youthful offender program should be developed as an alternative sentencing option for juveniles convicted of crimes in adult court.
- All judges should enforce case processing and speedy trial rules.
- Post conviction proceedings should be streamlined.
- Changes should be made to enhance the quality of service to children and families.
- A comprehensive effort should be undertaken to protect the victims of domestic abuse.
- Expedited case processing for domestic relations cases, utilizing mediation when possible, should be established.

ACCESS/INFORMATION TO THE USERS OF THE COURT

- Public education programs should be developed.
- The judicial system's responsiveness to the public should be enhanced.
- Statewide filing system should be developed.

FISCAL ISSUES

- The entire court system should become state funded with July, 1995, as the target date.
- Statewide funding proposal for technology and automation should be developed.
- Judicial salaries should be increased to attract and retain the most qualified individuals to the bench.

* *for Maricopa and Pima Counties, any county exceeding 150,000 population or voter approval to implement.*

Reprinted from the Fiscal 1990 *Arizona Annual Judicial Report.*

D. Selected Readings

1. *History*

Arizona Judicial Coordinating Committee. *1981 Arizona Judicial Plan.* Phoenix: Arizona Supreme Court, (1981).

Arizona Supreme Court. *The Superior Court in Arizona, 1912-84.* Phoenix: Arizona Supreme Court, Administrative Office of the Courts, (1985)

"Discipline and Removal of Judiciary in Arizona," 1973 *Arizona Law and Social Order* 85.

Gorski, Peter M. "Arizona Lower Court Study Completed," 18 *Arizona Bar Journal* 35, (June, 1982)

Hink, Heinz, R. "Judicial Reform in Arizona-Selection of Judges," 6 *Arizona Law Review* 13, (1964).

"Judicial Selection and Tenure-A Merit Selection Plan For Arizona," 9 *Arizona Law Review* 297, (1967).

Lee, Stephen E. "Judicial Selection and Tenure in Arizona," 1973 *Law & Social Order* 51.

"Lower Court Improvement in Arizona," 19 *Arizona Bar Journal,* No. 1, p. 1 (1984).

Udall, Morris, K. "Modern Courts-Where Do We Go From Here?," 2 *Arizona Law Review* 166, (1960).

2. *Present*

Arizona Supreme Court. Commission on the Courts. *Report of the Commission on the Courts, 1989.* Phoenix: Arizona Supreme Court, 1989.

Arizona Supreme Court. Commission on the Courts. *Report of the Task Force on Children and Families in the Courts.* Phoenix: Arizona Supreme Court, 1989.

Arizona Supreme Court. Commission on the Courts. *Report of the Task Force on Court Organization and Administration.* Phoenix: Arizona Supreme Court, 1989.

Arizona Supreme Court. Commission on the Courts. *Report of the Task force on Court Productivity.* Phoenix: Arizona Supreme Court,1989.

Arizona Supreme Court. Commission on the Courts. *Report of the Task Force on Dispute Resolution.* Phoenix: Arizona Supreme Court, 1989.

Arizona Supreme Court. *Arizona Annual Judicial Report, FY 90 Judicial Report.* Phoenix: Arizona Supreme Court, 1990.

Gordon, Frank X., Jr. "Commission on the Courts," 26 *Arizona Attorney* 13, (February, 1990).

E. Directory of Courts

1. *Federal Courts*

United States District Court for Arizona
230 N. First Street
Phoenix, AZ 85025
(602)379-3342

Tucson Office
44 East Broadway
Tucson, AZ 85701
(602) 670-6536

2. *State Courts*

Arizona Supreme Court
1501 West Washington
Phoenix, AZ 85007
(602) 542-9396

Arizona Court of Appeals
Division One
1501 W. Washington
Phoenix, AZ 85007
(602) 542-4821

Arizona Court of Appeals
Division Two
State Office Building
416 West Congress, Room 181
Tucson, AZ 85701
(602) 628-1999

3. *Arizona Superior Courts*

Maricopa County Superior Court
201 W. Jefferson
Central Court Building
Phoenix, AZ 85003-2205
(602) 506-3253

Maricopa County Superior Court
Southeast Judicial District
222 East Javelina Drive
Mesa, AZ 85210-6201
(602) 506-2086

Juvenile Court, Durango Facility
3125 W. Durango
Phoenix, AZ 85009-6292
(602) 506-4011

Juvenile Court, Southeast Facility
1810 South Lewis Street
Mesa, AZ 85210-6234
(602) 506-2500

Apache County Superior Court
P.O. Box 365
St. Johns, AZ 85936
(602) 337-4364

Cochise County Superior Court
P.O. Drawer CK
Bisbee, AZ 85603
(602) 432-5471

Coconino County Superior Court
Superior Courthouse
Flagstaff, AZ 86001
(602) 779-6535

Gila County Superior Court
1400 East Ash
Globe, AZ 85501
(602) 425-3231

Graham County Superior Court
Courthouse
Safford, AZ 85546
(602)428-3100

Greenlee County Superior Court
P.O. Box 1027
Clifton, AZ 85533
(602) 865-4242

La Paz County Superior Court
P.O. Box 730
Parker, AZ 85344
(602) 669-6131

Pima County Superior Court
110 W. Congress
Tucson, AZ 85701
(602) 740-3200

Pima County Superior Court
Juvenile Court
2225 East Ajo Way
Tucson, AZ 85701
(602)740-6280

Mojave County Superior Court
401 East Spring Street
Kingman, AZ 86401

Navajo County Superior Court
S. Hwy. 77
Navajo County Complex
Holbrook, AZ 86025
(602) 524-6161

Pinal County Superior Court
P.O. Box 889
Florence, AZ 85232
(602) 868-5801

Santa Cruz County
Superior Court
P.O. Box 1265
Nogales, AZ 85628

Yavapai County Superior Court
Prescott, AZ 86301
(602) 771-3312

Yuma County Superior Court
168 S. 2nd Avenue
Yuma, AZ 85364
(602) 329-2164

Illustration A

Organic Act of 1863

Feb. 24, 1863.

CHAP. LVI. — *An Act to provide a temporary Government for the Territory of Arizona, and for other Purposes.*

Territory of Arizona.

Be it enacted by the Senate and House of Representatives of the United States of America in Congress assembled, That all that part of the present Territory of New Mexico situate west of a line running due south from the point where the southwest corner of the Territory of Colorado joins the northern boundary of the Territory of New Mexico to the southern boundary line of said Territory of New Mexico be, and the same is hereby, erected into a temporary government by the name of the Territory of Arizona: *Provided,* That nothing contained in the provisions of this act shall be construed to prohibit the Congress of the United States from dividing said Territory or changing its boundaries in such manner and at such time as it may deem proper: *Provided, further,* That said government shall be maintained and continued until such time as the people residing in said Territory shall, with the consent of Congress, form a State government, republican in form, as prescribed in the Constitution of the United States, and apply for and obtain admission into the Union as a State, on an equal footing with the original States.

Boundaries.

May be divided hereafter.

Territorial government to remain until, &c.

SEC. 2. *And be it further enacted,* That the government hereby authorized shall consist of an executive, legislative, and judicial power. The executive power shall be vested in a governor. The legislative power shall consist of a council of nine members, and a house of representatives of eighteen. The judicial power shall be vested in a supreme court, to consist of three judges, and such inferior courts as the legislative council may by law prescribe; there shall also be a secretary, a marshal, a district attorney, and a surveyor-general for said Territory, who, together with the governor and judges of the supreme court, shall be appointed by the President, by and with the advice and consent of the Senate, and the term of office for each, the manner of their appointment, and the powers, duties, and the compensation of the governor, legislative assembly, judges of the supreme court, secretary, marshal, district attorney, and surveyor-general aforesaid, with their clerks, draughtsman, deputies, and sergeant-at-arms, shall be such as are conferred upon the same officers by the act organizing the Territorial government of New Mexico, which subordinate officers shall be appointed in the same manner, and not exceed in number those created by said act; and acts amendatory thereto, together with all legislative enactments of the Territory of New Mexico not inconsistent with the provisions of this act, are hereby extended to and continued in force in the said Territory of Arizona, until repealed or amended by future legislation: *Provided,* That no salary shall be due or paid the officers created by this act until they have entered upon the duties of their respective offices within the said Territory.

Government, executive, legislative, judicial.

Officers, how appointed, &c.

Acts governing New Mexico extended to this territory.

Proviso.

SEC. 3. *And be it further enacted,* That there shall neither be slavery nor involuntary servitude in the said Territory, otherwise than in the punishment of crimes, whereof the parties shall have been duly convicted; and all acts and parts of acts, either of Congress or of the Territory of New Mexico, establishing, regulating, or in any way recognizing the relation of master and slave in said Territory, are hereby repealed.

Slavery not to exist therein.

APPROVED, February 24, 1863.

Reprinted from *United States Statues at Large.*

Illustration B

CHAP 131.—An act to provide for an additional associate Justice of the supreme court of Arizona.

February 11, 1891.

Be it enacted by the Senate and House of Representatives of the United States of America in Congress assembled, That hereafter the supreme court of the Territory of Arizona shall consist of a chief justice and three associate justices, any three of whom shall constitute a quorum: but no justice shall act as a member of the supreme court in any action or proceeding brought to such court by writ of error, bill of exception, or appeal from a decision, judgment, or decree rendered by him as judge of a district court, unless one of the other justices is disqualified to sit in such action.

Supreme court and judicial districts of Arizona Territory. Vol. 12, p. 665 amended. Composition of supreme court. Quorum. Disqualified to sit.

SEC. 2. That it shall be the duty of the President to appoint one additional associate justice of said supreme court in manner now provided by law, who shall hold his office for the term of four years, and until his successor is appointed and qualified.

Appointment of additional associate justice. Term of office.

SEC. 3. That the said Territory shall be divided into four judicial districts, and a district court shall be held in each district by one of the justices of the supreme court thereof, at such time and place as is or may be prescribed by law. Each judge, after assignment, shall reside in the district to which he is assigned.

Division into four judicial districts. Terms of court. Residence.

SEC. 4. That the present chief justice and his associates are hereby vested with power and authority, and they are hereby directed to divide said Territory into four judicial districts, and make such assignments of the judges provided for in the first section of this act as shall in their judgment be meet and proper: *Provided*, That said districts shall be subject to such changes as the Territorial Assembly of the said Territory may enact.

Division and assignments. *Proviso.* Changes in districts.

SEC. 5. That the said district court shall have jurisdiction, and the same is hereby vested, to hear, try, and determine all matters and causes that the courts of the other districts of the Territory now possess; and for such purposes two terms of said court shall be held annually, at such places within said district as may be designated by the chief justice and his associates, or a majority of them; and grand and petit jurors shall be summoned thereon in the manner now required by law.

Jurisdiction of district courts. R. S., sec. 1910, p. 337. Terms. Jurors.

SEC. 6. That all offenses committed before the passage of this act shall be prosecuted, tried, and determined in the same manner and with the same effect (except as to the number of judges) as if this act had not passed.

Pending offenses, etc.

Approved, February 11, 1891.

Reprinted from *United States Statutes at Large.*

Illustration C

AN OVERVIEW

CHART I
STATE OF ARIZONA
JUDICIAL DEPARTMENT
ORGANIZATION AND ADMINISTRATION , 1973

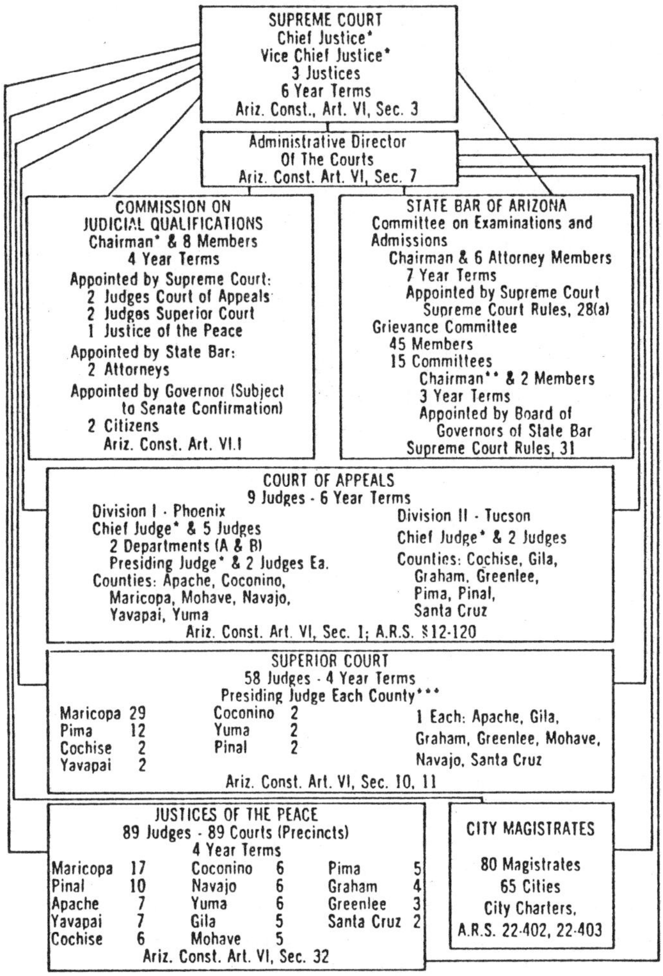

* Elected by Their Members
** Appointed by the Board of Governors
*** Appointed by the Supreme Court

— 7 —

Reprinted from the Report of the *Twenty-second Arizona Town Hall on the Adequacy of Arizona's Court System.*

Illustration D

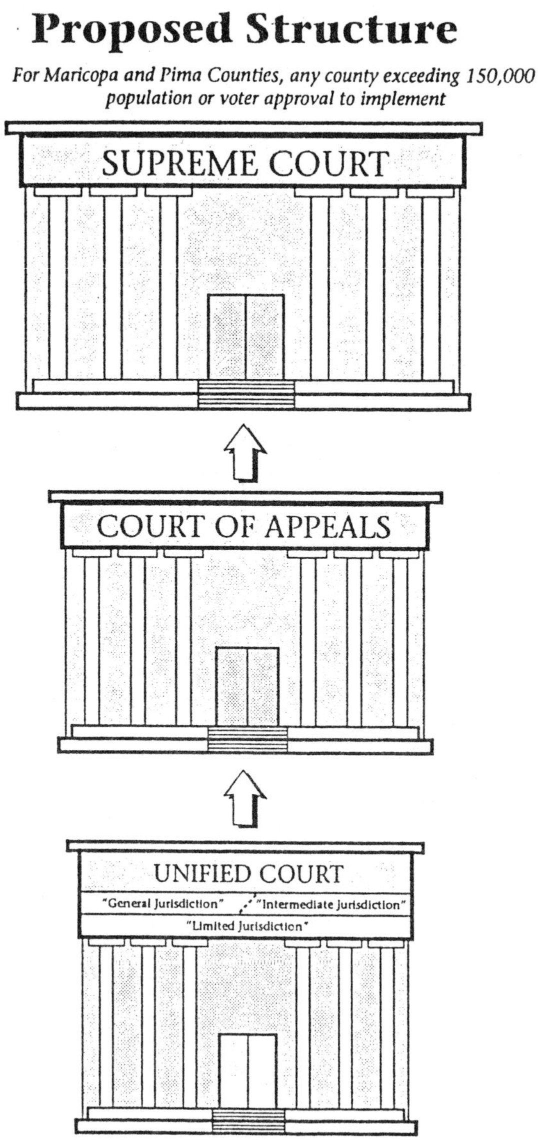

Reprinted from the *Arizona Annual Judicial Report,* FY 90.

Illustration E

The Courts of Arizona

Arizona Judiciary
Organizational Chart
June 30, 1990

SUPREME COURT
5 Justices, 6-Year Terms

Chief Justice*
Vice Chief Justice*
3 Associate Justices

Ariz. Const., Art. VI, Sec. 3

COURT OF APPEALS
21 Judges, 6-Year Terms

Division One - Phoenix
Chief Judge* & 14 Associate Judges
5 Departments (A, B, C, D & E)
Presiding Judge* & 2 Judges Each

Counties: Apache, Coconino, La Paz, Maricopa, Mohave, Navajo, Yavapai, Yuma

Division Two - Tucson
Chief Judge* & 5 Associate Judges
2 Departments (A & B)
Presiding Judge* & 2 Judges Each

Counties: Cochise, Gila, Graham, Greenlee, Pima, Pinal, Santa Cruz

Ariz. Const., Art. VI, Sec. 1; A.R.S. § 12-120

SUPERIOR COURT
116 Judges, 4-Year Terms

Presiding Judge in Each County**

County	Judges	County	Judges	County	Judges
Apache	1	Greenlee	1	Pima	23
Cochise	3	La Paz	1	Pinal	4
Coconino	3	Maricopa	64	Santa Cruz	1
Gila	2	Mohave	3	Yavapai	3
Graham	1	Navajo	3	Yuma	3

Ariz. Const., Art. VI, Secs. 3, 10 and 11

JUSTICES OF THE PEACE
84 JUDGES / [illegible] COURTS (PRECINCTS), 4-YEAR TERMS

County	Judges	County	Judges
Apache	4	Mohave	4
Cochise	6	Navajo	5
Coconino	4	Pima	7
Gila	5	Pinal	12
Graham	2	Santa Cruz	2
Greenlee	2	Yavapai	7
La Paz	3	Yuma	3
Maricopa	18		

Ariz. Const., Art. VI, Secs. 32

MUNICIPAL COURTS
137 Full and Part Time Judges, 83 Cities/Towns

County	Judges	Cities/Towns	County	Judges	Cities/Towns
Apache	3	3	Mohave	4	4
Cochise	8	7	Navajo	6	6
Coconino	5	4	Pima	16	4
Gila	5	5	Pinal	9	8
Graham	3	3	Santa Cruz	2	2
Greenlee	2	2	Yavapai	8	8
La Paz	1	1	Yuma	4	4
Maricopa	61	22			

A.R.S. §§ 22-402 and -403

page 10

*Elected by their members
** Appointed by the Supreme Court

Reprinted from the *Arizona Annual Judicial Report,* FY 90.

Chapter 5

Arizona Court Reports and Case Finders

Marianne Sidorski Alcorn

A. History

James M. Murphy in his book *Laws, Courts, & Lawyers: Thru the Years in Arizona* referred to a book entitled *Arizona Reports: Prospectus* which purports to record the written opinions of the Arizona Supreme Court at Mesilla. It is dated January 1858 - six years prior to the creation of the Arizona territory when the state was still a part of New Mexico.[1] The printers of the proposal, Vlaes & Green of Pittsburgh, stated, "The extreme ability of many of the Judges has now induced the undersigned, at great expense, to undertake the regular publication of their opinions for the future."[2]

1 *Arizona Reports:Prospectus* located in the Munk Collection of Arizoniana, Southwest Museum Library, Los Angeles, California.

2 Murphy, James M. *Laws, Courts, & Lawyers.* (Tucson:University of Arizona Press, 1970), p. 88.

According to Mr. Murphy, the modern series of *Arizona Reports* were born when Governor Safford requested the ninth territorial legislature to provide for the publication of Supreme Court decisions. Nothing was done at this time, but in 1879 the tenth legislature appointed Charles B. Rush territorial reporter of the Supreme Court. When enough decisions were accrued to form a volume of convenient size, Rush was instructed to have 300 copies printed and published, the cost of publication not to exceed $1000." [3] However by 1989, *Arizona Reports* comprised up to five volumes annually; containing the Supreme Court and Court of Appeals decisions, at a cost of $36.75 per volume (or $183.75 for all five). Should the state now decide to order 300 copies such as the tenth legislature did, the cost would be $55,125 instead of $1000.

Volume 1 of the *Arizona Reports* was published by the Bancroft-Whitney Company in 1884. It includes cases beginning in 1866 although, the cases from those early years are scattered and not cumulative. Certainly this is clear from studying volume one of the *Arizona Reports* which includes reports covering 1866 to 1884. At the back of the volume there is a section entitled "Additional Cases" which were cases found after the volume had been prepared. (See Illustration A, p.107.) E.W. Lewis, the Court Reporter for Volume 2, wrote in the preface, "The difficulties in now preparing complete and accurate reports have not been few. In the earlier years the (Supreme) court held its sessions in various parts of the Territory, at Tucson, Prescott and Phoenix, and doubtless this largely accounts for the regrettable lack of completeness in the files prior to 1894, when the court established its permanent seat at the capital, the original papers are missing; in others but a portion are to be found....No opinions have been recorded in permanent form from 1877 to 1886, and a few opinions which appear in the first volume of these reports, as well as in the later Pacific Reporters, cannot now be found."

The following is a list of the *Arizona Reports* and the court reporters for historical interest. It is possible that before the publication of the *Arizona Reports* in 1884 nominative report citations were used, (i.e., the court reporters name and the page number).

Volume	Years	Court Reporter
1	1866-1884	F.P. Dann
2-10[4]	1885-1906	E.W. Lewis
11-13	1907-1911	James R. Dunseath
14-16	1911-1914	Paul C. Thorne
16-43	1914-1933	Alice M. Birdsall
44-53	1934-39	Pearl H. Collier
54-62	1939-45	Loretta C. Savage
62-63	1945	John F. Sullivan

3 Ibid, p.89.

4 Volume 10 contains a cumulative digest for volumes 1 thru 10. It starts after page 256. All the pages are renumbered from that point. It is 359 pages in length.

In 1947 (the 1945 decisions), the *Arizona Reports* ceased publication by Bancroft-Whitney Company. After World War II, the cost of publishing the *Arizona Reports* had risen to $3,750 per volume for 250 copies.[5] As an alternative to ending its publication, Dean Byron McCormick of the University of Arizona College of Law negotiated with West to publish the *Arizona Reports* in addition to their *Pacific Reporters.*[6]

Chapter 92 of the Session Laws of Arizona was adopted on March 25, 1947 and in an emergency clause became effective immediately allowing the Supreme Court to contract for the publication and sale of their decisions "on the terms most advantageous to the state." This allowed the Supreme Court to contract with West to become their publisher.

The decisions of the highest court in the state, the Arizona Supreme Court and the decisions of the Arizona Court of Appeals and the Arizona Tax Court are reported in the *Arizona Reports.* The format of the *Arizona Reports* has been consistent from their beginning: Officials (Judges, Attorney Generals, Marshals), Table of Cases Reported, Table of Cases Cited, Table of Arizona Cases Cited, and Table of Statutes Construed. At the end of each volume there also has been a case digest. (See Illustrations B-H, pp.108-114) When West Publishing Company began publishing the *Arizona Reports* they added key numbers to the digests found at the end of the volumes.

The volumes' information listing attorneys, judges and Arizona Attorney Generals is certainly of historical value. The courts can be followed from the earliest days when the Territorial Court consisted of Justice of the Peace courts, probate and district courts and the Supreme Court. The three original judicial districts, were in La Paz, Tucson and Prescott. Once a year the three judges from the three courts sat together as the Territorial Supreme Court.[7] The interesting point is that the lower court judge also heard the same case when he was acting as a Supreme Court Justice. Jumping further ahead to 1963 there are three judges listed for Division I of the Arizona Court of Appeals and three listed for Division II. By 1990, however, Division I had 12 judges and Division II had 6. In volume 2 of the *Arizona Reports* for the year 1885, there is one Attorney General listed; Clark Churchill. In 1963, 32 Attorney Generals are listed and as of December 19, 1989, volume 161 lists 248 Attorney Generals.

B. Current Court Reports

West Publishing Company began publication of volume 64 and continues to publish the Court of Appeals and Supreme Court decisions. It was not until 1964 that a Court of Appeals was created and judges were elected to sit on it. West introduced a new reporter, *Arizona Appeals Reports,* in 1965 for the decisions of the new Court of Appeals. This set lasted until 1976 and contained volumes 1-27. At this point, the Appeals decisions were merged into the *Arizona Reports* and have remained there ever since.

5 Murphy, *Laws, Courts, & Lawyers,* 89.
6 Ibid., p.89.
7 Murphy, James M. *Laws, Courts & Lawyers* (Tucson: University of Arizona Press, 1970), 19.

The Arizona Tax Court Cases have been published in the *Arizona Reports* since its first decision in March of 1989. The Arizona Tax Court was established by the 38th legislature (1988) in Chapter 330 of the Arizona Session Laws (Ariz. Rev. Stat. Ann. §§12-161 thru 12-174). The Tax Court is housed in the Maricopa County Superior Court and is under its budget and administration. But the court may hold hearings in any county seat. It is the tax department of the Superior Court exercising original jurisdiction over cases of equity and at law which involve the legality of any tax, impost or assessment. The Tax Court will hear Appeals from the Board of Tax Appeals while appeals from the Tax Court are heard by a department of Division I of the Arizona Court of Appeals. A taxpayer may elect to use a simplified, small claims procedures in some cases (Ariz. Rev. Stat §12-172). Decisions of the Tax Court are reported in *Arizona Reports, Pacific Reporter, Arizona Advance Reports,* and are also on WESTLAW.

1. *Advance Sheets (See Illustrations I-J)*

Code Co Law Publishers of Orem, Utah are authorized by the Arizona Supreme Court to publish the recent opinions of the Arizona Supreme Court, Arizona Court of Appeals and Arizona Tax Court. Occasionally changes may be made by the court before the opinions are published in the official reporter. The *Arizona Advance Reports* began publication with issue number one on February 15, 1988. The reports are printed every other Tuesday (26 times a year). Each issue contains all the new cases issued through the preceding Friday. Cases from the Supreme Court are cited:

Cabrera v. Cottrell, 1 Ariz. Adv. Rep. 5 (Jan. 15, 1988)

Cases from the Arizona Court of Appeals are cited in the form:

Cabrera v. Cottrell, 49 Ariz. Adv. Rep.5 (Ct. App. Feb. 5, 1988).

The price for a subscription to the *Arizona Advance Reports* is currently $150. per year.

Each advance sheet contains:

Table of Cases Reported

The cases

Statute Index located after the reported cases. This index contains all references to any statute, rule, constitutional provision or administrative rule cited in the advance sheets and is cumulative for a year.

The Case Name Index is also cumulative for the preceding year and reflects if a case has been vacated, amended or modified.

2. *Slip Opinions*

The Supreme Court and Court of Appeals print slip opinions which are distributed to the state, county and university law libraries and some firms. These opinions are without editorial enhancements such as a syllabus or headnotes. (See section G. Accessing the Arizona Courts)

3. *Arizona Business Gazette*

The *Arizona Business Gazette,* Law/Courts section prints the decisions of the Arizona Supreme Court and Court of Appeals. The time lag on these varies, some cases are included within two weeks of the decision while others are months behind. In the past not all cases from the courts have been included in the *Arizona Business Gazette.* The publisher's new goal is to include all the cases from these courts. At this time, in an effort to catch up, some older cases are being printed. When the backlog has been eliminated all Arizona Supreme Court and Court of Appeals cases should be published in this newspaper.

4. *Computerized Access*

Arizona Supreme Court, Court of Appeal and Arizona Tax Court Decisions can be accessed on LEXIS and on WESTLAW.

LEXIS - ARIZ

Supreme Court	1898 - current
Court of Appeals	1965 - current
Board of Tax Appeals	Dec. 1982 - current

WESTLAW - AZ-CS

Supreme Court	1899 - current
Court of Appeals	1965 - current

AZTX-TCT

Arizona Tax Court	1989 - current

5. *Pacific Reporter*

The *Pacific Reporter* is a part of the West Publishing Company's National Reporter System. It is one of the seven regional reporters contained in this System. A regional reporter includes the decisions of the highest courts of its states. The *Pacific Reporter* prints the decisions of the Arizona Supreme Court, Arizona Court of Appeals and Arizona Tax Court. The contents page found at the beginning of the *Pacific Reporter* Advance Sheets, also contains the recent federal cases from the Pacific Reporter states. The cases are listed by originating state and the federal cite is given. The following is a list of the state decisions included in the *Pacific Reporter*, the corresponding volume of the state reports (when applicable), and the date publication began in the *Pacific Reporter:*

Alaska (1960), Alaska Appellate (1981), 1 Arizona (1866), 1 Arizona Appeals (1965), 64 California (1883), 1 California Appellate (1905), 7 Colorado (1883), 1 Colorado Appellate (1891- 1905, 1912-15, 1970-date), 44 Hawaii (1959), 1 Hawaii Appellate (1980), 2 Idaho (1881), Idaho Appeals (1882), 30 Kansas (1883), 1 Kansas Appeals (1895-1901 and 1977-date), 4 Montana (1882),17 Nevada (1882), 3 New Mexico (1883), New Mexico Appeals (1967), 1 Oklahoma (1890), Oklahoma Appeals (1969), 1 Oklahoma Criminal Appeals ((1908), 11 Oregon (1883), 1 Oregon Appeals (1969), 3 Utah (1881), 2 Washington Territory (1880), 1 Washington (1889), 1 Washington Appellate (1969), 3 Wyoming (1883).

Arizona attorneys often look to California law when no applicable law can be found in Arizona. Therefore researchers should be aware that the decisions of the California Courts of Appeal (California District Courts of Appeal and the Appellate Department of the Supreme Court) were removed from the Pacific Reporter in 1960. In addition, the *Pacific Digest* only contains California Supreme Court Decisions. To search for California Appellate Decisions use *West's California Digest 2d, California Digest of Official Reports, 3d series,* WESTLAW or LEXIS.

C. Digests

Years ago as an undergraduate student I worked at the University of Washington Law Library with a third year law student. This student taught me his unique method of locating pertinent cases. For example, he mentioned certain volumes of the *Southern Reporter;* and said that if I went to that set and picked up one of these volumes, it would automatically open to the most often read cases (which correspondingly were also the most perverse).

In *Finding the Law* a story is told regarding Otto Preminger's classic movie 'Anatomy of a Murder.' It "features a scene in which one of the defense attorneys, who is hoping to bolster an insanity defense in a murder trial, paces excitedly around a law library, then spins on his heel and snatches a book from a shelf, seemingly guided only by instinct. Opening it, he finds a case in point and exclaims in joy."[8]

I, personally, would prefer it if we could all follow the "LA Law" legal research method. We would then have the books but be able to prepare dramatic summations and briefs without ever opening them.

Since none of the above actually bares results we must return to the question of how to locate Arizona cases. The applicable indexes are the *Arizona Digest* and the *Pacific Digest.* It is a fairly easy task to use either of them since they are both published by West Publishing Company. Once a researcher is familiar with one West digest it is simple to use any of the others whether state, regional or federal.

The first digest of Arizona cases occurs in 1909 at the back of volume ten of the *Arizona Reports.* It was prepared by Charles L. Thompson a member of the San Francisco Bar and consist of a 359 page subject digest.

In 1915 Bancroft-Whitney published a separate volume called *Arizona Digest* covering volumes 1-16 of the *Arizona Reports.* This edition was also prepared by a member of the San Francisco Bar, Peter V. Ross. It adopted the *American Digest* Classification as set out by West. It included a table of cases and tables showing where the Arizona decisions, constitution, codes, and statutes had been cited and construed.

Another edition of the *Arizona Digest* was published by Bancroft-Whitney in the 1920's and authored by Albert R. Smith a member of the Arizona Bar, covering the cases in volumes 1 to 25 of the *Arizona Reports.* This edition contained not only the decisions of the Arizona Supreme Court but also of the

8 Cohen, Morris L., Robert C. Berring, and Kent C. Olson, *Finding the Law.* (St. Paul: West Publishing Co., 1989), p. 82.

U.S. Courts originating in Arizona. The Table of Cases included a citator showing where each case had been cited in later decisions of the Arizona Supreme Court. Another Table had cases overruled, reversed, modified, limited, criticized and disapproved.

In 1939 the *Arizona Digest* reached its current level. It was initially jointly published by Bancroft-Whitney and West Publishing Co. and, therefore, included the West Key Number System. It covered Arizona cases from 1866 with the *Arizona Reports* and *Pacific Reporter* cites, as well as Arizona Cases decided in the Federal District Court, Circuit Court of Appeals and U.S. Supreme Court. This edition is currently being replaced with *Arizona Digest 2d,* by West Publishing Company.

For the inexperienced researcher Cohen, Berring and Olson's, *Finding the Law* or the free publication from West Publishing Co., *West's Law Finder* give in-depth instructions on locating cases through the digests. Briefly there are three ways to use any of the digests which West publish (again for Arizona cases you would be using either the *Pacific Digest* or the *Arizona Digest*).

1. *Subject*

Every digest has a Descriptive Word Index. The researcher has to determine which words describe the facts or legal issues of the case. The most descriptive words will be connected with the five elements of the case; Parties, Places and Things, Basis of Action or Issue, Defense, and Relief Sought. If this seems difficult, try thinking of a legal problem and then picking out the four or five words that seem most important to the problem. Look the words up in the Descriptive Word Index. Usually even if the word is not precise or correct, there will be "see references" to other terms that may ultimately yield relevant cases. Basically think about your legal problem and try to look for various synonyms in the Descriptive Word Index. One of the tasks law librarians find themselves doing is discussing the researcher's legal question so they mutually arrive at words to search for in the index. (See Illustrations K-M, pp.117-119)

2. *Table of Cases*

If you have the name of a case, you can go to the volumes labeled "Table of Cases" to locate the reporter citation. The key numbers (under which the various points of case law have been classified) will also be listed, enabling you to go to any of the other West's Digests and research the same point of law.

3. *Topic method*

There are two methods to locate the correct topic. (See Illustrations N-O, pp.120-121)

A. Studious analysis of the Key Number System Law Chart may direct you to the correct topic.

B. In using Descriptive-Word Indexes, you may, on occasion be unable to locate the precise Key Number which carries that point of law. In every instance, however, the Descriptive Word Index will refer to other appropriate topics.[9]

Digests are updated by annual pocket parts and supplementary pamphlets. The *Arizona Digest* has a supplementary pamphlet (issued each July). It can be further updated by using the Key Number Digests in each volume and advance sheets of the West Reporters.

Each pocket part or pamphlet will list the last reporters that were included in the digest. (See Illustration P) From this list the researcher should examine the next issued reporter volume and search by key number from the back of each reporter volume or advance sheet. In updating Arizona state and federal cases the following would be searched:

Pacific Reporter or *Arizona Reports* (Note - *Pacific* is updated more frequently than the *Arizona Reports*).

Supreme Court Reporter
Federal Reporter
Federal Supplement
Federal Rules Decisions
Bankruptcy Law Reporter
Arizona Advance Reports

Generally, the *Pacific Reports* and *Arizona Advance Reports* would be the two sets used most often for updating.

The *Arizona Digest* is the most advantageous to use however for several reasons:

1. It is the only digest that brings all Arizona cases together in one set (federal and state).

2. It has a defendant-plaintiff table which the Pacific Digest does not include.

D. Parallel Citations

The bound *Pacific Reporters* will provide the parallel citation to the *Arizona Reports* above the name of the case and correspondingly, the bound *Arizona Reports* will give the *Pacific Reporter* cite.

Another way of obtaining parallel cites for Arizona cases would be to Shepardize the case. The parallel citation will be listed in parenthesis in the first Shepard's in which the case appears. West also publishes the *Arizona Blue and White Book.* One section goes from the *Pacific Reporter* to the *Arizona Reports,* the other section reverses the process and goes from the *Arizona Reports* to the *Pacific Reporter.* (See Illustrations Q & R). The *National Reporter Blue Book* also published by West, enables the researcher to go from the state reports citation to the regional reporter citation. In addition Auto-Cite in LEXIS and Insta-Cite in WESTLAW provides parallel citations to cases.

9 *West's Law Finder* (St. Paul: West Publishing Co., 1988).

E. Shepard's Citations

An essential facet of legal research is determining the current status of any case relevant to the issue involved. The researcher can use *Shepard's Arizona Citations* to determine this for Arizona legal sources. Information on the mechanics of using Shepard's citators can be found in two free pamphlets published by Shepard's, "How to Use Shepard's Citations," and "Questions and Answers." Legal research books will also discuss how to use Shepard's Citations.

Shepard's Arizona Citations consist of two volumes and supplements. The first volume is the case edition which shows all the citations to Arizona cases reported in the *Arizona Reports* or the *Pacific Reporter* as cited in the Arizona and federal courts, law reviews, legal texts and annotations. The second volume is the statute edition. It shows citations to the Arizona Constitution, codes, laws, municipal charters, ordinances, court rules, jury instructions, law review articles, several legal texts, annotations and in the laws of Arizona.[10]

Shepard's Arizona Case Names Citator is an alphabetical listing of all cases reported in the official Arizona reports from 1940. Both the defendant's and plaintiff's names are listed and a citation to both the official Arizona reports and Pacific Reporter are shown.

Shepard's bound volumes are updated by pamphlet supplements bimonthly. Check the cover of the latest supplement to be sure of what your set should contain.

In order to meet the need for faster delivery of the citations Shepard's has introduced the monthly *Shepard's Arizona Express. Arizona Express* provides the latest analyzed citations to Arizona cases, statutes and the Arizona Constitution, even quicker than using Shepard's online. This service, however, does not replace the red and white covered supplements of *Shepard's Arizona Citations.* The researcher uses the *Arizona Express* in the same method as the *Shepard's Arizona Citations.* For example to shepardize 102 Ariz. 518, use the *Arizona* Express in exactly the same way i.e., volume numbers are in the upper corner (here, vol. 102) with the first page of the case listed underneath (here 518). Beneath the citation is the name of the case *Hartford Accident & Indem. v. Aetna Casualty & Sur. Co.* No. CV-89-0101-T/AP. Beside the name of the case is an (o) showing that the case has been overruled, and listed under the docket number is the citation to the overruling case, 62 Ariz. Adv. Rep. 7 (Ariz. May 29, 1990). (Illustration S, p.125)

Shepard's can be accessed on WESTLAW or LEXIS. Using Shepard's on either of these two systems eliminates the need to use several books and pamphlets, as all the citing entries are cumulated in one listing. The researcher can also choose a particular "history" or "treatment" to be displayed. For example, only the cases that have been overruled or reversed can be displayed. An additional advantage is that the cases can be retrieved and read at the same time. The *Shepard's Arizona Express* now makes the printed version more up to date than

10 *Shepard's Arizona Citations,* preface. Colorado Springs:Shepard's/McGraw-Hill, February, 1991.

the online Shepard's version. However, WESTLAW and LEXIS can be used as citators to retrieve the most recent cases, (see Chapter 10 for more information).

F. Auto-Cite and Insta-Cite

Auto-Cite (LEXIS) and Insta-Cite (WESTLAW) are two cite-checking systems. When only verification of a case is needed Auto-Cite or Insta-Cite can be used. These are time saving devices which eliminate sorting through Shepard's for case history and current status. Auto-Cite and Insta-Cite give the history of the case from the lower courts onward and provide any decisions that have direct effect upon the case. Therefore they can be used to obtain parallel citations and to confirm if the case has been appealed or directly affected by any connected case.

G. Accessing Arizona Court Documents

Case law is not the only information needed from the courts. Case files contain a wide variety of documents beneficial to the researcher from briefs to listings of evidence. The following are the locations and directions for acquiring materials from Arizona Courts.

1. Arizona Supreme Court
Courts Building
1501 West Washington
Phoenix, AZ 85007
Clerk - phone # (602)542-9396
Copies are presently 50 cents per page.

a. Documents can be retrieved from the Clerk's Office, 4th floor of the Courts Building, Room 402.

b. Request the case by docket number (either Supreme Court or lower court) or by case name.

c. Information available in the case files include:

i. Motions
ii. Pleadings
iii. Briefs
iv. Depositions
v. Writs
vi. Minutes
vii. Orders
viii. Complaints
ix. Judgments
x. List of evidence

d. Retention - Civil cases are kept in hard copy for three years, while criminal cases are maintained for four years. After this time, the cases are placed on microfiche and the hard copies sent to the Department of Library, Archives and Public Records on 19th Avenue and Jefferson.

e. The Supreme Court Clerk's office has only a microfiche viewer. Another set and microfiche copier are located in the State Library in the Courts Building.

f. In addition, the Arizona State University Law Library, University of Arizona Law Library have Arizona Supreme Court and Court of Appeals briefs on microfilm. Some briefs are also available in hard copy.

2. Arizona Court of Appeals - Division One
1501 West Washington
Phoenix, AZ 85007
Clerk (602) 542-4821
Copies are presently $1.15 per page (whether from microfilm or hard copies). Copying is limited to 10 pages.

a. Documents can be retrieved from the clerk's office, 2nd floor of the Courts Building.

b. Request the case by docket number or names of the parties.

c. Information available in the case files includes:

i. All filings made to the Court of Appeals.

ii. Original briefs. Briefs can not be copied. However, they can be examined and photocopied at Arizona State University Law Library, University of Arizona Law Library and at the State Law Library in the Courts Building.

iii. Superior Court files are sent to the Court of Appeals when the case is appealed and are returned to the Superior Court when the appeal is decided.

d. Retention - The court anticipates that all files will remain in hard copy for three years and then be placed on microfilm. However presently filming has been delayed and the files have remained in hard copy for a longer period.

Arizona Court of Appeals - Division Two
State Office Building
416 West Congress, Room 181
Tucson, AZ 85701
Clerk (602) 628-1999
Basically, follow the same procedure given above. Copy charges remain the same.

3. Maricopa County Superior Court
201 W. Jefferson
Central Court Building
Phoenix, AZ 85003
Clerk (602) 506-3253
Copies are presently $1.15 for both hard copy or microfiche.

a. Documents can be retrieved from the Clerk's Office. The Information Desk is located on the lower level.

b. Request the case by docket number on the slips provided. The clerk will pull the file. If the requester does not have the docket number, there are computers accessible to obtain it.

c. Information available in the case files;

i. Motions
ii. Pleadings
iii. Briefs
iv. Depositions
v. Writs
vi. Minutes
vii. Orders
viii. Complaints
ix. List of Evidence
x. Subpoenas
xi. Subpoena Duces Tecum
xii. Interrogatories
xiii. Summons
xiv. Opinion
xv. Judgment

d. Retention - From the late 1800's until 1930 the files are in hard copy format. Civil cases are kept on hard copy for three years and then microfilmed. Criminal cases, however, are microfilmed and the hard copies also retained.

Pima County Superior Court
110 West Congress
Tucson, AZ 85701
Clerk (602) 740-3201
Documents from Pima County Superior Court can be retrieved in a similar manner.

4. United States District Court; District of Arizona
230 N. 1st Avenue
Phoenix, AZ 85025
Clerk (602)379-3341
Copies are presently 50 cents per page.

Note: The copies are made by the court employees and copying is a low priority item. Therefore the clerk has suggested that copies be made by their off-site copy service at 15 cents per page. The forms for this service are available at the court and the service can deliver the finished copies directly to law offices.

Tucson Division
44 East Broadway
Tucson, AZ 85701
Clerk (602)670-6559
Photocopy fees are presently 50 cents per page and off-site copy service is available.

Note: the Bankruptcy Court is at a different location, 110 S. Church Avenue, phone (602)670-6304.

a. Documents can be retrieved from the Phoenix Clerk's Office, Room 1400. Bankruptcy records are found on the 5th floor.

b. The information available is similar to the list above for Maricopa County Superior Court. All file materials are available except for the items sealed by the judge.

c. Retention — Case files are kept in Phoenix for five years. After five years they are sent to California for storage. There is a $25 out-of-state retrieval fee per file.

Illustration A

ADDITIONAL CASES.

NOTE.—The following decisions were found among the records of the court after the preceding portion of the volume was stereotyped, and for that reason they appear out of the order of date.

TERRITORY OF ARIZONA, Respondent, *v.* MICHAEL KENNEDY, Appellant.

[25 Pac. 517.]

IN CRIMINAL CASE, COURT MUST COMMIT CHARGE TO JURY TO WRITING and read it to the jury, unless the defendant expressly waive his right to have it so given; and where this is not done at the trial, the error is not cured by subsequently reducing the charge to writing.

APPEAL from the district court of the first judicial district, county of Pima. The opinion states the case.

J. E. McCaffry, Attorney General, for the Respondent.

The act approved October 5, 1867, does not require that the charge shall be filed before the jury leaves the box; it is sufficient that it be written and filed.

The rights of the defendant have not been infringed; the charge is in writing and filed with the papers in the case.

The statute of October 5, 1867, was made to enable the defendant to except to any portion of the charge; no exceptions have been taken, and it is not claimed that the charge filed is not the identical charge delivered to the jury.

The decisions cited by counsel for appellant were made upon a law wholly different from this. Hittell's General Laws of California, sec. 1949.

The true intent of our laws in regard to proceedings in criminal cases is that the defendant can not take advantage of any

Illustration B

REPORTS OF CASES

ARGUED AND DETERMINED IN THE

SUPREME COURT

OF THE

TERRITORY OF ARIZONA

FROM

JANUARY TERM, 1866

TO

JANUARY TERM, 1884, INCLUSIVE

F. P. DANN
REPORTER

VOLUME ONE
Reprinted

SAN FRANCISCO
BANCROFT-WHITNEY COMPANY
LAW PUBLISHERS AND LAW BOOKSELLERS
1905

Illustration C

LIST OF THE JUDGES

WHO HAVE BEEN APPOINTED FOR THE TERRITORY OF ARIZONA SINCE ITS ORGANIZATION.

1. WILLIAM F. TURNER, Chief Justice........Appointed in 1865.
2. HENRY T. BACKUS, Associate Justice.. ....Appointed in 1865.
3. JOSEPH P. ALLYS, Associate Justice.......Appointed in 1865.
4. HARLEY H. CARTTER, Associate Justice....Appointed in 1867.
5. JOHN TITUS, Chief Justice.... ....Appointed in 1871.
6. C. A. TWEED, Associate Justice...........Appointed in 1871.
7. ISHAM REAVIS, Associate Justice..........Appointed in 1871.
8. DE FOREST PORTER, Associate Justice....
   Appointed in 1873; reappointed 1877 and 1881; resigned 1882.
9. E. F. DUNNE, Chief Justice............ ..Appointed in 1875.
10. C. G. W. FRENCH, Chief Justice...........
    Appointed in 1875; reappointed in 1880.
11. CHARLES SILENT, Associate Justice........Appointed in 1879.
12. W. H. STILWELL, Associate Justice........Appointed in 1881.
13. WILSON W. HOOVER..... ....Appointed in 1882.
14. A. W. SHELDON, Associate Justice.........Appointed in 1883.
15. DANIEL PINNEY, Associate Justice........Appointed in 1883.

(iii)

UNITED STATES MARSHALS

FOR THE

TERRITORY OF ARIZONA.

EDWARD PHELPS..... ....Appointed June 18, 1866.
ISAAC Q. DICKINSON.... .. ..Appointed April 15, 1871.
GEORGE TYNG....... ....Appointed Jan. 30, 1874.
FRANCIS H. GOODWIN.......... ....Appointed Dec. 23, 1874.
W. W. STANDIFER..... ... .Appointed Aug. 15, 1876.
C. P. DAKE... ....Appointed June 12, 1878.
ZAN L. TIDBALL....... ....Appointed July 18, 1882.

(iv)

Reprinted with permission from 1 *Arizona Reports* (1905), by the Bancroft-Whitney Co.

Illustration D

LIST OF ATTORNEYS

PRACTICING IN THE SUPREME COURT OF THE TERRITORY OF ARIZONA FROM ITS ORGANIZATION UP TO THE YEAR 1883.

Able, Paul.
Ainza, Santiago.
Alexander, H. M.
Anderson, James.
Anderson, J. A.
Anderson, N. D.
Aram, E. W.
Baker, A. C.
Bashford, Coles.
Berry, George G.
Berry, W. J.
Bianwell, J. F.
Bruner, A. J.
Buell, James.
Campbell, A.
Cartter, Harley H.
Churchill, Clark.
Churchman, James.
Clark, J. W.
Culver, W. H.
Dann, F. P.
Darroche, J. R.
Davis, A. E.
Davis, D. E.
Davis, J. W.
Dibble, Henry C.
Dobbins, M. D.
Dofficy, Thos. P.
Dorsey, Caleb.
Drum, T. J.
Earll, Warner.
Farley, H.
Fitch, Thomas.
Furgeson, R. D.
Gauche, F.
Goodrich, Ben.
Goodrich, Briggs.
Graves, William.
Gray, Clarence.
Gregg, Frederick W.
Hancock, W. A.
Hargrave, Joseph P.
Haynes, W. M.
Hereford, B. H.
Herring, W. F.
Hicks, John C.
Hodge, Hiram C.
Howard, G. Hill.
Howard, John.
Hoyt, John P.
Hughes, L. C.
Krinchman, James.
Lacy, J. H.
Lemon, A. D.
Leonard, John W.
Lewis, James F.
Lowe, James R.
McCaffry, J. E.
McCarty, O. F.
McClusky, Franklin.
Marsh, Lucius P.
Masterson, Murat.

(v)

Mitchell, Thomas.
Morgan, Benjamin.
Neugass, Joseph N.
Noble, Edward.
Osborn, W. J.
Otis, James W.
Oury, Granville H.
Perry, Joseph C.
Pomroy, E. B.
Price, Lyttleton.
Reymert, J. D.
Risley, E. W.
Robinson, James F.
Robinson, James O.
Robinson, Joseph W.
Roman, John.
Rountree, John M.
Rowell, C. W. C.
Rush, John A.
Safford, A. P. K.
Satterwhite, T. D.
Scott, Chalmers.
Silcot, J.
Smith, F. M.
Smith, Horace.
Smith, Marcius A.
Spalding, G. W.
Stanford, S.
Stebbins, J. C.
Stephens, C. C.
Stiles, T. L.
Street, Webster.
Strong, E. D.
Struter, O. W.
Stuart, Charles D.
Summers, H. B.
Thurmond, Philip M.
Turner, P. M.
Tweed, C. A.
Van Voorhies, W.
Walsh, M. J.
Wells, Ed. W.
Wicks, Moye.
Williams, George R.
Willis, Henry M.
Wordude, P. K.
Zabriskie, J. A.

Illustration E

TABLE OF CASES REPORTED.

(vii)

Reprinted with permission from 1 *Arizona Reports* (1905), by the Bancroft-Whitney Co.

Illustration F

TABLE OF CASES CITED.

	Page
Adams v. Knowlton, 22 Cal. 283	273
Aitken v. Mendenhall, 25 Cal. 213	135
Allen v. Fennon, 27 Cal. 69	512
Allen v. MacPherson, 1 H. L. Cas. 191, 209	219
Allen v. MacPherson, 1 Phill. 133	219
Allison's Exr. v. Allison, 4 Hawks, 141	207
Alter's Appeal, 67 Pa. St. 341	188
American Fur Co. v. United States, 2 Pet. 358	37, 45
American Ins. Co. v. Canter, 1 Pet. 511	69
Atherton v. Fowler, 96 U. S. 513	407
Atkyns v. Horde, 1 Burr. 119	152
Baker v. Joseph, 16 Cal. 180	125
Baldwin v. Kramer, 2 Cal. 582	335
Bank of United States v. Moss, 6 How. 31	335
Batdorff v. Bank of Reading, 61 Pa. St. 179	125
Beal v. Nichols, 2 Gray, 264	131
Beckley v. Newland, 2 P. Wms. 182	198, 199, 200
Beckley v. Newland, 1 Story's Eq. 343	188, 199
Bell v. Red Rock T. & M. Co., 36 Cal. 219	146, 501
Benner v. Porter, 9 How. 235	69
Bickham v. Smith, 62 Pa. St. 45	125
Bohanan v. Hans, 26 Tex. 450	126
Brannan v. Paty, 58 Cal. 330	460
Brewer v. Baxter, 41 Ga. 212	188, 209
Broderick's Will, 21 Wall. 503	218, 226
Brown v. Burrus, 8 Mo. 26	131
Buckout v. Swift, 27 Cal. 433	425
Bundy v. Hyde, 50 N. H. 121	127
Buntain v. Baily, 27 Ill. 410	125
Burke v. Miller, 7 Cush. 550	137
Burlington University v. Barrett, 22 Iowa, 60, 72	208, 209
Burton v. Lies, 21 Cal. 87	273
Callis v. Tolson, 6 Gill & J. 80, 91	128
Camden v. Doremus, 3 How. 515, 530	125
Candler v. Rossiter, 10 Wend. 487	241
Carle v. Underhill, 3 Bradf. 101	207
Carroll v. City of Benicia, 40 Cal. 390	125
Case of Broderick's Will, 21 Wall. 503	218
Charauleau v. Woffenden, 1 Ariz. 243	354, 355
Cherokee Nation v. Georgia, 5 Pet. 1	37, 42, 45, 46
Christy v. Scott, 14 How. 292	153
Clark v. Conway, 23 Mo. 438	125
Colman v. Clements, 23 Cal. 248	146
Cordier v. Schloss, 12 Cal. 147	387
Cornell v. Barnes, 26 Wis. 480	126

(1)

Reprinted with permission from 1 *Arizona Reports* (1905), by the Bancroft-Whitney Co.

Illustration G

CITATIONS.

ARIZONA.

COMPILED LAWS.

	Page
Sec. 1, page 536	28
Sec. 2, page 306	272
Sec. 3, page 365	227
Sec. 4, page 365	227
Sec. 4, page 248	418
Sec. 5, page 250	188, 214
Sec. 5, page 375	51
Sec. 7, page 524	311
Sec. 8, page 179	313
Sec. 9, page 307	356
Sec. 13, page 250	215
Sec. 13, page 376	188, 218
Sec. 14, page 376	188, 218
Sec. 22, pages 362, 363	249
Sec. 24, page 369	355
Sec. 51, page 394	94
Sec. 60, c. x	68
Sec. 63, c. x	68
Sec. 66, pages 306, 310	235
Sec. 114, pages 267, 268	509
Sec. 152, page 409	93
Secs. 153, 154, 156	317
Sec. 170, page 412	317, 339
Sec. 205, page 417	228
Sec. 217, c. xi	66
Sec. 222, page 123	509
Sec. 247, page 126	97
Sec. 331. page 134	97
Sec. 338	57
Sec. 368, page 137	65, 75, 506
Secs. 340, 341	363
Secs. 344, 345, 347, 348, page 437	85, 362
Sec. 347, page 447	241
Secs. 361, 362, page 440	85

(7)

Reprinted with permission from 1 *Arizona Reports* (1905), by the Bancroft-Whitney Co.

Illustration H

INDEX.

(515)

Reprinted with permission from 1 *Arizona Reports* (1905), by the Bancroft-Whitney Co.

Illustration I

ARIZONA ADVANCE REPORTS

80 Ariz. Adv. Rep. **February 26, 1991**

Opinions from the **Arizona Supreme Court,**
Arizona Court of Appeals and the
Arizona Tax Court

CONTENTS

Table of Cases, with Comprehensive Summaries
Full Text of Opinions
Petitions, Writs, Rule Changes, etc. (if any)
Statute Index (Cumulative)
Case Name Index (Cumulative)

ISSN 0897-9235

CODE • CO
Law Publishers
P.O. Box 1471
Provo, Utah 84603-1471
Toll-free: 1-800-255-5294

Illustration J

80 Ariz. Adv. Rep. **February 26, 1991**

TABLE OF CASES REPORTED

Continued on next page

Illustration K

West's

ARIZONA DIGEST 2d

VOLUME 1

ABANDONED AND LOST PROPERTY—
APPEAL AND ERROR ⚷867

COVERING CASES FROM

STATE AND FEDERAL COURTS

ST. PAUL, MINN.

WEST PUBLISHING CO.

Illustration L

DIGEST TOPICS

See, also, Outline of the Law by Seven Main Divisions of Law, Page VII

The topic numbers shown below may be used in WESTLAW searches for cases within the topic and within specified key numbers.

---

1 Abandoned and Lost Property
2 Abatement and Revival
3 Abduction
4 Abortion and Birth Control
5 Absentees
6 Abstracts of Title
7 Accession
8 Accord and Satisfaction
9 Account
10 Account, Action on
11 Account Stated
11A Accountants
12 Acknowledgment
13 Action
14 Action on the Case
15 Adjoining Landowners
15A Administrative Law and Procedure
16 Admiralty
17 Adoption
18 Adulteration
19 Adultery
20 Adverse Possession
21 Affidavits
22 Affray
23 Agriculture
24 Aliens
25 Alteration of Instruments
26 Ambassadors and Consuls
27 Amicus Curiae
28 Animals
29 Annuities
30 Appeal and Error
31 Appearance
33 Arbitration
34 Armed Services
35 Arrest
36 Arson
37 Assault and Battery
38 Assignments
40 Assistance, Writ of
41 Associations
42 Assumpsit, Action of
43 Asylums
44 Attachment
45 Attorney and Client
46 Attorney General
47 Auctions and Auctioneers
48 Audita Querela
48A Automobiles
48B Aviation
49 Bail
50 Bailment
51 Bankruptcy
52 Banks and Banking
54 Beneficial Associations
55 Bigamy
56 Bills and Notes
57 Blasphemy
58 Bonds
59 Boundaries
60 Bounties
61 Breach of Marriage Promise
62 Breach of the Peace
63 Bribery
64 Bridges
65 Brokers
66 Building and Loan Associations
67 Burglary
68 Canals
69 Cancellation of Instruments
70 Carriers
71 Cemeteries
72 Census
73 Certiorari
74 Champerty and Maintenance
75 Charities
76 Chattel Mortgages
76A Chemical Dependents
76H Children Out-of-Wedlock
77 Citizens
78 Civil Rights
79 Clerks of Courts
80 Clubs
81 Colleges and Universities
82 Collision
83 Commerce
83H Commodity Futures Trading Regulation
84 Common Lands
85 Common Law
86 Common Scold
88 Compounding Offenses
89 Compromise and Settlement
89A Condominium
90 Confusion of Goods
91 Conspiracy
92 Constitutional Law
92B Consumer Credit
92H Consumer Protection
93 Contempt
95 Contracts
96 Contribution
97 Conversion
98 Convicts
99 Copyrights and Intellectual Property
100 Coroners
101 Corporations
102 Costs
103 Counterfeiting
104 Counties
105 Court Commissioners
106 Courts
107 Covenant, Action of
108 Covenants
108A Credit Reporting Agencies

XIII I-1

Illustration M

AIR

1 Ariz D—4

References are to Digest Topics and Key Numbers

Illustration N

1 Ariz D 2d

ALIENS

SUBJECTS INCLUDED

Persons of foreign allegiance; their rights and disabilities in general

Exclusion or expulsion from the country

Regulation and restriction of immigration

Admission to citizenship

SUBJECTS EXCLUDED AND COVERED BY OTHER TOPICS

Alien enemies, see WAR AND NATIONAL EMERGENCY

Domicile, application of law of, see titles of particular subjects involvec

Escheat proceedings, see ESCHEAT

Federal courts, jurisdiction and venue, see FEDERAL COURTS

Particular kinds of property or particular remedies, rights and liabilities ir respect of, see MINES AND MINERALS, SHIPPING, PATENTS, COPY RIGHTS AND INTELLECTUAL PROPERTY, TRADE REGULATION anc other specific topics

Workmen's compensation acts, rights under, see WORKERS' COMPENSATION

Wrongful death, right of action for, see DEATH

For detailed references to other topics, see Descriptive-Word Index

---

Analysis

I. **DISABILITIES**, ⚬⇒1–17.

II. **EXCLUSION OR EXPULSION**, ⚬⇒18–38.

III. **IMMIGRATION**, ⚬⇒39–59.

IV. **NATURALIZATION**, ⚬⇒60–72.

I. **DISABILITIES.**

⚬⇒1. Who are aliens.
2. Evidence of alienage.
3. Status in general.
4. Protection of persons and personal rights.
5. Real property.
6. —— Disabilities in general.
 (1). In general.
 (2). Who may question capacity.
7. —— Right to take by purchase or devise.
8. —— Right to dower or curtesy.
9. —— Right to take or transmit by descent.

Illustration O

1 Ariz D 2d—269 **ALIENS**

I. DISABILITIES.—Continued.

10. —— Constitutional and statutory restrictions.
11. —— Grants from the state.
12. —— Enabling acts.
    (1). Existence and validity of acts.
    (2). Persons affected by statutes.
    (3). Repeal.
    (4). Construction and operation of statutes.
13. —— Effect of treaties.
14. Personal property.
15. Subjection to law of the country.
16. Actions.
17. Criminal prosecutions.

II. EXCLUSION OR EXPULSION.

⇐18. Power to exclude or expel aliens in general.

III. IMMIGRATION.

⇐39. Power to regulate or restrict immigration; head taxes.
40. Constitutional and statutory provisions.
41. Immigration officers.
42. —— Appointment and qualification.
43. —— Compensation and expenses.
44. —— Powers, duties, and proceedings.
45. Immigrants excluded.
46. —— In general.
47. —— Convicts.
49. —— Liable to become a public charge.
50. —— Imported under contracts to labor.
51. —— Prostitution.
51½. Restriction of number permitted to enter within given time.
52. Detention, supervision and deportation.
53. —— In general.
53.1. —— Grounds and defenses in general.
53.2. —— Crime and immorality.
    (1). In general.
    (2). Turpitude of offense.
    (3). Number and nature of prosecutions or punishment; clemency or recommendation against deportation.
53.3. —— Disloyalty; grounds affecting security or foreign relations.
53.4. —— Improper entry or breach of condition; change of status.
53.5. —— Limitations and time element in general.
53.6. —— Mode of landing or entry.
    (1). In general.
    (2). Re entry and re-entry permits.
    (3). Involuntary entry or re-entry.
53.7. —— Seamen and similar transients.
53.8. —— Arrest.
53.9. —— Custody and supervision; security, temporary admission and parole.

Illustration P

CLOSING WITH CASES REPORTED IN

Pacific Reporter, Second Series	798 P.2d
Supreme Court Reporter	111 S.Ct. 312
Federal Reporter, Second Series	915 F.2d
Federal Supplement	745 F.Supp.
Federal Rules Decisions	131 F.R.D.
Bankruptcy Reporter	118 B.R.

Reprinted with permission from *West's Arizona Digest,* copyright© 1991 by West Publishing Co.

Illustration Q

Arizona
Blue & White Book

Pacific Reporter References

FOR CASES REPORTED IN

Arizona Reports

This table contains in one column a list of pages of the state reports on which each case begins, and in a parallel column gives the volume and page of the Pacific Reporter where the case appears.

If a search is made by means of the title of the case only, then use WESTLAW or consult Tables of Cases in your Arizona Digest or Decennial Digests covering these reports.

VOL. 1, ARIZONA REPORTS

Ariz. Rep.	Pac. Rep.		Ariz. Rep.	Pac. Rep.		Ariz. Rep.	Pac. Rep.		Ariz. Rep.	Pac. Rep.		Ariz. Rep.	Pac. Rep.		Ariz. Rep.	Pac. Rep.		Ariz. Rep.	Pac. Rep.	
Pg.	Vol.	Pg.	Pg.	Vol.	Pg.	Pg.	Vol.	Pg.	Pg.	Vol.	Pg.	Pg.	Vol.	Pg.	Pg.	Vol.	Pg.	Pg.	Vol.	Pg.
35	25	535	87	25	530	237	25	647	340	25	522	397	25	797	426	25	794	506	25	617
31	25	517	96	25	476	239	25	476	346	25	652	399	25	528	444	3	748	507	25	473
49	25	527	99	25	616	240	25	537	361	25	650	401	25	648	482	5	751	509	25	583
53	25	528	161	25	640	243	25	662	362	25	534	404	25	793	485	3	755	510	25	473, 796
56	25	516	175	25	800	274	25	536	364	25	537	411	25	797	488	3	757	511	25	859, 790
58	25	478	227	25	648	319	25	522	377	25	538	413	25	539	490	3	809			
74	25	473	229	25	649	328	25	646	381	25	534	421	25	529	491	3	810			
81	25	790	232	25	651	336	25	536	388	25	534	428	25	798	496	4	180			

VOL. 2, ARIZONA REPORTS

Ariz. Rep.	Pac. Rep.		Ariz. Rep.	Pac. Rep.		Ariz. Rep.	Pac. Rep.		Ariz. Rep.	Pac. Rep.		Ariz. Rep.	Pac. Rep.		Ariz. Rep.	Pac. Rep.		Ariz. Rep.	Pac. Rep.	
Pg.	Vol.	Pg.	Pg.	Vol.	Pg.	Pg.	Vol.	Pg.	Pg.	Vol.	Pg.	Pg.	Vol.	Pg.	Pg.	Vol.	Pg.	Pg.	Vol.	Pg.
1	6	478	57	76	1126	144	11	177	222	76	1125	288	15	23	335	76	1124	392	17	564
4	6	479	58	76	1124	147	11	312	223	12	567	299	15	141	335	76	1126	394	18	276
6	7	176	59	10	359	154	11	314	225	12	607	306	15	129	336	76	1124	399	18	373
8	7	496	62	10	368	162	11	351	229	12	614	308	15	712	336	76	1125	407	18	596
10	7	718	69	10	367	169	11	396	233	12	686	315	15	862	337	76	1125	411	18	597
16	8	187	71	11	44	171	11	545	239	12	694	319	15	672	339	16	309	415	19	4
27	8	160	75	11	58	202	11	397	246	12	671	326	16	45	344	16	369	420	19	6
29	8	295	82	11	119	204	11	671	248	12	730	331	76	1125	347	16	370	428	19	157
44	8	302	88	11	62	207	11	763	253	14	300	331	76	1126	350	16	371	438	19	325
50	8	351	89	11	61	210	11	863	257	14	299	332	76	1124	354	16	366	441	76	1126
55	76	1125	91	11	117	213	76	1130	259	14	364	332	76	[illegible]	358	16	434	442	17	72
55	76	1126	96	11	110	214	12	65	262	14	799	333	76	[illegible]	362	16	565	442	76	1126
56	76	1125	100	11	108	221	11	46	264	15	373	333	76	[illegible]	371	17	453	443	17	363
56	76	1126	107	11	114	221	76	1124	273	15	98	334	76	[illegible]	381	17	10	443	76	1124
57	76	1124	114	11	122	221	76	1125	275	15	87	334	76	1125	390	17	87	444	76	1126
57	76	1125	127	11	473	222	76	1124												

Illustration R

Arizona
Blue & White Book

Section II

Arizona Reports
and
Arizona Appeals Reports
Cases reported in
Pacific Reporter

2 P.

2 P. Page	State Report
748	1 Ariz. 464
751	1 Ariz. 482
755	1 Ariz. 455
757	1 Ariz. 484

3 P.

3 P. Page	State Report
399	1 Ariz. 490
610	1 Ariz. 491

4 P.

4 P. Page	State Report
130	1 Ariz. 483

6 P.

6 P. Page	State Report
478	2 Ariz. 1
479	2 Ariz. 4

7 P.

7 P. Page	State Report
176	2 Ariz. 6
496	2 Ariz. 8
718	2 Ariz. 10

8 P.

8 P. Page	State Report
160	2 Ariz. 27
187	2 Ariz. 16
396	2 Ariz. 29
802	2 Ariz. 44
861	2 Ariz. 60

Ariz.B.& W.

10 P.

10 P. Page	State Report
259	2 Ariz. 59
267	2 Ariz. 69
868	2 Ariz. 68

11 P.

11 P. Page	State Report
44	2 Ariz. 71
45¹	2 Ariz. 221
58	2 Ariz. 75
61	2 Ariz. 69
62¹	2 Ariz. 88
105	2 Ariz. 100
110	2 Ariz. 93
114	2 Ariz. 107
117	2 Ariz. 91
119	2 Ariz. 82
122	2 Ariz. 114
177	2 Ariz. 114
212²	2 Ariz. 147
214	2 Ariz. 154
271	2 Ariz. [illegible]
306	2 Ariz. 169
307	2 Ariz. 202
472	2 Ariz. 127
480	2 Ariz. 127
545	2 Ariz. 171
671	2 Ariz. 204
753	2 Ariz. 207
863	2 Ariz. 210

12 P.

12 P. Page	State Report
65	2 Ariz. 214
567	2 Ariz. 223
607	2 Ariz. 225
614	2 Ariz. 229
671	2 Ariz. 246
858	2 Ariz. 233
694¹	2 Ariz. 239
730	2 Ariz. 248

14 P.

14 P. Page	State Report
290	2 Ariz. 257
340	2 Ariz. 253
356	2 Ariz. 259
799	2 Ariz. 262

15 P.

15 P. Page	State Report
26	2 Ariz. 272
28	2 Ariz. 263
37	2 Ariz. 275
139	2 Ariz. 305
141	2 Ariz. 279
273	2 Ariz. 268
673	2 Ariz. 319
712	2 Ariz. 305
862	2 Ariz. 315

16 P.

16 P. Page	State Report
45	2 Ariz. 326
209	2 Ariz. 339
226	2 Ariz. 354
269	2 Ariz. 344
270	2 Ariz. 347
271	2 Ariz. 350
434²	2 Ariz. 353
665	2 Ariz. 302

17 P.

17 P. Page	State Report
10	2 Ariz. 353
72¹	2 Ariz. 442
97¹	2 Ariz. 390
263	2 Ariz. 443
433²	2 Ariz. 371
664¹	2 Ariz. 392

18 P.

18 P. Page	State Report
273	2 Ariz. 399
276	2 Ariz. 394
595	2 Ariz. 407
597	2 Ariz. 411

19 P.

19 P. Page	State Report
4	2 Ariz. 415
6	2 Ariz. 420
157	2 Ariz. 428
225	2 Ariz. 426

20 P.

20 P. Page	State Report
83	3 Ariz. 6
94	3 Ariz. 1
183	3 Ariz. 9
189	3 Ariz. 20
310	3 Ariz. 5
311	3 Ariz. 27
607	3 Ariz. 48
673	3 Ariz. 57
803	3 Ariz. 62

21 P.

21 P. Page	State Report
152²	3 Ariz. 92
177	3 Ariz. 100
232	3 Ariz. 84
228	3 Ariz. 96
465	3 Ariz. 109
765	3 Ariz. 117
815	3 Ariz. 122
866	3 Ariz. 80

22 P.

22 P. Page	State Report
363¹	3 Ariz. 132

23 P.

23 P. Page	State Report
680	3 Ariz. 143

24 P.

24 P. Page	State Report
182	3 Ariz. 178
183	3 Ariz. 199
184	3 Ariz. 182
257¹	3 Ariz. 176
257²	3 Ariz. 176
320	3 Ariz. 182
324	3 Ariz. 184

Illustration S

Vols. 101–104 ARIZONA REPORTS

-156-
Arizona v. Anaya, No. CA-CR 88-1274, 110:46 Ariz. Bus. Gaz. 27 (Ariz. Ct. App. June 28, 1990).

-225-
Boyle v. Parsons, No. 1 CA-CV 89-178, 67 Ariz. Adv. Rep. 51, 110:44 Ariz. Bus. Gaz. 36 (Ariz. Ct. App. Aug. 23, 1990).

-268-
Orme School v. Reeves, No. CV-89-0403-SA, 75 Ariz. Adv. Rep. 5, 110:52 Ariz. Bus. Gaz. 22 (Ariz. Dec. 6, 1990).

-282-
DKI Corp. v. Industrial Comm'n, No. 1 CA-IC 89-024, 78 Ariz. Adv. Rep. 44 (Ariz. Ct. App. Jan. 17, 1991).

-301-
Hartford Accident & Indem. Co. v. Aetna Casualty & Sur. Co., No. CV-89-0101-T/AP, 62 Ariz. Adv. Rep. 7 (Ariz. May 29, 1990).

-309-
In re Maricopa County Juvenile Actions No. JV119590 & No. JV118201, No. CA-JUV 90-006, 73 Ariz. Adv. Rep. 17, 111:3 Ariz. Bus. Gaz. 22 (Ariz. Ct. App. Nov. 6, 1990).

-366-
Boyle v. Parsons, No. 1 CA-CV 89-178, 67 Ariz. Adv. Rep. 51, 110:44 Ariz. Bus. Gaz. 36 (Ariz. Ct. App. Aug. 23, 1990).

Mid Kansas Fed. Sav. & Loan Ass'n v. Dynamic Dev. Corp., No. CV-89-0447-PR, 78 Ariz. Adv. Rep. 3 (Ariz. Jan. 10, 1991).

-444-
In re Marriage of Cooper, No. 2 CA-CV 89-0217, 75 Ariz. Adv. Rep. 76 (Ariz. Ct. App. Nov. 29, 1990).

Volume 102

-78-
Orme School v. Reeves, No. CV-89-0403-SA, 75 Ariz. Adv. Rep. 5, 110:52 Ariz. Bus. Gaz. 22 (Ariz. Dec. 6, 1990).

Arizona v. Carr Constr. Corp., No. 1 CA-TX 90-001, 75 Ariz. Adv. Rep. 39 (Ariz. Ct. App. Dec. 6, 1990).

In re Marriage of Nanini, No. 2 CA-CV 90-0075, 75 Ariz. Adv. Rep. 82 (Ariz. Ct. App. Nov. 29, 1990).

-93-
Maricopa County v. Barkley, No. 1 CA-CV 89-251, 75 Ariz. Adv. Rep. 48 (Ariz. Ct. App. Dec. 11, 1990).

-102-
Arizona v. Peraskov, No. 1 CA-CV 90-002, 72 Ariz. Adv. Rep. 16, 111:1 Ariz. Bus. Gaz. 35 (Ariz. Ct. App. Oct. 23, 1990).

-192-
Maricopa County v. Barkley, No. 1 CA-CV 89-251, 75 Ariz. Adv. Rep. 48 (Ariz. Ct. App. Dec. 11, 1990).

-272-
(d) *Havasu Heights Ranch & Dev. Corp. v. Desert Valley Wood Prods.*, No. 1 CA-CV 89-274, 76 Ariz. Adv. Rep. 46 (Ariz. Ct. App. Dec. 20, 1990).

-299-
Arizona v. Garcia, No. CA-CR 89-326, 110:48 Ariz. Bus. Gaz. 31 (Ariz. Ct. App. Sept. 20, 1990).

-312-
Andrews v. Casagrande, No. CA-CV 88-515, 110:48 Ariz. Bus. Gaz. 35 (Ariz. Ct. App. Sept. 20, 1990).

-330-
Orme School v. Reeves, No. CV-89-0403-SA, 75 Ariz. Adv. Rep. 5, 110:52 Ariz. Bus. Gaz. 22 (Ariz. Dec. 6, 1990).

-377-
Arizona v. McCain, No. 1 CA-CR 89-431, 77 Ariz. Adv. Rep. 33 (Ariz. Ct. App. Jan. 8, 1991).

-472-
Arizona v. Fierro, No. CR-87-0051-AP, 76 Ariz. Adv. Rep. 12 (Ariz. Dec. 18, 1990).

-495-
Arizona v. Jimenez, No. 88-0005-AP, 67 Ariz. Adv. Rep. 3 (Ariz. Aug. 7, 1990).

-508-
Hartford Accident & Indem. Co. v. Aetna Casualty & Sur. Co., No. CV-89-0101-T/AP, 62 Ariz. Adv. Rep. 7 (Ariz. May 29, 1990).

-518-
(o)* *Hartford Accident & Indem. Co. v. Aetna Casualty & Sur. Co.*, No. CV-89-0101-T/AP, 62 Ariz. Adv. Rep. 7 (Ariz. May 29, 1990).

-575-
(d) *Circle K Corp. v. City of Mesa*, No. 1 CA-CV 88-205, 76 Ariz. Adv. Rep. 34 (Ariz. Ct. App. Dec. 18, 1990).

Volume 103

-13-
Exodyne Properties, Inc. v. City of Phoenix, No. 1 CA-CV 88-421, 70 Ariz. Adv. Rep. 15 (Ariz. Ct. App. Sept. 25, 1990).

-37-
Arizona v. Jimenez, No. 88-0005-AP, 67 Ariz. Adv. Rep. 3 (Ariz. Aug. 7, 1990).

-125-
Arizona v. Angelo, No. 1 CA-CR 89-871, 72 Ariz. Adv. Rep. 13 (Ariz. Ct. App. Oct. 23, 1990).

-204-
Circle K Corp. v. City of Mesa, No. 1 CA-CV 88-205, 76 Ariz. Adv. Rep. 34 (Ariz. Ct. App. Dec. 18, 1990).

-435-
Orme School v. Reeves, No. CV-89-0403-SA, 75 Ariz. Adv. Rep. 5, 110:52 Ariz. Bus. Gaz. 22 (Ariz. Dec. 6, 1990).

Volume 104

-59-
Morrison v. Shanwick Int'l Corp., No. CA-CV 89-326, 110:46 Ariz. Bus. Gaz. 36 (Ariz. Ct. App. Sept. 11, 1990).

-69-
Miller v. State Farm Fire & Casualty Co., No. 2 CA-CV 90-0063, 70 Ariz. Adv. Rep. 58 (Ariz. Ct. App. Sept. 28, 1990).

-209-
Arizona v. City Court, No. CV-90-0003-PR, 71 Ariz. Adv. Rep. 19, 110:49 Ariz. Bus. Gaz. 30 (Ariz. Oct. 11, 1990).

-238-
(f) *Arizona v. McCain*, No. 1 CA-CR 89-431, 77 Ariz. Adv. Rep. 33 (Ariz. Ct. App. Jan. 8, 1991).

-250-
McDonald v. Campbell, No. 1 CA-SA 90-172, 73 Ariz. Adv. Rep. 28 (Ariz. Ct. App. Nov. 13, 1990).

McDonald v. Arizona, No. CA-SA 90-172, 111:5 Ariz. Bus. Gaz. 33 (Nov. 13, 1990).

-297-
(f) *Arizona v. Comer*, No. CR-88-0136-AP, 799 P.2d 333, 110:41 Ariz. Bus. Gaz. 26 (Ariz. July 31, 1990).

Arizona v. Thomas, No. 1 CA-CR 89-1625, 71 Ariz. Adv. Rep. 27, 110:44 Ariz. Bus. Gaz. 44 (Ariz. Ct. App. Oct. 11, 1990).

Arizona v. Ross, No. 1 CA-CR 88-442, 67 Ariz. Adv. Rep. 38 (Ariz. Ct. App. Aug. 21, 1990).

Arizona v. King, No. 1 CA-CR 89-615, 67 Ariz. Adv. Rep. 56, 110:44 Ariz. Bus. Gaz. 37 (Ariz. Ct. App. Aug. 23, 1990).

(f) *Arizona v. Amaya-Ruiz*, No. CR-86-0095, 800 P.2d 1260, 110:44 Ariz. Bus. Gaz. 27 (Ariz. Sept. 6, 1990).

Arizona v. Barnes, No. 90-0133-PR, 78 Ariz. Adv. Rep. 21 (Ariz. Jan. 10, 1991).

-362-
Arizona v. Comer, No. CR-88-0136-AP, 799 P.2d 333, 110:41 Ariz. Bus. Gaz. 26 (Ariz. July 31, 1990).

-380-
Arizona v. Fierro, No. CR-87-0051-AP, 76 Ariz. Adv. Rep. 12 (Ariz. Dec. 18, 1990).

-561-
McDonald v. Campbell, No. 1 CA-SA 90-172, 73 Ariz. Adv. Rep. 28 (Ariz. Ct. App. Nov. 13, 1990).

16 * For further information on this citation, see the cited authority in the Citation Summaries section.

Chapter 6

Rules of Court, Evidence, Practice and Procedure

Kathy Shimpock-Vieweg

A. Introduction

Court rules govern the practice and procedure associated with litigation. In Arizona, the Supreme Court has been empowered with promulgating these rules for "all courts of the state for the purpose of simplifying such pleading practice and procedure and promoting speedy determination of litigation upon its merits."[1] The court's authority is limited to procedural rather than substantive regulation, although court rules do have the effect of statutes.[2] In addition,

1 Ariz. Rev. Stat. Ann. § 12-109(A) (1982). Note: The *Victims' Bill of Rights,* Ariz. Const. art II, § 2.1(11) (West supp. 1991) subjects the Rules of Criminal Procedure to amendment or repeal by the Legislature.

2 *Brown v. Haymore,* 43 Ariz. 466, 32 P.2d 1027 (1934).

Arizona also has numerous statutes dealing with civil and criminal procedure.[3] *Arizona Revised Statutes* § 12-111 states that all such statutes are rules of court unless later modified or suspended by the Supreme Court.[4] The State Bar of Arizona's Committee on Civil Practice and Procedure and its Committee on Criminal Code and Rules act as advisory boards to the court.[5]

B. Historical Background

Arizona's Territorial Supreme Court authorized its first compilation of court rules in 1865. Thirty-two rules were drafted by three Arizona attorneys, Coles Bashford, James Anderson and Joseph Hargrave. These attorneys were later ordered to prepare rules for the district courts: rules which were in effect until an 1879 revision.[6]

The next major development occurred in 1913. The *Revised Statutes of Arizona* began to separately compile legislation on civil and criminal procedure, evidence, jurisdiction and appeals into the civil and penal codes.[7] And, finally, in 1956 the West Publishing Company issued separate volumes of court rules with its *Arizona Revised Statutes Annotated.* These rules were published with all the West "amenities" including indexing, annotations and tables. The rules have continued to be part of this set to the present day.

Prior versions of court rules can be located in the *Arizona Revised Statutes.* (See Chapter 2 on Arizona Statutory Research for further information.) Superseded court rules from May 1988 can be found at the office of the Clerk of Court for the Arizona Supreme Court. The major Arizona law libraries (ASU, U of A, Maricopa County and Pima County) also contain superseded court rules from 1977 to date.

C. Sources for Court Rules

There are numerous published sources for Arizona state and federal court rules. The more common ones are listed below.

1. *Arizona Revised Statutes Annotated.* St. Paul, MN: West Publishing Co., 1956- . 43v.[8]

These statutes contain four volumes of court rules (volumes numbered 16, 17, 17A and 17B). Each includes annotations, State Bar Committee notes, source notes, cross references, reviser's notes and law review commentaries. There is a separate index, although all rules are also included within the *A.R.S.* general

3 See Title 12 and Title 22, Chapter 2 of the *Arizona Revised Statutes.*

4 Ariz. Rev. Stat. Ann. § 12-111 (1982).

5 Ariz. Rev. Stat. Ann. § 12-110 (1982).

6 Murphy, *Laws, Courts and Lawyers,* 21.

7 Samuel L. Pattee, comp., *Revised Statutes of Arizona: Civil Code* (Phoenix, AZ: The McNeil Co., 1913), 3v. Samuel L. Pattee, comp., *Revised Statutes of Arizona: Penal Code* (Phoenix, AZ: The McNeil Co., 1913), 1v.

8 Note: The Michie Co.'s set of unannotated *Arizona Revised Statutes* includes all statutory titles dealing with civil and criminal procedure, but does not contain any court rules.

index. Tables locate comparable Federal rules and Wright and Miller's *Federal* Practice and *Procedure* sections. Additional tables locate those sections of the *Revised Code of 1928* (not included within the *Arizona Code Annotated 1939*), within the Rules of Civil Procedure and/or the Rules of Civil Appellate Procedure. A similar table locates sections of the *Arizona Code Annotated 1939* within the current *A.R.S.*, the Rules of Civil Procedure, Rules of the Supreme Court, Rules of Evidence and the Rules of Civil Appellate Procedure. Obviously all applicable statutory provisions are also found within this set. (See Illustration A, page 139.)

2. *Arizona Rules of Court State and Federal.* St. Paul, MN: West Publishing Co., 1977- annual. pamphlet.

The source for Arizona court rules, these one-volume, unannotated editions include most of the court rules for Arizona state and federal courts. The State Bar Committee Notes, source references and separate indices are also provided. (See Illustration B, page 140.)

3. *Arizona Criminal Law and Rules.* St. Paul, MN: West Publishing Co., 1987 - annual. pamphlet.

The West unannotated edition includes the Arizona Criminal Code, applicable provisions from the Constitution and Revised Statutes; the Rules of Criminal Procedure; Rules of Evidence; and the Rules of Procedure for the Juvenile Court. There is also a combined index. (See Illustration C, p. 141.)

4. *Federal Civil Judicial Procedure and Rules.* St. Paul, MN: West Publishing Co., 1950 - annual. pamphlet.

The West's Federal Rules edition includes the following unannotated federal rules: Civil Procedure, Multi-district Litigation Rules, Habeas Corpus Rules, Motion Attacking Sentence Rules, Temporary Emergency Court of Appeals, Evidence, Appellate Procedure and Supreme Court Rules. Local rules, however, are not contained. The book also reprints Title 28 of the *U.S.C.* dealing with the Judiciary and Judicial Procedure. There is a consolidated index.

5. *Federal Criminal Code and Rules.* St. Paul, MN: West Publishing Co., 1946 - annual. pamphlet.

Each paperback edition contains the Federal Rules of Criminal Procedure, Habeas Corpus Rules, Motion Attacking Sentence Rules, Misdemeanor Trials Before U.S. Magistrates, Evidence, Appellate Procedure, and Supreme Court Rules. In addition, notes are set out following each rule. The applicable titles of the *U.S.C.* are also included. There is a consolidated index.

D. Updating

Arizona rules of court become effective sixty days after distribution by the Supreme Court.[9] Any additions, deletions or modifications of existing court rules can be found in the following sources: 1) the *West's Legislative Service,*

9 Ariz. Rev. Stat. Ann. § 12-109(C) (1982).

2) the paper supplements to the *Pacific Reporter 2d* and the annual pocket parts and paper supplements to the *Arizona Revised Statutes Annotated.* Less frequently, court rules can also be located in: 1) the bound volumes of the *Arizona Reports;* 2) the *Arizona Advance Reports*; and 3) the *Arizona Attorney.* The *Arizona Advance Reports* also provides the most current source for court interpretation in their "Statute Index." In addition, updates are often obtained directly from the applicable court or from the Arizona State Bar.[10]

Copies of local federal rule changes can be obtained from the office of the Clerk of Court for the District Court in Phoenix or Tucson. In addition, district court amendments can be found in the advance sheets to the *West's Supreme Court Reporter, Federal Reporter, Federal Supplement* and *Federal Rules Decisions.* The *Federal Reporter* advance sheets also reprints rule changes for the Ninth Circuit. Other sources for federal rules include the *Cyclopedia of Federal Procedure* (Vol. 16A), and pamphlets to the *United States Code Advance Service* and the *U.S. Code Congressional and Administrative News.*

However, the best source for local rule changes can be found in Callaghan's *Federal Local Court Rules.*[11] This service compiles all the local rules of the U.S. Court of Appeals and District Courts, and is frequently updated.

E. Arizona Court Rules

A listing of Arizona's court rules, federal and state, is as follows:[12]

1. *Federal Court Rules*

The U.S. Supreme Court has the authority to promulgate all rules for federal courts.[13] However, each U.S. District Court or U.S. Court of Appeals may also issue separate rules, providing these rules are not inconsistent with those issued by the Supreme Court. The local rules for Arizona can be found in the *Arizona Rules of Court: State and Federal,* and Callaghan's *Federal Local Court Rules* (U.S. District Court only). Other federal rules may be found in numerous sources, but most commonly in West's *Federal Civil Judicial Procedure and Rules,* or *Federal Criminal Code and Rules.*

Court interpretations can be found within the annotated versions of the *United States Code* (i.e., the *U.S.C.A.* or *U.S.C.S.*). They can also be located in *Moore's Rules Pamphlets,* Lawyer's Co-Op's *Digest of United States Supreme Court Reports* (1987), Wright and Miller's *Federal Practice and Procedure,* Moore's *Federal Practice* and in Callaghan's *Federal Rules of Evidence Digest, Federal Rules Digest 3d, Federal Rules of Evidence Service,* and *Federal Rules Service 3d.*.

a. Rules of Practice for the United States District Court for the District of Arizona. (Effective 1982).

10 ARIZ. REV. STAT. ANN. § 12-109(B) (1982).

11 Pike & Fischer,Inc. eds. *Federal Local Court Rules* (Deerfield, IL: Callaghan & Co., 1964-) 3v.

12 *See also* the "Checklist of Court Rules" found in Charles Marshall Smith, *Civil Trial Practice,* vol. 2 of *Arizona Practice* (St. Paul, MN: West Publishing Co., 1986), 13-15.

13 28 U.S.C. § 2072 (1982), 18 U.S.C. §§ 3771-3772 (1985).

See: *Arizona Rules of Court: State and Federal,* or Callaghan's *Federal Local Court Rules.*

All trials in Federal District Courts are conducted according to the Federal Rules of Civil Procedure (28 U.S.C.) or the Federal Rules of Criminal Procedure (18 U.S.C.). Rule 83 of the Federal Rules of Civil Procedure authorizes each District Court to "make and amend rules governing its practice not inconsistent with these rules."

b. Federal Rules of Evidence, 28 U.S.C. (Effective July 1, 1975).

See: *Arizona Rules of Court: State and Federal, Federal Civil Judicial Procedure and Rules,* or *Federal Criminal Code and Rules.*

The Rules of Evidence apply to all proceedings in federal courts, and to those before bankruptcy judges and U.S. Magistrates.[14]

c. Local Rules of Bankruptcy Procedure for the District of Arizona. (Effective December 15, 1983).

See: *Arizona Rules of Court: State and Federal.*

These rules were based on the federal rules (11 U.S.C.).

d. Rules of Procedure for the Trial of Misdemeanors Before U.S. Magistrates, 18 U.S.C. (Effective June 1, 1980).

See: *Federal Criminal Code and Rules.*

e. Rules of Procedure of the Judicial Panel on Multi-district Litigation, 28 U.S.C. § 1407, 28 U.S.C. § 2112(a)(3). (Effective July 6, 1988.)

See: *Arizona Rules of Court: State and Federal,* or *Federal Civil Judicial Procedure and Rules.*

f. Federal Rules of Appellate Procedure with Ninth Circuit Rules, 28 U.S.C. (Effective July 1, 1990.)

See: *Arizona Rules of Court: State and Federal.*

Local rules are promulgated under the authority of Rules 2 and 47 of the Federal Rules of Appellate Procedure. They govern the appellate process from the U.S. District Courts, U.S. Tax Court, Bankruptcy Appellate Panel, review of administrative agencies, etc. A major restructuring of the Ninth Circuit rules occurred in 1986, while in 1989 the court's internal operating procedure was reviewed and incorporated into the Advisory Committee Notes.

g. Rules of the United States Bankruptcy Appellate Panel of the Ninth Circuit. (Adopted November 15, 1984.)

See: *Arizona Rules of Court: State and Federal.*

2. *Arizona State Courts.*

Arizona state rules of court can be found in the *Arizona Revised Statutes,* and the *Arizona Rules of Court: State and Federal.* Criminal rules are also located

14 Fed. R. Evid. 101.

in *Arizona Criminal Law and Rules.* The Arizona rules of court listed below include their *A.R.S.* citation only.

a. Justice and Municipal Courts

i. Rules of Procedure in Traffic Cases. (Effective July 1, 1963.) See vol. 17B *Arizona Revised Statutes Annotated.*

ii. Rules of Procedure in Civil Traffic Violation Cases. (Effective January 1, 1984.) See vol. 17B *Arizona Revised Statutes Annotated.*

iii. Local Rules of Practice and Procedure, City Court of Phoenix. (Effective September 27, 1973.) See vol. 17B *Arizona Revised Statutes Annotated.*

iv. Local Rules for Pima County Justice of the Peace Courts Providing for Pre-Trial Conferences in Criminal Cases. (Effective July 1, 1978.) See vol. 17B *Arizona Revised Statutes Annotated.*

v. Local Rules of Procedure, Bullhead City Municipal Court. (Approved and Effective October 20, 1989.)

vi. In addition, the following *Arizona Revised Statutes* sections should be examined: for civil proceedings in justice courts *A.R.S.* §§ 22-201 to 22-283(1990); for criminal proceedings in justice courts *A.R.S.* §§ 22-301 to 22-375 (1990); for municipal courts *A.R.S.* §§ 22-401 to 22-428(1990), and for the small claims division of justice courts *A.R.S.* §§ 22-501 to 22-523 (1990).

b. Superior Courts

i. Rules of Civil Procedure. (Effective January 1, 1956.) See vol. 16 *Arizona Revised Statutes Annotated.*

The Arizona Rules of Civil Procedure regulate practice for civil actions at the trial court level. These rules are based substantially on the Federal Rules of Civil Procedure. Modifications from the federal involve court designations and specific procedures found not applicable to Arizona. These differences are designated in the reviser's notes. The numbering of the Arizona rules is based on the federal rules, although rule subdivisions may not correspond.

ii. Rules of Criminal Procedure. (Effective September 1, 1973.) See vol. 17 *Arizona Revised Statutes Annotated.*

Based largely on the American Law Institute's "Model Code of Criminal Procedure". These rules apply to all criminal offenses with the exception of specific traffic violations.

iii. Arizona Rules of Evidence. (Effective September 1, 1977.) See vol. 17A *Arizona Revised Statutes Annotated.*

Based on the Federal Rules of Evidence. Michie's *Evidence in America: The Federal Rules in the States*[15] serves as a source for all state versions of these Federal Rules.

15 Gregory P. Joseph, Stephen A. Saltzburg and the Trial Evidence Committee of the A.B.A. Section of Litigation, *Evidence in America: The Federal Rules in the States* (Charlottesville, VA: The Michie Co., 1988 -) 4v.

iv. Uniform Rules of Practice of the Superior Court of Arizona. (Effective 1962.) See vol. 17B *Arizona Revised Statutes Annotated.*

These rules supplement the Rules of Civil Procedure and focus on pretrial practice, civil motions, setting of civil cases for trial, pretrial statements and interrogatories.

v. Arizona Tax Court Rules of Practice. (Effective September 30, 1988.) See vol. 17B *Arizona Revised Statutes Annotated* pocket part.

The Arizona Tax Court is the Tax Department of the Superior Court in Maricopa County. Rule 1 of the Local Rules of Practice for Maricopa County also applies to this court.

vi. Local Rules of Practice for the Superior Courts. (Effective January 1, 1962.) See vol. 17B *Arizona Revised Statutes Annotated.*

Rule XIV of the Uniform Rules of Practice of the Superior Court authorizes the presiding judge in each county to supplement the Uniform Rules with local rules. These local rules must be approved by a majority of judges of the county, then promulgated and published upon approval of the Chief Justice of the Supreme Court. Local rules vary with each county depending upon the county's size and case load.[16]

Local rules are available for the following counties:

Apache County (Effective January 1, 1962)

Cochise County (Effective September 1, 1987)

Coconino County (Effective September 1, 1978)

Gila County (Effective January 1, 1962)

Graham County (Effective January 1, 1962)

Greenlee County (Effective January 1, 1962)

La Paz County (Effective March 31, 1983)

Maricopa County (Effective September 1, 1978)

Maricopa County has specific local rules for its Northeast Judicial District and its Southeast Judicial District.

Superior Court in Maricopa County. Mandatory Alternate Dispute and Discovery Track Rules. (the Zlaket Rules.) These are proposed rules issued by the Arizona Supreme Court Special Committee on Civil Litigation Abuse, Cost and Delay. The Zlaket Rules are in effect for all cases assigned to the Maricopa County Superior Court after January 1, 1991 and will remain in use until the Supreme Court ends this experimental program. The rules may be obtained from the Court Administrator's Office and this Division.

16 Smith, *Civil Trial Practice,* 17.

Maricopa County Superior Court Criminal Judges. Rule 8 Guidelines. (See vol. 17 *Arizona Revised Statutes Annotated* pocket part after Rule 8.6 of the Rules of Criminal Procedure.)

Maricopa County Superior Court Civil Judges. Rule V Inactive Calendar Guideline. (See vol. 17B *Arizona Revised Statutes Annotated* pocket part following Rule V of the Uniform Rules of Practice of the Superior Court of Arizona.)

Mohave County (Effective January 1, 1962)

Navajo County (Effective January 1, 1962)

Pima County (Effective June 1, 1986)

Pinal County (Effective April 1, 1986)

Santa Cruz County (Effective February 15, 1988)

Yavapai County (Effective May 1, 1984)

Yuma County (Effective October 1, 1975)

vii. Rules of Procedure for Special Actions. (Effective January 1, 1970.) See vol. 17B *Arizona Revised Statutes Annotated.*

These include extraordinary writs, certiorari, mandamus and prohibition.

viii. Special Actions and Proceedings by Individual Persons. See vol. 12 *Arizona Revised Statutes Annotated* §§601 to 694.

Special actions include the following: change of name; death by wrongful act; establishing identity; motor vehicle subleasing; injury to child or ward; libel, slander, and invasion of privacy; libel and slander correction and resulting damages; torts of minors; insufficient funds check; product liability and shoplifting.

ix. Uniform Rules of Procedure for Arbitration. (Effective February 1, 1974.) See vol. 17B *Arizona Revised Statutes Annotated.*

These rules are available when a county Superior Court decides to provide for arbitration of claims by majority vote. Jurisdictional limits must be established pursuant to *A.R.S.* § 22-133.[17]

x. Uniform Rules of Procedure for Medical Liability Review Panels in the Superior Court. (Effective March 1, 1977.) See vol. 17B *Arizona Revised Statutes Annotated.*

xi. Rules of Procedure for the Juvenile Court. (Effective April 15, 1970.) See vol. 17B *Arizona Revised Statutes Annotated.* See also *A.R.S.* §§ 8-201 to 8-278 for Juvenile Court General Provisions, General Procedure, Delinquency and Alcohol Offense Complaints, Juvenile Hearings, Disposition and Commitment, Family Counseling Programs and Juvenile Intensive Probation.

17 Ariz. Super. Ct. Uniform Prac. R.1.

xii. Local Rules of Procedure for the Pima County Juvenile Court. (Effective June 1, 1974.) See vol. 17B *Arizona Revised Statutes Annotated.*

xiii. Uniform Rules of Practice for Medical Malpractice Cases. (Effective January 1, 1990.) See vol. 17B *Arizona Revised Statutes Annotated.*

Includes Uniform Interrogatories for Use in Medical Malpractice Cases (Defendant to Plaintiff), and (Plaintiff to Defendant).

xiv. Superior Court Rules of Appellate Procedure - Civil. (Effective April 1, 1980.) See vol. 17B *Arizona Revised Statutes Annotated.*

These rules govern the procedures for all civil appeals taken to the Superior Court from the final judgment of a justice court (*A.R.S.* § 22-261), or municipal court (*A.R.S.* § 22-425B).[18]

xv. Superior Court Rules of Appellate Procedure - Criminal. (Effective April 1, 1980.) See vol. 17B *Arizona Revised Statutes Annotated.*

These rules govern appeals in a criminal action taken to the Superior Court from the final judgment of a justice or police court (*A.R.S.* § 22-371) where either a transcript or a statement has been made.[19]

c. Court of Appeals

i. Arizona Rules of Civil Appellate Procedure. (Effective January 1, 1978.) See vol. 17B *Arizona Revised Statutes Annotated.*

These rules govern civil appellate procedure in the Court of Appeals and the Supreme Court. See also Appeals *A.R.S.* §§ 12-2101, 12-2101.01, 12-2107.

ii. Rules of Procedure for Special Actions. (Effective January 1, 1970.) See vol. 17B *Arizona Revised Statutes Annotated.*

iii. Rules of Procedure for the Juvenile Court Appeals: Rule 24-29. (Effective April 15, 1970.) See vol. 17B *Arizona Revised Statutes Annotated.*

iv. Rules of Criminal Procedure. (Effective September 1, 1973.) See vol. 17 *Arizona Revised Statutes Annotated* Rule 31: appeal from Superior Court.

d. Supreme Court

i. Arizona Rules of Civil Appellate Procedure. (Effective January 1, 1978.) See vol. 17B *Arizona Revised Statutes Annotated.* See also *A.R.S.* §§ 12-2102 to 12-2107 on Appeals.

ii. Rules of Criminal Procedure. (Effective September 1, 1973.) See vol. 17 *Arizona Revised Statutes Annotated.* Rule 31 covers Appeals from the Superior Court.

iii. Rules of the Supreme Court. (Effective January 1,1956.) See vol. 17A *Arizona Revised Statutes Annotated.*

Application for Issuances of Writs Under Original Jurisdiction or for Certiorari to Industrial Commission (Rule 1)

18 Ariz. Super. Ct. Civ. App. Proc. R.1(a).
19 Ariz. Super. Ct. Crim. App. Proc. R.1 (a).

Civil Appeals (Rule 3-14)

Criminal Appeals (Rule 15-24)

General Provisions (Rule 25-30)

Rules of Court of Appeals (Rule 101-110)

Opinions (Rule 111-120)

Appeals in Groundwater Cases (Rule 121)

3. *Miscellaneous Rules*

a. Admission and Discipline of Attorneys. Rules of the Supreme Court, Rule 31-80. (Effective February 1, 1985.) See vol. 17A *Arizona Revised Statutes Annotated.*

These rules have been adopted from the ABA Model Rules of Professional Conduct with some modification. Rule 42 encompasses the Arizona Rules of Professional Conduct. Individual rules within Rule 42 are called Ethical Rules or "ERs." Rule 45 outlines Arizona's Mandatory Continuing Legal Education requirements.

b. Adoption of Code of Judicial Conduct of the American Bar Association. Rules of the Supreme Court, Rule 81. (Effective February 1, 1985.) See vol. 17A *Arizona Revised Statutes Annotated.*

Rule 81 sets forth the Code of Judicial Conduct of the American Bar Association. Includes Canons 1-7.

c. Court Commissioners. Rules of the Supreme Court, Rules 82-90. (Effective February 1, 1985.) See vol. 17A *Arizona Revised Statutes Annotated.*

d. Rules of Procedure for the Commission on Judicial Conduct. (Effective July 1, 1990.) See vol. 17B *Arizona Revised Statutes Annotated.*

> Note: The Rules of Procedure for the Commission on Judicial Qualifications are no longer in effect.

e. Rules of Procedure for Judicial Nominating Commission on Appellate Court Appointments. (Effective July 1, 1975.) See vol. 17B *Arizona Revised Statutes Annotated.*

f. Rules of Procedure for Judicial Nominating Commission on Maricopa County Superior Court Appointments. (Adopted July 9, 1975.) See vol. 17B *Arizona Revised Statutes Annotated.*

g. Rules of Procedure for Judicial Nominating Commission on Pima County Superior Court Appointments. (Effective July 1, 1975.) See vol. 17B *Arizona Revised Statutes Annotated.*

h. Rules of Procedure for the Foster Care Review Boards. (Effective January 31, 1979.) See vol. 17B *Arizona Revised Statutes Annotated.*

i. Supplemental Rules of the State Foster Care Review Board. (Adopted April 3, 1980.) See vol. 17B *Arizona Revised Statutes Annotated.*

j. State Bar of Arizona Trust Account Guidelines. Rules of the Supreme Court, Rule 43. (Revised May 1, 1984.) See vol. 17A *Arizona Revised Statutes Annotated.*

F. Citators

The statute portions of *Shepard's Arizona Citations* includes citations to both Arizona and federal court rules and to jury instructions. Citations are from Arizona and federal courts, Arizona laws, periodical articles and annotations.

Shepard's *United States Citations'* statutes volumes include numerous federal court rules. Ninth Circuit Rules and District Court rules are provided separately. Citations are from federal cases, *United States Statutes at Large,* the *American Bar Association Journal* and various annotations.

Citations to the Federal Rules of Civil Procedure, the Federal Rules of Criminal Procedure, the Federal Rules of Evidence and the Federal Rules of Appellate Procedure are found in *Shepard's Federal Rules Citations.* In addition, citations are provided for states having corresponding rules. (See Illustration D, page 142.) Applicable law review citations are also included.

G. Jury Instructions

The Board of Governors of the State Bar of Arizona have approved the use of civil instructions found in *Recommended Arizona Jury Instructions* (RAJI).[20] These instructions were first introduced in 1974, revised in 1987 and supplemented in 1988.

The Civil Jury Instructions Committee of the State Bar, however, issued a new edition in 1991.[21] The committee has added several new instructions and four new sections - Preliminary, Fault, Bad Faith, and Contract. Notes and comments are now included. A forms diskette is also available.

The *Recommended Arizona Jury Instructions (Criminal)*[22] provides a complete series of instructions for use in felony criminal trials. This was first published in 1980 with a major revision in 1989 by the Arizona Criminal Jury Instructions Committee of the State Bar. Instructions are arranged in three sections - Standard Instructions, Title 13 Instructions, and Criminal Offenses Outside Title 13. These instructions are also available on diskette. *RAJI (Criminal)* has received a qualified approval from the Arizona Supreme Court. The Bar Committee intends to review and revise it annually. *Shepard's Arizona Citations: Statutes* edition includes citations to civil and criminal jury instructions.

20 *Recommended Arizona Jury Instructions (Civil)* (Phoenix, AZ.: Continuing Legal Education, State Bar of Arizona, 1987 -). looseleaf.

21 *Recommended Arizona Jury Instructions (Civil),* 2d ed. (Phoenix, AZ: Civil Instructions Committee, State Bar of Arizona, 1991). looseleaf.

22 *Recommended Arizona Jury Instructions (Criminal)* (Phoenix, AZ: Continuing Legal Education, State Bar of Arizona, 1989).

Although the federal courts have no uniform set of approved instructions, the Ninth Circuit has prepared both model civil and criminal jury instructions.[23] West's *Federal Jury Practice and Instructions*[24] and Matthew-Bender's *Modern Federal Jury Instructions*[25] provides the unofficial civil and criminal instructions.

H. Online Resources

WESTLAW contains both Arizona state and federal court rules. The AZ-RULES database includes rules as found in the current *Arizona Rules of Court State and Federal.* The AZ-ORDERS database provides the court orders which updates these rules. WESTLAW also includes court rules in their AZ-ST-ANN database which is comprised of the complete *Arizona Revised Statutes Annotated.*

The 9th Circuit Online is available free to subscribers of *9th Circuit Update* (published by Judicial Update). This database includes the most recent version of local rules and can be accessed by any computer with a modem. The Ninth Circuit Court of Appeals Service, ACES (Appeals Court Electronic Service) also contains court rule changes.

LEXIS, however, presently does not have Arizona court rules online.

I. Citation Form

The *Uniform System of Citation* suggests the following abbreviated format for Rules of Court:

Arizona Rules of Evidence:

Ariz. R. Evid. x

Arizona Rules of Civil Procedure:

Ariz. R. Civ. P. x

Arizona Rules of Criminal Procedure:

Ariz. R. Crim. P. x

In addition, at the beginning of each *A.R.S.* rules volume a complete listing of alternative citations is also given. For example, the Civil Appellate Procedure Rules would be cited as 17B A.R.S. Civil Appellate Proc. Rules, Rule x.

23 *Manual of Model Jury Instructions for the Ninth Circuit* (St. Paul, MN: West Publishing Co., 1985). The civil instructions are still in effect. *Manual of Model Criminal Jury Instructions for the Ninth Circuit,* (St. Paul, MN: West Publishing Co., 1989).

24 Devitt, Edward J., Charles B. Blackmar and Michael A. Woolf, *Federal Jury Practice and Instructions: Civil and Criminal* (St. Paul, MN: West Publishing Co., 1977 -).

25 Sand, Leonard B., et. al., *Modern Federal Jury Instructions - Civil and Criminal* (Albany, NY: Matthew-Bender, 1986 -).

Illustration A

Pursuant to Article VI, Section 5 of the Arizona Constitution, the Supreme Court of Arizona adopts the following rules to be known as the Uniform Rules of Practice of the Superior Court:

Rule I. Presiding Judge, Associate Presiding Judge

(a) The presiding judge in each county, in addition to exercising general administrative supervision over the court and the judges thereof, shall:

(1) Make regular and special assignments of all judges, except as otherwise provided by Arizona Revised Statutes Section 8–202(B), and, unless otherwise directed by the Chief Justice, assign judges within the county to other counties;

(2) Exercise general supervision over all court personnel;

(3) Prescribe the powers and duties of the clerk of the court, in addition to those prescribed by law and the Supreme Court;

(4) Appoint with the approval of the Supreme Court an associate presiding judge to act in his place during his absence or unavailability as presiding judge;

(5) Promulgate such local rules as a majority of the judges of the county may approve or as the Supreme Court shall direct;

(6) Determine the need for and approve (i) the allocation of space and furnishings in the court building; (ii) the construction of new court buildings, courtrooms and related physical facilities; and (iii) the modification of existing court buildings, courtrooms and related physical facilities.

In order to facilitate the business of the court the presiding judge or associate presiding judge may delegate the duties prescribed in these rules to other judges.

(b) The associate presiding judge shall serve at the pleasure of the presiding judge and shall exercise and discharge all powers and duties of the presiding judge, except he may not appoint court commissioners or appoint judges permanently to special assignments.

Amended Jan. 22, 1971, effective Feb. 1, 1971; March 22, 1972, effective April 1, 1972.

Historical Note

Arizona Const. Art. 6, § 5 provides, in part, that the Supreme Court shall have:

"Power to make rules relative to all procedural matters in any court."

Notes of Decisions

Administrative power and authority 3
Assignment judge 5
Construction and application 1
Grand jury 4
Purpose 2

1. Construction and application

Uniform rules promulgated by supreme court under authority of Const. Art. 6, § 5 have force and effect of a statute and are binding on court, parties, and counsel. 17A A.R.S.Super. Ct.Uniform Prac.Rules, Rules 4(a), 5(h), 12(c), (c) (3). Valley Nat. Bank of Arizona v. Meneghin (1981) 130 Ariz. 119, 634 P.2d 570.

Uniform Rules for Superior Courts have effect of statutes so far as they are applicable to any case, and any violation thereof has same effect as violation of a statute. Kinman v. Grousky (1935) 46 Ariz. 191, 49 P.2d 624.

Illustration B

STATE BAR COMMITTEE NOTES
1961 Amendment

[**Rule 54(b)**] The Arizona State Bar Committee adopts as its own the relevant materials from the comment of the Federal Committee whose note in the relevant portion is as follows:

"This rule permitting appeal, upon the trial court's determination of 'no just reason for delay,' from a judgment upon one or more but less than all the claims in an action, has generally been given a sympathetic construction by the courts and its validity is settled. Reeves v. Beardall, [62 S.Ct. 1085] 316 U.S. 283 [86 L.Ed. 1478] (1942); Sears, Roebuck & Co. v. Mackey, [76 S.Ct. 895] 351 U.S. 427 [100 L.Ed. 1297] (1956); Cold Metal Process Co. v. United Engineering & Foundry Co., [76 S.Ct. 904] 351 U.S. 445 [100 L.Ed. 1311] (1956).

"A serious difficulty has, however, arisen because the rule speaks of claims but nowhere mentions parties. A line of cases has developed in the circuits consistently holding the rule to be inapplicable to the dismissal, even with the requisite trial court determination, of one or more but less than all defendants jointly charged in an action, i.e., charged with various forms of concerted or related wrongdoing or related liability. See: Mull v. Ackerman, 279 F.2d 25 (2d Cir.1960); Richards v. Smith, 276 F.2d 652 (5th Cir.1960); Hardy v. Bankers Life & Cas. Co., 222 F.2d 827 (7th Cir.1955); Steiner v. 20th Century-Fox Film Corp., 220 F.2d 105 (9th Cir.1955). For purposes of Rule 54(b) it was arguable that there were as many 'claims' as there were parties defendant and that the rule in its present text applied where less than all of the parties were dismissed, cf. United Artists Corp. v. Masterpiece Productions, Inc., 221 F.2d 213, 215 (2d Cir.1955); Bowling Machine, Inc. v. First Nat. Bank, 283 F.2d 39 (1st Cir.1960); but the Courts of Appeals are now committed to an opposite view.

"The danger of hardship through delay of appeal until the whole action is concluded may be at least as serious in the multiple-parties situations as in multiple-claims cases, see Pabellon v. Grace Line, Inc., 191 F.2d 169, 179 (2d Cir.1951), cert. denied, [72 S.Ct. 201] 342 U.S. 893 [96 L.Ed. 669](1951), and courts and commentators have urged that Rule 54(b) be changed to take in the former. See: Reagan v. Traders & General Ins. Co., 255 F.2d 845 (5th Cir.1958); Meadows v. Greyhound Corp., 235 F.2d 233 (5th Cir.1956); Steiner v. 20th Century-Fox Film Corp., supra; 6 Moore's Federal Practice Par. 54.34(2) (2d ed.1953); 3 Barron & Holtzoff, Federal Practice & Procedure Sec. 1193.2 (Wright ed. 1958); Developments in the Law—Multiparty Litigation, 71 Harv.L.Rev. 874, 981 (1958); Note, 62 Yale L.J. 263, 271 (1953); Ill.Ann.Stat. ch. 110, Sec. 50(2) (Smith-Hurd 1956). The amendment accomplishes this purpose by referring explicitly to parties."

1970 Amendment

[**Rule 54(f)**] (1) Rule 54(f). The amended rule is designed expressly to settle the present conflict between this rule and A.R.S. § 12-346 pertaining to statements of costs.

(2) Prior to this amendment, Rule 54(f) provided that costs could be taxed by the clerk on one day's notice. There is no similar provision in A.R.S. § 12-346.

(3) A.R.S. § 12-346 provides that the statement of costs shall be filed and served within ten days after judgment, unless for good cause shown the time is extended by the court. Prior to this amendment, Rule 54(f) placed no time limit upon filing the statement of costs.

(4) The five-day period provided in the original Rule 54(f) and A.R.S. § 12-346 for objecting to the statement of costs began to run from differing events. The amendment to Rule 54(f) eliminates this procedural inconsistency.

(5) The original Rule 54(f) provided that costs against the state, its officers, and agencies could be imposed only to the extent permitted by law. This portion of the rule has been deleted by the amendment since the subject is completely covered in A.R.S. § 12-345.

(6) In Hurst v. Hurst, 1 Ariz.App. 227, 401 P.2d 232 (1965), the Court of Appeals held that under the provisions of the original Rule 54(f), which provided that costs should be allowed to the prevailing party "unless the court otherwise directs," the taxing of costs in favor of the prevailing party was discretionary with the trial court. No similar language is found in A.R.S. § 12-346 giving the court the same discretion in the matter of taxing costs. Therefore, in order to eliminate the conflict and avoid the possibility of altering a substantive right by a rule of procedure, the discretionary language has been omitted by the amendment to Rule 54(f).

(7) The substantive law on taxing costs is covered in A.R.S. § 12-341 through A.R.S. § 12-347. Reference should be had to these sections to determine when and to what extent a party has the right to costs in a given case.

RULE 55. DEFAULT

(a) Application and Entry. When a party against whom a judgment for affirmative relief is sought has failed to plead or otherwise defend as provided by these Rules, the clerk shall enter that party's default in accordance with the procedures set forth below. All requests for entry of default shall be by written application to the clerk of the court in which the matter is pending.

(1) *Notice.*

(i) To the Party. When the whereabouts of the party claimed to be in default are known by the party requesting the entry of default, a copy of the application for entry of default shall be mailed to the party claimed to be in default.

(ii) Represented Party. When a party claimed to be in default is known by the party requesting the entry of default to be represented by an attorney, whether or not that attorney has formally appeared, a copy of the application shall also be sent to the attorney for the party claimed to be in default. Nothing herein shall be construed to create any obligation to undertake any affirmative effort to determine the existence or identity of counsel representing the party claimed to be in default.

(iii) Whereabouts of Unrepresented Party Unknown. If the whereabouts of a party claimed to be in default are unknown to the party requesting the entry of default and the identity of counsel

Illustration C

I. GENERAL PROVISIONS

RULE 1. SCOPE, PURPOSE AND CONSTRUCTION, COMPUTATION OF TIME, DEFINITIONS, SIZE OF PAPER

Rule 1.1. Scope

These rules shall govern the procedure in all criminal proceedings in all courts within the State of Arizona except that the Rules of Procedure in Traffic Cases shall continue to apply.

Rule 1.2. Purpose and construction

These rules are intended to provide for the just, speedy determination of every criminal proceeding. They shall be construed to secure simplicity in procedure, fairness in administration, the elimination of unnecessary delay and expense, and to protect the fundamental rights of the individual while preserving the public welfare.

Rule 1.3. Computation of time

In computing any period of time of more than 24 hours prescribed by these rules, by order of court, or by any applicable statute, the day of the act or event from which the designated period of time begins to run is not to be included. The last day of the period so computed shall be included, unless it is a Saturday, Sunday or legal holiday, in which case the period shall run until the end of the next day which is neither a Saturday, Sunday nor a legal holiday. When the period of time prescribed or allowed is less than 7 days, intermediate Saturdays, Sundays, and legal holidays shall be excluded in the computation. Whenever a party has the right or is required to take some action within a prescribed period after service of a notice or other paper and such service is allowed and made by mail, 5 days shall be added to the prescribed period.
Amended May 7, 1975, effective Aug. 1, 1975.

Rule 1.4. Definitions

Whenever they appear in these rules the terms below shall carry the following meaning:

a. **Minor Traffic Offense.** Any offense contained in Arizona Revised Statutes Annotated Title 28, except those punishable by imprisonment for more than 30 days.

b. **Presiding Judge.** For the Superior Court: The judge, in counties having only one Superior Court judge. In other counties, the judge designated by the Supreme Court as presiding judge, or another judge appointed by him regularly to handle a particular duty. For other courts: the judge, or, in courts having more than one judge, the judge designated as presiding judge by the appropriate authority. The presiding judge for the Superior Court is the presiding judge of the county.

c. **Non-Record Court.** Any justice of the peace, city magistrate or police court.
Amended May 5, 1981, effective July 15, 1981.

Rule 1.5. Size of paper

All pleadings and other papers filed in any proceeding governed by these rules shall be on paper measuring 8½ inches × 11 inches. Notwithstanding the foregoing, exhibits or attachments to pleadings may be folded and fastened to pages of the specified size. An exhibit or attachment not in compliance with the foregoing provisions may be filed only if it appears that compliance is not reasonably practicable.
Amended Oct. 20, 1981, effective July 1, 1982.

II. PRELIMINARY PROCEEDINGS

RULE 2. COMMENCEMENT OF CRIMINAL PROCEEDINGS

WESTLAW Computer Assisted Legal Research

WESTLAW supplements your legal research in many ways. WESTLAW allows you to

- update your research with the most current information
- expand your library with additional resources
- retrieve direct history, precedential history and parallel citations with the Insta-Cite service

For more information on using WESTLAW to supplement your research, see the WESTLAW Electronic Research Guide, which follows the Preface.

523

Reprinted with permission from *West's Arizona Criminal Law and Rules*, Copyright© 1990 by West Publishing Co.

Illustration D

FEDERAL RULES OF CIVIL PROCEDURE

Art. 5
Rule 34

634P2d378
636P2d1170
638P2d668
Subd. a
526P2d31
Subd. b
645P2d204

Arizona Rules of Civil Procedure for the Superior Courts 1955 as Amended 1973

Rule 34
84Az104
87Az1
91Az120
97Az122
97Az169
98Az85
127Az436
134Az426
135Az545
136Az438
137Az330
148Az339
1AzA298
5AzA286
6AzA280
7AzA277
7AzA363
10AzA564
11AzA62
11AzA136
12AzA411
17AzA120
19AzA169
324P2d764
347P2d565
370P2d273
397P2d624
398P2d671
402P2d212
402P2d233
425P2d856
431P2d921
438P2d424
439P2d526
460P2d670
461P2d706
462P2d829
471P2d296
495P2d1327
505P2d1060
621P2d942
657P2d414
662P2d1052
666P2d538
670P2d728
714P2d832
7AzL48
1978AzS245
73Æ104n

Rule 34(a)
87Az1
347P2d565

Rule 34(b)
A135Az
lxix

Arkansas Rules of Civil Procedure 1979

Rule 34
267Ark857
281Ark334
7AkA133
591SW2d668
644SW2d641
663SW2d743
33AkL32
38AkL579
Subd. a
37AkL772
Subd. c
33AkL50

Colorado Rules of Civil Procedure 1970 as Amended 1977

Rule 34
Cir. 6
30FRD392
126Col32
128Col23
135Col489
138Col450
152Col180
158Col531
161Col386
186Col226
187Col298
189Col284
192Col227
193Col289
199Col167
199Col224
199Col304
31CoA62
31CoA499
38CoA456
39CoA156
246P2d620
259P2d863
313P2d1000
334P2d1090
381P2d36
408P2d992

422P2d46
478P2d705
497P2d723
507P2d479
526P2d1336
530P2d496
540P2d327
540P2d352
557P2d415
558P2d447
562P2d763
565P2d926
607P2d985
607P2d986
612P2d1086
619P2d771
619P2d772
627P2d1122
633P2d496
638P2d848
638P2d1376
644P2d29
670P2d762
676P2d1203
686P2d1320
710P2d1098
10CoL2492
14CoL526
14CoL949
1973CoL(1)4
1972CoL(3)
[14
37Dic27
51DJ384
73Æ122n
Subd. a
193Col290
540P2d354
565P2d926
668P2d6
703P2d648

Connecticut Practice Book 1978 as Amended 1983

§ 227
155Ct88
156Ct169
157Ct230
24CS381
25CS284
26CS2
27CS90
27CS241
28CS212
1Cir614
2Cir370
4Cir669
190A2d918
199A2d358
202A2d901
209A2d681
230A2d13
230A2d441
235A2d330
238A2d811
239A2d516

253A2d22
257A2d29
284A2d893
288A2d686
37CBJ129
37CBJ142
44CBJ193
73Æ12s

Delaware Superior Court (Civil) 1947 as Amended 1974

Rule 34
Cir. 3
8FRD616
39FRD43
6Ter184
8Ter283
8Ter583
9Ter367
10Ter540
11Ter275
3Sto1
3Sto461
3Sto578
5Sto554
40DCh451
70A2d262
90A2d672
95A2d464
103A2d333
121A2d310
128A2d808
163A2d526
171A2d910
173A2d883
184A2d91
188A2d679
223A2d390
229A2d568
249A2d436
307A2d807
438A2d1234
73Æ12s
73Æ105n
Subd. b
A1981June1

District of Columbia Rules of Civil Procedure 1971

Rule 34
431A2d7
439A2d467
Subd. a
503A2d1251

Florida Rules of Civil Procedure 1967 as Amended 1985 Revised

Rule 1.350
Cir. 2
482FS716
Cir. 11
776F2d949
1FlS111
12FlS107
14FlS170
19FlS26
30FlS121
32FlS64
34FlS125
46FlS85
49FlS132
50FlS190
46So2d390
47So2d306
50So2d169
61So2d426
63So2d308
82So2d734
92So2d818
93So2d374
97So2d693
107So2d798
108So2d791
115So2d448
117So2d34
121So2d675
122So2d216
123So2d574
123So2d685
123So2d686
135So2d434
135So2d857
141So2d19
141So2d617
143So2d217
144So2d865
145So2d506
158So2d771
166So2d832
167So2d116
168So2d200
173So2d682
176So2d578
182So2d498
186So2d87

187So2d388
190So2d62
191So2d487
200So2d619
203So2d54
203So2d618
213So2d491
213So2d902
214So2d629
226So2d217
227So2d51
227So2d705
247So2d474
251So2d899
255So2d557
270So2d433
279So2d374
280So2d493
289So2d18
298So2d525
318So2d200
326So2d242
327So2d804
346So2d100
358So2d1095
359So2d1202
365So2d418
369So2d93
380So2d1306
402So2d1362
402So2d1370
416So2d1277
420So2d904
427So2d275
427So2d1014
445So2d1069
464So2d185
471So2d575
478So2d383
479So2d240
486So2d655
488So2d523
488So2d887
492So2d423
7FLR136
23FLR297
3FSU94
14MiL260
16MiL617
18MiL243
18MiL761
18MiL780
20MiL611
22MiL210
22MiL478
22MiL579
24MiL553
24MiL555
26MiL523
28MiL295
31MiL881
73Æ105n
83Æ313n
83Æ321n
86Æ189n
Subd. a
50So2d170
280So2d484
308So2d634
318So2d200
352So2d934
393So2d654
435So2d369
478So2d493
488So2d523
488So2d887

28MiL288
30MiL37
¶ 1
359So2d1202
¶ 2
433So2d607
¶ 3
359So2d1202
Subd. b
280So2d484
289So2d19
292So2d400
314So2d642
323So2d654
402So2d1370
458So2d317
463So2d291
28MiL295
30MiL37
Subd. c
278So2d652
Subd. 1
479So2d240

Hawaii Rules of Civil Procedure 1953 as Amended 1984

Rule 34
45Haw335
49Haw514
56Haw227
66Haw275
367P2d473
422P2d99
533P2d871
660P2d1316

Idaho Rules of Civil Procedure 1975 as Amended 1980

Rule 34(a)
94Ida515
96Ida400
492P2d54
529P2d1272

Illinois Supreme Court 1967 as Amended 1985

Rule 214
63Il2d455
Va78Il2d372
90IlA348
112IlA325
118IlA456
132IlA708
29IlA195
29IlA239
31IlA648
32IlA1075
38IlA578
48IlA964
59IlA383
64IlA427
65IlA671
68IlA174
71IlA988
74IlA563
74IlA961
80IlA987
81IlA1147
82IlA665
89IlA385
92IlA283
94IlA154
97IlA211
103IlA608
105IlA594
111IlA294
112IlA196
114IlA130
118IlA413
140IlA523
145IlA587
6IlD833
16IlD668
20IlD898
21IlD803
24IlD746
28IlD2
30IlD467
30IlD649
Va35IlD801
36IlD305
37IlD65
37IlD949
44IlD641
47IlD869
49IlD790
52IlD667
59IlD321
61IlD370
67IlD26
68IlD72
69IlD876
73IlD634
94IlD823
99IlD530
102IlD183
39NE2d122
232NE2d771
251NE2d88
254NE2d803
270NE2d123
330NE2d266
330NE2d271

Continued

367

Chapter 7

Arizona Administrative and Executive Publications

Kathy Shimpock-Vieweg

A. Introduction

Arizona's state executive and administrative publications emulate the design of similar federal documents. The Governor issues executive orders, vetoes and proclamations (i.e., executive publications), while state departments and agencies issue rules, regulations, orders, and decisions (i.e., administrative publications).

Administrative law is critical, for these rules and regulations carry forward legislation affecting an agency. Regulations often have a direct impact on citizens in areas ranging from labor and business, to public health, taxation and the environment. And, although Arizona has codified its administrative regulations, they are published slowly. Decisions tend to be even more ephemeral.

This chapter, therefore, will discuss the available resources for executive and administrative law. The best initial step, however, can be taken by examining the following state publications. These guides provide an overview of executive and administrative departmental responsibility, some also give biographical information and directory listings.

Arizona Blue Book. Phoenix, AZ: Arizona Secretary of State, 1986. 1988/1989 supplement. irregular.

Arizona Yearbook: A Guide to Government in the Grand Canyon State. Eugene, OR: Information Press, 1989-1990. annual.

Arizona Administrative Register. Annual Index. Phoenix, AZ: Office of the Secretary of State, 1976-date. annual.

B. Executive Publications

1. *In General*

Article V of the Arizona Constitution designates the composition of the Executive Office to include the Governor, the Secretary of State, the Attorney General, the State Treasurer and the Superintendent of Public Instruction. For administrative purposes, however, the State Mine Inspector and the three members of the Arizona Corporation Commission have also been added.

2. *Office of the Governor*

Office of the Governor
Capitol West Wing
Phoenix, AZ 85007
(602) 542-4331

Statutory Authority:

Ariz. Const. art V, §§ 3-8;
Ariz. Rev. Stat. Ann. §§ 41-101 to 41-106.

The Governor is the chief executive officer of the state. He/she also acts as chief legislator (executing veto power), state spokesperson, commander-in-chief of the militia and party leader. The Governor makes appointments and supervises all executive officers. He/she convenes the state legislature for extraordinary sessions, and requests that the Attorney General appear or investigate various issues. The Governor has the power to grant pardons, reprieves and commutations for all crimes (other than treason or impeachment). In addition, the Governor is responsible for the faithful execution of state laws.

A.R.S. § 41-102 states that the Governor shall retain a record of official acts, an accounting of official expenses and disbursements, and a register listing all appointments and documents received in an official capacity. Executive publications, however, include executive orders, proclamations, veto messages and the "state of the state" address. Various topical studies and reports are often published.

a. Executive Orders

Executive orders are renumbered sequentially each year (e.g., 90-1). Orders are printed in West's *Arizona Legislative Service* and the *Arizona Administrative Register*. They are also cited within *A.R.S.* annotations and historical notes. Recent executive orders may be obtained from the Secretary of State. Older documents are found at the Department of Library, Archives and Public Records. There is no status table for executive orders.

b. Proclamations

Proclamations are printed in the West's *Arizona Legislative Service* and the *Arizona Administrative Register*. The Governor's Office issues a monthly "Proclamation Summary," (i.e., a dated alphabetical title listing of proclamations). Proclamations of the current administration are available from the Governor's office, while those for prior administrations are found at the Department of Library, Archives and Public Records. There is no index available.

c. Veto Messages

The Governor's veto message regarding specific legislation can be found in West's *Arizona Legislative Service* and the official session laws volumes.

d. "State of the State" Address

A copy of the Governor's address at each new legislative session can be found in the official session laws volume.

3. *Secretary of State*

Secretary of State
Capitol West Wing
Phoenix, AZ 85007
(602) 542-4285

Statutory Authority:
Ariz. Const. art V, § 1;
Ariz. Rev. Stat. Ann. §§ 41-121 to 41-131.

The Secretary of State acts as the chief elections officer. He/she is also responsible for retaining all non-financial records and for publishing state legal documents (including slip laws, statutes, and administrative rules and regulations). The Secretary of State attests to the Governor's signature on official documents and affixes to official documents the Great Seal of Arizona. Certificates of trademarks, UCC secured transactions and other business documents are also filed in this office. The Secretary of State succeeds the Governor and serves as the Acting Governor when needed.

a. Publications

The Secretary of State publishes the *Arizona Administrative Code,* the *Arizona Administrative Register* and the *Arizona Blue Book.* The office also reprints sections from selected *A.R.S.* titles and the *Administrative Code* in pamphlet form. Under *A.R.S.* § 41-121, the Secretary must keep a register of the Governor's official acts, a book of fees and compensation collection, and report annually all official actions taken. The annual report may be obtained from the Office of the Secretary of State. Outdated materials are transferred to the Department of Library, Archives and Public Records. (See Chapter 7, Section C.)

4. *Attorney General*

Attorney General
1275 West Washington
Phoenix, AZ 85007
(602) 542-4266

15 South 15th Avenue
Phoenix, AZ 85007
(Civil, Liability Defense and Tax Divisions)

Statutory Authority:
Ariz. Const. art V, § 1;
Ariz. Rev. Stat. Ann. §§ 41-191 to 41-196.

Administrative Regulations:
A.A.C. R10-1-101 to R10-4-404.

The Attorney General is the state's chief legal officer, administering the Department of Law. This office acts as a legal advisor to the Executive Department and to most state agencies. The Attorney General also represents the State in certain legal transactions. The office has the power to enforce various laws, prosecute criminal offenses, and certify administrative rules.[1]

The Department of Law is composed of the following divisions:

Civil Division — (Administration, Consumer Protection and Antitrust, Complaint Investigation, Land and Natural Resources, Liability Defense, Licensing Enforcement, Solicitation and Opinions, Tax and Transportation)

Human Services Division — (Civil Rights, Mediation, Economic Security (Child Support), Economic Security (Child Welfare))

Criminal Division — (Criminal Appeals, Criminal Trials, Drug Enforcement, Environment Enforcement, Organized Crime and Fraud, Special Investigations)

1 For more information on the powers and duties of the Attorney General, *see:* Arizona Office of the Attorney General, *Arizona Agency Handbook* (Phoenix, AZ: Office of the Attorney General, 1989).

a. Legal Opinions

Legal opinions have been issued by the Attorney General since 1883. *A.R.S.* §41-193(A)(7) requires the Attorney General's office to render opinions to the legislature, state public officers, and county attorneys on legal questions pertaining to their offices. In addition, *A.R.S.* §§15-253(B) and 15-1448 require the Attorney General to review school opinions.

There are three types of Attorney General opinions: formal, letter and concurring. Formal opinions concern issues of major statewide importance. Letter opinions are those of limited importance. Concurring opinions are those issued on various school matters by county attorneys and "concurred" with by the Attorney General. The Attorney General may either "concur, revise, or decline" review of a County Attorney's "school" opinion. Failure to act within 60 days results in an opinion's affirmation. If the Attorney General affirms an opinion, it is applicable for the entire state. But, if the Attorney General denies an opinion, it is applicable only for the issuing county. In addition, legal advice rendered orally is never considered an official opinion.[2]

The procedure for issuing an opinion is as follows: Special Counsel first assigns a request to an Assistant Attorney General for research and writing. Each request is assigned an "R number" for reference (e.g., R90-001). The draft opinion is reviewed and edited by the Attorney General's Opinion Review Committee. The opinion must then be approved by the Special Counsel and Chief Assistant Attorney before it is forwarded to the Attorney General for final signature. Once an actual opinion is issued, an "I number" is designated and the opinion filed (e.g., I81-111). Both R and I numbers are usually found on an opinion. (See Illustration A, p.184.) Rarely has an opinion been issued with only an R number. There is a conversion table, however, at the Department of Library, Archives and Public Records to convert the cite into the proper I number. In addition, some letter and concurring opinions have been designated with a suffix. Letter opinions had an L suffix (e.g., 72-9-L) from 1953 to 1973, and concurring opinions a C suffix (e.g., 62-1-C) from 1962 to 1976. Since that time only the R and I numbers have been used.

Written opinions are issued to public officials on questions of law relating to their offices.[3] Opinions are never issued on any matter pending before a court[4] and are not generally given on the constitutionality of legislation. Opinions of the Attorney General are advisory only and not judicially binding.[5] Public officials, however, are protected from personal liability for any official acts based on a good faith reliance on these opinions.[6]

A.R.S. §§41-194(A) and 39-121.01 require the Attorney General to make copies of these opinions available for public distribution. Although requests for opinions regarding violations of conflict of interest laws are confidential, the issued opinion is a public record (*A.R.S.* §38-507). Most major law libraries in Arizona

2 *Ibid.*, 1-10.

3 *See* Ariz. Atty. Gen. Op. I80-231 (1980), stating that opinions are not issued on factual matters.

4 Ariz. Atty. Gen. Op. I81-137(1981).

5 *Green v. Osborne,* 157 Ariz. 363,758 P.2d 138 (1988).

6 *Marston's Inc. v. Roman Catholic Church,* 132 Ariz. 90,94, 644 P.2d 244,248 (1982).

have a good collection of these documents, while the Department of Library, Archives and Public Records has the most complete inventory.

A listing of Arizona Attorney General's Reports and Opinions is as follows:[7]

Volume	Dates of Coverage	Pages	Notes
1883-84	Jan.1883-Dec.1884	41-45p	Report only in Governor's Message, 1885.
1888-89	Jan.1888-Dec.1889	7p	Report published by Tribune Publishing Co., Phoenix, 1889.
1899	Jan.-Dec.1899	10p	Report only
1902	Jan.-Dec.1902	1p	Report only in Governor's Report, 1902. Published by Citizen Printer Publishing Co., Tucson. 22-23p.
1903	Jan.-Dec.1903	44p	Report only in Governor's Report, 1903.
1907-08	July 1, 1907 - Oct. 1, 1908	2p	Report only
1910-11	July 1, 1910 - June 30, 1911	5 leaves	Report only
1912-14	No record found of published reports.		
1915-16	Jan. 1, 1915 - Dec. 31, 1916	viii + 136p	
1917-18	Jan. 1, 1917 - Dec. 31, 1918	xi + 246p	
1919-20	Jan. 1, 1919 - Dec. 31, 1920	182p	Opinions only
1921-22	Jan. 1, 1921 - Dec. 31, 1922	6+5-119+12p	
1922-36	No record found of published reports.		
1937-38	Jan. 4, 1937 - Dec. 31, 1938	57p	
1939-40	Jan. 4, 1939 - Dec. 31, 1940	45 leaves	
1941	Jan.-Dec. 1941	32 leaves	

7 This chart is a corrected and updated version of Meira Pimsleur's *Checklists of Basic American Legal Publications* (Littleton, CO: Fred Rothman & Co., 1988), and reprinted with permission from the American Association of Law Libraries.

Volume	Dates of Coverage	Pages	Notes
1942	Jan.-Dec. 1942	29 leaves	
1943	Jan.-Dec. 1943	23 leaves	
1944-52	No record found of published reports. Typed script opinions begin being issued in 1950.		
1953	Jan.-Dec. 1953	41 leaves	Report only
1954	Dec. 1, 1953 - Dec. 1, 1954	40 leaves	Report only
1955	Dec. 1, 1954 - Dec. 1, 1955	288p	Report only
1956	Dec. 1, 1955 - Dec. 1, 1956	143p	
1957	Dec. 1, 1956 - Dec. 1, 1957	161p	
1958	Dec. 1, 1957 - Dec. 1, 1958	133p	
1959	Dec. 1, 1958 - Dec. 1, 1959	242p	
1960	Dec. 1, 1959 - Dec. 1, 1960	141p	
1961	Dec. 1, 1960 - Nov. 15, 1961	168p	
1962	Nov. 15, 1961 - Nov. 15, 1962	274p	
1963	Nov. 15, 1962 - Nov. 15, 1963	99p	Concurring Opinions ceased, not included again until 1980.
1964	Nov. 16, 1963 - Nov. 15, 1964	97p	
1965	Nov. 16, 1964 - Nov. 15, 1965	v + 146p	
1966	Nov. 16, 1965 - Nov. 15, 1966	[15] + vii + 129p	
1967	Nov. 16, 1966 - Nov. 15, 1967	[15] + viii + 120p	
1968	Nov. 16, 1967 - Nov. 15, 1968	[22] + ix + 96p	
1969	Nov. 16, 1968 - Nov. 15, 1969	[12] + vii + 125p	
1970	Nov. 16, 1969 - Nov. 15, 1970	[15] + vi + l + 120p	

Volume	Dates of Coverage	Pages	Notes
1971	Nov. 16, 1970 - Nov. 15, 1971	[12] + viii + 171p	
1972	Nov. 16, 1971 - Nov. 15, 1972	[12] + vi + 138p	
1973	Nov. 16, 1972 - Nov. 15, 1973	xxiii + 150p	
1974	Nov. 16, 1973 - Nov. 15, 1974	xxii + 162p	
	(No record found regarding Nov. 16, 1974 - June 30, 1975)		
1975-76	Nov. 18, 1974- April 7, 1976	xxii + 162p	Incomplete
1976-77	Aug. 4, 1976 - May 31, 1977	[iii] + 183p	Incomplete
1978	Jan.-Dec., 1978	var. pag.	Typed script
1979	Jan.-Dec., 1979	var. pag.	Typed script
1980	Jan.-Dec., 1980	232 + 9p	Published again by State Bar. All opinions now included. No report.
1981	Jan.-Dec., 1981	119 + 9p	Published by Attorney General's Office. Opinions only.
1982	Jan.-Dec., 1982	129 + 10p	Opinions only
1983	Jan.-Dec., 1983	96 + 10p	Opinions only
1983	1982-83	125p	Report only
1984	Jan.-Dec., 1984	183 + 11p	Opinions only
1985	Jan.-Dec., 1985	var. pag.	Typed script
1986	Jan.-Dec., 1986	var. pag.	Typed script
1987	Jan.-Dec., 1987	282p	Opinions only
1988	Jan.-Dec., 1988	194p	Opinions only
1989	Jan.-Dec., 1989	224p	Opinions only
1990	Jan.-Dec., 1990	169p	Opinions only

The Attorney General's Office also releases "slip opinions" (i.e., typed and photocopied opinions released prior to the bound volumes). Copies can be found at most major law libraries within the state and at the Department of Library,

Archives and Public Records. These opinions are often more complete than the official compilations. Libraries usually bind the opinions, but without an index.

In addition, Attorney General opinions can be obtained on microform from the William S. Hein & Co. From 1915 to 1977 they are available on microfilm; after that date, on microfiche.

i. Index

Prior to 1980 most volumes of opinions contained a subject index. Some also included an index of statutes construed. A one-volume subject index was published by the Attorney General's Office in 1984 covering all opinions issued from 1975 - 1983. This index provided a listing of cited prior opinions, state and federal statutes and regulations, and constitutional provisions. Since this date, each volume of opinions has contained a similar index. A current index can also be found in the *Arizona Administrative Register.*

ii. Summary of Attorney General Opinions

The Attorney General's Office periodically issues summaries of recent opinions. These summaries indicate the opinion number, requesting agency or person, prior opinions cited, statutes construed or cited and a brief summary. The summaries are published in the *Arizona Register,* the *Yellowsheet Report* and the *Arizona Capitol Times.*[8]

iii. Updating

The Attorney General's Office sends monthly photocopies of opinions to those on a mailing list for a charge.

iv. Online Resources

WESTLAW has Arizona Attorney General Opinions (AZ-AG) online from 1977 to date. LEXIS has the opinions from September 1975 to date (ARIZ;AG). In addition, LEXIS also has Arizona Attorney General Opinions on insurance in their Insurance Law Library (INSRLW;AG) from 1970 to date.

b. Arizona Attorney General Annual Report

Until 1977, the annual report was usually contained within the bound opinion volumes. Later reports are found at the Department of Library, Archives and Public Records. Copies of current annual reports may be obtained from the Office of the Attorney General for a nominal charge.

8 The *Yellowsheet Report* and *Arizona Capitol Times* are both published by the Arizona News Service, 14 North 18th Avenue, Phoenix, AZ 85007. (602)258-7026.

5. *Superintendent of Public Instruction*

Superintendent of Public Instruction
1535 West Jefferson
Phoenix, AZ 85007
(602) 542-4361

Statutory Authority:
Ariz. Const. art. V, §1;
Ariz. Rev. Stat. Ann. §§15-251 to 15-255.

The Superintendent of Public Instruction acts as the chief administrative officer for public education. He/she is responsible for administering the policies promulgated by the Arizona State Board of Education. The Superintendent is an ex officio member of several education boards. He/she distributes funding and publications to counties for public schools and may authorize the Auditor General to investigate any school accounts. He/she also holds an annual meeting of school superintendents.

a. Legal Opinions

The Superintendent of Public Instruction must furnish concurring Attorney General Opinions and County Attorney Opinions (submitted for Attorney General review) to requesting parties (*A.R.S.* §15-253). These opinions deal only with school matters. The Programs and Projects Specialist at the Department of Education will fax copies of opinions when needed. Opinions are available from the Department of Education from 1948 to date. Older materials can be obtained from the Department of Library, Archives and Public Records, as well as an in-house index of opinions.

b. Annual Report

The Superintendent of Public Instruction is required to make an annual report to the Governor and Legislature. A copy of the current report can be obtained from the Central Distribution Service at the Department of Education. Older items can be located at the Department of Library, Archives and Public Records.

6. *State Treasurer*

State Treasurer
Capitol West Wing
Phoenix, AZ 85007
(602) 542-5815

Statutory Authority:
Ariz. Const. art. V §§1, 10;
Ariz. Rev. Stat. Ann. §§41-171 to 41-175.

The State Treasurer is the state's chief financial officer. He/she is responsible for all state funds not managed by another official. The State Treasurer authenticates certified writings and documents with the official seal. He/she pays warrants and maintains accounts of monies received and disbursed. The Treasurer also delivers receipts for monies paid. He/she must give a written report on the condition of the state treasury, or on any other official duties when requested by a state legislator.

The State Treasurer may also provide assistance to communities for water and waste water facilities, especially in regards to budgeting and capital planning.

a. Reports

A.R.S. §41-172(A)(8) requires the State Treasurer to prepare a monthly and an annual financial statement for the Governor and the Department of Administration. Current reports are available from the State Treasurer's Office. Earlier materials can be obtained from the Department of Library, Archives and Public Records.

7. *State Mine Inspector*

State Mine Inspector
Capitol West Wing
Phoenix, AZ 85007
(602) 542-5971

Tucson Office:
416 West Congress, Rm 187
Tucson, AZ 85701
(602) 628-5990

Statutory Authority:
ARIZ. CONST. art. XIX;
ARIZ. REV. STAT. ANN. §§27-121 to 27-128.

Administrative Regulations:
A.A.C. R11-1-101 to R11-1-2235.

The State Mine Inspector administers all state and federal mining rules and regulations governing the safety and health of mine workers and the general public. He/she is responsible for the inspection of individual mines for possible violations, and the preparation of inspection reports recommending preventative actions. The Mine Inspector is required to submit an annual report to the Governor. A current report may be obtained from the Office of the State Mine Inspector. Earlier reports can be found at the Department of Library, Archives and Public Records.

8. *The Corporation Commission*

The Corporation Commission
1200 West Washington
Phoenix, AZ 85007
Info: (602) 542-3931
Securities Div: (602) 542-4242
Docket Control: (602) 542-3477

Southern Arizona Office:
402 West Congress Street
Tucson, AZ 85701
(602) 628-5555

Statutory Authority:
Ariz. Cont. art XV, §§1 to 19;
Ariz. Rev. Stat. Ann. §§40-101 to 40-112; 40-201 to 40-206.

Administrative Regulations:
A.A.C. R14-1-101 to R14-5-205.

The Corporation Commission is composed of three elected officials. The Commission retains the public records of all corporations doing business within the state and issues to Arizona corporations certificates of incorporation and licenses foreign corporations. The Corporation Commission also sets rules, regulations and orders regarding public service corporations. The Commission has the power to investigate and hold hearings on rate setting, financing and other public service actions. Examples of public service corporations include the intrastate telephone company and corporations furnishing power or waste disposal. The Commission also regulates securities brokers and dealers, and issues applications for security registration.

Presently the Corporation Commission has the following divisions: Administrative Division, Corporations Division, Hearing Division, Legal Division, Securities Division, and Utilities Division. There is also an Executive Secretary and Controller/Deputy Executive Secretary.

a. Annual Report

A.R.S. §40-105(B)(4) requires the Executive Secretary of the Corporation Commission to prepare an annual report for the Governor and Legislature. This report can be obtained from the Corporation Commission. Earlier reports are available at the Department of Library, Archives and Public Records.

b. Corporate Public Record

These include annual reports and the articles of incorporation for Arizona corporations, and licenses for foreign corporations. A written request must be submitted to obtain copies of broker/dealer registrations. The Commission requires prior notice to retrieve public offerings materials. Earlier reports are available at the Department of Library, Archives and Public Records.

c. Hearings/Orders

The Corporation Commission holds hearings on securities issues, rate setting for public service corporations, etc. Information discovered during the initial investigation is not public information. However, once the file is brought before the Hearing Division, certain parts do become public. Both civil and criminal decisions (orders) can be picked up from the Docket Control Division (1st Floor, Rm 130). The Division has decisions from 1986 to date. Phone requests are taken and copies will be made for a fee. Copies must be paid for in person, as none will be sent out with an invoice.

d. Arizona Corporation Commission Securities Division

Arizona Securities Act and Rules and Regulations of the Arizona Corporation Commission Governing Administration of the Securities Statutes (Phoenix, AZ: Imperial Financial Printing, irregular). pamphlet.

A reprint of the applicable sections from the *Arizona Revised Statutes* and the *Arizona Administrative Code.* This cannot be updated.

e. Online Resources

WESTLAW includes Arizona Corporation Commission Orders regarding securities law (AZSEC-ADMIN) from 1985 to date. Arizona Public Utilities Reports (AZ-PUR) are also online. This includes Arizona cases and administrative decisions from the *Public Utilities Reports,* Fourth Series and the National Reporter System. Headnotes and full text are provided when available.

LEXIS has the Arizona Corporation Commission orders on securities law (ARIZ; AZSEC) from September 1975 to date.

C. Administrative Publications

1. *Introduction*

Black's Law Dictionary describes an administrative agency as "a governmental body charged with administering and implementing particular legislation."[9] An administrative agency may be part of the executive, legislative or judicial branch or it may be an independent entity. Arizona agencies vary both in their format and in their responsibilities. They may be involved in issuing rules, regulations, and orders and in holding hearings.

Most Arizona administrative agencies are not authorized by the Constitution.[10] Many are merely assumed to be part of the executive branch, and their duties delineated by statute.

9 *Black's Law Dictionary*, 6th ed. (St. Paul, MN: West Publishing Co., 1990).

10 An exception is the Corporation Commission (Ariz.Const., art. XV,§1-19), and for other Commissions *see* (Ariz. Const., art.V,§12.).

2. *Rules and Regulations*[11]

Statutory Authority:
Ariz. Rev. Stat. Ann. §§41-1001 to 41-1066.

Administrative Regulations:
A.A.C. R1-101 to R1-6-206.

Arizona enacted the Model State Administrative Procedure Act (known as the Arizona Administrative Procedure Act) in 1987 (*see A.R.S.* §§41-1001 to 41-1066). *A.R.S.* §41-1030 states that an administrative rule is invalid unless adopted and certified in substantial compliance with this act's provisions. The act defines a rule as "an agency statement of general applicability that implements, interprets or prescribes law or policy, or describes the procedure or practice requirements of an agency." [12] *A.R.S.* §41-1003 requires each agency to adopt rules for all formal procedures available to the public. Rules regulating an agency's internal affairs, however, are not controlled by this act. [13]

a. Rule Adoption Procedure

All agencies are required to file an "R101" (i.e., a Notice of Proposed Rule Making) form prior to the adoption, repeal, or amendment of a rule. Also attached to this form are the following: a summary of the proposed rule to be published in the *Arizona Administrative Register,* the rule's text, an economic impact statement, a statement of impact on small business and a copy of any documents to be incorporated by reference.

Many agencies are first required to file this notice with the Governor's Regulatory Review Council (GRRC). [14] The GRRC may require an agency representative to attend a council meeting and answer questions regarding the proposed rule. [15] Note: *A.R.S.* §41-1055 enumerates those agencies exempt from GRRC review. If GRRC approval is obtained the "R101" is forwarded to the Secretary of State.

Once the Secretary of State has received the Notice, it is compared against those requirements found within the *A.A.C.* Title 1, Chapters 1 and 2. If the requirements are met, the "R101" is filed. The Secretary of State is then responsible for publishing notice of rule changes in the *Administrative Register.* [16] This notice must be given at least 30 days prior to any oral proceeding or deadline for written statements. [17] *A.R.S.* §41-1022 lists the requirements for the Notice of Proposed Rule Adoption. Additional notice requirements may be statutorily defined for some agencies.

11 For more information on agency rule making and hearings, *see* Arizona Office of the Attorney General, *Arizona Agency Handbook* (Phoenix, AZ: Office of the Attorney General, 1989).

12 Ariz.Rev.Stat.Ann.§41-1001(12)(1985).

13 Ariz.Rev.Stat.Ann.§41-1005(A)(4)(1985).

14 Ariz.Rev.Stat.Ann.§41-1052(1985).

15 Ariz.Rev.Stat.Ann.§41-1052(D)(1985).

16 Ariz.Rev.Stat.Ann.§41-1013(1985).

17 Ariz.Rev.Stat.Ann.§41-1023(C)(1985).

An agency must give the public an opportunity to comment on any potential rule change. This may be in the form of an oral proceeding, an opportunity for written statements, or both. [18] *A.R.S.* §41-1023(B) states that hearings are not required unless requested in writing by at least five persons. However, location cites for hearings must be generally accessible. More than one location is often needed.

Either an agency representative or another designated official will preside at any oral proceeding. If the agency representative does not preside, the designated official is required to prepare a memorandum summarizing the proceeding's events. In addition, oral proceedings must either be open to the public or recorded in some manner. [19] The agency is required to review this record, all written and oral submissions, the economic impact statement and statement of the rule's effect on small businesses, prior to its final adoption. [20]

During this process the agency is required to maintain both a public rule making docket and a rule making record. *A.R.S.* §41-1021 details the information contained in the rule making docket and *A.R.S.* §41-1029 sets out the contents of the rule making record.

An agency may not adopt a rule until the rule making record is closed. [21] After closure, however, the agency has 120 days to adopt the rule and issue a concise explanatory statement.[22] The rule is then sent to the Attorney General's Office for certification. Each proposed rule must be certified for 1) proper format, 2) clear and understandable text, 3) subject matter within the agency's authority, and 4) compliance with statutory procedures. [23] And finally, the rule is forwarded to the Secretary of State for filing. [24] A rule is not effective until the Secretary of State affixes to it the filing time and date. [25] Rules have the effect of law once certified and filed, or as prescribed by law.[26]

Special procedures for the adoption of emergency rules can be found in *A.R.S.* §41-1026 and §41-1041(B) (D).

b. Agency Documents and Publications

i. Public Rule Making Docket - *A.R.S.* §41-1021

By statute, each agency is required to maintain a current rule making docket. The docket lists the subject matter for each rule under active consideration. It provides the name and address of agency personnel to contact for further information, indicates the rule's current status, and lists rule making proceedings for pending rules. Information on where the following documents may be inspected is also available: 1) written submissions, 2)

18 Ariz.Rev.Stat.Ann.§41-1023(A)(1985).
19 Ariz.Rev.Stat.Ann.§41-1023(D)(1985).
20 Ariz.Rev.Stat.Ann.§41-1024(C)(1985).
21 Ariz.Rev.Stat.Ann.§41-1024(A)(1985).
22 Ariz.Rev.Stat.Ann.§41-1024(B),41-1027(1985).
23 Ariz.Rev.Stat.Ann.§41-1041(1985).
24 Ariz.Rev.Stat.Ann.§41-1041(C)(1985).
25 Ariz.Rev.Stat.Ann.§41-1031(1985).
26 Ariz.Rev.Stat.Ann.§41-1032(1985).

the economic impact statement, 3) the statement of the rule's effect on small business, and 4) pertinent GRRC meeting minutes.

ii. Rule Making Record - *A.R.S.* §41-1029

Agencies are required to maintain an official rule making record for proposed rules (i.e., those published in the *Administrative Register*), and for each rule certified and filed. This information is available to the public. The record includes copies of the following: 1) the initial notice, 2) all applicable *Register* publications, 3) relevant portions of the agency's rule making docket, 4) the agency's written petitions, requests, submissions and comments, 5) any other written materials considered or prepared by the agency, 6) official transcripts, tape recordings or other records of all proceedings, 7) memoranda summarizing the contents of oral proceedings, 8) all materials submitted to the GRRC, 9) GRRC meeting minutes, 10) certified rule and explanatory statement, and 11) information regarding the agency's experience, technical competence, specialized knowledge and judgment (under *A.R.S.* §41-1024(D)).

In addition, *A.R.S.* §41-1028 states that an agency may incorporate by reference, any part of a code, standard, rule or regulation adopted by another agency or organization. A copy of the matter incorporated by reference is available for public inspection as part of the agency's rule making record.

iii. Statements and Analysis

The full text of the economic impact statement, impact on small business statement and cost/benefit analysis are available from the Office of the Secretary of State.

iv. Administrative Rules and Regulations

The first law requiring a central filing of administrative rules was found in the Laws of 1952, Chapter 97. This initial version of the Administrative Procedure Act required agencies to hold hearings and file in the Office of the Secretary of State a certified copy of every rule adopted and in effect at the time of filing. The Laws of 1972, Chapter 35, Section 1 provided for a single publication of all administrative rules and regulations. However, the *Official Compilation of Administrative Rules and Regulations* was not completed until 1975. In 1986, the Legislature again revised the Administrative Procedure Act (Laws of 1986, Chapter 232). The act became effective in 1987, and completely revised the rule making process and procedures. The *Arizona Administrative Code* was born of this revision.

Today the Office of the Secretary of State is solely responsible for the publication and distribution of administrative rules and regulations, including their codification, format and style. [27] An agency must draft rules to conform with this format. [28]

27 Ariz.Rev.Stat.Ann.§41-1012(1985).
28 Ariz.Rev.Stat.Ann.§41-1011(D)(1985).

Rules remain in the codification until either repealed by the agency or judicially construed to be unconstitutional. The effective date for a rule is found following the Historical Notes. The absence of an Historical Note indicates that the rule has been in effect since 1975. The Secretary of State's publication of a rule constitutes *prima facie* evidence of its adoption and filing.[29]

Rules and regulations prior to the official compilation in 1975 are available on microfiche at the Office of the Secretary of State. They are arranged by agency. Sources for Arizona administrative rules and regulations are as follows:

Superseded Regulations

Official Compilation of Administrative Rules and Regulations. Phoenix, AZ: Office of Secretary of State, 1975-1986. 9 vols. looseleaf.

The codified version of administrative rules and regulations filed with the Secretary of State. There is no subject index. The first volume has a master table of contents, and a table of agencies indicating corresponding regulation titles. The Department of Library, Archives and Public Records and the Maricopa County Law Library maintain the superseded pages of this compilation from 1975.

Arizona Administrative Digest. Phoenix, AZ: Office of Secretary of State, 1979-1986. Issues numbered 79-1 to 81-6; v.1, no. 1 (1981) - v.6, no. 12 (1986).

This was the monthly publication updating the *Official Compilation of Administrative Rules and Regulations.* It contained summaries of proposed rules, hearing notices, emergency rules and a listing of permanent rules. Also included were the Governor's executive orders and proclamations, a summary of Attorney General opinions, and a listing of State Appointed Officials, etc.

The first Cumulative Index was compiled for volume 3 covering January 3 to December 3, 1983. The index was comprised of four sections: Agency Index (arranged by A.C.R.R. chapter heading), Permanent Rule Index, Attorney General's Opinion Index (topical arrangement), and a listing of State Appointed Officials, State Boards and Commissions. An index was subsequently published twice a year. The *Arizona Administrative Digest* is continued by the *Arizona Administrative Register.*

Current Regulations

Arizona Administrative Code. Phoenix, AZ: Office of Secretary of State, 1986 - date. 7 v. looseleaf.

A.R.S. §41-1012 states the code shall contain the full text of each approved rule certified and filed. There are presently 18 titles divided into major subject areas. There is no subject index, but volume 1 contains a Table of Contents subdivided into titles and chapters, and an alphabetical index of agencies. (See

29 Ariz.Rev.Stat.Ann.§41-1012(B)(1985).

Illustration B, p.185.) Each additional volume contains a Table of Contents and a Table of Chapter, Articles and Rules.

The *Arizona Administrative Code's* numbering system is hyphenated, similar to the *A.R.S.* A typical citation would be *A.A.C.* R3-1-50, which translates as the *Arizona Administrative Code,* Title 3, Chapter 1, Rule 50. (See Illustration C, p.186.)

Quarterly supplements include all rule changes. Each supplement contains the rules filed with the Secretary of State since the previous issue. Because there is a delay in the publication of rules, the *Arizona Administrative Register* should always be consulted.

The full text copies of all published rules are available at the Secretary of State, Publication Division and the promulgating agency. In addition, the Code itself can be purchased from the Secretary of State, in a full set, by the volume, title, chapter, or section. Superseded pages from 1986 can be found at the Department of Library, Archives and Public Records and the Maricopa County Law Library.

Arizona Administrative Register. Phoenix, AZ: Office of Secretary of State, 1976 - date. monthly. pamphlet.

Formerly known as the *Arizona Digest,* the *Arizona Administrative Register* includes the following information: the full text of Governor's executive orders and proclamations of general applicability; digests of Attorney General opinions; notices of proposed rules; emergency rule certification; lists of permanent and terminated rules; and lists of appointed officers, state boards and commissions. The *Administrative Register* also provides publication schedules for notice closing dates,issue dates and hearing dates. It is published on the first working day of each month and includes information filed the preceding 30 days.

The *A.A.R.* is cited by volume and page number. For example, *A.A.R.*90-20 would translate as volume 90 of the *Arizona Administrative Register* beginning on page 20 (1990). (See Illustration D, p.187.) The pages run consecutively throughout the year.

An index is published both semi-annually and annually. The index is divided into several sections: Governor (listing executive orders and proclamations), Attorney General Opinions (subdivided into subject and cites from federal law, *A.R.S.*, Arizona session laws, Attorney General Opinions, *A.A.C* and the Arizona Constitution), Proposed Rule Index, Emergency Rules, Temporary Rules (as adopted by the Department of Environmental Quality), Permanent Rules, Terminated/Rejected Rules and a listing of Boards and Commissions.

The Register can be purchased by individual copy or by subscription. Back issues are available from the Secretary of State until their supply is depleted. In addition, the full text of all documents included within the *Administrative Register* is available at the Secretary of State, Publication Division. Superseded issues can be found at the Department of Library, Archives, and Public Records and at the Maricopa County Law Library.

Arizona Capitol Times. Phoenix, AZ: Arizona News Service, 1945 - date. weekly. newspaper.

The *Arizona Capitol Times* also contains articles on state agencies, including new appointments, policy changes, etc.

Yellowsheet Report. Phoenix, Az: Arizona News Service, 1906 - date. [Wednesday-Friday] weekly, newspaper. (Published when the Legislature is not in session).

The "Yellowsheet" contains administrative rules and regulations along with a report of agency and Corporation Commission meetings.

C. Administrative Adjudicatory Proceedings *A.R.S.* §§41-1061 to 41-1066[30]

The Arizona Administrative Procedure Act governs the adjudicatory process for many state agencies. Other agencies, however, rely on internal procedural rules (either in addition to or instead of the Arizona Administrative Procedure Act). Therefore, it is suggested that the agency itself be contacted for applicable regulations.

Agencies use adjudicatory proceedings to ascertain whether enforcement or disciplinary actions should be taken in areas of licensing or regulation. Hearings are also used for rate setting and to settle disputes between private parties. A hearing may be held before an agency official, a board, or hearing officer to make findings of fact and conclusions of law. However, the agency itself is generally responsible for making a decision based upon the evidence. When warranted, an agency may impose a sanction (e.g., a fine or order) or deny, suspend or revoke a license. Arizona's Open Meeting Law provides for public attendance at administrative adjudicatory proceedings.[31]

Most administrative decisions are subject to judicial review under the Administrative Review Act.[32] Although a court is not bound by an agency's decisions, weight may be given to a long held statute or rule interpretation. (*Long v. Dick,* 87 Ariz. 25, 29, 347 P. 2d 581, 583-84 (1959)).

The documents associated with the adjudicatory process are as follows:

1. Notice: A.R.S. §41-1061(A)

This section requires an agency to give 20 days prior notice of a hearing (unless otherwise provided by statute).

2. Hearing Officer Procedures

Agencies generally adopt rules and prepare manuals describing adjudicatory procedures for hearing officers. For example, see the procedures set out by the State Accountancy Board.

30 For more information on the adjudicatory process, *see Arizona Agency Handbook* (Phoenix, AZ: Office of the Attorney General, 1989).

31 Ariz.Rev.Stat.Ann. §§38-431 to 38-431.09(1985).

32 Ariz.Rev.Stat.Ann.§§12-901 to 12-914(1982).

3. *Transcript of Hearing: A.R.S.* §41-1061(F)

When a hearing ofhicer presides over a hearing, a transcript or tape recording must be made for the agency decision makers. Recordings will be transcribed for requesting parties for a fee.

4. *Procedural Rules for Adjudicatory Proceedings*

Large agencies authorized to conduct hearings generally adopt their own procedural rules. For example, see the *Rules of Procedure for Workmen's Compensation Hearings Before the Industrial Commission of Arizona* (A.A.C. R4-13-101 to R4-13-163) or *Rules of Practice and Procedure Before the Superintendent of Banks* (A.A.C. R4-4-1201 to R4-4-1220). For information regarding similar agency rules, contact each agency directly.

5. *Record of Proceeding: A.R.S.* §41-1061(E)(F)

Each agency is required to maintain a formal record of the proceedings (whether manually or mechanically recorded). The record should include: 1) all pleadings, motions and interlocutory rulings, 2) evidence received or considered, 3) a statement of matters officially noticed, 4) objections and offers of proof and corresponding rulings, 5) proposed findings and exceptions, 6) any decision, opinion or report issued by the presiding officer, and 7) all staff memoranda (with the exception of various privileged communications).

6. *Order or Decision: A.R.S.* §41-1063

The final order or decision must either be made in writing or stated in the record. It should include a separate statement of the findings of fact and the conclusions of law.

D. Online Resources

WESTLAW includes the following administrative decisions online:

Arizona Board of Tax Appeals (AZTX-ADMIN). Includes the Board's Division II Decisions (from 1982 to date).

Arizona Public Utilities Reports (AZ-PUR).

Arizona cases and administrative decisions from the *Public Utilities Reports*, Fourth Series; the *P.U.R. Digest*, Third Series, and the *West's National Reporter System* are provided. Headnotes and full text are included when available.

LEXIS administrative database holdings are as follows:

Arizona Board of Tax Appeals (ARIZ;AZTAX) (from December 1982 to date).

Arizona Insurance Department Regulations (INSRLW;REGS) (current year only).

Arizona Insurance Department Miscellaneous Circulars, Bulletins, Letters and Memoranda (INSRLW;MISC) (from 1976 to date).

E. Citation Form

The Uniform System of Citation[33] suggests the following abbreviated format for citing administrative and executive publications:

Official Compilation Administrative Rules and Regulations	Ariz. Comp. Admin. R. & Regs. x(19xx)
Arizona Administrative Code (cited by title, chapter and rule number)	Ariz. Admin. C. Rx-xx-xxx (19xx)
Administrative Digest	___ Ariz. Admin. Dig.___ (19xx)
Administrative Register	___ Ariz. Admin. Reg.___(19xx)
Governor's Executive Order (cited by year and number)	Ariz. Exec. Order [yr.-no.] (19xx)
Governor's Proclamation (unnumbered, but dated)	Ariz. Proclamation [mo., day, yr.]
Attorney General Opinions (cite by volume and page)	___ Ariz. Op. Att'y Gen. ___ (19xx)

However, an alternative system of citation recommended in the official documents is as follows:

Arizona Administrative Code (cited by title, chapter, and rule number)	*A.A.C.* Rxx-xx-xxx (19xx)
Administrative Register (cited by volume and page)	*A.A.R.* [vol.-page] (19xx).
Attorney General Opinions (opinions are usually cited with an R or I prefix)	Ariz. Att'y Gen.Op. Ixx-xxx (19xx)

F. Arizona Administrative Agencies, Boards, or Commissions

Orders and decisions issued by most state agencies are ephemeral and difficult to locate. Often agency files are closed from public review until a final decision is made. Requests for orders and decisions must generally be made in writing.

33 *The Bluebook: A Uniform System of Citation,* 15th ed. (Cambridge, MA: The Harvard Law Review Association, 1991), 343 p.

The following is a listing of the major Arizona administiative agencies, boards and commissions. Requirements for document retrieval is provided for the most commonly used agencies. Contact each individual agency for additional information. There is usually a charge for photocopying.

Accountancy, State Board of
3110 North 19th Avenue, Suite 140
Phoenix, AZ 85015
(602) 255-3648
Statutory Authority: *A.R.S.* §§32-701 to 32-707.

Disciplinary hearings are available from 1978 to present. Requests for copies must be made in writing. A photocopy request form will be returned along with price information. Once the Board receives the photocopy request form and check, copies will be issued.

Administration, Department of
State Capitol, West Wing, Room 801
Phoenix, AZ 85007
(602) 542-1500
Statutory Authority: *A.R.S.* §§41-701, 41-621.

Affirmative Action, Governor's Office of
State Capitol, West Wing, Room 104
1700 West Washington
Phoenix, AZ 85007
(602) 542-3711
Authority: Ariz. Exec. Order 77-11.

Aging, Advisory Council on
1720 West Madison, Room B-6
Phoenix, AZ 85007
(602) 542-4710
Statutory Authority: *A.R.S.* §§46-183 to 46-184.

Agricultural Employment Relations Board
1937 West Jefferson, Bldg. E
Phoenix, AZ 85007
(602) 542-5989
Statutory Authority: *A.R.S.* §§23-1386 to 23-1388.

Settles labor disputes among agricultural employers, employees and labor unions. Transcripts from Hearing Officer's decisions may be available. Call to ascertain what information may be found in the file. The Board will send photocopy project to off-site copy center. Charges will vary.

Agriculture and Horticulture, Arizona Commission of
1688 West Adams, Room 421
Phoenix, AZ 85007
(602) 542-4373
Statutory Authority: *A.R.S.* §§3-101 to 3-104; 3-142; 3-362 to 3-363.

Hearings are held on issues involving pesticide use. The pesticide records are stored in the Agricultural Chemical and Environmental Services Division. Decisions are sent to the Attorney General's Office. *A.R.S.* §3-374 states that records, reports and other information from this agency are public unless determined to be confidential by the Attorney General.

Air Pollution Control Hearing Board
2005 North Central, Room 700
Phoenix, AZ 85004
(602) 257-2308
Clerk: (602) 257-6917
Statutory Authority: *A.R.S.* §§49-423 to 49-424.

Hearing documents are filed at the Board for the current six years only. A request form must be signed prior to copies being made. The form can either be mailed or picked up at the Board.

Appeal Board (Unemployment Insurance and Economic Assistance)
1140 E. Washington, Suite 104
P.O. Box 14
Phoenix, AZ 85034
(602) 229-2806

Previously the Unemployment Insurance Appeals Board, this board hears appeals on unemployment insurance and economic assistance. Only claimants' attorney(s) can obtain photocopies of transcripts, etc.

Appellate Court Appointments, Commission On
1700 West Washington
Capitol, West Wing
Phoenix, AZ 85007
(602) 542-4531
Statutory Authority: Ariz. Const. art VI, §36.

Arizona Mexico Commission
P.O. Box 13564
Phoenix, AZ 85002
(602) 542-1345

Arts, Arizona Commission on the
417 West Roosevelt
Phoenix, AZ 85003
(602) 255-5882
Statutory Authority: *A.R.S.* §§41-981 to 41-985.

Banking Department
3225 North Central, Suite 815
Phoenix, AZ 85012
(602) 255-4421
Statutory Authority: *A.R.S.* §§6-101 to 6-161.

Barbers, Arizona Board of
1645 West Jefferson, Room 418
Phoenix, AZ 85007
(602) 542-4498
Statutory Authority: *A.R.S.* §§32-301 to 32-305.

Beef Council, Arizona
1401 North 24th Street, Suite 4
Phoenix, AZ 85008
(602) 273-7163
Statutory Authority: *A.R.S.* §§3-1231 to 3-1239.

Behavioral Health Examiners, Board of
1624 West Adams, Room 100-A
Phoenix, AZ 85007
(602) 542-1882
Statutory Authority: *A.R.S.* §§32-3251 to 32-3254.

Boxing Commission, Arizona State
1645 West Jefferson, Room 212
Phoenix, AZ 85007
(602)542-1417
Statutory Authority: *A.R.S.* §§5-221 to 5-240.

Budget Committee, Joint Legislative
1716 West Adams
Phoenix, AZ 85007
(602) 542-5491
Statutory Authority: *A.R.S.* §§41-1271 to 41-1274.

Building and Fire Safety, Department of
1540 West Van Buren
Phoenix, AZ 85007
(602) 255-4072

Holds administrative hearings on violations of the state fire code. All requests for transcripts must be made in writing.

Children, Advisory Council to the Governor's Office of
1700 West Washington, Fourth Floor
Phoenix, AZ 85007
(602) 542-3191
Authority: Ariz. Exec. Order 88-22.

Chiropractic Examiners, Board of
5060 North 19th Avenue, Suite 413
Phoenix, AZ 85015
(602) 255-1444
Statutory Authority: *A.R.S.* §32-900 to 32-907.

Hearings are held regarding licenses. Request must be made in writing. For extensive copies, payment must be received in advance.

Civil Rights Advisory Board
1275 West Washington
Phoenix, AZ 85007
(602) 542-5263
Statutory Authority: *A.R.S.* §§41-1401 to 41-1403.

Hearings are held on civil rights infringement. Contact the agency directly for more information.

Climatologist, State
ASU Laboratory of Climatology
Tempe, AZ 85287-1508
(602) 965-6265

Coliseum and Exposition Center Board, Arizona
1826 West McDowell Road
Phoenix, AZ 85007
(602) 252-6771
Statutory Authority: *A.R.S.* §§3-1001 to 3-1013.

Commerce, Department of
3800 North Central
Phoenix, AZ 85012
(602) 280-1300
Statutory Authority: *A.R.S.* §§41-1501 to 41-1528.

Community Colleges, State Board of Directors for
Century Plaza, Ste. 1220
3225 North Central Avenue
Phoenix, AZ 85012
(602) 255-4037
Statutory Authority: *A.R.S.* §§15-1421 to 15-1428.

Compensation Fund Board
3031 North Second Street
Phoenix, AZ 85012
(602) 631-2000
Statutory Authority: *A.R.S.* §23-981.01.

Compensation Fund, State
3031 North Second Street
Phoenix, AZ 85012
(602) 631-2000
Statutory Authority: *A.R.S.* §§23-981 to 23-987.

Contractor's Recovery Fund Board
800 West Washington, 6th Floor
Phoenix, AZ 85007
(602) 542-1525
Statutory Authority: *A.R.S.* §32-1134.

Contractors, Registrar of
800 West Washington, 6th Floor
Phoenix, AZ 85007
(602) 542-1525
Statutory Authority: *A.R.S.* §§32-1101 to 32-1107.

Holds administrative hearings regarding formal complaints. Can place phone orders. Written complaints are held in the Complaint Department prior to a hearing. The Hearing Department maintains transcripts of hearings, judgments, and complaints (for hearings once held).

Correctional Industries, Arizona
1601 West Jefferson
Phoenix, AZ 85007
(602) 255-5786
Statutory Authority: *A.R.S.* §§41-1621 to 41-1630.

Corrections, Department of
1601 West Jefferson
Phoenix, AZ 85007
(602) 542-5536
Statutory Authority: *A.R.S.* §§41-1601 to 41-1675.

Corrections, Department of Juvenile
1645 West Jefferson Street, 2nd Floor
Phoenix, AZ 85007
(602) 542-5306
Statutory Authority: *A.R.S.* §§41-2801 to 41-2842.

Cosmetology, Board of
1645 West Jefferson, Room 125
Phoenix, AZ 85007
(602) 542-5301
Statutory Authority: *A.R.S.* §§32-501 to 32-507.

Complaint may be filed by customer. A hearing is held if necessary. No photocopies may be made until the hearing goes before the Board. A request for information must be made in writing on the Board's form.

Criminal Justice Commission, Arizona
1700 North Seventh Avenue, Suite 250
Phoenix, AZ 85007
(602) 255-1928
Statutory Authority: *A.R.S.* §§41-2401 to 41-2416.

Deaf and Blind, Arizona State School for,
Board of Directors
Box 5545
Tucson, AZ 85703
(602) 628-5357
Statutory Authority: *A.R.S.* §15-1321.

Dental Examiners, State Board of
5060 North 19th Avenue, Suite 406
Phoenix, AZ 85015
(602) 255-3696
Statutory Authority: *A.R.S.* §§32-1201 to 32-1212.

Attorneys representing the doctor have access to the entire file, while those representing the complainant have access only to public information. Must request information in writing. Minutes of preliminary hearings are kept for 3 years at the Board, and 10 years are maintained at Records Management (19th Avenue and Jefferson). Invoice is sent with copies.

Developmental Disabilities, Governor's Council on
1717 West Jefferson, Code 0742
Phoenix, AZ 85007
(602) 255-4049
Statutory Authority: *A.R.S.* §§41-2451 to 41-2454.

Disease Control Research Commission
c/o Department of Health
1740 West Adams, Room 407
Phoenix, AZ 85007
(602) 542-1024
Statutory Authority: *A.R.S.* §§36-272 to 36-273.

Economic Security, Department of
1717 West Jefferson
Phoenix, AZ 85007
(602) 542-4791
Statutory Authority: *A.R.S.* §§41-1951 to 41-2022.

Education, Department of
1535 West Jefferson
Phoenix, AZ 85007
(602) 542-5393
Statutory Authority: *A.R.S.* §§15-231 to 15-239.

Transcripts of hearings before the State Board become public record (with the exception of student names and testimonies) and are available.

Education, Postsecondary, Arizona Commission for
3030 North Central Avenue, Suite 1407
Phoenix, AZ 85012
(602) 255-3109
Statutory Authority: Ariz. Exec. Order 88-23.

Education, Private Postsecondary, Board for
East Annex
1624 West Adams, Room 102
Phoenix, AZ 85007
(602) 542-5709
Statutory Authority: *A.R.S.* §§32-3001 to 32-3004.

Education, State Board of
1535 West Jefferson
Phoenix, AZ 85007
(602) 542-5057
Statutory Authority: Ariz. Const., art XI, §3; *A.R.S.* §§15-201 to 15-214.

Education, Vocational, State Council on
4725 North 19th Avenue, Suite 2
Phoenix, AZ 85015
(602) 255-5040
Statutory Authority: *A.R.S.* §§15-781 to 15-790.

Emergency and Military Affairs, Department of
5636 East McDowell Road
Phoenix, AZ 85008
(602) 267-2710
National Guard: (602) 267-2700
Emergency Services Division: (602) 244-0504
Statutory Authority: *A.R.S.* §§26-101 to 26-102; 26-305.

Employment and Training Council, Arizona
1300 West Washington, Second Floor
Phoenix, AZ 85007
(602) 542-5945
Statutory Authority: U.S. Pub. L. No. 47-300.

Environment, Commission on Arizona
1645 West Jefferson, Room 416
Phoenix, AZ 85007
(602) 542-2102
Statutory Authority: *A.R.S.* §49-121.

Environmental Quality, Department of
2005 North Central Avenue
Phoenix, AZ 85004
(602) 257-2300
Statutory Authority: *A.R.S.* §§49-101 to 49-161.

Hearings are held on major environmental issues. Transcripts are available at Court Reporter Service. Contact individual subdepartment for information on other retrieval and photocopying. The Department issued a brochure entitled the "Guide to Program Information" to assist with due diligence searches.

Foster Care Review Boards
Supreme Court
1314 North Third Street, Suite 200
Phoenix, AZ 85004
(602) 253-5700
Statutory Authority: *A.R.S.* §§8-515.01 to 8-515.04.

Fruit and Vegetable Standardization
2720 West Weldon Avenue
Phoenix, AZ 85017
(602) 264-0556

Funeral Directors and Embalmers, Board of
1645 West Jefferson, Room 410
Phoenix, AZ 85007
(602) 542-3095
Statutory Authority: *A.R.S.* §§32-1301 to 32-1310.

Public records are only available after Board has made a decision. Must fill out a request form for photocopies. There may be a charge for researching.

Game and Fish Commission
2222 West Greenway Road
Phoenix, AZ 85023
(602) 942-3000
Statutory Authority: *A.R.S.* §17-201.

Game and Fish, Department of
2222 West Greenway Road
Phoenix, AZ 85023
(602) 942-3000
Statutory Authority: *A.R.S.* §§17-201 to 17-281.

Governor's Regulatory Review Council
West Wing, Room 801
1700 West Washington
Phoenix, AZ 85007
(602) 542-5822
Statutory Authority: *A.R.S.* §§41-1051 to 41-1055.

Grain Research and Promotion Council, Arizona
c/o Agriculture and Horticulture Commission
1688 West Adams, Room 421
Phoenix, AZ 85007
(602) 542-4373
Statutory Authority: *A.R.S.* §§3-581 to 3-594.

Health Care Cost Containment System Administration (AHCCCS)
801 East Jefferson
Phoenix, AZ 85034
(602) 234-3655
Statutory Authority: *A.R.S.* §§36-2901 to 36-2974.

Health, Physical Fitness and Sports, Governor's Council on
1740 West Adams, Room 409
Phoenix, AZ 85007
(602) 542-6396
Authority: Ariz. Exec. Order 85-1.

Health Services, Department of
1740 West Adams
Phoenix, AZ 85007
(602) 542-1000
Statutory Authority: *A.R.S.* §§36-101 to 36-118.

Hearing Impaired, Arizona Council for
1300 West Washington, Second Floor
Phoenix, AZ 85007
(602) 542-3323
Statutory Authority: *A.R.S.* §§36-1941 to 36-1947.

Highway Safety, Representative, Governor's
3010 North Second Street, Suite 105
Phoenix, AZ 85012
(602) 255-3216
Statutory Authority: *A.R.S.* §28-611 (1989); Ariz. Exec. Order 87-7.

Historical Society, Arizona
949 East Second Street
Tucson, AZ 85719
(602) 682-5774
Statutory Authority: *A.R.S.* §§41-821 to 41-825.

Historical Society, Prescott
415 West Gurley Street
Prescott, AZ 86301
(602) 445-3122
Statutory Authority: *A.R.S.* §§41-831 to 41-834.

Homeopathic Medical Examiners, Board of
1645 West Jefferson, Room 410
Phoenix, AZ 85007
(602) 542-3095
Statutory Authority: *A.R.S.* §§32-2901 to 32-2907.

Must first submit a written request, then return the Board's photocopy request form before copying will be initiated. There may be an additional charge for researching.

Humanities Council, Arizona
1242 North Central
Phoenix, AZ 85004
(602) 257-0335
Statutory Authority: U.S. Pub. Law No. 94-462.

Indian Affairs, Commission of
1645 West Jefferson, Room 422
Phoenix, AZ 85007
(602) 542-3123
Statutory Authority: *A.R.S.* §§41-541 to 41-543.

Industrial Commission of Arizona
800 West Washington
Phoenix, AZ 85007
(602) 542-4661
Statutory Authority: *A.R.S.* §§23-101 to 23-110.

Portions of files are available for public review. Representing attorneys must make a written request for entire file. Call one day prior for file retrieval. An invoice will be sent with copies. Hearing transcripts are available at Court Reporter Service. *Arizona Advance Reports* publishes administrative decisions.

Insurance, Department of
3030 North Third Street, Suite 1100
Phoenix, AZ 85012
(602) 255-5400
Statutory Authority: *A.R.S.* §§20-101 to 20-173.

Hearings are for revocation of agent's license and company audit. Make appointment with the Complaint Division to view file, then ask for the examination of a specific company (give name). By state law, you must sign form before copies can be made. No phone or mail-in requests.

Land Department
1616 West Adams, Room 329
Phoenix, AZ 85007
(602) 542-4621
Statutory Authority: *A.R.S.* §§37-101 to 37-108.

Land Department Board of Appeals
1616 West Adams, Third Floor
Phoenix, AZ 85007
Info.: (602) 542-4603
Public Records: (602) 542-4631
Statutory Authority: *A.R.S.* §§37-213 to 37-215.

Hearings are held on property reclassification and state land sales. The hearings are taped and a copy can be purchased. Transcripts are made only when a case goes to the Superior Court. Call to view file. The file number or name is needed to access.

Law Enforcement Merit System Council
2102 West Encanto Boulevard, Suite 250
P.O. Box 6638
Phoenix, AZ 85005
(602) 223-2286
Statutory Authority: *A.R.S.* §§28-234.01 to 28-240.

Law Enforcement Officer Advisory Council
3001 West Indian School Road, Suite 17
Phoenix, AZ 85005
(602) 223-2514
Statutory Authority: *A.R.S.* §§41-1821 to 41-1828.01.

Library, Archives and Public Records, Department of
State Capitol
Third Floor
Phoenix, AZ 85007
(602) 542-3701
Statutory Authority: *A.R.S.* §§41-1331 to 41-1354.

Liquor Board, State
800 West Washington, Room 500
Phoenix, AZ 85007
(602) 542-5141
Statutory Authority: *A.R.S.* §§4-111 to 4-119.

Hearings are on audio cassettes. Copies are also available of transcripts. Files containing application for license, questionnaires and disposition report may be copied. A certified copy is available for a separate charge.

Liquor Licenses and Control, Department of
800 West Washington, Fifth Floor
Phoenix, AZ 85007
(602) 542-5141
Statutory Authority: *A.R.S.* §§4-111 to 4-119.

Lottery Commission, Arizona State
4740 East University
Phoenix, AZ 85034
(602) 921-4400
Statutory Authority: *A.R.S.* §§5-501 to 5-512.01.

Manufactured Housing, Board of
701 East Jefferson, Room 200
Phoenix, AZ 85034
(602) 255-4072
Statutory Authority: *A.R.S.* §41-2143 to 41-2144.

Medical Examiners, Board of
2001 West Camelback Road, Suite 300
Phoenix, AZ 85015
(602) 255-3751
Statutory Authority: *A.R.S.* §§32-1401 to 32-1407.

Requests must be submitted in writing. Public information includes the file of individual doctors and the transcripts of any actions the Board took resulting in discipline or advisory action. An invoice may be sent with photocopies. *See also* Allen G. Minker, "Medical Malpractice: How the Board of Medical Examiners Investigates," *Arizona Bar Journal* 20, no. 5 (February/March 1985): 11-12.

Medical Radiologic Technology, Board of Examiners
4814 South 40th Street
Phoenix. AZ 85040
(602) 255-4845
Statutory Authority: *A.R.S.* §32-2802.

Mines and Mineral Resources, Department of
Minerals Building, Fairgrounds
Phoenix, AZ 85007
(602) 255-3791
Statutory Authority: *A.R.S.* §§27-101 to 27-111.

Motion Picture and Television Advisory Board, Arizona Governor's
3800 North Central
Phoenix, AZ 85012
(602) 280-1300
Authority: Ariz. Exec. Order 77-1.

Naturopathic Physician's Board of Examiners
1645 West Jefferson, Room 410
Phoenix, AZ 85007
(602) 542-3095
Statutory Authority: *A.R.S.* §§32-1501 to 32-1506.

No telephone requests. A copy request form must be filled out prior to the initiation of any photocopying. An additional charge may be placed on lengthy documents.

Nursing, Board of
2001 West Camelback Road, Suite 350
Phoenix, AZ 85015
(602) 255-5092
Statutory Authority: *A.R.S.* §§32-1601 to 32-1611.

Written requests are preferred. Copies are available of hearings, formal complaints, notice, pleadings, witness list and exhibit list.

Nursing Care Institution Administrators, Licensing Board of
1645 West Jefferson, Room 410
Phoenix, AZ 85007
(602) 542-3095
Statutory Authority: *A.R.S.* §36-446.02.

No phone requests. Must fill out a photocopy request form prior to the issuance of copies. There may be an additional charge depending upon the length of the request.

Occupational Safety and Health Review Board
800 West Washington
Phoenix, AZ 85007
(602) 542-5795
Statutory Authority: *A.R.S.* §§23-422 to 23-423.

Each judge maintains his/her separate files. Call the secretary of the deciding judge for information on document retrieval. Phone requests for photocopies are allowed. Files can also be reviewed at the Board.

Oil and Gas Conservation Commission
5150 North 16th Street, Suite B-141
Phoenix, AZ 85016
(602) 255-5161
Statutory Authority: *A.R.S.* §§27-514 to 27-527.

Minutes of meetings and hearings can be reviewed at the Commission.

Opticians, Board of Dispensing
1645 West Jefferson, Room 410
Phoenix, AZ 85007
(602) 542-3095
Statutory Authority: *A.R.S.* §§32-1671 to 32-1674.

Optometry, State Board of
1645 West Jefferson, Room 410
Phoenix, AZ 85007
(602) 542-3095
Statutory Authority: *A.R.S.* §§32-1701 to 32-1705.

No phone request. Must fill out a copy request form prior to the issuance of photocopies. There may be an additional charge depending upon the length of the request.

Osteopathic Examiners in Medicine and Surgery, Arizona Board
1830 West Colter, Suite 104
Phoenix, AZ 85015
(602) 255-1747
Statutory Authority: *A.R.S.* §§32-1800 to 32-1806.

Board minutes and disciplinary actions taken against doctors are available. Must send a written request for copies of hearings. Appointments are necessary to review files.

Outdoor Recreation Coordinating Commission, Arizona
800 West Washington, Suite 415
Phoenix, AZ 85007
(602) 542-4174
Statutory Authority: *A.R.S.* §§41-511.25 to 41-511.26.

Pardons and Paroles, Board of
1645 West Jefferson, Suite 326
Phoenix, AZ 85007
(602) 542-5656
Statutory Authority: *A.R.S.* §§31-401 to 31-402.

Inmate files including letters of support, hearing officer report, pre-sentencing report, and progress reports are available to the public. Medical records, psychological and victim records are not included. Call one day ahead of visit to make sure a file is available.

Parks Board, Arizona State
800 West Washington, Suite 415
Phoenix, AZ 85007
(602) 542-4172
Statutory Authority: *A.R.S.* §§41-511 to 41-511.23.

Personnel Board, State
5050 North 19th Avenue, Room 208
Phoenix, AZ 85015
(602) 255-3888
Statutory Authority: *A.R.S.* §§41-781 to 41-786.

The Hearing Officer hears appeals, disciplinary actions, etc. and makes recommendations to the Board. There may be either an open or closed hearing. The Board renders the final decision. Files are available for viewing for open hearings only. No photocopying is possible at the Board. Arrangements can be made, however, to borrow files.

Pharmacy, Arizona State Board of
5060 North 19th Avenue, Suite 101
Phoenix, AZ 85015
(602) 255-5125

402 West Congress, Room 213A
Tucson, AZ 85701
(602) 628-5471
Statutory Authority: *A.R.S.* §§32-1901 to 32-1908.

No information is given out for ongoing investigations except to a client. Once the decision is rendered, however, the file becomes public. A written request must be submitted for photocopying.

Physical Therapy Examiners, Board of
1645 West Jefferson, Room 410
Phoenix, AZ 85007
(602) 542-3095
Statutory Authority: *A.R.S.* §§32-2001 to 32-2005.

Must fill out a copy request form prior to the issuance of photocopies. Need name of case to retrieve file. There may be an additional charge, depending upon the length of the request.

Physician's Assistants, Joint Board on the Regulation of
2001 West Camelback Road, Room 300
Phoenix, AZ 85015
(602) 255-3751
Statutory Authority: *A.R.S.* §§32-2501 to 32-2506.

Information available includes actions, transcripts and dismissals. Must submit a written request for photocopies. Transcripts must be requested specifically. Information on dismissals are found in Board minutes. Without reference to a name and specific date, the Board will not research dismissals. The files are available, however, for public examination. Copies can be invoiced.

Pioneers Home and Disabled Miners Hospital
Superintendent
300 S. McCormick Street
Prescott, AZ 86303
(602) 445-2181
Statutory Authority: *A.R.S.* §§41-921 to 41-925.

Podiatry Examiners, Board of
1645 West Jefferson, Room 410
Phoenix, AZ 85007
(602) 542-3095
Statutory Authority: *A.R.S.* §§32-801 to 32-806.

No phone requests. Must fill out a copy request form prior to the issuance of photocopies. Need the name of the party to retrieve file. There may be an additional charge, depending upon the length of the request.

Power Authority Commission, Arizona
1810 West Adams Street
Phoenix, AZ 85007
(602) 542-4263
Statutory Authority: *A.R.S.* §§30-105 to 30-108.

Prosecuting Attorneys Advisory Council
3001 West Indian School Road
Phoenix, AZ 85017
(602) 265-4779
Statutory Authority: *A.R.S.* §§41-1830 to 41-1830.05.

Psychologist Examiners, Board of
1645 West Jefferson, Room 410
Phoenix, AZ 85007
(602) 542- 3095
Statutory Authority: *A.R.S.* §§32-2061 to 32-2063.

Must fill out a copy request form prior to the issuance of photocopies. Need the name of the party to retrieve file. There may be an additional charge, depending upon the length of the request.

Public Safety, Department of
2102 West Encanto
Phoenix, AZ 85009
or
P.O. Box 6638
Phoenix, AZ 85005
(602) 223-2000
Statutory Authority: *A.R.S.* §41-1711.

Public Safety Personnel Retirement System, Fund Managers
1020 East Missouri
Phoenix, AZ 85014
(602) 255-5575
Statutory Authority: *A.R.S.* §§38-848; 38-850.

Racing Commission, Arizona
500 West Washington, Suite 515
Phoenix, AZ 85007
(602) 542-5151
Statutory Authority: *A.R.S.* §§5-102 to 5-104.

Disciplinary actions are heard before a Hearing Officer, and may be appealed to the Racing Commission. Must submit a written request for photocopying. Copies cannot be made until the file is closed and the information becomes public.

Racing, Department of
800 West Washington, Suite 515
Phoenix, AZ 85007
(602) 542-5151
Statutory Authority: *A.R.S.* §5-101.01.

Radiation Regulatory Authority
4514 South 40th Street
Phoenix, AZ 85040
(602) 255-4845
Statutory Authority: *A.R.S.* §§30-652; 30-654.

Radiation Regulatory Hearing Board
4514 South 40th Street
Phoenix, AZ 85040
(602) 255-4845
Statutory Authority: *A.R.S.* §§30-653; 30-655.

No phone request. Preference is for requestor to place order in person for copies. Need the name of the licensee for request.

Real Estate, Department of
202 East Earll Drive, Suite 400
Phoenix, AZ 85012
(602) 255-4345
Statutory Authority: *A.R.S.* §§32-2101 to 32-2112.

Information is available on actions against a licensee. Must go in person to view a hearing file and place order for photocopying.

Regents, Arizona Board of
3030 North Central, Suite 1400
Phoenix, Az 85012
(602) 255-4082
Statutory Authority: *A.R.S.* §§15-1621 to 15-1646.

Residential Utility Consumer Board
34 West Monroe, Suite 512
Phoenix, AZ 85003
(602) 255-1431
Statutory Authoriry: *A.R.S.* §40-463.

Residential Utility Consumer Office
34 West Monroe, Suite 512
Phoenix, AZ 85003
(602) 255-1431
Statutory Authority: *A.R.S.* §§40-461 to 40-464.

Retirement System Board, State
3815 North Black Canyon Highway
Phoenix, AZ 85015
(602) 255-5131
Statutory Authority: *A.R.S.* §§38-742 to 38-743.01.

Retirement System Investment Advisory Council
3815 North Black Canyon Highway
Phoenix, AZ 85015
(602) 255-5131
Statutory Authority: *A.R.S.* §38-743.05.

Revenue, Department of
1600 West Monroe
Phoenix, AZ 85007
(602) 542-3572
Statutory Authority: *A.R.S.* §§42-101 to 42-110.

Solar Energy Advisory Council
c/o Department of Commerce
State Capitol, West Wing
Phoenix, AZ 85007
(602) 542-5371
Statutory Authority: *A.R.S.* §41-1510.

Structural Pest Control Commission
1150 South Priest, Suite 4
Tempe, AZ 85281
(602) 255-3664
Statutory Authority: *A.R.S.* §§32-2301 to 32-2306.

Tax Appeals, State Board of
1645 West Jefferson
Phoenix., AZ 85007
Division 1: (602) 542-5462
Division 2: (602) 542-3288
Statutory Authority: *A.R.S.* §§42-171 to 42-176.

For Division 1 (property valuation) requests, either walk-in or written requests will be honored. Can be invoiced for photocopies.

For Division 2 (incomes, sales and use, etc.) requests, either phone or written requests will be honored. Can be invoiced for photocopies. Both WESTLAW and LEXIS have Division 2 decisions from 1982 to date. The State Law Library also gets copies of these decisions.

Technical Registration, State Board of
1951 West Camelback Road, Suite 50
Phoenix, AZ 85015
(602) 255-4053
Statutory Authority: *A.R.S.* §§32-101 to 32-110.

Prior to the file being closed, a written request must be sent for the release of public information for non-commercial use. Once the file is closed, it becomes public and copies can be made without the release.

Tourism, Office of
1100 West Washington
Phoenix, AZ 85007
(602) 542-8687
Statutory Authority: *A.R.S.* §§41-2301 to 41-2306.

Transportation, Department of
206 South 17th Avenue
Phoenix, AZ 85007
(602) 255-7011
Statutory Authority: *A.R.S.* §§28-103 to 28-104.

Uniform State Laws, Commission on
6900 East Camelback Road, Suite 1040
Phoenix, AZ 85251
(602) 949-8998
Statutory Authority: *A.R.S.* §§41-1306 to 41-1307.

Utility Consumer Office, Residential
34 West Monroe, Suite 512
Phoenix, AZ 85003
(602) 255-1431
Statutory Authority: *A.R.S.* §40-462 (1985).

Veterans' Service Commission, Arizona
3225 North Central Avenue, Suite 910
Phoenix, AZ 85012
(602) 255-4713

Veterinarian, State
1688 West Adams, Room 21
Phoenix, AZ 85007
(602) 542-4293
Statutory Authority: *A.R.S.* §§3-1211 to 3-1213.

Veterinary Medical Examining Board
1645 West Jefferson, Room 410
Phoenix, AZ 85007
(602) 542-3095
Statutory Authority: *A.R.S.* §§32-2201 to 32-2206.

Must fill out a copy request form prior to the issuance of photocopies. Need name of party to pull file. There may be an additional charge, based on the length of the request.

Water Commission, Arizona
15 South 15th Avenue
Phoenix, AZ 85007
(602) 542-1553
Statutory Authority: *A.R.S.* §§45-121 to 45-125.

Water Quality Appeals Board
Clerk (located at Department of Administration)
(602) 542-0056
Statutory Authority: *A.R.S.* §§49-322 to 49-324.

Appeals are from the decisions of the Department of Environmental Quality. A three-page request form must be submitted when requesting the "Notice of Appeals." Call and the form will be mailed out.

Water Resource, Department of
15 South 15th Avenue
Phoenix, AZ 85007
(602) 542-1550
Statutory Authority: *A.R.S.* §§45-101 to 45-113.

Weights and Measures, Department of
1951 West North Lane
Phoenix, AZ 85021
(602) 255-5211

Women's Services, Governor Office of
Capitol, West Wing, Room 601
Phoenix, AZ 85007
(602) 542-1755

Illustration A

STATE OF ARIZONA

OFFICE OF THE ATTORNEY GENERAL

1275 WEST WASHINGTON, PHOENIX 85007

GRANT WOODS
ATTORNEY GENERAL

MAIN PHONE : 542-5025
TELECOPIER : 542-4085

February 13, 1991

Ronald W. Dalrymple
Executive Director
Board of Technical Registration
1951 West Camelback Road, Suite 250
Phoenix, Arizona 85015

RE: I91-011 (R90-132)

Dear Mr. Dalrymple:

You have asked our opinion on two questions relating to the licensing of professional engineers and private investigators. You first require whether an engineer who is called upon to investigate the origin of fires involving electrical apparatus, and then testify at trial as an expert witness regarding the cause and origin of fires involving electrical components, must have a private investigator's license. Next, you inquire whether a licensed private investigator who investigates a matter involving engineering must become a licensed professional engineer.

For the reasons that follow, we conclude that an engineer so engaged need not become licensed as a private investigator. We further conclude that private investigators normally need not become licensed professional engineers in order to investigate matters involving engineering.

Chapter 24 of Title 32, Arizona Revised Statutes, regulates the conduct of private investigators. A private investigator is defined in A.R.S. § 32-2401(7), which provides in pertinent part:

> "Private investigator" means a person . . . who, for any consideration, engages in business or accepts employment to furnish, or agrees to make, or makes, any investigation for the purpose of obtaining information with reference to:
>
> (d) The cause or responsibility for fires, libels, losses, accidents, or damage or injury to persons or property.

Reprinted from *Arizona Attorney General Opinion,* 1991.

Illustration B

Arizona Administrative Register

Proposed Rules

Dated: January 16, 1991 /s/ Leonard J. Kirschner, M.D., M.P.H., Director

Filed in the Office of the Secretary of State 2/12/91

TITLE 14. PUBLIC SERVICE CORPORATIONS; CORPORATIONS AND ASSOCIATIONS; SECURITIES REGULATION

CH. 2. CORPORATION COMMISSION FIXED UTILITIES

The undersigned hereby gives notice that, pursuant to the statutory authority of A.R.S. §§ 28-202 and 28-1571, the following action is proposed:

Adopt

Article 8.	Customer owned pay telephones
R14-2-801.	Definitions
R14-2-802.	Application for certificate of convenience and necessity
R14-2-803.	Grant of certificate of convenience and necessity
R14-2-804.	Application for adjudication not a public service corporation
R14-2-805.	Generic (Streamlined) COPT Tariff
R14-2-806.	Special (Non-Streamlined) COPT Tariff
R14-2-807.	Reporting requirements
R14-2-808.	Violations

Summary

The Arizona Corporation Commission proposes to add Article 8 to its fixed utility rules to establish procedures for streamlined regulation of Customer Owned Pay Telephones (COPTs). The primary Commission objective is to promote uniform standards of service and pricing for public pay telephones.

Governor's Regulatory Review Council

Not applicable.

Opportunity for Public Comment

Notice is given that any person may file written comments on the proposed rulemaking with the agency contact person on or before April 12, 1991.

Contact: Richard Kauffman, 1200 West Washington Street, Phoenix, Arizona 85007, (602) 542-0853.

The Agency has scheduled oral proceedings to be held at the Arizona Corporation Commission, 1200 West Washington Street, Phoenix, Arizona, at the hour of 1:00 p.m. on the fifth day of April, 1991.

Dated: February 14, 1991 /s/ James Matthews, Executive Secretary

Filed in the Office of the Secretary of State 2/14/91

TITLE 16. TAX APPEALS

CH. 2. BOARD OF TAX APPEALS-DIVISION ONE (PROPERTY VALUATION)

The undersigned hereby gives notice that, pursuant to the statutory authority of A.R.S. §§ 42-172(B) and (C) and 41-1003, the following action is proposed:

Repeal

Article 1.	Appeals Hearing
R16-2-101.	In general
R16-2-102.	Hearings before Division One
R16-2-103.	Hearings before one member of Division One or a hearing officer
R16-2-104.	Priority of cases
R16-2-105.	Order of assignment of hearing dates
R16-2-106.	Form of petition
R16-2-107.	Procedure upon receipt of petition or appeals
R16-2-108.	Proof of service of notice of appeal
R16-2-109.	Service of pleadings and motions
R16-2-110.	Subpoenas
R16-2-111.	Answer by State
R16-2-112.	Testimony under oath
R16-2-113.	Order of proceedings in hearings
R16-2-114.	Right of cross-examination
R16-2-115.	Continuances and recesses
R16-2-116.	Objections
R16-2-117.	Use of copies as evidence
R16-2-118.	Dismissal for lack of jurisdiction, withdrawals
R16-2-119.	Submission of case on the record
R16-2-120.	Decisions of Division One
R16-2-121.	Representation before Division One
R16-2-122.	Record of proceedings

Adopt

Article 1.	General Provisions
R16-2-101.	Definitions
R16-2-102.	Filing with and appearing before the Board
R16-2-103.	Appeal forms and filing procedures
R16-2-104.	Rules of evidence
R16-2-105.	Motions and pleadings
R16-2-106.	Proof of service by the Assessor or the Department
R16-2-107.	Subpoena
R16-2-108.	On the Record hearing
R16-2-109.	Transcripts and records of proceedings
R16-2-110.	Order of hearing procedure
R16-2-111.	Testimony under oath
R16-2-112.	Request for additional information
R16-2-113.	Withdrawals
R16-2-114.	Decisions of the Board

Summary

The Board is proposing new rules to enhance and support existing statutory provisions and provide additional guidance to taxpayers and government agencies who file with and appear before the Board. The proposed rules are structured to direct taxpayers through a complex system of procedures.

Instituting the rulemaking statutes and guidelines resulted in disjointed flow of the existing rules. Because of extensive changes, the Board is proposing to repeal existing rules R16-2-101 through R16-2-122 and replace them with language which is clear, concise, understandable, and reorganized to follow chronological steps in filing an appeal. With the exception of a new definition Section, no new requirements have been introduced.

Governor's Regulatory Review Council

The proposed rules with the economic impact, cost/benefit analysis, and impact on small businesses, were heard by the Governor's Regulatory Review Council on February 5, 1991.

Reprinted from *Arizona Administrative Code,* 1991.

Illustration C

ARTICLE 8. RESERVED

ARTICLE 9. ADMINISTRATIVE HEARINGS, REHEARINGS AND APPEAL

ARTICLE 1. RESERVED

ARTICLE 2. TITLES AND REGISTRATION

R17-4-201. Reserved

R17-4-202. Reserved

R17-4-203. Reserved

R17-4-204. Certificate of Title

A. Security features -- Certificate of Title will be printed on paper utilizing security features which hinder counterfeiting or alteration.

B. Contents of certificate -- The State of Arizona, Motor Vehicle Division, Certificate of Title shall contain space for the following information:
   1. Title information -- title number, issue date, title control number, previous title number, state of previous title and date, month and year first registered and type of title being issued.
   2. Vehicle information -- type, status, vehicle identification number, model year, make, body style, model, fuel type, odometer code, month and year of manufacture, factory list price, previous vehicle mechanical or structural condition and gross vehicle weight.
   3. Lienholder information -- names and addresses of all lienholders.
   4. Vehicle owner information -- name and street address of owner(s).
   5. Mailing information -- name and mailing address of owner or owner's legal designee.
   6. Ownership change information -- date of sale, name and address of purchaser, new lienholder information, odometer statement, signature of seller, notary statement, and dealer reassignment information.

Historical Note

Adopted effective November 10, 1986 (Supp. 86-6). Former Section R17-4-75 renumbered without change as Section R17-4-204 (Supp. 87-2).

R17-4-205. Application for Arizona Certificate of Title and Registration

A. The application for Arizona Certificate of Title and Registration shall contain space for the following:
   1. Vehicle information -- title number, license number, tab number and year of tab number, tab expiration date, the month and year first registered, make, year, body style, model, status, list price, gross vehicle weight, fuel type, Motor Vehicle Division Tax Account Number, Division index number, vehicle identification number, odometer reading, previous title number, state of previous title, previous title date, whether the vehicle was acquired new or used, name and address of person from whom procured, whether vehicle will be rented without a driver and whether the vehicle is specially constructed or reconstructed.
   2. Applicant information -- first, middle and last name, legal status of ownership, date of birth, driver's license or federal identification number, current street address, city, county, state, zip code number, and whether applicant's registration rights are under suspension.
   3. Lienholder information – name and address of all lienholders, amount of each lien and date of each lien.
   4. Mobile home information -- name of mobile home manufacturer, site of physical location of mobile home.
   5. Motor Vehicle Division information -- information needed for in-house agency use.
   6. Joint tenancy information -- whether the applicants intend to hold the title as joint tenants with rights of survivorship.
   7. Duplicate title information -- whether the original title was lost, destroyed, mutilated or has become illegible and certifying that the title has not been assigned or surrendered.
   8. Certification -- applicant certification that applicant is the owner of the vehicle, has listed all liens and encumbrances and acknowledges the odometer reading as qualified by the seller and has met mandatory insurance requirements.
   9. Signature and verification -- signatures of applicants and a notary public or Motor Vehicle Division agent.
   10. Joint ownership instructions -- printed information defining joint ownership conditions shown by "or" -- "and" -- "and/or".
   11. Odometer -- printed information explaining odometer reading codes.

B. Except as provided for in subsection (C), no Application for Arizona Certificate of Title and Registration will be processed and no certificate of title or registration will be issued unless all information required on the application has been provided by the applicant.

C. The applicant may provide the following information on a voluntary basis:
   1. Applicant's date of birth.
   2. Applicant's driver's license number.
   3. Applicant's federal employer identification number, if the applicant is an organization taking title as a sole proprietor partnership, corporation or other legal entity.

Historical Note

Adopted effective November 13, 1986 (Supp. 86-6). Former Section R17-4-75 renumbered without change as Section R17-4-205 (Supp. 87-2).

R17-4-206. Title sign-off by owner must be witnessed

Requiring a verification by owner when transferring title to a motor vehicle.
   1. Section 66-211, A.C.A. 139 as amended, relating to transfer of Title, reads in part and provides that the owner "shall also endorse on the back of the Certificate of Title to such vehicle, if issued, any assignment thereof, with the warranty of Title in the form printed thereon, and shall deliver the same to the purchaser or transferee at the time of delivery to him of such motor vehicle, except as provided in section 1640a".
   2. It is of prime importance that the purchaser or transferee, referred to in the above quoted section, have assurance of the genuineness of the assignment and warranty.

Reprinted from *Arizona Administrative Code,* 1990.

Illustration D

TABLE OF TITLES AND CHAPTER HEADINGS

9. Livestock Board
10. Agricultural Chemicals and Environmental Services Division, Arizona Commission of Agriculture and Horticulture
11. Veterinary Medical Examining Board
12. Cotton Research and Protection Council
13. Grain Research and Promotion Council, Arizona

TITLE 4. COMMERCE, PROFESSIONS, AND OCCUPATIONS

Chap.
1. Accountancy, Board of
2. Agricultural Employment Relations Board
3. Boxing Commission, State
4. Banking Department
5. Barber Examiners, Board of
6. Reserved
7. Chiropractic Examiners, Board of
8. Reserved
9. Contractors, Registrar of
10. Cosmetology, Board of
11. Dental Examiners, State Board of
12. Funeral Directors and Embalmers, Board of
13. Industrial Commission of Arizona
14. Insurance, Department of
15. Liquor Licenses and Control, Department of
16. Medical Examiners, Board of
17. Physician's Assistants, Joint Board on the Regulation of
18. Naturopathic Physicians Board of Examiners, State
19. Nursing, Board of
20. Opticians, Board of Dispensing
21. Optometry, Board of
22. Osteopathic Examiners in Medicine and Surgery, Board of
23. Pharmacy, Board of
24. Physical Therapy Examiners, Board of
25. Podiatry Examiners, Board of
26. Psychologist Examiners, Board of
27. Racing Commission, Arizona
28. Real Estate Department
29. Structural Pest Control Board
30. Technical Registration, Board of
31. Weights and Measures, Department of
32. Joint Underwriting Plan Board of Directors
33. Nursing Care Institution Administrators, Board of Examiners for
34. Building and Fire Safety, Department of

6/30/87 Supp. 87-2 xviii © 1987 Arizona Secretary of State

Reprinted from *Arizona Administrative Register,* 1987.

Chapter 8

Municipal and Local Legislation

Kathy Shimpock-Vieweg

A. Introduction and Definitions

The resolution of legal issues often involves not only state and federal laws, but also an examination of local legislation. This legislation is generally comprised of charters, ordinances and codes promulgated by municipal or county governments as authorized by the state legislature.[1]

Charters are a city's organic law: a fundamental law analogous to a state's constitution. Charters delineate the powers vested in local governments.

Ordinances are local laws promulgated within limited areas of authority.[2] These are issued primarily in the areas of infrastructure; i.e., building, transportation, municipal services, education, environmental issues, taxation and zoning. Ordinances are analogous to state statutes.

1 In Arizona, *see generally,* Ariz. Rev. Stat. Ann. §§ 9-801 to 9-813, 9-240, 9-499.01, 11-251.05 (1990).

2 For example, Ariz. Const. art. 4, § 19; Ariz. Rev. Stat. Ann. §§ 9-219, 9-240, 11-251.05 (1990).

Codes are subject compilations of ordinances, sometimes containing annotations and other references. Charters are frequently included. Codes are compiled of ordinances current at the date of publication, but are usually designed for updating.

B. Local Government Structure

1. *Cities and Towns*

In Arizona cities and towns are statutorily classified into five groups: 1) towns of less than 600 voters, 2) towns between 600 to 850 voters, 3) towns between 850 to 3,000 in population, 4) cities over 3,000 in population, and 5) cities over 3,500 in population. Arizona law designates each community a "town" until its population has reached 3,000 and its council and voters have approved the incorporation. In actuality, there is little difference between a town and a city's government structure. Yet only a city has the ability to adopt a charter or the ward system for selecting council members. Arizona presently has 43 incorporated cities and 43 incorporated towns.[3]

Towns with a population less than 3,000 have a common council type of government. *Arizona Revised Statutes* § 9-240 enumerates the general powers delegated to the common council. These include the promulgation of regulations. A brief description of the government structure for cities and towns is given below.

a. Towns of less than 600 voters, *A.R.S.* §§ 9-201 to 203

Officers include a mayor, one council member from each ward and either a marshal or chief of police. The chief of police or marshal acts as the ex officio town license/tax collector, pound master, street commissioner and fire warden. Appointive officers include a clerk and treasurer.

b. Towns of 600 to 850 voters, *A.R.S.* §§ 9-20

Officers include a mayor, four council members, a chief of police, a treasurer and a recorder (who is the ex officio city auditor and police judge).

c. Towns of 850 to 3,000 in population, *A..R.S.* §§ 9-231 to 255

Officers include a mayor and five council members if the population is less than 1500. This can be increased to seven council members once the population exceeds 1500. Appointed officers are the town clerk (who acts as treasurer), the town marshal (who acts as the tax collector), and the town engineer. In towns less than 3,000, the town marshal may also act as the town engineer.

d. Cities over 3,000 in population, *A.R.S.* §§ 9-271 to 276

Once a town has obtained a population over 3,000 it may by resolution and majority vote assume a "city" organization. City officers include seven elected council members and a mayor. Appointed officers consist of a city clerk (who

3 *Local Government Directory* (Phoenix, AZ: The League of Arizona Cities and Towns, The Arizona Association of Counties, 1990).

acts as the ex officio treasurer), a city attorney, a city marshal or chief of police, a city physician and a city engineer. When required, a city health or sanitary officer, a superintendent of streets and a fire chief may also be hired. In addition, a city may elect to follow the ward system, thereby dividing the city into wards from which council members are elected.

e. Cities over 3,500 in population, *A.R.S.* §§ 9-281 to 285

Cities of this size may draw up a charter and submit it to their voters for approval. The governor must also approve the charter, after ascertaining whether it is in conflict with the constitution or any state law. Once approved, however, the charter operates as a repeal or suspension of any inconsistent laws. In addition, the office of city or town manager can now be created.

2. *Counties A.R.S. §§11-251, 11-401 et seq.*

County governments are important in Arizona for they serve a population located in largely uninhabited areas. Arizona has fifteen counties: Mohave, La Paz, Yuma, Coconino, Yavapai, Maricopa, Pinal, Pima, Santa Cruz, Navajo, Apache, Graham, Gila, Greenlee and Cochise.

Each county has the following officers: a sheriff, a county attorney, a county recorder, a treasurer (who acts as the ex officio tax collector), an assessor, a superintendent of schools, and a small board of supervisors (with 3 members unless a county's population is over 200,000, when it is increased to 5 members).[4] Non-elected county officers include a county manager and assistants; clerks of various boards; and heads of boards, commissions, or departments.

Arizona Revised Statutes § 11-251 lists all the powers and duties delegated to the Board of Supervisors. This includes to "make and enforce necessary rules and regulations for the government of its body, the preservation of order and the transaction of business."[5] In essence, the Board acts as an administrative unit of the state and is responsible for supervising county elections, law enforcement, transportation, and health and welfare services.

3. *Disincorporated cities or towns, A.R.S. §§ 9-211 to 226*

A Board of Trustees government is formed after the disincorporation of a city or town. This Board may pass ordinances to govern the area. The ordinances must be within its delegated corporate limits and not conflict with state law.

C. Local Publications and Records

County and municipal officers are required by law to "maintain all records reasonably necessary or appropriate to maintain an accurate knowledge of their official activities and of any activities which are supported by funds from the state or any political subdivision thereof."[6] These records must be transcribed,

4 Ariz. Rev. Stat. Ann. § 11-211 (1990).
5 Ariz. Rev. Stat. Ann. § 11-251(21) (1990).
6 Ariz. Rev. Stat. Ann. § 39-121.01(B) (1985).

maintained and stored in a manner conforming to the standards established by the Director of the Department of Library, Archives and Public Records.[7]

Public records and "other matters" may be open to public inspection during office hours.[8] Inspection may be denied, however, when a record is confidential under statute,[9] or when there are other countervailing considerations.[10]

A.R.S. § 39-121.01 authorizes charging a fee for copies, printouts, etc. of public records.

1. Cities and Towns

The *Arizona Revised Statutes* requires cities and towns to maintain the following records and publications:

a. Power of Council to Regulate Proceedings Records, *A.R.S.* §§ 9-234(B), 9-811

The clerk of the common council must maintain a journal of its proceedings and a record of all ordinances adopted. The proceedings of the common council are public. These minutes may be published as the council directs.

b. Publication of Financial Statement, *A.R.S.* § 9-246

The common council must publish or post a full statement of all monies received into the town treasury at least ten days before each biennial election. This statement will include all sources of funding, disbursements/expenditures and the accounts drawn upon.

c. Zoning Regulations, *A.R.S.* § 9-462.01

Enumerates the various areas subject to municipal zoning regulations.

d. Audits of Cities and Towns, *A.R.S.* § 9-481

An audit by a certified public accountant must be made each fiscal year for all incorporated cities, and at least every two fiscal years for incorporated towns. One copy of this report will be treated as a public record and available for inspection.

e. Enactment of Code of Public Record by Reference, *A.R.S.* §§ 9-801 to 804

These sections deal with technical trade codes (e.g., the building code, plumbing code, or fire prevention code).[11] It allows a municipality to adopt a technical code without actually setting forth its provisions. Instead, the technical code is incorporated by reference in the adopting ordinance. It must be published in full and at least three copies filed with the city clerk and available for public

7 Ariz. Rev. Stat. Ann. § 39-101 (1985).

8 Ariz. Rev. Stat. Ann. § 39-121 (1985).

9 *Berry v. State,* 145 Ariz. 12, 699 P.2d 387 (App. 1985).

10 *Mitchell v. Superior* Ct., 142 Ariz. 332, 690 P.2d 51 (1984).

11 Examples of these codes include: *The Uniform Building Code, The Uniform Mechanical Code* and *The Uniform Plumbing Code* (issued by the International Conference of Building Officials), and *The National Electric Code* (issued by the National Fire Protection Association).

inspection. A code or public record enacted by reference may be amended in the same manner.

f. City Charter, *A.R.S.* § 9-283(B)

A city charter, once certified and authenticated, must be filed with the Secretary of State, the city archives and the county recorder's office.

g. City and Town Ordinances, *A.R.S.* § 9-812

Requires the "publication" of laws and ordinances. Publication generally refers to notice placed within a newspaper of any changes or amendments.

The publication of municipal ordinances is somewhat of an enigma in Arizona. Every possible system for maintaining and storing these laws is employed. In small towns ordinances may be filed chronologically with no central compilation of current laws and no available index. Larger cities, however, may have professionally published codes containing historical notes, cross references, indexes, and disposition tables. (See Illustration A, p.204.) Some compilations are designed for easy supplementation but others are not updated between revisions. Most are reprinted irregularly. The League of Arizona Cities and Towns publishes many municipal ordinances but does not sell them commercially.

Current ordinances, therefore, are often difficult to locate due to their ephemeral nature. The Maricopa County Law Library and the State Department of Library Archives and Public Records have adequate collections but even these may not be current. Individual ordinances can best be obtained from the city or town clerk's office. In larger cities, zoning ordinances and technical codes may be obtained directly from the corresponding city director or officer.

Cities and towns usually charge a fee for photocopying current ordinances, and often shipping and handling charges. Compilations of ordinances or codes are more expensive. Contact the city clerk's office for pricing information.

Ordinances generally are in effect 30 days after passage by the council and after receiving mayoral approval. The corresponding council meeting minutes must also be certified by the clerk during this 30 day period.[12]

The best source for locating needed municipal and county directory listings is the *Local Government Directory* prepared by the League of Arizona Cities and Towns and the Arizona Association of Counties. This pamphlet is reprinted annually.

Another excellent source for community profiles and statistical data can be found in the *Arizona Community Profiles* issued by the Arizona Office of Economic Planning and Development. This book also includes information on Indian tribal communities. And finally, any local phone directory's governmental section provides an adequate listing of municipal and county offices.

A listing of municipal codes or ordinance compilations available for purchase is as follows. Complete bibliographic entries are provided only for larger cities. Unless stated otherwise, individual ordinances are available for purchase from

12 League of Arizona Cities and Towns, *Local Laws: How to Prepare, Pass and Publish* (Phoenix, AZ: The League, 1988), 3.

the clerk's office. Note: All out-of-zone telephone numbers must be prefixed by 602.

- Apache Junction (City) . . . . Clerk: 982-8002

  The City Code of Apache Junction. Apache Junction, AZ: League of Arizona Cities and Towns; 1990- 1 v. looseleaf.

  Updated regularly. Apache Junction also issues a *Land Development Code* (Zoning Ordinances).

- Avondale (City) . . . . Clerk: 932-2400

  A city code is available and updated quarterly.

- Benson (City) Clerk: 586-2245

  No city code is available.

- Bisbee (City) . . . . Clerk: 432-5446

  There is no printed city code available, however, the clerk's office is willing to photocopy the entire code (or the tax code) at a per page charge. Amendments and changes are sent to those on the city's mailing list for a small fee.

- Buckeye (Town) . . . . Clerk: 256-2488

  A city code is available. Annual supplements are mailed to purchasers.

- Bullhead City (City) . . . . Clerk: 763-9400

  A city code is available with updates.

- Camp Verde (Town) . . . . Clerk: 567-6631

  A city code, planning and zoning ordinances, and a zoning map are available. Call the clerk's office for any changes.

- Carefree (Town) . . . . Clerk: 488-3686

  There is no town code available.

- Casa Grande (City) . . . . Clerk: 421-8600

  A city code was adopted August 5, 1991 and is available for a charge. The code will be updated bi-annually.

- Cave Creek (Town) . . . . Clerk: 257-9011

  A town code is available. It is updated annually.

- Chandler (City) . . . . Clerk: 786-2231

  The Code of the City of Chandler, Arizona. Tallahassee, FL: Municipal Code Corporation, 1990-

  Looseleaf updated regularly. Chandler also issues the *Chandler Subdivision Code, Zoning Code* and *Tax Code.*

- Chino Valley (Town) . . . . Clerk: 636-2646

  There is no town code.

- Clarksdale (Town) . . . . Clerk: 634-9591

  A town code is available. Updates are mailed free of charge to purchasers on a mailing list.

- Clifton (Town) . . . . Clerk: 865-4146

  There is no town code.

- Colorado City (Town) . . . . Clerk: 875-2646

  There is no town code.

- Coolidge (City) . . . . Clerk: 723-5361

  A city code is available. Updates are mailed free of charge to purchasers.

- Cottonwood (City) . . . . Clerk: 634-5526

  There is no city code.

- Douglas (City) . . . . Clerk: 364-7501 Ext. 35

  There is no city code.

- Duncan (Town) . . . . Clerk: 359-2791

  There is no published town code.

- Eagar (Town) . . . . Clerk: 333-4128

  There is a town code published by the Book Publishing Co. of Seattle, WA (206-343-5700).

- El Mirage (City) . . . . Clerk: 972-8116

  A city code is available. There is a mailing list for updates.

- Eloy (City) . . . . Clerk: 466-9201

  There is no city code.

- Flagstaff (City) . . . . Clerk: 774-5281

  The city is in the process of codifying its ordinances. The *City of Flagstaff Charter* was issued as a pamphlet in 1978.

- Florence (Town) . . . . Clerk: 868-5889

  The town is in the process of codifying its ordinances with a completion date of 1992 expected. The clerk's office will not make copies of current information but will send out the older edition of the code.

- Fountain Hills (Town) . . . . Clerk: 837-2003

  A town code is not available. The clerk's office, however, will photocopy any or all ordinances for a fee.

- Fredonia (Town) . . . . Clerk: 643-7241

  There is no town code.

- Gila Bend (Town) . . . . Clerk: 683-2255

  There is no town code.

- Gilbert (Town) . . . . Clerk: 892-0802

  City Code of Gilbert. Gilbert, Az: City Planning Dept., 1984- 1 v. looseleaf. Updated regularly. There is also a *Zoning Code* and *Tax Code* issued.

- Glendale (City) . . . . Clerk: 435-4251

  City Code of Glendale. Tallahassee, FL: Municipal Code Corporation, 1985- 1 v. looseleaf. Updated regularly.

- Globe (City) . . . . Clerk: 425-7991

  There is no city code available.

- Goodyear (City) . . . . Clerk: 932-3910

  There is a city code and available updates. Note: There is no charge for the lst update received after purchase.

- Guadalupe (Town) . . . . Clerk: 730-3080

  There is no town code available.

- Hayden (Town) . . . . Clerk: 356-7801

  There is no town code available.

- Holbrook (City) . . . . Clerk: 524-6225

  There is a city code, but it is not available for purchase.

- Huachuca City (Town) . . . . Clerk: 456-1354

  There is no town code available.

- Jerome (Town) . . . . Clerk: 634-7943

  There is no town code available.

- Kearny (Town) . . . . Clerk: 363-5547

  There is no town code available.

- Kingman (City) . . . . Clerk: 753-8113

  City of Kingman, Arizona: General Ordinances of the City. Tallahassee, FL: Municipal Code Corporation, 1980- looseleaf.

  Updated regularly.

- Lake Havasu City (City) . . . . Clerk: 453-4142

  There is a city code issued with updates available.

- Litchfield Park (City) . . . . Clerk: 935-5033

  There is a city code available. Updates are issued.

- Mammoth (Town) . . . . Clerk: 487-2331

  The town code is presently being codified. There is no photocopying service available.

- Marana (Town) . . . . Clerk: 682-3401

  There is no town code available.

- Mesa (City) . . . . Clerk: 644-2381

  City Code of Mesa. Weiser, ID: Sterling Codifiers, Inc., 1990- 1 v. looseleaf. Updated regularly.

- Miami (Town) . . . . Clerk: 473-4403

  There is no town code available.

- Nogales (City) . . . . Clerk: 287-6571

  The city code is presently being codified.

- Oro Valley (Town) . . . . Clerk: 297-2591

  There is a town code available. Amendments will be issued at no charge.

- Page (City) . . . . Clerk: 645-8861

  There is a city code available. Amendments will be issued at no charge.

- Paradise Valley (Town) . . . . Clerk: 948-7411

  There is a town code available. Paradise Valley also issues zoning ordinances.

- Parker (Town) . . . . Clerk: 669-9265

  There is a town code available. Updates are sent free with the purchase price.

- Patagonia (Town) . . . . Clerk: 394-2229

  There is no town code available.

- Payson (Town) . . . . Clerk: 474-5242

  There is no town code available.

- Peoria (City) . . . . Clerk: 979-3720

  The city is in the process of compiling a code.

- Phoenix (City) . . . . Clerk: 262-6811

  City Code of Phoenix. Phoenix, AZ: Law Department City of Phoenix, 1951- 2 v. looseleaf. Updated regularly.

  Fire Prevention Code for the City of Phoenix Phoenix, AZ: City of Phoenix, Division of Fire Prevention, 1990- 1 v. looseleaf.

  City of Phoenix: Construction Code. Phoenix, AZ: City of Phoenix, Building Safety Department, 1980- 1 v. looseleaf.

  City of Phoenix: Model City Tax Code. Phoenix, AZ: City of Phoenix, 1987.

  The Zoning Ordinance of the City of Phoenix. Phoenix, AZ: City of Phoenix, 1991- 1 v.looseleaf.

  Note: The Phoenix City Clerk's office is the depository for all ordinances enacted by the council.

- Pima (Town) . . . . Clerk: 485-2611

  There is no town code available, although certain sections are preprinted (e.g., planning and zoning).

- Pinetop-Lakeside (Town) . . . . Clerk: 368-8696

  There is no town code available.

- Prescott (City) . . . . Clerk: 445-3500

  City Code of Prescott. Weiser, ID: Sterling Codifiers, Inc., 1964- 1 v. looseleaf. Updated regularly. A separate charter and a Zoning Code are also issued.

- Prescott Valley (Town) . . . . Clerk: 772-9207

  There is no town code available.

- Quartzsite (Town) . . . . Clerk: 927-4333

  There is no town code available.

- Queen Creek (Town) . . . . Clerk: 899-0077

  Town Code of the Town of Queen Creek, Arizona. Queen Creek, AZ: the Town, 1990-

- Safford (City) . . . . Clerk: 428-2762

  There is no city code available.

- St. Johns (City) . . . . Clerk: 337-4517

  There is no city code available.

- San Luis (City) . . . . Clerk: 627-2027

  The city is in the process of compiling a code.

- Scottsdale (City) . . . . Clerk: 994-2412

  Scottsdale Revised Code: General Ordinances of the City. Tallahassee, FL: Municipal Code Corporation, 1987- 2 v. looseleaf. Updated regularly.

  Scottsdale Zoning Ordinance No. 455. Scottsdale, AZ: City of Scottsdale, 1970? 1 v. looseleaf.

- Sedona (City) . . . . Clerk: 282-3113

  There is no city code available.

- Show Low (City) . . . . Clerk: 537-5724

  There is a city code available which is updated annually published by Municipal Code Corporation.The Zoning and Subdivision Ordinances can be purchased separately.

- Sierra Vista (City) . . . . Clerk: 458-3315

  There is no city code available.

- Snowflake (Town) . . . . Clerk: 536-7103

There is no town code available.

- Somerton (City) . . . . Clerk: 627-8866

  There is no city code available.

- South Tucson (City) . . . . Clerk: 792-2424

  South Tucson City Code: General Ordinances of the City. Tallahassee, FL: Municipal Code Corporation, 1989.

- Springerville (Town) . . . . Clerk: 333-2656

  There is no town code available.

- Superior (Town) . . . . Clerk: 689-5752

  There is no town code available.

- Surprise (Town) . . . . Clerk: 977-8369

  There is a town code available with supplements provided at no charge.

- Taylor (Town) . . . . Clerk: 536-7366

  There is no town code available.

- Tempe (City) . . . . Clerk: 350-8241

  The Code of the City of Tempe. Tallahassee, FL: Municipal Code Corporation, 1986- 2 v. looseleaf. Updated regularly. Tempe also issues annual zoning ordinances.

- Thatcher (Town) . . . . Clerk: 428-2290

  The town is in the process of compiling a code.

- Tolleson (City) . . . . Clerk: 936-7111

  The city is in the process of revising its code. There are zoning ordinances also available.

- Tombstone (City) . . . . Clerk: 457-3562

  There is a city code available published by Sterling Codifier, Inc. (1-800-338-7458).

- Tucson (City) . . . . Clerk: 791-4213

  Tucson Code. Tallahassee, FL: Municipal Code Corporation, 1987- 1 v. looseleaf. Updated regularly. This code contains annotations, cross references, charter references, an index and tables.

  Tucson Zoning Code. Tallahassee, FL: Municipal Code Corporation, 1987.

  The Tucson Public Library's Governmental Reference Library acts as a depository for Tucson municipal documents. The library is located at 255 W. Alameda in Tucson. Telephone: 791-4041, 791-4393.

- Wellton (Town) . . . . Clerk: 785-3348

  There is no town code available.

- Wickenburg (Town) . . . . Clerk: 684-5451

  There is no town code available.

- Willcox (City) . . . . Clerk: 384-4271

  There is no city code available.

- Williams (City) . . . . Clerk: 635-4451

  There is no city code available.

- Winkelman (Town) . . . . Clerk: 356-7854

  There is no town code available.

- Winslow (City) . . . . Clerk: 289-2422

  There is no recent city code available. *See Code of Ordinances, City of Winslow, Arizona.* Tallahassee, FL: Municipal Code Corporation, 1987.

- Youngtown (Town) . . . . Clerk: 933-8286

  There is no town code. Zoning ordinances are available.

- Yuma (City) . . . . Clerk: 783-1274

  There is a city code.

2. *Counties*

The *Arizona Revised Statutes* requires counties to maintain the following records and publications:

a. Minutes of Proceedings, *A.R.S.* § 11-217

The Board of Supervisors is required to record all proceedings in a minute book. These minutes are published once in the official county newspaper no later than one month after the meeting. Each newspaper that publishes minutes must supply a copy to the public libraries in every "city, town and county." *A.R.S.* § 11-221 requires all books, records and accounts of the Board be kept in the clerk's office and open to public inspection.

b. Publications of Ordinance Adopting Code, *A.R.S.* §§ 11-861, 11-864

Any building or technical code may be enacted by reference.[13] The adopting ordinance must be published in full and three copies filed in the clerk's office of the Board of Supervisors and available for public inspection. Such a code may be amended in the same manner. Many counties issue amendments to codes enacted by reference. These can be obtained from the applicable county department.

c. Recorder: Records, *A.R.S.* §§ 11-461, 11-473

The county recorder must make all books of records, indices, instruments and papers available for public inspection without charge.

13 *See* note 11 above.

d. Ordinances, *A.R.S.* § 11-251.05

Authorizes the Board of Supervisors to "adopt, amend and repeal all ordinances necessary or proper to carry out the duties, responsibilities and functions of the county." A county ordinance may apply to both unincorporated and incorporated areas if the ordinance does not conflict with existing local or state laws. A city or town's council must first review such an ordinance and approve by resolution the application or enforcement of the ordinance within its boundaries.

Ordinances may be obtained from the Board of Supervisors' "record center." *A.R.S.* § 11-251.03 requires the Board to establish a central records center for the preservation, storage and handling of all records required by law to be kept by the county officers and justice of the peace. These public records must be open to inspection.

Unfortunately, county ordinances are almost as ephemeral as municipal laws. Counties do not generally publish codes of their ordinances, however, they do issue various subsections (e.g., planning and zoning, flood plan regulations, or health codes). (See Illustration B, p.205.) To obtain these documents it is necessary to contact the applicable county department. Individual ordinances can be obtained from the Board of Supervisors.

3. *Public Notices*

Arizona Revised Statutes require both municipal and county governments to publish legal notices in a variety of areas including new ordinances and resolutions, elections, zone changes, bids, contracts, property sales, etc.[14] This publication is usually made in the "official" newspaper and must follow specific guidelines regarding the time and frequency of publication.[15] In Maricopa County official newspapers are the *Arizona Business Gazette* and the *Court Reporter.* In Pima County official newspapers are the *Tucson Daily Star,* the *Tucson Citizen* and the *Territorial News.*

4. *Miscellaneous Local Publications*

Model City Tax Code (Master Version): Intended for Tax Attorneys and Tax Practitioners. Phoenix, AZ: League of Arizona Cities and Towns, 1987- 1 v. looseleaf.

This volume contains a master version of the Model City Tax Code with both model and local options. It also includes a charter displaying which options each Arizona town or city has chosen.

Local Government Handbook. Phoenix, AZ: Office of the Attorney General, 1987. 1 v. looseleaf.

This book contains information on local government law including employees and officers, public records, open meetings, conflict of interest, de-

14 For example, *see* Ariz. Rev. Stat. Ann. §§ 9-811 to 813, 11-217, 11-251.05, 11-829, 18-217 (1990).

15 Ariz. Rev. Stat. Ann. §§ 39-203 to 204 (1985).

tection and reporting of criminal or fraudulent conduct, antitrust laws, procurement, and liabilities and immunities.

D. Citators and Annotations

The following sources provide citations and annotations to local laws.

1. *Shepard's Arizona Citations: Statutes. Colorado Springs, CO: Shepard's/McGraw-Hill, 1985-*

Shepard's provides citations to cases and annotations interpreting Arizona municipal charters and ordinances. These are arranged alphabetically by city and town and subdivided topically. There are also separate subject indexes for municipal charters, and one for municipal ordinances. (See Illustration C, p.206.)

2. *Ordinance Law Annotation: A Comprehensive Digest of American Cases that Interpret or Apply City and County Ordinances. Colorado Springs, CO: Shepard's/McGraw-Hill, 1970- 12 v.*

This treatise discusses local laws. It is arranged topically and provides annotations to applicable court decisions. There is also a geographical table of cases.

3. *McQuillin, Eugene, The Law of Municipal Corporations. 3d ed. Wilmette, IL: Callaghan & Co., 1987- 20 v.*

A subject treatment of municipal corporation law is provided in this treatise along with state and federal case annotations.

4. *Antieau, Chester James. Municipal Corporation Law. New York: Matthew Bender & Co., 1989- 4 v. looseleaf.*

Both municipal and county law are discussed in this treatise. Annotations are provided to local laws.

5. *Municipal Codes*

Some municipal codes (e.g., Tucson) provide annotations to individual ordinances.

E. Online Resources

Neither WESTLAW nor LEXIS has a database containing municipal or county laws. However, cases interpreting local laws can be found by using WESTLAW or LEXIS as a citator. (See Chapter 10 for more information.)

F. Citation Form

The Uniform System of Citation suggests the following abbreviated format for Codified Ordinances:

Tucson, Ariz., CODE Ch. x, art. x, § x (19xx).

Phoenix, Ariz., CODE Ch. x, § x,(19xx).

For uncodified ordinances:

Anytown, Ariz., Ordinance xx (date of adoption)

Anytown, Ariz., Ordinance to Regulate ... (date of adoption)

In addition, at the beginning of many codes a suggested format for citation is provided.

Illustration A

Article VII. Solar System Code

Article VIII. Spa/Pool Code

ARTICLE I. IN GENERAL

Sec. 6-1. Administrative code adopted.

The documents entitled "Uniform Administrative Code, 1988 Edition" published by the International Conference of Building Officials and "1988 Uniform Administrative Code Modifications," a copy of which modifications is attached to Ordinance No. 7180 as exhibit A, are adopted, except for those provisions of the modifications which are designated for use by the county, by reference as the Building Safety Administrative Code of the City of Tucson.
(Ord. No. 5334, § 2, 5-11-81; Ord. No. 5770, § 1, 5-23-83; Ord. No. 6566, § 1, 11-10-86; Ord. No. 7180, § 1, 4-24-89)

Editor's note—Exhibit A, referred to in this section, is not printed herein but is on file with the original ordinance.

Further amendments to the Uniform Administrative Code have been made by the following ordinances:

Ord. No. 5382, §§ 1, 2, 6-1-81; Ord. No. 5396, §§ 1, 2, 6-29-81; Ord. No. 5523, §§ 1—7, 2-22-82; Ord. No. 6344, § 3, 12-2-85; Ord. No. 6720, § 1, 6-8-87.

Cross reference—Technical division of administrative hearing office to have exclusive jurisdiction over alleged violations of administrative code, § 28-4(1).

Sec. 6-2. Clerk to keep copies of administrative code.

Three (3) copies of the Building Safety Administrative Code of the City of Tucson adopted in section 6-1 shall be filed in the office of the city clerk and are made public records and shall be available for public use and inspection during regular office hours.
(Ord. No. 5334, § 2, 5-11-81)

Sec. 6-3. Amendments of administrative code.

The Building Safety Administrative Code adopted in section 6-1 may be amended from time to time by the mayor and council. Three (3) copies of current ordinances amending the Building Safety Administrative Code shall be kept on file by the city clerk as public records and shall be kept available for public use and inspection during regular office hours.
(Ord. No. 5334, § 2, 5-11-81)

Sec. 6-4. Reserved.

Editor's note—Former § 6-4, pertaining to self-regulating building and electrical permits, was repealed by Ord. No. 5770, § 2, adopted May 23, 1983. The former section was derived from Ord. No. 4914, § 1, adopted Dec. 18, 1978.

Sec. 6-5. Violation.

It shall be a civil infraction for any person to violate any of the provisions of chapter 6 of the Tucson Code.
(Ord. No. 5334, § 3, 5-11-81; Ord. No. 5718, § 2, 2-28-83)

Cross reference—General penalty, § 1-8.

Sec. 6-6. Records of applications, permits, inspections required.

A complete record of all applications for permits, of all permits issued and of all inspections made under each permit shall be kept in the building safety division of the city in accordance with applicable law.
(Ord. No. 5531, § 3, 3-22-82)

Reprinted from the *Tucson Code,* 1987.

Illustration B

ARTICLE I. AUTHORITY, PURPOSE AND TITLE

Section 101. Statutory Authority.

Sections 48-3603 and 48-3609 of the Arizona Revised Statutes directs each County Flood Control District Board of Directors to adopt and enforce floodplain regulations. Therefore, the Board of Directors of the Flood Control District of Maricopa County, Arizona adopts this Regulation.

Section 102. Statement of Purpose.

It is the purpose of this Regulation to comply with the directive of ARS 48-3603 and to promote and protect the health, peace, safety, comfort, convenience, and general welfare of the citizens within the jurisdictional area of Maricopa County, Arizona and to minimize public losses due to flood conditions in specific areas.

Section 103. Title.

This Regulation may be referred to as the Floodplain Regulation for Maricopa County.

ARTICLE II. RULES, CONSTRUCTION AND INTERPRETATION

Section 201. Rules.

When not inconsistent with the context, words used in the present tense include the future tense, words in the singular number include the plural; words in the plural number include the singular. Words or phrases used in this Regulation shall be interpreted so as to give them the meaning they have in common usage and to give this Regulation its most reasonable application; the word "building" includes the word "structure"; the word "shall" is mandatory and the word "may" is permissive. No provision of this Regulation shall be construed to require written authorization for those exemptions set forth in ARS 48-3613 (B) nor shall the Board of Directors have authority to prohibit said exemptions.

Section 202. Construction and Interpretation.

1. This Regulation shall be liberally construed to effectuate its purposes. The requirements set out herein shall be construed as minimum requirements.

2. Nothing contained in this Regulation shall be construed to limit or repeal any powers granted to the Flood Control District of Maricopa County under state statute. If the provisions of this Regulation conflict with or overlap with other regulations, ordinances and statutes, the regulation, ordinance or statute which imposes the more stringent requirement or restriction shall prevail.

Reprinted from *Floodplain Regulations for Maricopa County,* as adopted August 4, 1986 and Amended September 18, 1989.

Illustration C

MUNICIPAL CHARTERS — Phoenix

FLAGSTAFF

City Employees
Merit System-Regulations
116Az382
569P2d812

GLENDALE

Council
Powers-Duties
14AzA4
480P2d27

MESA

City
Powers
111Az29
121Az65
523P2d57
588P2d358

Planning
Land-Regulations
1973AzS785

Property
City-Sale
21AzA58
515P2d355

NOGALES

Budget
Annual-Limitation
49Az146
65P2d1154

Land
Use Regulations
1973AzS786

PHOENIX

Boundaries
City-Definition
36Az21
282P42
—Enlargement
36Az21
282P42

Charter
Construction-Effect
84Az382
329P2d1103

City
Powers
121Az65
588P2d358
—General-Successor Corporation
18Az35
24Az155
156P75
207P611
—General Welfare Clause
38Az466
300P1010
—Legislative-Limitation
60Az530
141P2d852
—Regulation-Signs
121Az65
588P2d358
—Utilities-Acquisition
128Az201
624P2d879

City Attorney
Duties
110Az111
515P2d856

City Commission
Legislation-Power-Restriction
98Az329
404P2d414

City Council
Consent Orders-Approval-Requirements-Formal Session
133Az339
651P2d867
Legislative Powers
124Az162
602P2d827
—Offensive Conduct-Prohibition
124Az162
602P2d827

City Court
Jurisdiction
110Az111
115Az351
515P2d856
565P2d531

City Magistrates
Absence-Substitute-Appointment
73Az420
242P2d546

City Manager
Removal-Cause
18Az298
44Az40
158P845
34P2d385

Civil Service
Commission-Establishment-Authority
98Az329
404P2d414
Rules-Appointments-Temporary
46Az500
52P2d1155

Claims
Municipal Liability Exemption
4Az283
C16Az511
18Az35
36P916
C147P732
156P75
Payment-Procedure
41Az537
20P2d296
Presentation-Necessity
46Az200
49P2d626

Commission
Actions-Requirement
18Az298
37Az194
158P845
291P1000
Powers-Enumeration
35Az214
36Az251
38Az135
46Az106
47Az133
57Az350
276P325
284P350
297P1037
47P2d442
54P2d258
113P2d935
—Extent
38Az135
46Az106
297P1037
47P2d442
—Limitation
37Az194
291P1000
—Offenses-Punishment
38Az466
300P1010

Common Council
Powers-Real Property-Acquisition
24Az155
207P611
Streets-Sidewalks-Exclusive Control
16Az511
147P732

Contracts
Bids-Advertising
216F2d928
—Advertising-Notice
216F2d928
—Consideration
20AzA1
509P2d1038
Execution-Registration
37Az194
291P1000
—Requirements
46Az200
52Az291
55Az374
49P2d626
80P2d695
102P2d82

Council
Meetings-Recording Votes
14AzA457
484P2d226
Member-Failure to Vote
14AzA457
484P2d226
Powers-Scope
18Az35
156P75
Quorum
130Az355
14AzA457
484P2d226
636P2d133

Courts
Police-Jurisdiction-Limitation
46Az106
47P2d422
Recorder's-Jurisdiction
1AzA334
402P2d1010

Elections
Ballot-Candidates-Arrangement
72Az360
236P2d48
—Form-Provisions
110Az160
515P2d1180
Canvassing Board-Members-Duties
64Az125
166P2d831
Electors-Residence Qualifications
39Az457
7P2d588
Majority Vote-Effect
34Az528
C64Az125
72Az360
74Az269
273P10
C166P2d831
236P2d48
247P2d617
—Insufficiency-Effect
34Az528
273P10
Nominating Petitions-City Clerk-Duties
39Az457
7P2d588
—Filing-Time
39Az457
7P2d588
—Signers-Qualifications
39Az457
7P2d588
Registration Laws-Enactment-Duty
39Az457
7P2d588

Electors
Register
107Az514
489P2d853

Chapter 9

Selected Secondary Sources for Arizona Legal Research

Victoria K. Trotta

A. Introduction

Legal researchers often find that a good secondary source can lead them to the primary authority of a jurisdiction, and give them a procedural roadmap to travel to answer a legal question. Researchers also need statistics or business information to complete their analysis. Historically, legal researchers have not had a large variety of secondary sources to choose from in researching Arizona law. This is always a source of amazement to out-of-state researchers. There is to date no Arizona legal encyclopedia or multi-volume treatise that outlines Arizona legal jurisprudence. Researchers of Arizona law have had to rely on seminar and professional program papers and proceedings for much of their analytical information.

Arizona researchers now have a new wave of secondary sources from which to choose. This has been prompted by the advent of mandatory continuing legal education, the growth of the legal community in Arizona, and the demand for more in-depth materials on legal matters.

The following bibliography is a selective representation of some of these secondary sources. It includes not only traditional legal treatises and program materials, but governmental, historical and statistical finding tools that are routinely useful to legal researchers. Other strictly secondary sources and finding tools that are used more directly in Arizona legal practice (i.e. jury instructions) are located elsewhere in this volume.

Whenever possible, the bibliography includes treatises that are still in print, currently supplemented, or available from a lending library. See Appendix A for information on how to contact those libraries. Researchers are also encouraged to contact the State Bar of Arizona, the Center for Legal Development (distributors of Professional Publishing Company titles), or the Maricopa County or Pima County Bar Associations for current or backlisted titles that may address the issue under study. For an excellent, annotated bibliography that includes more historical entries, see Torres and Elliott, "Arizona Practice Materials: A Selective Annotated Bibliography " 80 *Law Library Journal* 577 (1988).

B. Secondary Sources by Subject

AIDS

Media Law Seminar Hypothetical (1989 : Tempe, AZ.) *AIDS and privacy: tough issues for police, media, courts & victims* / Media Law Seminar Hypothetical, held Saturday, February 11, 1989, Fiesta Inn, Tempe. -- [Tempe, AZ.? : n.p.], 1989. xi, 98 p. ; 28 cm.

Bankruptcy

Shill, Otto S. *The fate of debtors' qualified retirement plan benefits in personal bankruptcy* / Otto S. Shill . -- Phoenix, AZ. : Professional Publishing Group, 1990. ii, 23 p. : 22 cm. -- (LEGALbits)

Business and Economics

Arizona blue chip economic forecast : blue chip consensus. -- Vol. 3, no. 2 (Feb. 1987-). -- Tempe, AZ. : Economic Outlook Center, College of Business, Arizona State University, 1987- . Monthly.

Arizona business / Center for Business Research, College of Business. -- Tempe, AZ. : Arizona State University, 1953- . Monthly.

Arizona business directory, 1990-91 / rev. ed. -- Omaha, Neb. : American Directory Publishing Co., 1990. Annual.

Arizona Labor Market Information Directory. / Arizona Department of Economic Security Research Administration. -- Phoenix, AZ. : Arizona Department of Economic Security, Research Division, [1987]. 18 p.

Arizona's economy / Division of Economic and Business Research, College of Business and Public Administration, University of Arizona. -- Tucson, AZ. : The Division. Monthly.

Cole's cross reference directory for Phoenix and suburbs. -- Phoenix, AZ. : Cole's Publications. 2 v. Annual.

Researching Arizona's economy : a guide to basic sources. / Phoenix Chamber of Commerce, Arizona Department of Commerce. -- Phoenix, AZ. : The Phoenix Chamber, c1989. 232 p. ; 26 cm.

Business Enterprises

Arizona Source Book./ compiled and edited by Klute Communications ; editor, Pete Klute -- Rancho Bernardo, CA : Bernardo Press, 1989- . Annual. A guide to local clubs, groups, organizations and associations in Arizona.

Arizona business entities / Matthew P. Feeney, Snell & Wilmer, et al. -- Phoenix, AZ.: Professional Publishing Group, 1990. iv, 71 p. ; 22cm. -- (BAR-Bites)

Going public in Arizona / Paul J. Roskha, Jr., Chairman . -- Phoenix, AZ. : State Bar of Arizona, Continuing Legal Education, 1985. 1 v. (various pagings) ; 28 cm.

Construction

Horne, Thomas C. *Arizona construction law* / by Thomas C. Horne. -- Phoenix, AZ. : State Bar of Arizona, 1988. xvi, 480 p. ; 26 cm. Supplemented.

Horne, Thomas C. *Mechanics' lien law* / by Thomas C. Horne ; sponsored by Continuing Legal Education of the State Bar of Arizona. -- Phoenix, AZ. : The Bar Association, c1981. 1 v. (various pagings) ; 28 cm.

Slavin, Francis J. *Arizona construction law* / Francis J. "Buzz" Slavin Jr., Dwayne L. Burton. -- Eau Claire, WI. : Professional Education Systems, c1983. 1 v. (various pagings) : forms ; 27 cm.

Courts

Arizona Administrative Office of the Courts. *Annual judicial report.* -- Phoenix, AZ. : Published on behalf of the Arizona Supreme Court by the Administrative Office of the Courts, 1977- . Annual.

Arizona limited jurisdiction: a reference guide. -- Phoenix, AZ. : Arizona Administrative Office of the Courts, 1988 - . 2 v.

Arizona Trial Lawyers Association. *Guide to the Maricopa County Superior Court*/ Arizona Trial Lawyers Association. -- 1989 ed. -- [Phoenix, AZ.] : The Association, 1989. iii, 168 p. ; 30 cm. Earlier edition published in 1983.

Bluff, Guy W. *Arizona Courts Manual: A Guide to Filing Documents and General Procedures.* -- Phoenix, AZ: State Bar of Arizona, 1991. 1 v. (various pagings): forms.

King, Kamla J. *BNA's Directory of state courts, judges, and clerks : a state-by-state listing* / compiled by Kamla J. King and Judith Springberg with the BNA Library Staff. -- 3rd ed. -- Washington D.C. : BNA Books, 1990.

State Bar of Arizona. Civil Jury Instruction Committee. *Recommended Arizona Jury Instructions (Civil)* / State Bar of Arizona. --2nd ed.-- Phoenix, AZ. : The State Bar. 1 v. (looseleaf). 1991. Earlier edition published in 1987.

State Bar of Arizona. Arizona Criminal Jury Instructions Committee. *Reccomended Arizona jury instructions (Criminal).* / State Bar of Arizona. -- Phoenix, AZ. : The State Bar, 1989. 1 v.

Domestic Relations

Arizona. Supreme Court. *Arizona child support guidelines* / adopted by the Arizona Supreme Court July, 1987. -- [s.l. : s.n., 1987]. 8 p. ; 28 cm.

Domestic relations handbook / Maricopa County Superior Court, Arizona, revised June 1, 1983. -- [Phoenix, AZ.] : Maricopa County Bar Association, c1983. 33 p. ; 22 cm.

Smith, Charles Marshall. *Marriage dissolution practice* / by Charles Marshall Smith and Irwin Cantor. -- St. Paul, MN. : West Publishing Co., 1988. xviii, 654 p. : ill, ; 27 cm. -- (Arizona practice ; v. 3) Supplemented.

Education

Arizona Educational Directory. -- Phoenix, AZ. : Arizona Department of Education, 1989- . annual.

Environmental Law

Arizona environmental law letter. -- Nashville, TN.: M. Lee Smith Publishers + Printers, 1990- . Monthly.

Hazardous waste in Arizona / National Business Institute, Inc. -- Eau Claire, WI.: The Institute, 1988. 1 v.

Forms

Arizona legal forms. -- St. Paul, MN. : West Publishing Co., 1988- . Civil Procedure (vols. 1,2); Debtor Creditor (vol. 3); Domestic Relations (vol. 4); Commercial Transactions (vols. 5,6); Criminal Procedure (vol. 7); Business Organizations (vols, 8,9).

Industrial Development

Arizona Industrial Development Authority handbook / Molly Armstrong, principal editor . -- Phoenix, AZ. : Arizona Office of Economic Planning and Development, Office of the Governor, 1981. 98 p. ; 28 cm.

Insurance

Title insurance in Arizona / Marcia Busching, Larry Dahl, Co-Chairpersons. -- Phoenix, AZ. : State Bar of Arizona, Continuing Legal Education, 1986. 1 v. (various pagings) ; 28 cm.

Land Use

Jordan, Douglas A. *Arizona Land Use Law* / Douglas A. Jordan and Michael D. House. -- [Phoenix, AZ.]: State Bar of Arizona, Continuing Education. c1988. 1 v. (various pagings) ; 23 cm. Kept up to date with supplementation.

Land use : regulation and litigation in Arizona / S.L. Schorr, Chairman. -- [Phoenix, AZ.] : State Bar of California, c1986. ix, 519, [14] p. ; 28 cm.

Legal Practice

Arizona Attorney / State Bar of Arizona . -- Phoenix, AZ. : The State Bar, 1988 - (monthly, except August/September). Current manifestation of Arizona's bar journal. Previous titles include *Arizona Bar Journal* and *Arizona Bar Briefs.*

Arizona handbook for legal secretaries / Arizona Association of Legal Secretaries. -- Phoenix, AZ. : The Association, 1985. 2 v. (looseleaf); 28 cm.

Arizona legal skills / Garrick Gallagher, Christina Hamilton, Mark Jewett, Co-chairpersons. -- Phoenix, AZ. : State Bar of Arizona, Continuing Legal Education, 1989. 1 v. (various pagings) ; 28 cm.

Arizona legal service practice manual / Ann M. Davis, editor. -- 2nd ed. -- Phoenix, AZ. : Arizona Statewide Legal Services Project, 1989- .

State Bar of Arizona. Subcommittee on Rendering Legal Opinions in Business Transactions. *Report of the State Bar of Arizona Corporate, Banking and Business Law Section, Subcommittee on Rendering legal opinions in business transactions.* -- Phoenix, AZ.: State Bar of Arizona, 1989. ii, 63 p.

Guide to Arizona Statutes of Limitation / Young Lawyers Division, Maricopa County Bar Association. -- Phoenix, AZ. : Maricopa County Bar Association, 1991. 1 v.

Medical Associations

Arizona. Board of Medical Examiners. *Arizona State medical directory.* -- Phoenix, AZ. : Board of Medical Examiners, 1935 - Annual.

Arizona Osteopathic Medical Association. *Annual Membership Directory.* -- Phoenix, AZ. : The Association, 19 - Annual.

Maricopa County Medical Society. *Pictorial membership directory.* -- Phoenix, AZ.: the Society. Annual.

Medical Malpractice

Personal Injury Verdict Survey / Arizona ed. -- Solon, OH. : Jury Verdict Research, Inc., 1984?- . Annual.

Stephan, Robert. *The Arizona law of medical malpractice, with a practical appendix* / by Robert Stephan, Jr. -- Phoenix, AZ. : Medilex Co., c1983- . 1 v. (looseleaf) ; 26 cm. Supplemented.

Mental Health

Miller, Michael O. *Law and mental health professionals, Arizona.* / Michael O. Miller and Bruce D. Sales. -- Washington, DC : American Psychological Association, c1986.

Minerals And Mining

The Copper industry's impact on the Arizona economy in ... Marana, AZ.: Southwest Economic Information Center, 19 - Annual.

On record : a newsletter about Arizona's mining and industry. -- 1987- . -- Phoenix, AZ. : AMIGOS, 1987- . Quarterly.

Native American Indians

Goodman, James Marion. *The Navajo Atlas : environments, resources, people, and history of the Dine Bikeyeh* / by James M. Goodman. -- 1st ed. -- Norman, OK.: University of Oklahoma Press, c1982.

Navajo Tribe. *Navajo Tribal Code* / edited and published by Equity Publishing Corporation. -- 1977 ed. [3rd ed.]. -- Oxford, New Hampshire: The Corporation, c1978. [Last supplemented in 1985. New edition forthcoming by Butterworths.]

Navajo Tribe. *Navajo court rules.* -- 3rd ed. -- [Window Rock, AZ.] : Judicial branch of the Navajo Nation, c1978.

Tribal Directory / Arizona Commission of Indian Affairs. -- Phoenix, AZ. : The Commission, 19 - . Annual.

Newspapers

Arizona Business Gazette. -- Phoenix, AZ. : Phoenix Newspapers. Vol. 81, no. 6 - (Sept. 30, 1980) - . weekly. "Arizona's business and court newspaper." Continues *Arizona Weekly Gazette.*

Arizona Capitol Times . -- Phoenix, AZ. : Arizona News Service, 1945 - . Weekly.

Arizona Daily Star . -- Tucson, AZ. : L.C. Hughes. Vol. 1, no. 1 - (Dec. 21, 1879) - . daily. Also a weekly edition called *Arizona Weekly Star.*

Arizona Newspapers Association. Directory. -- Phoenix, AZ. : Arizona Newspapers Association, 1977- Annual. Directory and advertising rates for Arizona's newspapers, magazines, and other periodicals.

Arizona Republic . -- Phoenix, AZ. : Phoenix Newspapers. Vol. 1, 1890 - . daily.

Business Journal . -- Phoenix, AZ. : Business Journal. Vol. 1, 1980- . 53 issues per year.

Tucson Citizen . -- Tucson, AZ. : Citizen Publishing Co., 1977- . v. 107, no. 130 (June 1, 1977) - daily (except Sunday).

Politics And Government

Arizona Agency Handbook/ rev. ed. -- [Phoenix, AZ.] : State of Arizona, Office of the Attorney General, [1983]. 1 v. (looseleaf).

Arizona community profiles / Arizona Office of the Governor, Office of Economic Planning and Development. -- Phoenix, AZ. : Community Development Program, Arizona Department of Commerce, 1987. 1 v. (looseleaf) ; 28 cm. Includes state, community and Native American Indian profiles.

Arizona. Legislature. Legislative Council. *Arizona legislative bill drafting manual.* -- Phoenix, AZ. : The Arizona Legislative Council, 1987. xi, 133 p.

Goff, John S. *The Supreme Court Justices, 1863 - 1982* / by John S. Goff. -- Cave Creek, AZ. : Black Mountain Press, c1975. 200 p. : ill. ; 26 cm. -- (Arizona Territorial Officials. v.1).

State of Arizona Directory / Arizona Department of Administration Telecommunications. -- Phoenix, AZ. : Arizona Secretary of State. Annual.

Arizona Town Hall / Arizona Academy . -- [Phoenix, AZ.]: The Academy, 1962- . Semiannual. Working papers that cover issues of current relevancy, e.g. the environment, education, business, status of women. Serves as an advisory body to the State Legislature.

A Guide for Annexation . -- [Phoenix, AZ. : League of Arizona Cities and Towns], 1988. 33 p. : forms ; 28 cm.

Legislative process / sponsored by the State Bar of Arizona. -- Phoenix, AZ. : State Bar of Arizona, Continuing Legal Education, 1980. 1 v.(various pagings); 28 cm.

Local government handbook / [Local Government Handbook Committee]. -- [Phoenix, AZ. : Office of the Attorney General, [1989?]. 1 v. (looseleaf) : charts, forms ; 30 cm.

Local laws : how to prepare, pass and publish. -- [Phoenix, AZ.] : League of Arizona Cities and Towns, 1988. 17 p. : ill. ; 28 cm.

Municipal budget and finance manual / prepared by the League of Arizona Cities and Towns. -- [Phoenix, AZ.] : The League, 1989. 1 v. (looseleaf) : forms ; 28 cm.

Municipal election manual / prepared by the League of Arizona Cities and Towns. -- [Phoenix, AZ.] : The League, 1980. 1 v. (various pagings) : forms; 30 cm.

Reference handbook : improvement districts . -- Phoenix, AZ. : Burgess & Niple, Inc., 1988. 19 p. : ill. ; 28 cm.

Selected state officials and the legislatures . -- Lexington, KY. : Council of State Governments. Biennial.

Tapping officials' secrets : the door to open government in Arizona / Reporters Committee for Freedom of the Press. -- Washington, D.C. : The Committee, 1989. 1 v. (various pagings); 30 cm.

You As a Public Official: open meetings, conflict of interest, incompatibility of offices, nepotism, financial disclosure / League of Arizona Cities & Towns . -- Phoenix, AZ. : The League, 1988. 1 v. (various pagings) : 28 cm.

Probate

Geiser, Jeannette K. *Arizona probate code practice manual* / by Jeannette K. Geiser, David J. Estes, Louis F. Comus, Jr., Eleanor ter Horst. -- 3rd ed. -- [Phoenix, AZ.] : State Bar of Arizona, c1989,. 1 v. (various pagings) : ill. ; 23 cm.

Wiley, Thomas W. and Robert J. Rosepink. *Arizona probate.* -- Thomas W. Wiley and Robert J. Rosepink. -- San Francisco, CA. : Bancroft Whitney Co., 1980- . 1 v. (looseleaf)

Procedure

Arizona appellate handbook / Appellate Handbook Committee. --[Phoenix, AZ.] : Continuing Legal Education of the State Bar of Arizona, [1978]- 3 v. (looseleaf) : ill., forms ; 30 cm. Supplemented.

Arizona litigation guide / by the lawyers of Fennemore Craig. -- Phoenix, AZ. : Arizona Institute of Continuing Legal Education, Maricopa County Bar Association, 1989- . 1 v. (looseleaf) ; 28 cm.

Arizona attorneys' fees manual / Scott Butler, et al. -- Phoenix, AZ. : Continuing Legal Education, State Bar of Arizona, 1987. 1 v. (various pagings) ; 30 cm.

Arizona practice manual / Continuing Legal Education of the State Bar of Arizona ; in cooperation with the Maricopa County Young Lawyers. -- [Phoenix, AZ.] : State Bar of Arizona, 1984. 1 v. (looseleaf) ; 30 cm.

Udall, Morris K. *Arizona law of evidence* / by Morris K. Udall and Joseph M. Livermore. -- 2nd ed .-- St. Paul, MN. : West Publishing Co., 1982 . -- (Arizona Practice , Vol. 1). Supplemented.

McClennen, Crane. *Arizona courtroom evidence manual* / Crane McClennan. -- 2d ed. -- [Phoenix, AZ.]; Continuing Legal Education, State Bar of Arizona, 1988- 1 v. (looseleaf) ; 30 cm.

Smith, Charles Marshall. *Civil trial practice* / by Charles Marshall Smith. -- St. Paul, MN. : West Publishing Co., 1986. xxiii, 686 p. ; 26 cm. -- (Arizona Practice, Vol. 2). Supplemented.

Guide to Arizona Statutes of Limitation / compiled by Maricopa County Bar Association, Young Lawyers Division . -- 1991 ed. -- Phoenix, AZ.: Professional Publishing Co., 1991.

Murray, Stanley D. *Time limitations applicable to actions and procedures in the Arizona Superior Court* / by Stanley D. Murray. -- Phoenix, AZ. : Professional Publishing Co., 1991.

Trial Reporter... / Andy Anderson Editor. -- Phoenix, AZ. : The Trial Reporter. 1968 - . Biweekly. Editions for Central and Northern Arizona and Southern Arizona. Available to subscribers only. Tracks superior court judgements and awards.

Real Estate

Bender, Steven W. *Arizona guaranty actions* / by Steven W. Bender. -- Phoenix, AZ. : Professional Publishing Group, 1990. ii, 30 p. ; 23 cm. -- (BARBites)

Birringer, Steven. *Arizona guide to residential landlord-tenant law* / Steven Birringer. -- Phoenix, AZ. : Professional Publishing Group, 1991. 1 v. (looseleaf) ; 28 cm.

Commercial real estate transactions practice manual. -- [Phoenix, AZ.] : State Bar of Arizona, 1989. 2 v. (looseleaf) : ill. ; 29 cm.

Friedrich, Blair P. *The commercial lease* / by Blair P. Friedrich. -- Phoenix, AZ. : Professional Publishing Co., 1991.

Hinkel, Gregory E. *Receivers in Arizona : can they be appointed in conjunction with a non-judicial foreclosure?* / Gregory E. Hinkel. -- Phoenix, AZ. : Professional Publishing Group, c1990. 19 p. 23 cm. -- (BARBites).

Hinkel, Gregory E. *When to foreclose a deed of trust judicially* / Gregory E. Hinkel. -- Phoenix, AZ. : Professional Publishing Group, c1990. ix, 28 p. ; 23 cm. -- (BARBites).

Remedies

Arizona civil remedies / edited by Marilee Miller Clarke. -- [Phoenix, AZ.]: State Bar of Arizona, c1982. vi, 577 p. : ill. ; 24 cm.

Statistics

Arizona Blue Book / Arizona Secretary of State. -- Phoenix, AZ. : The Secretary, 1986- Irregular.

Arizona facts: a comprehensive look at Arizona today, county by county. / by John Clements. -- Dallas, TX. : Clements Research II, Inc. , c1989. viii, 215 p. ; 26 cm.

Arizona Statistical Abstract / University of Arizona, Division of Economic and Business Research. -- Flagstaff AZ. : Northland Press, 1979- . Annual.

Arizona Statistical Review / Valley National Bank, Economic Research Department. -- Phoenix, AZ. : The Bank, 1969- . Annual.

Arizona Yearbook: a Guide to government in the Grand Canyon State -- Eugene, OR. : Information Press, c1983- . Biennial. Ready reference source of tabular, pictorial, directory information . Arizona state song, Constitution, history, statistics, judicial rosters,government offices, maps of political boundaries. To supplement the *Arizona Blue Book.*

Book of Lists / The Business Journal. -- Phoenix, AZ.: The Journal, 1987 - . Annual. Compilation of lists published in the previous year's *Journal.* Ranks a host of business entities, by type. Includes rankings of accounting firms to women-owned businesses. Focus on Maricopa County (Phoenix), but many encompass state coverage.

Local Government Directory / The League of Arizona Cities and Towns and the Arizona Associations of Counties. -- Phoenix, AZ.: The League, 198? - . Annual. City, town, county government rosters. Also includes city, county and state affiliate groups.

Taxation

Arizona. Department of Revenue. Standards, Manuals, and Guidelines Unit. *Land Manual.* -- Phoenix, AZ. : The Department, 1987. 1 v. (looseleaf).

Arizona master income tax guide / Edited by Ira S. Feldman, Robert C. Hofman. -- 1990 edition, for 1988 and subsequent years, including tax reform provisions through 1989. -- Phoenix, AZ. : Phoenix Tax Workshop ; Toback & Company, c1990. 31. p. ; 28 cm.

Arizona sales and use tax / Lawrence F. Winthrop, et al. -- Eau Claire, WI. : Professional Education Systems Inc., 1990. 1 v. (various pagings) ; 28 cm.

Arizona sales & use tax guide / Patrick Derdenger . -- Phoenix, AZ. : Professional Publishing Co. Annual.

Arizona Tax Reports: State and Local / Chicago, IL.: Commerce Clearing House, 1986- . 2v. Monthly.

Arizona's corporation income tax : preliminary draft : a research paper / prepared for the Arizona Joint Select Committee on State Revenues and Expenditures. -- [Phoenix, AZ.]: The Committee, 1989. 17, [5] leaves ; 28 cm. (Fiscal 2000 Publication).

Arizona's personal income tax : preliminary draft : a research paper / prepared for the Arizona Joint Select Committee on State Revenues and Expenditures. -- [Phoenix, AZ.] : The Committee, 1989. 44 leaves ; 28 cm. (Fiscal 2000 Publication).

Feldman, Ira S. and Robert C. Hofman, eds. *Arizona Master Sales and Use Guide.* -- Phoenix, AZ. : The Phoenix Tax Workshop, 1990- .

Hoffman, Dennis. *The economic impact of four fiscal alternatives* / prepared by Dennis Hoffman, Lee McPheters, and Michael Ormiston. -- Tempe, AZ. : Department of Economics, Arizona State University, 1989. 1 v. (various pagings) ; 28 cm. (Fiscal 2000 Publication)

Ladd, Helen F. *Sales taxes in Arizona : report to the Arizona Joint Select Committee on State Revenues and Expenditures, March 29, 1989* / Helen F. Ladd, Dana Weist. -- Preliminary Draft. -- [Phoenix, AZ. : The Committee, 1989.] 1 v. (various pagings) ; 28 cm. (Fiscal 2000 Publication).

Taxation of financial industries in an era of change : preliminary draft : a research paper / prepared for the Arizona Joint Select Committee on State Revenues and Expenditures. -- [Phoenix, AZ. : The Committee, 1989]. 46 leaves ; 28 cm. (Fiscal 2000 Publication).

Water

Tellman, Barbara. *Where to get free (or almost free) information about water in Arizona* / Barbara Tellman. -- Tucson, AZ. : Water Resources Research Center, University of Arizona, 1990. vii, 58 p. ; 23 cm.

C. Publisher Information

American Directory Publishing Co.
5711 S. 86th Circle
P.O. Box 27347
Omaha, Nebraska 68127

American Psychological Association
202 E. McDowell Road
Phoenix, Arizona 85004
602-253-3210

AMIGOS
P.O. Box 25187
Phoenix, Arizona 85002
602-279-3197

Arizona Academy
111 W. Monroe Street
Suite 1216
Phoenix, Arizona 85003
602-252-9600

Arizona Administrative Office of the Courts
1314 N. 3rd Street
Suite 200 & 300
Phoenix, Arizona 85004
602-253-5700

Arizona Association of Counties
1910 W. Jefferson Street
Phoenix, Arizona 85004
602-252-6563
FAX: 602-254-0969

Arizona Association of Legal Secretaries
3358 N. Treat Circle
Tucson, Arizona 85716

Arizona Attorney General
1275 W. Washington St.
Phoenix, Arizona 85007
602-542-4266

Arizona Board of Medical Examiners
2001 W. Camelback Road,
Suite 300
Phoenix, Arizona 85015
602-255-3751

Arizona Commission of Indian Affairs
1645 W. Jefferson Street
Room 127
Phoenix, Arizona 85007
602-542-3123

Arizona Daily Star
P.O. Box 26887
Tucson, Arizona 85726

Arizona. Department of Commerce
State Capitol Tower
1700 W. Washington Street
Phoenix, Arizona 85007
602-255-5434

Arizona Department of Economic Security
1717 W. Jefferson Street
Phoenix, Arizona 85007
602-542-4791

Arizona Department of Education
1535 W. Jefferson
Phoenix, Arizona 85007
602-542-5393

Arizona Legislative Council
Legislative Services Wing,
Suite 100
1700 W. Washington St.
Phoenix, Arizona 85007
602-542-4236

Arizona News Service
14 N. 18th Avenue
Phoenix, Arizona 85007
602-258-7026

Arizona Newspapers Association
14 N. 18th Avenue
Phoenix, Arizona 85007
602-258-7026

Arizona. Office of Economic Planning and Development
State Capitol Tower
1700 W. Washington Street
Phoenix, Arizona 85007
602-255-4920

Arizona Osteopathic Medical Association
5057 E. Thomas Road
Phoenix, Arizona 85018
602-840-0460

Arizona Republic
Phoenix Newspapers
120 E. Van Buren Street
Phoenix, Arizona 85004
602-271-8000

Arizona Statewide Legal Services Project
402 W. Roosevelt Avenue
Suite "F"
P.O. Box 311
Phoenix, Arizona 85001

Arizona Trial Lawyers Association
1001 N. Central Street
Suite 590
Phoenix, Arizona 85007
602-257-8236

Bancroft Whitney
3250 Van Ness Avenue
San Francisco, CA 94109

Burgess & Niple, Inc.
5025 E. Washington Street
Suite 212
Phoenix, Arizona 85034
602-244-8100

Business Journal
3737 N. Seventh Street
Suite 200
Phoenix, Arizona 85014
602-230-8400

Butterworths
90 Stiles Road
Salem, New Hampshire 03079
603-898-9664
800-548-4001

Center for Business Research
College of Business
Arizona State University
Tempe, Arizona 85287-4406
602-965-3961

Clements Research II, Inc.
16850 Dallas Parkway
Dallas, Texas 75248

Cole's Publications
100 W. Camelback Road,
Suite 107
Phoenix, Arizona 85013
(602) 264-3407

Commerce Clearing House, Inc.
4025 W. Peterson Avenue
Chicago, Illinois 60646

Division of Economic and Business Research College of Business and Public Administration
University of Arizona
Tucson, Arizona 85721
602-621-2155

Economic Outlook Center
College of Business
Arizona State University
Tempe, Arizona 85027
602-965-5543

Information Press
P.O. Box 1422
Eugene, Oregon 97440-1422
503-689-0188

Jury Verdict Research, Inc.
5325 Naiman Parkway
Suite B
Solon, Ohio 44139

League of Arizona Cities and Towns
1820 W. Washington Street
Phoenix, Arizona 85007
602-258-5786
FAX: 602-253-3874

Maricopa County Bar Association
333 W. Roosevelt Street
Phoenix, Arizona 85003
602-257-4200
FAX: 602-257-0522

Maricopa County Medical Society
326 E. Coronado Road
Phoenix, Arizona 85004
602-252-2015

Medilex Corporation
371 E. Monte Vista Road
Phoenix, Arizona 85004
602-241-1400

National Business Institute, Inc.
P.O. Box 3067
Eau Claire, Wisconsin 54702
715-835-7909

Northland Press
2900 N. Fort Valley Road
Flagstaff, Arizona 86001
602-774-5251

Phoenix Chamber of Commerce
34 W. Monroe, Suite 900
Phoenix, Arizona 85003
602-254-5521

Phoenix Tax Workshop
3200 N. Central Avenue
Phoenix, Arizona 85012
602-264-9011

Pima County Bar Association
177 N. Church Street
Suite 101
Tucson, Arizona 85701
602-623-8258

Professional Education Systems, Inc.
200 Spring Street
P.O. Box 1208
Eau Claire, Wisconsin 54702
1-800-826-7155

Professional Publishing Group
1001 N. Central Street
Suite 810
Phoenix, Arizona 85004
602-258-0483
FAX: 602-258-0049

Reporters Committee for Freedom of the Press
P.O. Box 33756
Washington D.C. 20033

M. Lee Smith Publishers
P.O. Box 2678
Arcadia Station
Nashville, TN 37219

State Bar of Arizona
Continuing Legal Education
363 N. First Street
Phoenix, Arizona 85003
602-252-4804

Toback & Company
1839 S. Alma School Road
Mesa, Arizona 85210
602-264-9011

Trial Reporter
P.O. Box 8187
Phoenix, Arizona 85066-8187
602-276-7773 (Phoenix)
602-885-7773 (Tucson)
FAX: 602-276-5133

Tucson Citizen
Citizen Publishing Co.
4850 S. Park Avenue
P.O. Box 26767
Tucson, Arizona 85726

University of Oklahoma Press
1005 Asp Avenue
Norman, Oklahoma 73019
405-325-5111

Valley National Bank of Arizona Economic Planning Division
P.O. Box 71, Department A - 733
Phoenix, Arizona 85001
602-261-5043

Water Resources Research Center College of Engineering and Mines University of Arizona
350 N. Campbell Avenue
Tucson, Arizona 85721
602-621-7607

Chapter 10

Online Resources

Kathy Shimpock-Vieweg

A. Introduction

Online computer systems have become as much a part of legal research as their manual counterparts. Even small law firms now have access to a WESTLAW or LEXIS terminal. The Maricopa County Law Library has WESTLAW available for its patrons who are billed directly for their usage. Information brokers also provide database searching for those without access to a terminal.

Online systems are numerous and vary in scope. Because legal issues involve a wide range of topics, online research also reflects this need covering information in law, business, government documents, medicine, engineering and science. Databases also differ in the type of documents retrievable, cost, coverage, and search strategy. Some databases contain the full text of documents, while others hold merely abstracts or bibliographic excerpts. In addition, many databases do not provide full retrospective coverage. Some maintain the current year only.

Search strategies for some systems are "user friendly," employing simple English phrases (e.g., WESTLAW or LEXIS), but other systems require more abstract and abbreviated language (e.g., OCLC). And, although there is no uniformity of search strategies, most systems rely on Boolean operators (and, or, not).

In addition, subscription rates and database charges vary widely and change rapidly. Some services, however, do provide group discounts for law schools, governmental agencies or bar associations. Some even provide special usage packages.

Unfortunately, database searching requires constant practice for competency. For this reason it is often cheaper (and easier) to ask a librarian, information broker, or vendor representative, to run complicated searches or those needed in unfamiliar databases.

It should be emphasized that online systems are just another research tool. They are not a panacea and presently only supplement manual research. Rarely should a database search be the first or only step taken in any legal research project. Most information obtained online can also be found in hard copy, but there is the old tradeoff between time and money. For, although computer usage is costly, it is often cheaper in comparison with the person hours needed to locate the same information. For example, computers can more easily compile a cumulative listing of cases written by a particular judge, Shepardize a case, or retrieve cases dealing with a specific or unique factual situations.

Full text searching found with WESTLAW and LEXIS has its own unique problems. It is especially difficult because of the numerous words that can be used to describe the same item, the various spellings and other idiosyncrasies of the English language. It is also difficult to ascertain the relevance of found documents. What has actually been searched and what still needs to be found? What is the "best hit"; and what is, in reality, a "false drop"?[1] Therefore, it may be difficult to decide when to use an online resource. It changes with each researcher, law firm or client.

Attorneys, however, need to understand online systems to more wisely utilize them and explain their benefits to clients. Most vendors provide representatives and customer service numbers to provide training, equipment and assistance.

Updating database holdings can be a challenge. Changes, however, can be best ascertained from these directories: *Books and Periodicals Online;*[2] *Computer - Readable Databases;*[3] *The Directory of Periodicals Online: Indexed, Abstracted and Full-Text, News, Law and Business;*[4] and the online section of *Ulrich's International Periodicals Directory.*[5]

The following is a brief description of databases and online systems most likely to be useful for Arizona research. Vendors addresses and telephone numbers are also provided.[6]

1 A "false drop" has been defined as "an unwanted reference which does not pertain to the subject." (*See* Charles J. Sippl and Roger J. Sippl, *Computer Dictionary and Handbook,* 3rd ed. (Indianapolis: Howard W. Sams & Co., Inc., 1980), 197.) In essence, a "false drop" is a document retrieved from a database that meets all the search criteria but still is not relevant.

2 Nuchine Nobari, ed., *Books and Periodicals Online: A Guide to Publication Contents of Business and Legal Databases.* (New York, NY: Books and Periodicals Online, Inc., 1990).

3 Kathleen Young Marcaccio, ed., *Computer - Readable Databases: A Directory and Data Sourcebook,* 6th ed. (Detroit, MI: Gale Research Inc., 1990).

4 Anne Federer, *Directory of Periodicals Online: Indexed, Abstracted and Full-text, News, Law and Business,* 5th ed. (Toronto, Ontario: Info Globe, 1990).

5 *Ulrich's International Periodicals Directory,* 29th ed. (New York, NY: R.R. Bowker, 1990).

6 For information on start-up costs and search fees, contact the vendor.

B. Legal Systems

1. WESTLAW

West Services, Inc.
Two North Central, Suite 305
Phoenix, AZ 85004
(602) 257-4207/1-800-544-5330
Customer Service: 1-800-328-9833
FAX: (602) 340-0619

WESTLAW is a full-text online service available from the West Publishing Company. Its Arizona coverage and database identifiers (as of 3/1/91) are as follows:

a. Arizona State Case Law

i. Arizona Supreme Court (AZ-CS)

From 56 P (1885) to date.

ii. Arizona Court of Appeals (AZ-CS)

From 1 Ariz. App., 398 P.2d (inception 1965) to date.

iii. Arizona Tax Court (AZTX-TCT)

From 774 P.2d (inception, 1989) to date.

iv. Arizona cases can also be accessed through WESTLAW'S topical databases. These databases include (but are not limited to) cases in civil rights (AZCIV-CS), corporations (AZCORP-CS), criminal justice (AZCJ-CS), education (AZED-CS), energy (AZEN-CS), environmental law (AZENV-CS), family law (AZFL-CS), insurance (AZIN-CS), labor and employment (AZLB-CS), legal services (AZLS-CS), products liability (AZPL-CS), securities (AZSEC-CS), social security (AZCS-CS), taxation (AZTX-CS), workers' compensation (AZWC-CS), and health services (AZHTH-CS).

b. Arizona's Federal Case Law

Note: All reported federal cases are available online (ALLFEDS).

i. U.S. Court of Appeals for the Ninth Circuit (CTA9 and CTA9-OLD)

CTA9 from 146 F.2d (1945 to date).

CTA9-OLD from 47 F. (1891 to 1944).

* To limit a search to Arizona cases from CTA9, input: SY(arizona d.ariz) & ______. ("Sy" signifies a synopsis field query. Insert additional query term[s] in the blank.)

ii. U.S. District Courts (DCT)

DCT from 58 F. Supp. (1945), 4 F.R.D. (1945) and 1 B.R. (1979) to date. DCT-OLD (includes all documents released for publication) from 1789 to 1944.

*To limit a search to only Arizona District Court decisions, input: CO(AZ) & ______. ("CO" signifies a court field query. Insert additional query term[s] in the blank.)

*To limit a search to the district court cases decided by the states within the ninth Circuit, input: CO(9) or CO(ninth) &________. ("CO" signifies a court field query. Insert additional query term[s] in the blank.)

iii. U.S. Court of Appeals and U.S. District Court cases from the Ninth Circuit (in ALLFEDS and ALLFEDS-OLD database) input: CO(AZ) & ____________.

Coverage same as above.

Most cases on WESTLAW include the West synopsis and the topic and headnotes available in their hardcopy National Reporter system. In general, only those cases unreported or not yet formatted in hard copy are lacking these features.

In addition, the *Arizona Digest* and *West's Pacific Digest* can be easily updated or consolidated through WESTLAW. For example, searching for all headnotes under the topic adoption would be either: to(17) or to(adoption). [Note: There is no space between to(17) or to(adoption).]

One format for a topic and key number search would be: 101 k 61 .

This search would retrieve cases with the topic corporations (101) and key number (61) which pertain to "amount of capital."

c. Arizona Statutes - Current

i. *Arizona Revised Statutes Annotated* (AZ-ST-ANN)

Coverage corresponds with current hard copy *A.R.S.* with current pocket parts.

ii. Arizona Unannotated Statutes (AZ-ST)

Coverage corresponds with current hard copy *A.R.S.* with current pocket parts.

*Note: These databases include Arizona statutes, constitution and court rules.

iii. Arizona Statutes General Index (AZ-ST-IDX)

Coverage corresponds with current hard copy *A.R.S.* General Index.

iv. Arizona Insurance Statutes and Regulations (INSURLAW)

Includes full text of Arizona insurance statutes and regulations. The NILS Publishing Company database is also available. A standardized index is included to assist in document retrieval.

v. Arizona Legislative Service (AZ-LEGIS)

Current legislative session only.

Includes recent legislation, resolutions, governor's veto messages, proclamations, declarations of emergency, or initiative measures. Slip laws may be included into the database prior to receiving their full editorial enhancements.

d. Arizona Statutes-Historical

i. 1989 *Arizona Revised Statutes Annotated* (AZ-STAN89)

Complete through the First Regular Session of the Thirty-Ninth Legislature (1989). Titles 9 to 11, and 18 to 22 are current through the end of the First and Second Special Sessions of the Thirty-Ninth Legislature (1989).

ii. 1988 *Arizona Revised Statutes Annotated* (AZ-STAN88)

Complete through the Second Regular Session of the Thirty-Eighth Legislature (1988).

iii. 1990 *Arizona Legislative Service* (AZ-LEGIS90)

Includes documents and session laws passed during the Second Regular Session of the Thirty-Ninth Legislature (1990) and First through Fourth Special Sessions (1989-1990).

iv. 1989 Arizona Legislative Service (AZ-LEGIS89)

Includes documents and session laws passed during the First Regular Session of the Thirty-Ninth Legislature (1989) as found in corresponding hard copy. Coverage also includes proposed constitutional amendments passed during the 1988 session, and during the November 1988 election.

v. 1988 Arizona Legislative Service (AZ-LEGIS88)

Includes documents and session laws passed during the Second Regular Session of the Thirty-Eighth (1988) Legislature as found in corresponding hardcopy.

Note: The *Arizona Legislative Service* is placed online only after the issuance of the printed version.

e. Arizona Court Rules and Orders

i. Arizona Court Rules (AZ-RULES)

Corresponds with current edition of *Arizona Rules of Court, State and Federal.*

ii. Arizona Court Orders (AZ-ORDERS)

Updates court rules found in AZ-RULES database.

f. Arizona Administrative Law

i. Arizona Attorney General Opinions (AZ-AG)

From 1977 to date.

ii. Arizona Corporation Commission Order (AZSEC-ADMIN) (Securities law)

From 1985 to date.

iii. Arizona Board of Tax Appeals (AZTX-ADMIN) Includes Division II Board Decisions

From 1982 to date.

iv. Arizona Public Utilities Reports (AZ-PUR)

Selected cases from 1919, complete coverage of headnotes to cases and administrative decisions from 1953, full text of PUR begins with 1 PUR 4th (1974).

Arizona cases and administrative decisions from the *Public Utilities Reports,* Fourth Series; the *P.U.R.* Digest, Third Series and the *West's National Reporter System.* Includes headnotes and full text when available.

g. Shepard's

WESTLAW provides an online version of Shepard's for Arizona reports. The online coverage of Shepard's is generally only as current as the most recent paper supplement received. Shepard's Preview Service (SP) allows the researcher to update these citing cases. It provides Shepard's citations prior to the information appearing in the Shepard's online database. Shepard's Preview includes cases reported in *West's National Reporter* system but may exclude those issued within the last few months that have not yet been reported. Therefore, to be completely safe, it is necessary to either use WESTLAW itself as a citator, or use QuickCite. QuickCite, WESTLAW's newest citator service, retrieves the most current citing cases. Simply input "qc" and QuickCite will automatically search WESTLAW as a citator.

However, for "slip opinions," statutes, or other documents not available in Shepard's online version, WESTLAW itself must be used as a citator. A sample search to find the most recent Arizona cases citing the slip opinion *Smith v. Jones* in the Arizona database (AZ-CS) would be:

(Smith /s Jones) and ad(x/x/x)

Limit the added date restriction (i.e., ad) to the date of publication. "Ad" is used to retrieve only those cases added to WESTLAW since this date.

h. Insta-Cite

Insta-Cite provides case history and cite verification through WESTLAW. This system provides a chronological listing of case history with explanatory notes. It also includes other cases which may have had a negative impact on the citing case's precedential value. Case history information is included online within six working days after West's receipt of an opinion.

i. West's Legal Directory - Arizona (AZ-WLD)

Coverage includes only those profiles sent to West Publishing Co.

*Profiles Arizona law firms with biographical information on Arizona attorneys.

j. Arizona Periodicals (full-text of selected articles only)

Arizona Attorney (AZATT) previously *Arizona Bar Journal*

From Vol. 25 (1988) to date.

Arizona Bar Journal now *Arizona Attorney* (AZATT)

From Vol. 19 (1983) to Vol. 24 (1988).

Arizona Law Review (AZLR)

From Vol. 25 (1983).

Arizona State Law Journal (AZSLJ)

From Vol. 1982 (1982).

WESTLAW also has online periodical indexes:

CLIP (*Current Index of Legal Periodicals*)

Contains the eight most recent weekly editions.

Index to Legal Periodicals

From July 1981 to date.

Legal Resource Index

From December 1979 to date.

k. Gateway Services

WESTLAW also provides access to various other third-party online services through their "Gateway" service. These generally require a separate agreement, and sometimes a separate monthly charge. Contact the vendor for further information.

WESTLAW's Gateway Databases presently include:

*Dow Jones News/Retrieval

*DowQuest

*DIALOG Information Systems

One hundred twenty-nine DIALOG databases are currently available on WESTLAW and can be searched using WESTLAW commands. Additional ones will be added to the WESTLAW directory over time, but are currently available via the Gateway. (See Section E.(l) for further information.)

*Dun and Bradstreet Credit Service

*PaperChase

*PHINET: Prentice-Hall Information Network

*State Net

*Vu/Text

l. CD-ROM

WEST also produces compact disc libraries in the areas of Federal Civil Practice, Delaware Corporation Law, Federal Taxation, Bankruptcy, Federal Securities and Government Contracts. These discs contain comprehensive collections of legal materials. For example, the two-disc Federal Civil Practice Library includes the full text of the following: *Wright & Miller on Federal Practice and Procedure, Federal Rules Decisions, Federal Practice Digest, Federal Civil Judicial Procedure and Rules, Devitt & Blackman on Federal Jury Practice and Instructions,* and various treatises on evidence, complex litigation and appellate procedure. Full text searching is allowed using WESTLAW commands. The software also provides access to WESTLAW databases. Disks are reissued periodically.

2. *The LEXIS® SERVICE*

Mead Data Central, Inc.
234 North Central Avenue, Suite 113
Phoenix, AZ 85004
(602) 256-0454
Customer Service: 1-800-543-6862
FAX: (602) 252-2238

The LEXIS® Service is a full text online service available through Mead Data Central, Inc. Its Arizona's coverage and library file names (as of 3/1/91) are as follows:

a. Arizona State Case Law

i. Arizona Supreme Court (ARIZ; ARIZ)

From 1898 to date.

ii. Arizona Court of Appeals (ARIZ; APP)

From 2/65 to date.

iii. Arizona Supreme Court, Court of Appeals, Board of Tax Appeals decisions and Corporation Commission orders. (ARIZ; CASES)

Arizona Supreme Court

From 1898 to date.

Arizona Court of Appeals

From 2/65 to date.

Board of Tax Appeals

From 12/82 to date.

Corporation Commission

From 8/78 to date.

iv. Arizona Supreme Court, Court of Appeals, Board of Tax Appeals decisions, Corporation Commission orders and Attorney General opinions (ARIZ; AGCASE)

Arizona Supreme Court

From 1898 to date.

Arizona Court of Appeals

From 2/65 to date.

Board of Tax Appeals

From 12/82 to date.

Corporation Commission

From 8/78 to date.

Attorney General

From 9/75 to date.

v. Arizona cases can also be accessed through the LEXIS® Service's specialized legal libraries in selected topical areas. These libraries include:

corporate law (CORP; ARIZ), state employment (EMPLOY; ARIZ), health (HEALTH; ARIZ), insurance (INSRLW; ARIZ), public employment (PUBEMP; ARIZ), public utilities (UTILITY; ARIZ), state securities (STSEC; ARIZ), federal tax (FEDTAX; ARIZ), and state tax (STTAX; ARIZ).

b. Arizona's Federal Case Law

i. U.S. Court of Appeals for the Ninth Circuit (GENFED; 9CIR)

From Jan. 1912 to date.

ii. U.S. District Courts (GENFED; 9DIST)

From Jan. 1912 to date.

iii. U.S. Court of Appeals and U.S. District

Court cases from the Ninth Circuit (GENFED; 9th)

From Jan. 1912 to date.

c. Arizona Statutes

i. Arizona Statutes unannotated (ARIZ; CODE)

Current year only.

ii. Arizona Constitution unannotated (ARIZ; CONST)

Current year only.

iii. Arizona Advance Legislative Service unannotated (ARIZ; ALS)

Current year only.

iv. Arizona Bills (ARIZ; AZTRCK) (LEGIS; AZTRCK)

From 1/90 to date.

Pending bills are tracked from introduction to enactment or veto. Information provided includes the following: date of introduction, latest action, synopsis of text, chronological history, subject headings and sponsor. Updated daily.

v. Arizona Statutes, Constitution and Advance Legislative Service unannotated (ARIZ; AZCODE)

The LEXIS® Service has no online index for Arizona statutes. The court rules are also not included.

vi. Insurance codes (INSRLW; CODE)

Current year only.

*To access only Arizona statutes input: state (arizona)

vii. Insurance-related statutes - (INSRLW; RELLAW)

(Automobile financial responsibility)

Current year only.

*To access only Arizona statutes input: state (arizona)

d. Arizona Administrative Law

i. Arizona Attorney General Opinions (ARIZ; AG)

From 8/78 to date.

*Arizona Attorney General Opinions on insurance (INSRLW; AG) for Arizona opinions only input: state (arizona).

ii. Arizona Corporation Commission Orders (Securities Law) (ARIZ; AZSEC)

From 8/78 to date.

iii. Arizona Board of Tax Appeals (ARIZ; AZTAX)

From 12/82 to date.

iv. Arizona Insurance Department Regulations (INSRLW;REGS)

Current year only.

*To access only Arizona regulations input: state (arizona)

v. Arizona Insurance Department (INSRLW; MISC)

Miscellaneous circulars, bulletins, letters and memoranda.

From 1976 to date.

vi. Arizona Attorney General Opinions on Insurance Law (INSRLW; AZAG)

From 1970 to date.

e. Other Arizona Databases

i. *Martindale-Hubbell Law Directory* for Arizona (MARHUB; AZDIR)

Contains the same information available in hard-copy but can be accessed in its full-text format. MARHUB's files are broken into geographic regions.

ii. Arizona Periodicals

Arizona Business Gazette (ADPR; ARIZ) or (NEXIS; ARIZ), from June 1986.

Arizona Trend (ADPR; AZTR) or (NEXIS; AZTR), from Jan. 1986 - Jan. 1990.

Business Journal - Phoenix and the Valley of the Sun (ADPR; PBJ) or (NEXIS; PBJ), from Jan. 1986 to date.

The Phoenix Gazette (ADPR; PHNXGZ) or (NEXIS; PHNXGZ), from Jan. 1990 to date.

Arizona Republic (ADPRR; ARZREP) or (NEXIS; ARZREP), from 1990 to date.

Southwest Newswire (ADPR; SWNEWS) or (NEXIS; SWNEWS), from Feb. 1984 to date.

f. Shepard's

The LEXIS® Service provides an online version of Shepard's for Arizona reports. The online coverage of Shepard's, however, is generally only as current as the most recent paper supplement received. In order to update this information it is necessary to use the LEXIS® Service itself as a citator. A sample search to find the most recent Arizona cases citing *Smith v. Jones* in the Arizona library (ARIZ) would be (Smith w/15 Jones) and date (aft x/x/xx). Limit the date restriction to the last six months.

g. The Auto-Cite® Service

The LEXIS® Service also provides access to another valuable cite checking tool called Auto-Cite®. The Auto-Cite® service offers complete coverage of both appellate and treatment history for each citing case. The first paragraph in the Auto-Cite® display provides the case record including the case name, date, parallel cites, and subsequent history. The second paragraph provides the prior history of the case. Auto-Cite® also lists cases to which the cited case makes negative reference. Finally, Auto-Cite® lists references to ALR Annotations which have cited the case. The Auto-Cite® service is updated daily using cases from the LEXIS® Service, and includes references to over 300 reporters including many specialized areas of law.

h. The NEXIS® Service

NEXIS®, introduced in 1979, is a news and business information service with more than 750 full-text sources online. These include *The New York Times, The Washington Post, Los Angeles Times, Business Week, Fortune, The Economist,* and the news services TASS, Xinhau, AP, UPI and Reuters. In addition, the NEXIS® Service contains more than 2,000 sources of abstracts including the *Wall Street Journal.* Searches may be run which include all files, regional files, individual files, or a customized combination of files.

i. The MEDIS® Service

The MEDIS® Service offers the full-text of more than 40 current medical journals and textbooks. It also contains Medline® (MEDLNE), a bibliographic database produced by the National Library of Medicine and various other "libraries" with medical, drug and poison, pharmaceutical, cancer and health care administration information.

j. COMPANY Library

The COMPANY library (COMPNY) contains files providing business and financial information, and company and industry research reports from investment banks and brokerage houses. SEC company filings are also available, including the 10-Q, 10-K, proxy statements and annual reports to shareholders. Abstracts of new business articles, the Disclosure online database and Investext reports are also included.

k. NAARS

The National Automated Accounting Research System Service (NAARS) is available by the American Institute of Certified Public Accountants. The library provides annual reports of major public corporations and government entities. Accounting literature is also included.

l. County Assessor Public Records

This file (ARIZ;AZPROP) (ASSETS;AZPROP) includes property records for all fifteen Arizona counties. Brief record contains assessed valve, type of property, etc.

m. The LEXDOC™ Feature

The LEXDOC™ feature allows LEXIS/NEXIS subscribers to order copies of public records documents retrieved from any jurisdiction (whether state or local) in the country. Orders are handled by LEXIS® Document Services. The LEX-

DOC™ feature can be used from any point in LEXIS® research. Arizona corporate documents, UCC liens and name reservations filings can be retrieved through this service. (LEXIS® Document Services is a trade name of Illinois Code Company, a wholly owned subsidiary of Mead Data Central, Inc.) For more information, contact the LEXIS® Document Service at 1-800-634-9738.

n. The ECLIPSE™ Feature

The ECLIPSE™ feature (Electronic Clipping Service) automatically reports new materials that correspond to a saved search request. The reports can be issued daily, on business days, weekly or monthly.

3. Electronic Bulletin Board System (BBS)

State Bar of Arizona
363 North First Avenue
Phoenix, AZ 85003
(602) 252-4804

The Electronic Bulletin Board's usage is limited to Arizona law firms and lawyers. The system can either be accessed from a personal computer with a modem or from a dedicated WESTLAW or LEXIS terminal. The system can be used for electronic mail, electronic file transfer and also to provide access to various publications. The *Digest of Arizona Ethics Opinions* and its *Key Word Index* are online, but are updated irregularly. In addition, the system may provide information on upcoming bar events and MCLE programs. Contact the State Bar to register for this system.

4. ABA/NET

c/o iNet Company of America
14800 Conference Center Drive
Chantilly, VA 22021-3805

This is an international network designed and produced by the American Bar Association. It provides access to both WESTLAW and LEXIS and to over 1200 other databases. Practice handbooks, articles and monographs published by the ABA and the American Bar Foundation are also online. CLE programs are listed.

C. Court Databases

1. The Ninth Circuit Court of Appeals

Appeals Court Electronic Service (ACES)
Ninth Circuit Court of Appeals
P.O. Box 547
San Francisco, CA 94101
(415) 556-8355

This database contains the full text of Ninth Circuit slip opinions and orders from the past 30 days, oral argument calendars, Ninth Circuit appellate rules and procedures, lists of depositions; press releases and notices. Access on the system is first-come, first-served.

2. *Public Access to Court Electronic Records (PACER)*

United States District Court
District of Arizona
United States Courthouse, Rm 1400
230 N. First Avenue
Phoenix, AZ 85025
(602) 379-3547

This database provides access to federal civil dockets. For service and documentation, send a request on letterhead.

3. *9th Circuit Online*

Judicial Update
559 Douglass Street
San Francisco, CA 94114
(415) 282-4491

This service is provided free to all subscribers of *9th Circuit Update.* The database includes current local rules and the full text of Ninth Circuit slip opinions.

4. *United States Bankruptcy Court*

District of Arizona
Automated Public Access System
230 N. First Avenue, Rm 5000
Phoenix, AZ 85025
(closed daily 4:00-5:00 p.m.)
(602) 379-6965

The database provides information on the status of hearings, recent bankruptcy cases indexed by name or file number, administrative filings; adversary filings; case verification; name, address and telephone numbers of attorneys or trustees; docketed claims register and the judges' calendar for two weeks.

To access free software, send a self-addressed stamped envelope and blank diskette (5 1/4" or 3 1/2") to Doug Dickey's attention.

D. Arizona Government/Legislative Databases

1. *Arizona Legislative Information Service (ALES)*

Archives and Public Records
Department of Library
3rd Fl. Capitol Bldg.
1700 W. Washington
Phoenix, AZ 85007
(602) 255-3701

This database contains information on current Arizona legislation, including the full-text of bills, their status and history. It is available to the public at the State Documents Desk at the Department of Library, Archives and Public Records and at the State Law Library. Searches are run by librarians. There is no charge for usage.

2. *Electronic Legislative Search System (ELSS)*

Commerce Clearing House
CCH Legislative Products Group
4025 W. Peterson Avenue
Chicago, IL 60646
(312) 583-8500

Includes selection of current bills and their legislative histories. It is available for over 2100 different subjects. Searching can be by either subject, sponsor, date, type of action, or bill number. A hard copy service is also available.

3. *Legislation OnLine Arizona (LOLA)*

Arizona News Service
14 N. 18th Avenue
Phoenix, AZ 85007
(602) 258-7026

Summaries of Arizona bills can be accessed in this database by bill number, short title and *A.R.S.* code title. Bill histories and notes and calendars are also included. Access to the full text of bills is schedule for 1992.

4. *State Net*

Public Affairs, Inc.
1900 14th Street
Sacramento, CA 95814
(916) 444-0840
To access through WESTLAW: 1-800-937-8529

State Net includes all Arizona legislation introduced during the current session. The database contained an abstract of the bill and a chronological action listing. A summary of Arizona regulations are also included. Searches can be run by topic, bill number, or STATENET Net ID number (for regulations only).

E. Miscellaneous Databases

1. *DIALOG Information Services, Inc.*

3460 Hillview Avenue
Palo Alto, CA 94304
1-800-334-2564 /(415) 858-3785
FAX: (415) 858-7069
For access through WESTLAW: 1-800-937-8529

DIALOG contains over 300 databases in the areas of law, business, engineering, social sciences, science, medicine and technology. Some databases are full-text while others are bibliographic.

The "Papers" file (File PAPERS) is comprised of miscellaneous regional newspapers in full-text. Arizona newspapers included are as follows:

> *Arizona Republic* (AR), *Phoenix Gazette* (PG), *Arizona Business Gazette* (AB), *Arizona Republic/Phoenix Gazette* (File 492) (all from January 1988 to date).

The Business Dateline, (File 635) another DIALOG database, also includes the *Arizona Business Gazette,* the *Arizona Republic* and *Arizona Trends.* The Business Dateline provides these and other regional business publications in full text from 1985 to date.

DIALOG is also available as a Gateway on WESTLAW. In addition, 129 DIALOG databases are currently accessible on WESTLAW itself using WESTLAW commands and search techniques. More databases will be added in the future.

2. *Dow Jones News/Retrieval*

Dow Jones and Company, Inc.
P.O. Box 300
Princeton, N.J. 08543-0300
News/Retrieval Questions: 1-609-452-1511
Software Questions: 1-609-452-1511
For access through WESTLAW: 1-800-937-8529
Billing Questions: 1-609-520-4088

Includes late breaking business news stories and data on companies, industries and the economy. Current stock quotes and company profiles are also available.

The database contains seven major groups: online reference tools, news, company profiles and reports, company and industry statistics and forecasts, quotes and market averages, business services and general services. SEC filing extracts are available on the Disclosure Database. Dun and Bradstreet reports are available on over 750,000 companies.

DowQuest contains current information from selected business articles. *Arizona Trend* and the *Arizona Business Gazette* are included. In addition, Dow Jones Text-Search services contain the full text of the *Wall Street Journal* and other business publications.

3. *Dun & Bradstreet's Online Service*

1 Diamond Hill Road
Murray Hill, NJ 07974
1-800-255-1033
To access through WESTLAW: 1-800-937-8529

Provides business information reports on Arizona public and private companies. These reports contain the following data: capital and credit ratings, number of employees, payment history, banking history, public filings, company history and operations.

4. *Information America*

10940 Wilshire Boulevard, Suite 1600
Los Angeles, CA 90024
(213) 443-4111/1-800-235-4008

The database includes records from the Arizona Corporation Commission including good standing status, statutory agent's name and address, I.D. no., prior names,company doing business and filing history. This information is included for active corporations only. The "Name Availability Service" searches over 20 million corporate names nationally. The Business News database includes the full text of press releases from major international news sources. "People Finder" profiles over 111 million individuals in the U.S. The profiles include address, phone, type of residence (including length of time at each), date of birth and family members' dates of birth. The "Business Finder" profiles approximately 8.5 million companies. Profiles include company name, address, telephone, type business and SIC code. Duns Business Records Plus includes reports on operations, executives and any intracompany relationships for approximately 3 million national public and private businesses. DOX is Information America's express document ordering system.

5. *LEGI-SLATE*

777 North Capitol Street
Washington, D.C. 20002
1-800 -877-6999
FAX: (202) 842-4748

LEGI-SLATE contains the full text of federal legislative and regulatory documents including the following: Congressional bills and resolutions from the 99th Congress to date, "Current USC" files which updates the USC with each new public law enacted (retrospective coverage is available from the 1982 edition of the USC, 1986 supplement to date), the Federal Register from 1985 to date, and the "Daily CFR" which updates the Code of Federal Regulations on a daily basis (retrospective coverage is available from 1/1/90). In addition, Congressional profiles, voting records, Congressional hearings, a news service and a press briefing service are also available.

6. *PaperChase*

Longwood Galleria
350 Longwood Avenue
Boston, MA 02115
1-800-722-2075
For access through WESTLAW: 1-800-937-8529

PaperChase is a service of Boston's Beth Israel Hospital. It contains bibliographic entries of biomedical journals from the National Library of Medicine. Many of these contain abstracts.

7. PHINET

Thomson Professional Publishing
910 Sylan Avenue
Engelwood Cliffs, NJ 07632
1-800-562-0245

This tax research database includes an online version of the *All States Tax Guide* looseleaf service (formerly published by Prentice-Hall).

8. CCH ACCESS

Commerce Clearing House, Inc.
4025 West Peterson Avenue
Chicago, Illinois 60646
1-800-835-0105

The CCH electronic tax research system provides an online version of various CCH tax looseleaf services. It includes their state "publications": *CCH State Tax Reporters* (topical arrangement), *Laws-State Structures* (official statutory format arrangement), and the *Advance Release Legislative Summaries* (digests of recent bills and legislation).

9. Prentice Hall Online

1900 E. 4th Street
Santa Ana, CA 92705
Customer Service: 1-800-333-8356/(714) 547-0590

Contains Arizona bankruptcy public record information.

10. WILSONLINE

H.W. Wilson Company
950 University Avenue
Bronx, N.Y. 10452
(212) 588-8400/1-800-367-6770

Wilsonline is an online version of the H.W. Wilson periodical indexes including the *Index to Legal Periodicals.* The *Business Periodicals Index,* the *Social Science Index* and the *Readers' Guide to Periodical Literature.*

F. Newspaper Databases

1. DataTimes

14000 Quail Springs Parkway, Suite 450
Oklahoma City, OK 73134
1-800-642-2525/(405) 751-6400
FAX: (405) 755-8028

Includes the full text of newspapers, newswires, magazines, and financial databases. Arizona publications contained are as follows:

- *Arizona Republic* (PHX) from 9/1/89

Phoenix Gazette (PHX) from 9/1/89

Arizona Business Gazette (ABG) from 9/1/89

Arizona Daily Star (TUCS) from 10/1/90

Tucson Citizen (TUCC) from 10/1/90

Business Dateline (BUSD)

contains selected full-text articles from:

Arizona Trend (AZTR) from 1/87

Arizona Business Gazette (ARIZ) from 6/86

The Business Journal: Phoenix and the Valley of the Sun - (PBJ) from 1/86

Tucson Business Digest (TBD) from 4/85

2. *VU/TEXT Information Services, Inc.*

325 Chestnut Street, Suite 1300
Philadelphia, PA 19106
(215) 574-4400 /1-800-323-2940
For access through WESTLAW: 1-800-937-8529

Vu/Text is a full-text database of national newspapers containing the following Arizona titles:

Arizona Business Gazette (AZA) from 10/1/86

Arizona Republic (AZA) from 10/1/86

Phoenix Gazette (AZA) from 10/1/86

Business Dateline (BDL)

The Business Dateline contains selected full-text regional publications. For Arizona these include:

Arizona Trend: from 1/86-1/90.

The Business Journal: Phoenix and the Valley of the Sun from 1/86.

Tucson Business Digest: from 8/85-12/86.

G. Bibliographic Databases

1. *Arizona State Universities Online Catalog*

Hayden Library
Arizona State University
Tempe, AZ 85257
For Assistance: (602) 965-6164
For Technical Advice: (602) 965-6500

ASU has developed with the Colorado Alliance of Research Libraries (CARL) a free database primarily containing an online catalog for ASU and numerous

Colorado institutions. Also included are various reference files on Arizona statistics, the *Academic American Encyclopedia,* the Arizona and Southwest Index of Special Collections, and the Labriola National American Indian Data Center.

The database has dial-in and broadband access. The Wilson Journal indexes, however, are available only to registered borrowers of ASU. A password is necessary for access to these files. The indexes can be searched by anyone at an ASU library.

2. *GEAC*

University of Arizona
Main Library
(Located at Cherry and Third Street)
Tucson, AZ 85721
Library Systems Office: (602) 621-6403

GEAC is the University of Arizona's online circulation system containing all of the Library's holdings at all its branches. The system can be searched by author, title or call number. Information is also provided on an item's circulation status, and if checked out, its due date. Remote access is available.

3. *AHSC Library Remote Access*

University of Arizona
Tucson, AZ 85724
To Access: (602) 621-4357
For Reference: (602) 626-6125

The LS/2000 is a free online catalog for the Arizona Health Sciences Center Library. The catalog contains bibliographic information on books, journals and AV materials.

4. *SEL Online Catalog*

University of Arizona
Science-Engineering Library
Tucson, AZ 85721
Library Computer Operations: (602) 621-6403

SEL contains the holdings of the University of Arizona's Science-Engineering Library. Remote access of this online database is available.

5. *OCLC Online Union Catalog*

For Southwest Area Access Information, contact:

AMIGOS Bibliographic Council, Inc.
11300 North Central Expressway, Suite 321
Dallas, TX 75243
1-800-843-8482
FAX: (214) 750-7921

This database provides bibliographic records of the holdings of over 7900 libraries (including all major Arizona libraries and large law firm libraries). The EPIC service allows this database to be searched by subject.

H. Public Records Databases

1. CDB INFOTEK

701 S. Parker Avenue, Suite 4500
Orange, CA 92668
(714) 542-2727

This is an investigative database of public records. Arizona records include driver histories, vehicle registration, consumer public filings, court filings, F.A.A. Airmen directory, fictitious business name, property records, and corporation commission records.

2. Credit Data Southwest, Inc.

301 E. Virginia
P.O. Box 2070
Phoenix, AZ 85001
(602) 252-6951, Ext. 315

Business and consumer credit information is available. Public records (e.g., tax liens, judgments, UCC filings, bankruptcy, etc.) can also be accessed. Only businesses can subscribe.

3. DATA QUICK INFORMATION NETWORK

3200 E. Camelback Road
Phoenix, AZ 85018
(602) 381-0394
Sales: 1-800-765-9191
Services: 1-800-628-9337

Database for accessing real estate and business data in Maricopa and Pima counties. It will identify real property assets, determine "comps," locate owners, etc.

4. Dun & Bradstreet's Online Service

(*supra* E(3))

Business reports may include public records of suits, judgments, UCC filings and tax liens.

5. Information America

(*supra* E(4))

6. *Instant Access Information Services*

NCI Direct Access Package
3351 Carleton Road
Hillsdale, MI 49242
(517) 437-0400

The service contains Arizona credit reports, motor vehicle/driver records, online forwarding files, and social security information.

7. *LEXIS County Assessor Public Records*

(*supra* B (2) (l))

8. *Realtron Corp.*

2444 E. University Drive, Suite 130
Phoenix, AZ 85034
(602) 220-0707

Online microfiche service of property information for Maricopa County. The information can be assessed by address or subdivision.

9. *TRW Real Estate Information Service*

7227 North Sixteenth Street
Phoenix, AZ 85020
(602) 870-6400

This is a real estate database which provides information on Maricopa and Pima County property, including ownership, property characteristics, financing, sales, taxes and usage. The database is used primarily by title companies to access ownership information by parcel number, etc.

I. Citation Form

Documents retrieved from online resources are cited to their hardcopy equivalents with one exception: slip or unpublished opinions only found on WESTLAW and LEXIS. In this instance, the applicable WESTLAW or LEXIS cite should be given. *The Bluebook: A Uniform System of Citation,* 15th edition, Rule 10.8.1, states that this information should be given parenthetically.

For example:

Alegria v. Redcherries, 2 CA-CV 90-0230, 1991 WL 5985, at *1 (Ariz. App. Jan. 22, 1991).

or

Alegria v. Redcherries, 2 CA-CV 90-0230, 1991 Ariz. App. LEXIS 18, at *1 (Ariz. App. Jan. 22, 1991).

Chapter 11

Arizona State Government Publications: Non-Legal

Donna Larson-Bennett

The Arizona government publications librarians are always generous and helpful, and they have been especially so while I prepared this chapter. I would like to acknowledge the following people who contributed to this paper by providing me with expertise and advice: Janet Fisher, Arizona Department of Library, Archives and Public Records; Atifa Rawan, University of Arizona Main Library.

A. Introduction

State publications present complex problems to researchers and libraries. As continuing series they vanish and reappear at odd intervals, as works of lasting value they suffer from obscurity, and as publications meant for mass consumption they often combine obtuse grammar with simplistic format. Despite Arizona's brief existence as a state[1] and thus as a producer of publications, the frustrations encountered in finding or using Arizona publications equal if not exceed those encountered by the unwary in other states.

This chapter outlines the current dynamics of finding Arizona state publications, discusses the major indexes and guides available, and lists and describes a selection of the most important series and publications from state agencies and commissions.

B. Definitions

State publications differ from materials called "archives" and "records." Publications are published and distributed by a government entity. They do not have to be written or put together by a government entity, but must be produced at the expense or partial expense of a government entity. They can be in any format including electronic.[2] Archives differ from publications in that they were or are not items made "available" to the public. For example, the working papers of a governor or an agency administrator or a research specialist are or will be archives. They never were or will not be made available or never were or are not going to be published in that form. The final report of the governor, printed and distributed, or the final report of an agency or commission, printed and distributed is a publication. The papers and work of the governor or the commission used in preparing the report are archives. Some archives are not available for use immediately. For example, U.S. Supreme Court Justice Sandra Day O'Connor's papers are at the Arizona Department of Library, Archives, and Public Records [DLAPR], but are not available for use by researchers for a specified period of time. Publications, on the other hand, unless classified for security reasons, are available for use at the time of publication.

Records are defined by state law[3] as "all books, papers, maps, photographs or other documentary materials, regardless of physical form or characteristics, . . . made or received by any governmental agency in pursuance of law or in connection with the transaction of public business and preserved or appropriate for preservation by the agency or its legitimate successor as evidence or the organization, functions, policies, decisions, procedures, operations of other activities of the government, or because of the informational and historical value of data contained therein." All state records are managed by the State Records Center, a division of DLAPR. Those records determined by each agency to be of no further legal, administrative, historical or other value are disposed of at the

1 Arizona entered the Union as the 48th State, February 14, 1912.

2 The State Documents Depository Task Force, of the Statewide Library Planning Council, Arizona Dept. of Library, Archives and Public Records, approved in 1989, the following definition for state documents: "Any informational materials, regardless of format, method of reproduction, or source, which originate in or are produced with the imprint, by the authority, or at the total or partial expense of a state agency. "State publication" incorporates those publications that may or may not be financed by state funds but are released by private entities pursuant to a contract with or subject to the supervision of any agency, such as research and consulting firms under contract with a state agency. This does not include correspondence, intra-office or inter-office memoranda, or routine forms."

3 Ariz. Rev. Stat. Ann. § 41-1350 (1985).

direction of the agency. A list of records disposed of with a statement by the director of DLAPR that the disposal was in compliance with the law is filed with the agency and with DLAPR. Like archives, some records held by the Records Center until they have no further value are protected by privacy rights. However, for the most part while agency records are stored they are accessible at the Records Center.

To summarize, publications are those materials that are distributed by a governmental entity to those outside its offices. Publications can be in any format including electronic, micro, and print. Archives are the working papers of government and are of a permanent and historic value and can be in any format. Records are materials made by a department in connection with its public business and can also be in any format but are not kept beyond their usefulness. This chapter is devoted to a discussion of publications, but since there is a gray area of overlap between these three categories, I have provided a list in Appendix A of Arizona archival collections, and the address of the State Records Center.

C. Primary Collections and Primary Bibliographic Information Sources of Arizona State Publications

Three libraries in the state "comprehensively" collect and retain Arizona publications: DLAPR, Arizona State University Hayden Library, and University of Arizona Main Library. The libraries are listed with contact information in Appendix B. While it is comforting to believe that these three libraries have "comprehensive" collections, the term is really inaccurate. These libraries try to collect comprehensively, but do not have comprehensive collections of Arizona state publications. All other libraries, including the Maricopa County Law Library, the university law libraries, and the large public libraries, selectively collect Arizona publications, and mainly have the well known, current and heavily requested publications, but do not have large or extensive retrospective holdings or comprehensive holdings of recent date. A recent article by two librarians at the University of Arizona Library describes the mechanisms for selecting and acquiring government publications in Arizona, both state and local, and provides some guidelines for building a collection.[4]

Equally elusive is the comprehensive list or bibliography of state publications. While DLAPR provides a current checklist of publications, the list cannot be relied upon for being complete. Thus, while consulting the three large collections of state publications would be the first choice in searching for a particular report, a thorough search also involves contacting agency libraries and offices. If interest is in all publications in a subject area or from an agency, in order to be comprehensive it is necessary to scan agency newsletters and daily newspapers as well as to look at the monthly DLAPR list.

4 *Government Publications* Review. v. 18, No. 1, January-February 1991, "Building State and Local Publication Collections: the Arizona Experience", by Robert Mitchell and Atifa Rawan.

The following section discusses each of these approaches to locating state agency publications in the recommended order of attack.

1. Primary collections:

In reality, DLAPR has the most comprehensive collection of Arizona state publications because of the very nature of the agency and its proximity to other State entities. By law[5] State agencies are required to provide DLAPR with copies of reports and publications. The law even provides for a statewide depository system of state publications.[6] However, the law does not provide a mechanism for enforcement, and there never has been any funding available for a state depository system.[7] State publications at DLAPR are classified under the Arizona Classification Number (a number patterned after the U.S. Government Printing Office Superintendent of Documents Classification Number), and are in the process of being cataloged. Current access to the collection is primarily through the ASU online catalog, although current publications and some retrospective materials are in DLAPR's catalog.

In addition to DLAPR being the most comprehensive of the library collections, as a state agency and official source for state publications, DLAPR provides notarized copies of state publications on request. This service is not ordinarily or conveniently done by other libraries.

The University of Arizona's Library also has a strong collection of state publications. All pre-1985 state documents are in the Special Collections Department of that Library, while the post-1985 to date are in the Government Documents Department. Arizona publications in Special Collections are cataloged and are mainly classified by the Library of Congress Classification System while the more current publications in Government Documents are in the catalog and are classified by the Arizona Classification Number.

ASU Library's collection of state publications began to grow in the 1960's when ASU began to grow as a university. While some series of publications go back much further, the strength of the collection dates from the 1960's to date. All state publications at ASU are in the Government Documents Collection, appear in the online catalog, and are classified under the Arizona Classification. The ASU on-line catalog can be accessed off-campus by most computers with a modem. Specifications for this access to the catalog are available from ASU's Hayden Library.[8]

OCLC,[9] the on-line bibliographic utility used throughout the U.S. and by most of the public and academic libraries in the State, recognizes the Arizona Classi-

5 Ariz. Rev. Stat. Ann. §§ 41-1338 to 1339 (1985).

6 Ariz. Rev. Stat. Ann. § 41-1335(B)(1) (1985).

7 In 1988 the State Librarian, Director of the Department of Library, Archives and Public Records, appointed a Statewide Library Planning Council. The Council has several task forces, and one dealing directly with the state agency publications depository question: State Documents Depository Library Task Force.

8 Hayden Library, Library Technology and Systems Services, Arizona State University, Tempe, Arizona 85287, telephone: (602) 965-7693.

9 Online Computer Library Center, Inc., Dublin, Ohio. OCLC is a bibliographic utility to which most large libraries in Arizona subscribe for cataloging services.

fication Number. Thus, because ASU has cataloged its Arizona publications on OCLC, this utility can be used to verify the existence of a particular title and also to check for holdings at ASU and at DLAPR. The difficulty of access to bibliographic records in OCLC grows out of the use of AACR2[10] rules for corporate entries. Unless the AACR2 form of entry is known, finding a entry in OCLC's 22,000,000[11] bibliographic records for a corporate or agency author and/or for a nondescript title like 'annual report', can be very frustrating, dumping either too many or no citations. EPIC Services,[12] a on-line reference system from OCLC, includes subject access to the OCLC On-line Union Catalog and thus subject access to Arizona government publications which have been cataloged on OCLC. DLAPR's State Reference Center, headed by Beth Ellen Woodard,[13] provides subject access to the catalog file through EPIC on request and at her discretion for other libraries and the public. While this is of some help, access to state publications through OCLC would be a search of last resort, too difficult and time consuming for most uses.

2. *Primary Sources: Checklists and Indexes*

DLAPR's monthly selection list of state publications[14] provides libraries with a list of publications DLAPR has received and indicates which titles are available from them, from the agency, not available except on inter-library loan, or only available for use at DLAPR. The list is available free from DLAPR, and is the only selection tool that covers all of the state agencies. However, no periodicals are listed, and the entries are not necessarily the AACR2[15] form of entry. Since the list does not cumulate and since items are not necessarily listed when they are published but only listed when they are received by DLAPR, it is only useful for current selection or current awareness or state publications. DLAPR includes with the *Checklist* an agency address list as a appendix, and this feature makes the list a convenient tool to use for obtaining publications which are not available directly from DLAPR.

Some commercial indexes include Arizona publications, but not on a comprehensive basis. The familiar *PAIS*[16] includes major studies from Arizona agencies. Congressional Information Service's *SRI*[17]includes a elite selection of state publications which have statistical material. If statistics are needed, the advantage of using *SRI* is that a microfiche collection of all the material indexed is

10 *Anglo-American Cataloging Rules;* prepared by the American Library Association, et. al., edited by Michael Gorman and Paul W. Winkler. 2d ed. 1978.

11 According to OCLC Reference Services, 2 million records are added each year: *Fact Sheet: Search CD450,* September 1990.

12 *Fact Sheet: The Epic Service.* OCLC Online Computer Library Center, Inc., References Services. September 1990.

13 Beth Ellen Woodard, Head, State Reference Center, telephone (602) 542-4416.

14 *Checklist of Publications of the State of Arizona.* Arizona. Department of Library, Archives and Public Records. monthly. 1976 -

15 *Anglo-American Cataloging Rules, supra* note 10.

16 *Public Affairs Information Service Bulletin.* New York. Public Affairs Information Service, Inc. semimonthly with quarterly and annual cumulations. 1915 -

17 *Statistical Reference Index.* Washington, D.C. Congressional Information Service. monthly (with quarterly and annual cumulations). 1980 -

available. In Arizona, several libraries subscribe to the microfiche collection[18] and thus all state statistical publications indexed in *SRI* are available in micro format from 1980 to date.

The Library of Congress's *Monthly Checklist of State Publications*[19] keeps up its publication schedule but never was comprehensive and is now seldom used. It is compiled by the Exchange and Gift Division of the Library of Congress and lists those items sent for LC's collections by state agencies. As a selection tool or a index, the LC's long published and familiar *Checklist* is not recommended as a primary source for current publication information. The list is useful for a serious and thorough retrospective search and can be used as a safety net check for current items.

3. *Primary Sources: Agency Libraries, Directories, and Newsletters and Publications Lists*

a. Agency Libraries

State agency libraries exist mainly as research collections for the agency rather than as sources or repositories of the agency's publications. DLAPR is the official repository and distributor of state agency publications, but as mentioned above, there are no legal incentives for state agencies to deposit their publications at DLAPR and DLAPR does not have a budget that provides for a active acquisition program to enforce the law. Agency librarians are usually very helpful, sometimes have heard or have a copy of the reports of the agency, and can often give advice on who or how to obtain a copy. An organization called SAIL (State of Arizona Interagency Librarians) has existed for some time and provides an informal discussion structure for state librarians' interests and issues. Information on the organization, including who to contact for a list of members, is usually available from the state documents librarian at DLAPR.[20]

Not all state agencies have a library or a librarian. Also, agency libraries and librarians appear and disappear depending on the research or information need of the agency and the budget. Despite the sometimes transient nature of these libraries, they are a valuable resource when searching for state publications or information on state agency publishing activities. APPENDIX C provides a current list of agency libraries and librarians.

b. Agency Directories

If an agency does not have a library to contact, or if that contact has been unsuccessful, the next step in searching for a publication is to contact the agency

18 DLAPR Microforms Collection (1980 -); Phoenix Public Library, Business and Science Department, (1985 -); Arizona State University's Hayden Library, Current Periodicals and Microforms Service (1980 -); University of Arizona's Main Library, Government Documents Department (1980 -); Northern Arizona University's Cline Library, Microforms Department (1980 -).

19 Monthly Checklist of State Publications. U.S. Library of Congress. Gifts and Exchange Division. monthly with annual cumulative index. 1910 -

20 Arizona Department of Library, Archives and Public Records, Maps/State Documents, Research Division, 1700 W. Washington, Phoenix, AZ 85007, telephone (602) 542-4343.

office which produced the work or is familiar with the type of information wanted. There are three standard directories of Arizona government offices,[21] and one publication that can be used as a directory if the office needed regulates an activity.

When searching for information on a publication or information about a issue, the most efficient search requires approaching the most directly responsible bureaucratic entity or the smallest unit that may be able to help. A call to the operator or general information receptionist of a large or medium size agency can lead to a maze of intra-agency referrals and some time consuming experiences. Switchboard operators or general receptionists are often rushed and do not know a great deal about the work of each office within the agency. On the other hand, the person who answers the telephone of a small agency can often provide solid information and sometimes is even in charge of mailing copies of requested publications.

Some small agencies or offices within larger agencies maintain a general mailing list for announcements or publications. Once the existence of such a list is confirmed it is usually easy to add a name to the list. However, sole reliance on the mailing list to be a automatic comprehensive acquiring mechanism for publications can be a mistake. Mailing lists are sometimes skipped or exist in multiple versions depending on who is doing the mailing, and can be edited or discontinued without notice. Many state departments also have public information officers either listed in the directories or available through the main information or switchboard number. These officers can usually help in locating a particular function within the organization. The three statewide government directories cited above help locate these offices.

If a publication or piece of information needed is from a regulatory agency of the state, use the *Arizona Administrative Register*[22] (AAR) as a directory. AAR prints proposed rules and notices, and provides contact names and telephone numbers for each proposed rule. A "Permanent Rules Index" arranged by rule number provides access to the location of the proposed rule in AAR and thus provides access to an official who is familiar with that area of government regulation and who can likely provide the information or publication needed. AAR also lists new appointees. Astute use of AAR can save a lot of time and motion, and provides access to those employees who have expertise in a special area.

In addition to the above sources of directory information for state agencies, there are other more specialized directories. These special directories can be of great help if relevant to a search and are usually easy to obtain from the agency or organization publisher. Appendix D provides a list of the directories and the

21 *State of Arizona 1989 Directory*. annual. Arizona Department of Administration, Telecommunications Office, 1700 W. Washington, Phoenix, AZ 85007. *1989-90 Arizona Yearbook: a Guide to Government in the Grand Canyon State*; edited by Richard and Charity Yates. Biannual. Available from Information Press, P.O. Box 1422, Sisters, OR 97440. *Metro Phoenix Area Code 602 September 1989/90: The White Pages*. Annual. U.S. West. Blue pages are government listings.

22 *Arizona Administrative Register*. Arizona. Secretary of State. monthly. 1987 - Continues, *Arizona Administrative Digest*. Arizona. Secretary of State. 1981 - 1986.

procurement source for each. Only the most current and most useful directories are listed. The guide to Arizona directories cited immediately before the other listings provides a more comprehensive bibliography.

c. Agency Newsletters and Publications Lists

Publications lists provide excellent sources for retrospective bibliographic checking. If available for an agency, they usually are not printed with regularity, so that reliance on them can be a mistake. The public information officer or the research office of an agency will know if a list is prepared and send the list out on request.

Locating state publications by using agency newsletters and publications lists could be described as the "labor intensive" approach to state publication information. Despite the unappealing thought of sifting through newsletters, these publications are the most valuable sources of information on current agency activities, reports and publications. If the goal of an organization or library is to obtain all relevant state information on a particular issue, then obtaining and scanning the appropriate newsletters is the only thorough approach to the challenge in addition to consulting DLAPR's *Checklist.*[23] A problem with the method is that agencies and offices within state agencies, commissions and other official entities have a habit of beginning and ending periodicals and bibliographical series with no notice. Care must be taken to keep current with the reading, and if a newsletter stops publication, to call the office and inquire about a substitute or future plans. Frequently the information is simply added to another existing source and there is no loss of current news. Appendix E provides a list of currently issued newsletters arranged by agency. Note that often two or three departments or offices within a department may have functions relating to an interest area. Thus, more than one newsletter is needed. When dealing with areas like the environment or social and health services, this becomes apparent. Appendix E is not comprehensive, and since publications regularly materialize and disappear, an agency or office ought to be checked by telephone before concluding that no list or newsletter is available.

Coupled with the agency lists and newsletters, is the need to keep current and act on information in the newspapers and in the *Capitol Times*.[24] Printed reports often have very short runs, and while the report may eventually appear on DLAPR's monthly list, by the time it is listed it is often too late to obtain a copy. If the run is very short, DLAPR will not even loan its copy on interlibrary loan. Photocopying is always a backup, and usually a state publication is not copyrighted, however, it is a clumsy, costly and slow method of acquiring needed material.

23 *Checklist of Publications of the State of Arizona*, *supra* note 14.

24 *Arizona Capitol Times*. Phoenix. Arizona News Service. June 1982 - (formerly *Arizona Legislative Review*).

D. Arizona State Publications and Sources of Information: Those That Seem Useful for Most General and Special Libraries

1. Online sources: ALIS, LOLA, Arizona Statistics File, State Data Center

a. Preface

Although relevant to a topical search for information about Arizona or issues involving Arizona, federal data sources and indexes or data files of Arizona newspapers are not included. Only sources that are state generated or primarily include state generated material are listed.

b. ALIS (Arizona Legislative Information System)

Beginning with the Thirty Ninth Legislature, 1989, this system is designed to provide current information for the members and staff of the Arizona Legislature. The data base most interesting for outside use is the Bill Status System and is available to the public at the Reference Desk and the State Documents Desk at DLAPR.[25] The program provides for access by bill number, sponsor name, committee, ARS citation, or key word. Reports reveal the current status as well as a history of the bill in both houses. The system is full text, and provides the text of bill as introduced, as changed by the Senate and House, and the conference version. Like all systems, it is only as up to date as the input, and caution should be used in relying on the system for the most up to date information.

c. LOLA (Legislation on Line Arizona)

LOLA is a copyrighted product of the Arizona News Service.[26] Although not a full text system, it provides access to the current state legislative session and special sessions by bill number, committee, ARS citation and subject. Also entered are notes on debate calendars, and committee agendas. LOLA is updated daily and available 23 hours a day.

d. Arizona Statistics File

This file is part of the Arizona State University Library's on-line catalog system. The file is input from a variety of print sources, including both federal and state agencies, and is not flexible or programmable. Mainly directed toward the needs of ASU administrators, the data and the medium is useful if your need suits the series of tables. For example, enrollment data in schools is not given by grade, but by groups of grades, and most education tables are for higher education. The sources for the tables are cited, so the file can be used as a index to more detailed information.

25 DLAPR Reference, (602) 542-3701; DLAPR State Documents, (602) 542-4343.

26 For information on subscription price and access contact: Arizona News Service, P.O. Box 2260, Phoenix, AZ 85002, telephone (602) 258-7026.

e. State Data Center

The Center, part of the Arizona Department of Economic Security, acts as coordinator for U.S. Bureau of the Census data and Arizona access points, composed of five principal participants[27] and eighteen affiliates. The Center receives virtually all data products for Arizona from the Census Bureau, produces some standard data products itself, and can prepare special tabulations upon request at user cost.

f. Business and Industry Data Center (BIDC)

Like the State Data Center, but under the lead agency of the Arizona Department of Commerce, this center is in the process of being planned. The BIDC will act as a coordinator for federal data and Arizona access points. Inquiries about the status of this proposed center and its potential services should be addressed to the Department of Commerce or the State Data Center, Department of Economic Security.[28]

2. *Print sources by subject area: Business, Courts, Crime, Education, Environment, General Government (Budget, Administration, Legislature), Health and Vital Statistics, Labor, Population, Transportation*

a. Preface

The following discussion, under ten subject areas, presents a very subjective picture of Arizona government publications. Federal government and most commercial sources of information on Arizona are not included despite the fact that these sources sometimes add depth and perspective to an area. Despite its selective and biased content the discussion displays the 'multisource' structure of state government publishing sources. Usually it is the case that material needed on one subject area will be available from several agencies, each one gathering data and making reports on a different aspect of that topic. Thus for the most part one newsletter or one mailing list fail in covering a topic and fail in keeping current with the activities of government in a subject area. The following subject narrative cites to only the latest edition of a series. Frequency of publication is given if it is not discussed or indicated by the title. A price is provided if the publication is not free on request.

27 Arizona Department of Economic Security, 1300 West Washington, Room 102, P.O. Box 6123 (Site Code 045Z), Phoenix, AZ 85005, (602) 542-5984; Arizona Department of Library, Archives and Public Records, Federal Documents Section, 1700 West Washington, Phoenix, AZ 85007, (602) 542-4121; Arizona State University, Center for Business Research, College of Business Administration, Tempe, AZ 85287, (602) 965-3961; Northern Arizona University, College of Business Administration, P.O. Box 15066, Flagstaff, AZ 86011, (602) 523-3657; University of Arizona, Division of Economic and Business Research, College of Business and Public Administration, Tucson, AZ 85721, (602) 621-2155.

28 Mobin Qaheri, Arizona Department of Commerce, Research Department, 3800 N. Central, Suite 1400, Phoenix, AZ 85012, (602) 280-1321. Linda Strock, State Data Center, Department of Economic Security, 1300 W. Washington, Room 102, P.O. Box 6123 (Site Code 0452), Phoenix, AZ 85005, (602) 542-5984.

b. Business

The universities publish the bulk of material dealing with business and finance in Arizona. The University of Arizona produces a monthly periodical, *Arizona Economy,*[29] which reports a wide variety of data on both Phoenix, Tucson and two non-metropolitan regions. This periodical also includes brief articles on topics dealing with the economy and trends, however more extensive articles and analyses are printed in the annual serial, *Arizona Review.*[30] The subscription update released on a biannual schedule[31] expands the economic tables in the monthly periodical giving a wide and detailed statistical picture of the state. Arizona State University's *Arizona Business*[32] has brief articles on Arizona's economy, and provides a monthly snapshot of the Arizona business environment. The *Arizona Blue Chip Economic Forecast*[33] summarizes forecasts on Arizona's economy from twenty economists representing banks, universities, companies and state agencies, and includes a average figure of the projections. A *Western Blue Chip Economic Forecast*[34] includes the latest economic forecasts for nine western states so that comparisons can be made, and like the Arizona and Phoenix publications, includes articles on topics of special interest.

The Department of Economic Security does employment and labor force forecasts, and reports growth rates for the state, and Phoenix and Tucson, and non-metropolitan counties.[35] Also, the Department LMI Directory[36] includes a list of other state and private offices that produce economic forecasts and information about the Arizona business environment as well as a complete descriptive list of its own publications. The *LMI Newsletter*[37] reports business openings and closings in addition to providing data on labor and employment in the state. *Job Growth Update*[38] ranks state and metropolitan areas within states according to job growth in non-agricultural sectors: construction, manufacturing, transportation/communications/utilities, finance/insurance/real estate, services and

29 *Arizona Economy.* University of Arizona. College of Business and Public Administration. monthly except July & August.

30 *Arizona Review.* University of Arizona. College of Business and Public Administration. Division of Economic and Business Research. 1990.

31 *Arizona Economic Indicators.* University of Arizona. College of Business and Public Administration. Division of Economic and Business Research. biannual. $14/year.

32 *Arizona Business.* Arizona State University. College of Business. Center for Business Research. monthly.

33 *Arizona Blue Chip Economic Forecast.* Arizona State University. College of Business. Economic Outlook Center. monthly. $89/year (includes 2 supplement issues of *Phoenix Blue Chip Economic Forecast*).

34 *Western Blue Chip Economic Forecast.* Arizona State University. College of Business. Economic Outlook Center. 10 issues/year. $99/year.

35 *Arizona Employment Forecasts, 1990 - 1999.* Arizona. Department of Economic Security. Research Administration. September 1990; *Labor Force and Employment in Arizona, 1990 - 1999.* Arizona. Department of Economic Security. Research Administration. September 1990.

36 *LMI (Labor Market Information) Directory.* Arizona. Department of Economic Security. Research Administration. 1987.

37 *LMI (Labor Market Information) Directory.* Arizona. Department of Economic Security. Research Administration. monthly.

38 *Job Growth Update, Ranking of the States and MSAs.* Arizona State University. College of Business. Economic Outlook Center. monthly. $79/year.

government. Despite the fact that this is nationwide data, the implications for the Arizona economy are clear.

The Arizona Department of Commerce provides a useful bibliography of titles related to Arizona's economy, and includes citations to publications dealing with construction, employment, financial, housing/income/living costs, real estate data, and other areas.[39]

c. Courts

Along with the annual data report discussed below under "Crime", the *Judicial Report*[40] summarizes and presents data on the various functions of the state court system, including caseload and financial data. Particularly useful are the flow charts of the Superior Court adult probation and juvenile adjudication processes. In 1989, Arizona Supreme Court's Commission on the Courts, appointed by Chief Justice Frank X. Gordon, Jr., completed their report and published a long-range plan for the judiciary through the year 2000 which includes recommendations and strategies and a plan for implementing the changes.[41] Four task force reports expand the recommendations and analysis of the Commission.[42]

d. Crime

Information and data on the Arizona criminal justice system are reported in four agencies. The Department of Public Safety produces the *Uniform Crime Report.*[43] Data includes offenses and arrests by type of crime, place, and by age and sex of offender. A crime index and comparative data is also included for the previous year. Statistics cover a wide variety of topics, from information on law enforcement officers, value of property stolen and recovered, age and sex of victims, to types of weapons used, and location and time of offenses.

The Department of Corrections' *Annual Report,*[44] presents statistics on the Arizona prison population and population releases. Data includes average months served by type of crime and sex of offender. Juvenile offender information is also included.

The state attorney general also compiles a basic source for information on the criminal justice system.[45] Data, charts and graphs present a broad view of subjects dealing with crime rates, state and local government expenditures on

39 *Researching Arizona's Economy: A Guide to Basic Sources.* Arizona. Department of Commerce. 1989.

40 *The Arizona Courts, FY89 Judicial Report.* Arizona. Supreme Court. 1990.

41 *Report of the Commission on the Courts,* 1989. Arizona. Supreme Court. Commission on the Courts. 1989.

42 *Report of the Task Force on Children and Families in the Courts; Report of the Task Force on Court Organization and Administration; Report of the Task Force on Dispute Resolution; Report of the Task Force on Court Productivity.*

43 *Arizona Uniform Crime Report, 1989.* Arizona. Department of Public Safety. Arizona Criminal Justice Information System. 1990. annual.

44 *Arizona Department of Corrections 1989 Annual Report.* Arizona. Department of Corrections. 1990.

45 *The Facts About Crime and Punishment in Arizona.* Arizona. Attorney General. November 1988. irregular.

police and courts, and sentencing. Much of the information includes comparisons to national average figures.

The Arizona Supreme Court's *Data Report*[46] is a statistical addendum to the annual report and contains not only budget and personnel data on court operations, but also data on types of cases handled and disposition of cases including sentences. Juvenile adjudications, dispositions, and probation are included. Data on Superior Courts, Justice of the Peace Courts, Municipal Courts, as well as the District Courts and the Supreme Court are presented by court.

e. Education

Three state agencies publish material dealing with education topics. The Department of Education, headed by the elected office of the Superintendent of Public Instruction manages the general supervision over the school system,[47] while the Board of Regents directs the three state universities[48] and the State Board of Directors for Community Colleges administers the overall programs of the fourteen community college districts.[49]

The *Annual Report of the Superintendent of Public Instruction*[50] provides financial and enrollment statistics for all school districts, as well as summary statistics for the state. The annual *Statewide Report for Arizona Pupil Achievement Testing* and its *Appendix*[51] gives summary data and data by school district and school on Arizona students' testing scores by age, sex and ethnic background in reading, language and mathematics. A "quarterly" publication called *Ed. Stat*[52] presents an ongoing analysis and statistical data on Arizona schools and pupils. *Ed. Stat* has not kept its stated publication schedule, but it will hopefully be continued perhaps on a semi-annual basis.

The Arizona Board of Regents produces a policy manual, kept up to date by periodic filings, and available at the university libraries.[53] A publication produced by the Board of Regents and the Board of Directors for Community Colleges in conjunction with the Higher Education Coordinating Council[54] provides guidance to students who wish to transfer within the Arizona system.

46 *The Arizona Court's FY89 Data Report.* Arizona. Supreme Court. Administrative Office of the Courts. 1990.

47 Ariz. Rev. Stat. Ann. §§ 15-201 to 271 (1991).

48 Ariz. Rev. Stat. Ann. §§ 15-1601, 1625 to 1626 (1991).

49 Ariz. Rev. Stat. Ann. §§ 15-1421, 1424 to 1425 (1991).

50 *Annual Report of the Superintendent of Public Instruction for Fiscal year 1988-1989, Statistical Section, In compliance with Arizona Revised Statutes Sec. 15-255.* Arizona. Department of Education. December 1989.

51 *Statewide Report for Arizona Pupil Achievement Testing.* Arizona. Department of Education. June 1990 and *Appendix.*

52 *Ed. Stat: the Quarterly Statistical Report of the Arizona Department of Education.* Arizona. Department of Education. q. 1988 -

53 *Policy Manual.* Arizona. Board of Regents. 1983. kept up-to-date with periodic filings.

54 *Arizona Higher Education Course Equivalency Guide.* Arizona Board of Regents, Arizona State Board of Directors for Community Colleges in Arizona in conjunction with Arizona Higher Education Coordinating Council. 1974 -

The Commission on the Arizona Environment uses quarterly public forums to identify and study issues. Recommendations are then forwarded from the Commission to the Legislature and the Governor for consideration. Some reports on particular topics come from the Commission, as well as the regularly published directory.[55] While the Commission is largely advisory,[56] the Department of Environmental Quality, a completely separate body, is charged with the regulation and enforcement of state laws dealing with air, water quality, and with waste management.[57] The Department produces compliance status reports[58] and reports on environmental conditions.[59]

Arizona does not have an act that requires environmental impact assessments, but the Arizona State Clearinghouse, in the Department of Commerce,[60] coordinates all studies and comments on studies dealing with any federally funded projects in Arizona. Since a large part of Arizona's land is under federal control,[61] this is an important function in the state and for the process of environmental policy formation and enforcement. The Clearinghouse is also a source on all past Environmental Impact Statements, both the drafts and final versions.

The Department of Game and Fish periodically produces studies on wildlife. Although presently under budget constraints, the current data that had been in the game investigations[62] is available at the office. The annual report on hunting permits and game bagged is still being printed.[63]

The 1989 Arizona State Parks' *Arizona Statewide Comprehensive Outdoor Recreation Plan*[64] analyses serves as a common reference point for decisions relating to outdoor recreation. It also provides a framework for the orderly

55 See APPENDIX C, Environment.

56 Ariz. Rev. Stat. Ann. § 49-121(G) (1988).

57 Ariz. Rev. Stat. Ann. § 49-104 (1988).

58 *Arizona Drinking Water System Compliance Status Report, July 1988 through August 1989.* Arizona. Department of Environmental Quality. Office of Water Quality. Drinking Water Compliance Unit. November 15, 1990; *State of Arizona Water Quality Assessment for 1988 (Section 305(b)) Report.* Arizona. Department of Environmental Quality. Office of Water Quality. Water Assessment and Groundwater Hydrology Sections. June 30, 1989.

59 *1989 Air Quality Control for Arizona.* Arizona. Department of Environmental Quality. August 1990; *1989 Annual Report; Water Quality and Water Programs of the Arizona Department of Environmental Quality.* Arizona. Department of Environmental Quality. July 1, 1990.

60 Arizona State Clearinghouse, 1700 W. Washington, State Capitol, West Wing, Phoenix, AZ 85007, (602) 280-1300.

61 From *Arizona Yearbook: A Guide to Government in the Grand Canyon State.* Eugene, OR. Information Press. 1989: 18% of the land area in Arizona is under individual or corporate ownership, 16% - U.S. Forest Service, 17% - U.S. Bureau of Land Management, 13% - State, 23% - Indian, and 10% - Other (Military Reservation, National Parks, etc.).

62 *Arizona Big Game Investigations, 1984-1985.* Arizona. Game and Fish Department Wildlife Management Division. 1985 (last annual printed); *Arizona Small Game Investigations, 1985-1986.* Arizona. Game and Fish Department Wildlife Management Division. 1986 (last annual printed).

63 *Arizona Game Survey and Harvest Data Summary, 1989.* Arizona. Game and Fish Department Wildlife Management Division. 1990.

64 *SCORP: Arizona Statewide Comprehensive Outdoor Recreation Plan.* Arizona State Parks. 1989. Other components of the plan include: *Arizona Trails Plan, Arizona Rivers, Streams & Wetlands Study, Arizona Lakes Study, Arizona Outdoor Recreation Participation Study, Arizona Natural Areas Study.*

planning, acquisition, development, and administration of Arizona's outdoor recreation resources.

g. General Government: Budget, Administration, Legislature:

1. Budget

The budget documents for the state come from three sources: the Office of the Governor, the Legislature, and the Department of Administration. In January of each year, or within 5 days after the regular session to the legislature convenes,[65] the Governor submits to the Legislature an executive budget.[66] Budget preparation requirements for agency requests and statements, and for the Governor's submission to the Legislature, are found in the *Arizona Revised Statutes.*[67] This budget includes brief narratives for each department, commission or board, and a statement of program expenditures or estimates for the preceding two years, the requested amounts, and the Governor's recommendation for the next fiscal year. The narrative at the beginning of the document summarizes the changes requested and provides tables and analyses of revenues and expenditures in broad terms.

The next step of the budget process involves the Legislature with its Joint Legislative Budget Committee (JLBC). JLBC is directed by law to study and make recommendations to the Legislature regarding the expenditures and revenues of state agencies or divisions.[68] In conjunction with that responsibility, JLBC also performs a function of analyzing the fiscal impact of proposed legislation and regulation. As part of the budget process, JLBC submits to the Legislature a budget analysis with recommendations which is usually in several parts: a summary, a detailed report, capital outlay report, and non-appropriated funds and specific funds report.[69] State law requires this analysis be prepared and distributed as soon after the Governor's budget is presented as possible.[70] Naturally differences between the Governor's *Executive Budget* recommendations and JLBC's recommendations are discussed and highlighted. The outcome of the appropriations process is a general appropriations act[71] and other acts which are then put together by JLBC in the appropriations report.[72] This report not

65 Ariz. Rev. Stat. Ann. § 35-111 (1990).

66 *State of Arizona Executive Budget, Fiscal Year 1991, Containing the Recommendations of Rose Mofford, Governor, presented to the Second Regular Session of the 39th Legislature for the Fiscal Year, July 1, 1990 to June 30, 1991.* Arizona. Office of the Governor. January 1990.

67 Ariz. Rev. Stat. Ann., Title 35, Chapter 1.

68 Ariz. Rev. Stat. Ann. § 41-1272 (1985).

69 *Annual Budget FY 1991, Summary of Recommendations and Economic and Revenue Forecast.* Arizona. Joint Legislative Budget Committee. January 22, 1990; *Annual Budget FY 1991, Analysis and Recommendations.* Arizona. Joint Legislative Budget Committee. January 22, 1990; *Fiscal Year 199l, Capital Outlay Budget Recommendations.* Arizona. Joint Legislative Budget Committee. January 22, 1990?; *State of Arizona Annual Budget FY 1991, Non-Appropriated Funds and Special Funds Which Include Appropriated Dollars.* Arizona. Joint Legislative Budget Committee. January 22, 1990?.

70 Ariz. Rev. Stat. Ann. 41-1273(D) (1985).

71 *Session Laws 1990 Third Special Session.* Arizona. Secretary of State. 1990. Chapter 1 (SB 1008).

72 *State of Arizona Appropriations Report for the Fiscal Year Ending June 30, 1991.* Arizona. Joint Legislative Budget Committee. July 1990?

only provides the appropriation figures for each program, but also attempts to provide statements of legislative intent.

The final step in the budget process is the report on the actual budget outlays and expenditures. Two reports are produced by the Arizona Department of Administration, Accounting Office, one for the State funds[73] and the other for Federal funds.[74] The statement for State funds is submitted to the Governor on or before December 1, of each year[75] and provides a complete report of the financial transactions of the preceding fiscal year. The federal funds report is submitted to the Legislature at each regular session[76] and covers the preceding fiscal year as well as analyzes the adequacy of the programs in the state and makes recommendations regarding legislation necessary for improved operation or for activation of programs in which the state does not operate.

In addition to the regular budgetary and budget report process, the Auditor General, part of the JLBC office, makes regular financial and compliance audits of state agencies, commissions and boards, and also prepares special audit or performance audits at the request of the Joint Legislative Oversight Committee.[77] Since the special audits and performance audits are done on request, they usually highlight questions or problems with a program or operation. The *Annual Report of the Auditor General*[78] required by law,[79] lists the reports issued during the year by the Auditor's Financial Division and by the Performance Audit Division.

2. Administration

State government offices receive direction from many sources including the federal government. However, without going into the accounting and procedural requirements attached to federal money coming into the state, there are some general state administrative documents. The *Arizona Agency Handbook*[80] sets forth and explains the state laws that govern the operation of state agencies. Divided into major sections of functions, the manual includes indexes by cases, rules, Attorney General Opinions, and *Arizona Revised Statutes* and *Constitution* provisions. In addition, the Attorney General also publishes a *Local Government Handbook*[81] which details the laws, rules, procedures and policies set forth by the State for local governments. The *Arizona Blue Book*[82] provides a general guide to Arizona state and local government, elected offices, and state appointed boards and commissions, and includes a brief history of the state, a review of

73 *Annual Financial Report, 1988 - 1989.* Arizona. Department of Administration. November 1, 1989.

74 *State of Arizona Statement of Federal Funds, Fiscal Year 1990.* Arizona. Department of Administration. 1990.

75 Ariz. Rev. Stat. Ann. § 35-131(D) (1990).

76 Ariz. Rev. Stat. Ann. § 41-723 (1985).

77 Ariz. Rev. Stat. Ann. § 41-1279.03 (1985).

78 *State of Arizona Annual Report of the Auditor General, Year Ended June 30, 1989.* Arizona. Office of the Auditor General. December 22, 1989.

79 Ariz. Rev. Stat. Ann. § 41-1279.03(A)(4) (1985).

80 *Arizona Agency Handbook.* Arizona. Office of the Attorney General. 1988

81 *Local Government Handbook.* Arizona. Office of the Attorney General. [1988?].

82 *Arizona Blue Book.* Arizona. Secretary of State. January 1986; and *Arizona Blue Book Supplement.* Arizona. Secretary of State. 1988.

ballot measures and a list of all ballot propositions since statehood, as well as election totals and current voter registration requirements.

Like the *Annual Report of the Auditor General*,[83] annual reports of state agencies generally have useful information on governmental functions and activities. They often contain budget data and sometimes a directory for the agency itself, and information on publications and reports made during the past year.

Operations manuals used within agencies to perform various functions are usually not available for distribution or listed anywhere. Exceptions to this rule are several accounting manuals from the Office of the Auditor General mandated by Arizona law,[84] and a variety of other manuals usually produced in order to assist local government authorities in preparing requests or applications for grants, and reporting on activities.[85] Arizona does not have a freedom of information act, thus there is no formal mechanism or policy for gaining access to agency manuals if none are printed and distributed outside the agency as the above examples were. Manuals not in the State Documents Collection at DLAPR are likely to be only available at the agency office that produces the manual and available at the discretion of the officer in charge barring legal authority for making the material available.

3. Legislature

Keeping in mind the on-line legislative action tracking services described above, ALIS and LOLA, the primary publications of the Legislature are the bills, journals, and other legislative history information covered in Chapter 3 of this volume. The Legislative Council, however, provides three useful reports. The first is the *Arizona Legislative Bill Drafting Manual*[86] which provides guidance in the preparation of bills and other legislative proposals, and gives details on how to check for laws which will be affected by new provisions and what formal requirements must be followed to present a proposal. The Legislative Council's *Annual Report on Defects in the Arizona Revised Statutes and Constitution*[87] recommends or explains the lack of recommendation for blends or multiple legislative activity, and revision corrections of the current law. Blends are recommended when two or more chapters, free of Constitutional defect, are substantively compatible. Recommendations involving the Constitution are brief since changes are required to be passed by proposition to the electorate. Statute improvements are presented in order by ARS citation. A Proposed bill with all statutory provisions is included in the report. The Council's *Internal Reference Manual*[88] is a table of specifically interrelated statutory

83 *State of Arizona Annual Report of the Auditor General, supra* note 78.

84 Ariz. Rev. Stat. Ann. §§ 41-1270.03(B) and 41-1279.07 (1985).

85 For example: *Planning and Zoning Handbook.* Arizona. Department of Commerce. Community Development Program. January 1986; *Arizona Environmental Handbook: CDBG, Community Development Block Grant.* Arizona. Department of Commerce. Community Development Program Office. November 1986.

86 *Arizona Legislative Bill Drafting Manual.* Arizona. Legislative Council. January 1989.

87 *Annual Report on Defects in the Arizona Revised Statutes and State Constitution, Thirty-Ninth Legislature, Second Regular Session, 1990.* Arizona. Legislative Council. 1990.

88 *Arizona Revised Statutes Internal Reference Manual.* Arizona. Legislative Council. December 1989.

provisions in order by section number giving the section number in which the reference is located.

Copies of House and Senate bills, resolutions, and memorials during a session can be obtained from the Mail Room of the House.[89] Information on Committee calendars, consideration of proposed measures, or of floor action in either body can be obtained by calling the information desk or either house.[90] Both bodies also publish weekly progress reports on their respective bills.[91] The very current status of proposed legislation and the current schedule of consideration can be determined by either on-line service ALIS, or by calling the Chief Clerk of the House or Secretary of the Senate.[92] Status of bills is also reported in the *Arizona Capitol Times*[93] and in the *Arizona Legislative Reporting Service*.[94] The *Service* also provides House and Senate Committee calendars for the following week, and a print record of "Breakers" which show the line amendments and additions to bills under consideration. On an annual basis, the Senate provides a *Legislative Summary*[95] which abstracts action taken on Senate and House bills, on appropriations, and gives a short history of legislation enacted by subject. Indexes by bills, chapter number, and by ARS title are provided. Session Laws are available from the Office of the Secretary of State,[96] or from the West Publishing Company's *Arizona Legislative Service*.[97] West's publication is published periodically during the legislative session, and prints session laws, court rules, and executive orders. A cumulative subject index to the actions is also provided in each issue.

Senate and House rules[98] are printed periodically, not necessarily with each new legislature. When not printed for a legislature, the rules of the previous legislature are adopted by resolution. Both rule books are very broad, providing a outline of organization, procedure, reports, committees and legislative action needed for the passage of bills. Both the Senate[99] and the House[100] manuals

89 Arizona House of Representatives, Mail Room, State Capitol, House Wing, 1700 W. Washington, Phoenix, AZ 85007, (602) 542-4379.

90 Arizona Senate, Information Desk: (602) 542-3559; Arizona House of Representatives, Information Desk: (602) 542-4221.

91 *House Progress Report.* Arizona. House of Representatives. *Senate Progress Report.* Arizona. Senate. Obtain from: Arizona House of Representatives, Mail Room State Capitol, House Wing, 1700 W. Washington, Phoenix, AZ 85007, (602) 542-4379.

92 Arizona Senate Secretary: (602) 542-4231; Arizona House of Representatives Chief Clerk: (602) 542-3032.

93 *Arizona Capitol Times, supra* note 24.

94 *Arizona Legislative Reporting Service.* Phoenix. Arizona News Service. Daily during Legislative Session. This service is the print version of the on-line service LOLA, discussed above, *supra* note 26.

95 *1990 Legislative Summary, Thirty-Ninth Legislature, Second Regular Session.* Arizona. State Senate Research Staff. 1990.

96 Secretary of State, State Capitol, West Wing, Seventh Floor, 1700 W. Washington, Phoenix, AZ 85007. phone (602) 542-4285.

97 *Arizona Legislative Service.* West Publishing Company. 1974-

98 *Senate Rules, Thirty-Ninth Legislature, State of Arizona, 1989-1990.* Arizona. State Legislature. Senate. 1989; *Rules of the Arizona House of Representatives, Thirty-Ninth Legislature, 1989-90.* Arizona State Legislature. House of Representatives. 1989.

99 *Senate Rules, supra* note 98, Rule 24.

100 *Rules of the Arizona House of Representatives, supra* note 98, Rule 31.

refer to "Mason's Manual of Legislative Procedure"[101] for detailed parliamentary procedure guidelines. The *Arizona Legislative Bill Drafting Manual*[102] also gives details on legislative procedure with regard to new proposals.

h. Health and Vital Statistics

The Department of Health Services administers most of the health related programs in the state and produces most of the reports and studies related to health issues. The reports are roughly divisible into three categories: vital statistics and disease data, information on hospitals, patients and charges, and special reports. The annual report on vital statistics[103] gives county and population details for birth, marriage and divorce, and death. Particular problems or concerns are surveyed on a regular basis and reported yearly.[104] The Division of Disease Prevention reports annually on communicable diseases,[105] and also produces special reports dealing with particular prevention programs[106] and health problems.[107]

Hospital and patient reports are detailed by both specific hospital and by diagnosis category (DRG or Diagnosis Related Group).[108] Hospitals included in the reports are non-federal hospitals and those which have facilities of 50 beds or over. The annual report on the uniform reporting system[109] provides peer group and health service area comparisons between hospitals relating to costs and expenditures, manpower, and care costs which are reported uniformly for each institution. Directories of provider facilities are also available from the

101 *Manual of Legislative Procedure for Legislative and Other Governmental Bodies,* by Paul Mason, 1979, available from the Legislative Bill Room, California State Legislature, State Capitol, Sacramento, California 95814.

102 *Arizona Legislative Bill Drafting Manual,* supra note 86.

103 *Arizona Health Status and Vital Statistics, 1988.* Arizona. Department of Health Services. Office of Planning and Health Status Monitoring. 1990.

104 The Office of Planning and Health Status Monitoring of the Department of Health Services has produced the following reports on an annual basis, reporting a five year span of data: *Accidental Drowning Deaths in Arizona, Abortion Surveillance Report, Arizona, Drug-Related Mortality, Arizona, Firearm-related Fatalities, Arizona, Suicide Mortality, Arizona, Teenage Pregnancy Report, Arizona, Unintentional Injury Mortality Among Children and Adolescents, Arizona.*

105 *Communicable Diseases in Arizona, 1984-1988.* Arizona. Department of Health Services. Division of Disease Prevention. Infectious Disease Epidemiology Section. February 1989.

106 *Arizona Birth Defects Monitoring Program, Year 1986 Report.* Arizona. Department of Health Services. Division of Disease Prevention. 1990.

107 *Tuberculosis in Arizona, 1978-1987.* Arizona. Department of Health Services. Division of Disease Prevention. June 1988.

108 The Office of Health Economics and Facilities Review, Department of Health Services, prepares the following reports on an annual or biannual basis: *Arizona Hospital Statistics, Annual Report of Health Facilities: Hospitals; Arizona Hospital Statistics, Utilization-Cost-Services-Staffing: Hospitals; Arizona Nursing Care Institutions Statistics, Annual Report of Health Facilities: Nursing Care Institutions; Comparative Report of Hospital Charges, Based on 477 DRGs, biannual; Arizona Payer Report, Charge and Demographic Data by DRG Code and 26 Major DRG Groups for General Hospitals. biannual. Arizona Patient Origin Report by Zip Code and DRG Group for Arizona Hospitals.*

109 *Hospital Uniform Reporting System 1987 Annual Report.* Arizona. Department of Health Services. Office of Health Economics and Facilities Review. 1988?

Department of Health Services.[110]

Occasionally special reports on health problems or social issues with health implications are prepared by advisory councils or task forces appointed by the governor. Some current reports that have been published in the last few years deal with AIDS,[111] insurance coverage of long term care[112] and mismedication of the elderly.[113]

i. Labor

Data on wages and wage rates offered, employment and unemployment, and sex and minority status of the work force primarily come from the Department of Economic Security. Publications in the "Labor Market Information Series"[114] provide regular reports on these topics and are updated by two newsletters.[115] Employment forecasts are also done[116] as well as other studies which include information for those looking for employment.[117] The *Annual Planning Information*[118] summarizes labor force data for Arizona, the counties and the metropolitan areas, and includes information on race, age, income and education, poverty level and public assistance.

110 The following is a list of titles of the directories produced by the Department and updated at least annually: *Adult Day Health Care Facilities, Ambulatory Surgical Centers, Arizona Certified ESRD and Transplant Centers, Arizona Licensed Home Health Agencies, Arizona Licensed Non-Federal Hospitals, Arizona Licensed Nursing Care Institutions, Arizona Licensed Special Hospitals, Arizona Licensed Supervisory Care Homes, Arizona Medicare Certified Portable X-ray Units, Free Standing Facilities with 24-Hour Emergency Services, Health Care Services Organizations, Infirmaries, Licensed and Certified Hospice Agencies, Licensed Long Term Health Care Facilities Directory, Medicare Certified OTIP's, Medicare Certified Rehabilitation Clinics, Outpatient Treatment Clinics, Residential Care Homes, Rural Health Clinics, Unclassified Health Care Institutions, Arizona Certified ESRD & Transplant Centers.*

111 *State of Arizona Governor's Task Force on AIDS Report.* Arizona. Governor's Task Force on AIDS. November 1989.

112 *Report of the Governor's Private Sector Insurance Task Force on Long Term Care.* Arizona. Governor's Private Sector Insurance Task Force on Long Term Care. January 1986.

113 *A Report to the Governor: The Other Drug Problem, Mismedication of the Elderly.* Arizona. Governor's Advisory Council on Aging. March 1990.

114 *Maricopa County Employer Wage Survey,* annual; *Maricopa County Small Employer Wage Survey,* annual; *Pima County Employer Wage Survey,* annual; *Pima County Small Employer Wage Survey,* annual; *Affirmative Action Planning Information, Arizona: Maricopa County with Glendale, Mesa, Phoenix, Scottsdale and Tempe, Pima County and Tucson; Affirmative Action Planning Information, the Non-Metropolitan Counties,* annual; *Job Bank Wages,* annual.

115 *LMI [Labor Market Information] Newsletter.* Arizona. Department of Economic Security. Research Administration. monthly; *Arizona's Workforce; a News Release.* Arizona. Department of Economic Security. Research Administration. monthly.

116 *Occupational Employment Forecasts* (series). annual. Series is composed of a volume for Arizona and one for each county.

117 *Arizona Occupational Profiles* (series). Published every three years, it contains a pamphlet on each of the following occupations: construction, educational services, finance, insurance and real estate, government, hospitals, lodging, manufacturing, mining services, trade, transportation, communications, and public utilities.

118 *Annual Planning Information 1990-91.* Arizona. Department of Economic Security. Research Administration. 1990.

j. Statistics

General statistical almanac's for Arizona come from outside the state's offices. The annual abstract from the Valley National Bank[119] provides tables on topics ranging from climate to Social Security recipients and water supply and consumption. A section in the back provides data for each county, and the "Table of Contents" at the front is really a broad subject index. Sources for the data are footnoted so that the *Review* can be used as a index to data. A volume published annually by the University of Arizona[120] includes over four hundred tables on a variety of topics, also cites the sources of the tables, and includes a abbreviated subject index. A guide to Arizona sources of statistics has been compiled and revised by Atifa Rawan and Kenneth Furuta at the University of Arizona, and is available from them on request.[121]

Basic economic and population data is packaged by the Arizona Department of Commerce, along with information on services, education facilities, weather and attractions, for large and small communities in Arizona, including cities and towns located on the reservations.[122] The Department of Economic Security produces annual population estimates and projections.[123] The *Statistical Bulletin*[124] provides data on the recipients of programs managed by the Department, including, Aid to Families with Dependent Children, General Assistance, Emergency Assistance, Tuberculosis Control, Supplemental Payments, Food Stamp Program, and Medical Assistance.

In addition to the above sources, the federal government's role in statistics gathering and publishing cannot be ignored. Federal statistics come in all shapes and sizes, for states and local areas as well as for the nation and regions. The *American Statistics Index*[125] (ASI) provides comprehensive indexing and access to federal statistics, and the microfiche collection of ASI insures access to the publications.[126]

119 *Arizona Statistical Review*. Valley National Bank of Arizona. 1947-1989. annual. A 1992 edition is being planned by a private publisher. For information on price and availability contact: Arizona Statistical Review, P.O. Box 33363, Phoenix, AZ 85067-3363.

120 *Arizona Statistical Abstract, a 1989 Data Handbook*. University of Arizona. College of Business and Public Administration. Division of Economic and Business Research. 1989.

121 *Arizona Statistical Sources: A Guide* by Atifa Rawan and Kenneth Furuta. Revised edition, December 1989. Available from: Government Documents Department, University of Arizona Library, Tucson, AZ 85721, (602) 621-4871.

122 *Arizona Community Profiles*. Arizona. Department of Commerce. Community Development Program. 1988.

123 *Arizona Revised Population Estimates: 1981-1989 and Population Projections: 1989-2040*. Arizona. Department of Economic Security. Research Administration. Population Statistics Unit. May 1990.

124 *Statistical Bulletin*. Arizona. Department of Economic Security. Family Assistance Administration. monthly.

125 *American Statistics Index*. Washington, D.C. Congressional Information Service. monthly (with quarterly and annual cumulations). 1974 -

126 Arizona State University's Hayden Library, Government Documents Service (*Non-Depository ASI Microfiche Collection,* 1974 -); University of Arizona's Main Library, Government Documents Department (*Non-Depository ASI Microfiche Collection,* 1974 -); Northern Arizona University's Cline Library, Government Documents Department (*Depository and Non-Depository ASI Microfiche Collection,* 1974 -); Phoenix Public Library, Business and Science Department (*Non-Depository ASI Microfiche Collection,* 1989 -).

k. Transportation

In addition to the beautiful subscription magazine *Arizona Highways*,[127] the Arizona Department of Transportation produces the annual accident statistics report.[128] The Governor's Office of Highway Safety under the Department of Public Safety produces a report annually[129] which reviews traffic safety in Arizona and the contributing factors to accidents. Priorities and plans are also discussed in terms of identified problem areas. A biannual review from the Department of Transportation[130] includes summary data for transportation in Arizona by auto, airplane, and railroad. Figures on vehicle registration and road system milage and maintenance, as well as public transportation systems ridership and air passenger traffic are included.

E. Summary and Conclusion

The discussion has centered on two distinct approaches to state materials. The first is the approach to find or locate a particular publication or piece of information. The three major collections of Arizona publications offer the most hope for location followed by agency contacts from agency library to office.

The second approach to state documents centers on collecting the publications, either by agency or by subject matter. While using DLAPR's *Checklist* helps in this situation to pinpoint many titles, it is not reliable as a single source list, and agency contacts, newsletters and area newspapers need to used on a daily basis to keep current on state government activities and reports.

This paper presents a brief and logical analysis of the current situation of control over Arizona government agency publishing. While appointed task forces work on the problems of bibliographic control within state government and there is always hope that agency cooperation will be forthcoming or a enforcement provision added to the statutes, the past lack of control will continually have impact on a search or collection strategy. State governments are more notorious than the federal for their illusive publishing activities and Arizona is not the only state with bibliographic problems. The light at the end of the paper is simply that there are excellent professionals working in libraries throughout Arizona who not only can help, but enjoy helping all who want or need to use Arizona state documents.

127 *Arizona Highways*. Arizona. Department of Transportation. $16/year. Contact: Arizona Highways, 2039 W. Lewis, Phoenix, AZ 85009.

128 *Arizona Traffic Accident Summary*, 1988. Arizona. Department of Transportation. Traffic Records Unit. 1989?

129 *Arizona Highway Safety Plan, Fiscal Year 1991*. Arizona. Department of Public Safety. Governor's Office on Highway Safety. 1990.

130 *Arizona Transportation in Review, 1987*. Arizona. Department of Transportation. Transportation Planning Division. Policy and Research Section. September 1987. Note: A new edition of this will be published in 1992, but the title and format will change. The new title will be: *Arizona Transportation Fact Book*.

Appendix A

Arizona State Records

Records Management Division
Arizona Dept. of Library,
Archives and Public Records
1919 West Jefferson Street
Phoenix, AZ 85009
Phone: (602) 542-3741
Contact: Harold Holady

Arizona Archival Collections

Archives Division
Arizona Department of Library,
Archives and Public Records
Public Records
1700 West Washington
Phoenix, AZ 85007
Phone: (602) 542-4159
Official repository for historically valuable public records of Arizona state and local government.

Arizona Historical Foundation
Hayden Library
Arizona State University
Tempe, AZ 85287
Phone: (602) 966-8331

Arizona Historical Society
949 East Second Street
Tucson, AZ 85719
Phone: (602) 628-5775

Arizona Room
Phoenix Public Library
12 East McDowell
Phoenix, AZ 85004
Phone: (602) 262-6537, also 602) 262-4636

Arizona Room
Hayden Library
Arizona State University
Tempe, AZ 85287
Phone: (602) 965-3145

Special Collections
University Library
University of Arizona
Tucson, AZ 85721
Phone: (602) 621-6423

Appendix B

State Publications, Libraries with Primary Collections

Arizona State Library, Archives and Public Records
State Documents Collection
1700 West Washington
Phoenix, AZ 85007
Phone: (602) 542-4343
Attn: Janet Fisher or
Louise Muir

Hayden Library
Government Documents Service
Arizona State University
Tempe, AZ 85287-1006
Phone: (602) 965-3390
Attn: Mary Parhamovich

Main Library
Government Documents Department
University of Arizona
Tucson, AZ 85721
Phone: (602) 621-4871
Attn: Atifa Rawan

Appendix C

State Agency Libraries and Librarians

Lucy Trujillo, Librarian
Office of the Attorney General
1275 W. Washington
Phoenix, AZ 85007
Phone: (602) 542-1833

Nancy Markey
Water Rights Adjudication
Office of the Attorney General, Civil Division
1275 W. Washington
Phoenix, AZ 85005
Phone: (602) 542-1401

Martha DeMott
Corporation Commission
Utilities Division
1200 W. Washington
Phoenix, AZ 85007
Phone: (602) 542-5517

Jennie O'Leary
Coordinator of Library Services
Department of Corrections
1601 W. Jefferson, Rm. 102
Phoenix, AZ 85007
Phone: (602) 542-3159

Wes Rader, Librarian
Department of Economic Security
Authority Library 810z-1
1300 W. Washington
Phoenix, AZ 85007
Phone: (602) 542-4777

Linda Edgington, Librarian
Department of Education
Education Information Center
1535 W. Jefferson
Phoenix, AZ 85007
Phone: (602) 542-5416

Mary Alice Waldrip, Librarian
Department of Environmental Quality
2005 N. Central Avenue
Phoenix, AZ 85013
Phone: (602) 257-6959

Cathy LaBerge
Arizona Game and Fish
2222 W. Greenway Road
Phoenix, AZ 85023-4312
Phone: (602) 942-3000, ext. 349

Patricia Aiken, Library Manager
Department of Health Services
1740 W. Adams
Phoenix, AZ 85007
Phone: (602) 542-1013

Karen Jeffers, Librarian
Arizona State Hospital
Medical Library
2500 E. Van Buren
Phoenix, AZ 85008
Phone: (602) 220-6045

Del Taylor, Information Officer
Blank Forms and Publications Office
Department of Military Affairs
5636 E. McDowell Road
Phoenix, AZ 85008
Phone: (602) 267-2824

Sue Felts and Norleen Lara
Librarian
Department of Public Safety Library
2310 N. 20th Avenue
Phoenix, AZ 85009
Phone: (602) 223-2301

Alice McGarvey, Librarian
Salt River Project Library
ISB Branch
1600 N. Priest Drive
Tempe, AZ 85281
Phone: (602) 236-5676

Lloyd Anderson
Supreme Court
Staff Attorney's Office
Rm. 207 S.W. Wing State Capitol
Phoenix, AZ 85007
Phone: (602) 542-5028

Mary Silva, Librarian
Arizona Department of
Transportation
Transportation Research Center
Arizona State University
College of Engineering ERC 405
Tempe, AZ 85287
Phone: (602) 965-2372

Felice Bews, Librarian
Department of Water Resources
Library
15 S. 15th Avenue
Phoenix, AZ 85007
Phone: (602) 542-1541

Appendix D

For a Directory of Directories, Atifa Rawan, Government Documents Department, University Library, University of Arizona, has compiled and has kept updated a guide that is extremely useful: *Arizona Directories, Guidebooks, and Manuals*. It can be requested from: Atifa Rawan, Government Documents Department, University of Arizona, Tucson, Arizona 85721, (602) 621-2179.

Special Directories which include State Offices

COMMERCE: see also *Environment, Mining* and *Occupations*

Arizona Economic Development Directory. Arizona. Department of Commerce. Community Development Directory. July, 1989.

Obtain from: Arizona Department of Commerce, Community Development Division, 1700 West Washington, Phoenix, AZ 85007, (602) 542-5434.

Lists include name of the organization, address, names and titles of the principal officials and telephone numbers. Mainly contains non-governmental associations, the contacts can still be very useful when looking for information about a community or area. Lists included are: Chamber Associations, other Economic Development Organizations, Chambers of Commerce, Economic Development Organizations, Main Street Communities.

A Guide to State Licensing Requirements. Arizona. Department of Revenue, Forms Department. May, 1990.

Obtain from: Arizona Department of Revenue, Forms Department, 1600 W. Monroe, Phoenix, AZ 85007, (602) 542-4565.

Lists name, address and telephone number of state licensing entity, the subject or activity over which authority is held and a description or comment about the licensing activity or requirement. An index by profession is included.

COURTS

Arizona Courts Directory. Arizona. Supreme Court. Administrative Office of the Courts. 1989.

Obtain from: Arizona Supreme Court, Administrative Office of the Courts, 7 West Wing State Capitol, Phoenix, AZ85007, (602) 253-5700.

Lists names, titles, addresses and telephone numbers for the judges and staff of the following courts: Supreme Court, Administrative Office of the Courts, Court of Appeals, Superior Court, Justice of the Peace Courts, Municipal Courts, Arizona Court Associations, Arizona Commissions and Committees and National Organizations. A list of services of the Administrative Office is provided in the back of the volume.

Criminal Justice:

Arizona Criminal Justice Agencies, 1991 Directory. Arizona. Criminal Justice Commission. 1991.

Obtain from: Arizona Criminal Justice Commission, 1700 N. 7th Avenue, Ste. 250, Phoenix, AZ 85007, (602) 542-1928.

Provides names, office addresses, and telephone numbers for state and local government employees in the following areas: Enforcement and support agencies, courts, prosecutors and public defenders, federal agencies, Indian criminal justice agencies, college and university police and railroad police.

EDUCATION:

Arizona Educational Directory. Arizona. Department of Education. 1987.

Obtain from: Arizona Department of Education, 1535 West Jefferson, Phoenix, AZ 85007, (602) 542-4709.

A comprehensive list of educational agencies and officials in Arizona, entries include the name, address and telephone number of the organization, and the name and title of the principal official. A detailed "Table of Contents" helps locate particular lists. Among the sections in the volume are the following lists: Arizona State Board of Education; Arizona Department of Educational Personnel; Arizona County School Superintendents and County Attorneys; Arizona County Treasurers and County-Clerk-Board of Supervisors; Arizona School District Governing Boards; Arizona Public School Districts, Schools, and Administrators, by County; Special Services for Special Education; District Administrative Personnel; Council of Chief State School Officers; Arizona Board of Regents; Universities and Administrators; State Board of Directors for Community Colleges of Arizona; Arizona Community Colleges, District Governing Boards and Administrators; Arizona State Board for Private Post Secondary Education; Educational Organizations.

Indian Education Directory, 1990-91. Arizona. Department of Education. September 1990.

Obtain from: Arizona Department of Education, Indian Education Unit, 1535 West Jefferson, Phoenix, AZ 85007, (602) 542-4361.

The directory includes the names of officials, titles, office address and telephone for the following organizations: Tribal Contract/Grant Schools, Arizona Indian Head Start Programs, Bureau of Indian Affairs Schools, Indian Education Act-Title V and Johnson-O'Malley, Tribal Education Directors, Tribal Higher Education Staff, Colleges and Universities Financial Aid, American Indian Bilingual Education Projects.

ENVIRONMENT:

Arizona Environmental and Resource Conservation Directory: A List of Businesses, Organizations, and Agencies Concerned with Environmental Resources in the State of Arizona. Arizona. Commission on the Arizona Environment. April 1990.

Obtain from: Commission on the Arizona Environment, 1645 W. Jefferson, Suite 416, Phoenix, AZ 85007, (602) 542-2102.

Each entry includes the name and address of the organization, telephone number, name and title of a contact person and a brief abstract of the organization's interests and services. Organizations are listed alphabetically by name within the following categories: Business Groups, Citizen and Non-profit Organizations, Educational Institutions, Professional Associations, County and Local Government, State Government, Federal Government, Political Subdivisions of Arizona. A detailed "Table of Contents" at the front of the volume enables easy access to specific entries.

INDIANS:

Indian Education Directory, 1989-90. Arizona. Department of Education. 1990.

Obtain from: Arizona Department of Education, Indian Education Unit, 1535 W. Jefferson, Phoenix, AZ 85007, (602) 942-4391.

Names or directors or principals, titles, addresses and telephone numbers are listed for contacts in the following categories: Tribal Contract Schools, Arizona Indian Head Start Programs, BIA Schools, Indian Education Programs - Title IV Part A and Johnson-O'Malley, Tribal Education Directors, Tribal Higher Education Staff, College and Universities Financial Aid, and Indian Bilingual Education Projects.

1990 Tribal Directory. Arizona. Commission on Indian Affairs. 1990.

Obtain from: Arizona Commission on Indian Affairs, 1645 W. Jefferson, Phoenix, AZ 85005, (602) 542-3123.

Reservations are listed with the names and addresses of officials, council members, committee chairs and managers and directors. There is a statement regarding tribal council meetings and elections. Following the entries for tribal governments, federal, state, and association offices are listed that aid or interact with reservation governments or with individual tribal members. Most of the entries include personal names and titles of officials, addresses and telephone numbers. The directory is organized in alphabetical order by name of reservation.

LEGISLATURE:

Directory of the Thirty-Ninth Legislature, 1989-1990, State of Arizona. U.S. West Communications.

Price: 10 copies free, each additional copy $.35. Company will not mail out unless sent a postage-paid envelope; otherwise, copies must be picked up at the office.

Obtain from: U.S. West Communications, Government Relations Department, 3033 N. Third Street, Rm. 1015, Phoenix, AZ 85012, (602) 235-3687.

A handy pocket size directory, this pamphlet includes maps of the Congressional and State legislative districts, then the names, addresses and telephone numbers of the Congressional and state elected officials. Arizona Senate and House of Representative listings include: the seating arrangement in each house, directory information for the officers and staff of each house, members names, home city, district, room number, occupation, office telephone number, and committee assignments, committee membership, and each legislator's home office address and telephone number.

39th Legislature, 1989-1990. U.S. West Communications. Price: 20 copies free, each additional copy $.15. Company will not mail out unless a self-addressed postage-paid envelope is sent; otherwise, copies must be picked up at the office.

Obtain from: U.S. West Communications, Government Relations Department, 3033 N. Third Street, Rm. 1015, Phoenix, AZ 85012, (602) 235-3687.

Provides a list by District of the Arizona State Senate and House of Representatives. Each entry includes a photograph, name, address, party affiliation, and a very brief biographical statement. No telephone numbers are given.

LIBRARIES:

Arizona Library Directory, 1990. Arizona Department of Library, Archives and Public Records. 1990.

Obtain from: Arizona Department of Library, Archives and Public Records, State Capitol, Suite 200, 1700 W. Washington, Phoenix, AZ 85007, (602) 542-4035.

Lists with titles, addresses and telephone numbers, directors and librarians in DLAPR, and members of the Arizona State Advisory Council on Libraries. Public Libraries are listed alphabetically by the name of the library, address and telephone numbers are given along with the hours, names of the librarians and sometimes library staff, library board members or board president and friends' chair. Separate lists of "Presidents, Public Library Advisory Boards," and "Chairpersons, Friends of Arizona Libraries," with the name and mailing address, follow the public libraries listings. Academic libraries are listed alphabetically by name, with addresses, telephone numbers, hours open, and names and telephone numbers of the directors and department heads. Institutional libraries are listed by name with address and telephone number and sometimes with the name of a library director. Federal Depository libraries are listed last by name with telephone number, address and the name of the person responsible for the collection.

LOCAL GOVERNMENT: See also *Environment* and *Indians*

Local Government Directory. Prepared by the League of Arizona Cities and Towns and the Arizona Association of Counties. July 1990. Price: $10.00.

Obtain from: The League of Arizona Cities and Towns, 1820 West Washington Street, Phoenix, AZ 85007, (602) 258-5786 or Arizona Association of Counties, 1910 West Jefferson, Phoenix, AZ 85009, (602) 252-6523.

Although primarily listings of local government officials, the contacts can be extremely helpful in locating data or a publication dealing with a particular area or issue. Except for the lists of "County Affiliate Groups," and "League Affiliate Groups," listings in each category include the name, address and telephone number of the organization, names titles and telephone numbers of principal officers, regular meeting dates, term expirations, and hours of business if applicable. Each section is organized in alphabetical order. Sections are: City and Town Governments, County Governments, League Executive Committee, Arizona Association of Counties Board, County Affiliate Groups, League Affiliate Groups, Councils of Governments, Congressional Delegations, Selected State Offices and Other Agencies.

MINING:

State Agencies Concerned with Mining and Mineral Resources in Arizona. Arizona. Department of Mines and Mineral Resources. September 1989 (Circular 24).

Obtain from: Arizona Department of Mines and Mineral Resources, Mineral Building, State Fairgrounds, Phoenix, AZ 85007, (602) 255-3791.

Contains the agency and office name, address, telephone number and employee names of people in state government whose work includes the areas of mining and mineral resources. Personnel in the Department of Environmental Quality, the Industrial Commission, Department of Economic Security, as well as many other agencies are listed.

OCCUPATIONS:

Arizona Licensed Occupational Requirements. Arizona. Department of Economic Security. Research Administration. 1988.

Obtain from: Arizona Department of Economic Security, Research Administration Labor Market Publications 733A, P.O. Box 6123, Phoenix, AZ 85003, (602) 542-3871.

Occupations which require licenses in Arizona are listed in alphabetical order. Information for each license includes the name, address and telephone number of the licensed authority, the license or exam fee, and a brief statement of the licensing requirement.

SOCIAL SERVICES:

Note: Directories for local offices of State social service agencies and other organizations are available from a variety of sources. To obtain one for a particular area it is best to inquire first at the council of governments [COG] office of the area which is of interest. A list of COG organizations with telephone numbers and addresses is available in the *Local Governments Directory* listed above under "Local Government."

1990 Directory of Human Services, Maricopa County, Phoenix, Arizona. Community Information and Referral Services, Inc. 1990.

Obtain from: Community Information and Referral Services, Inc., 1515 E. Osborn, Phoenix, AZ 85014, (602) 263-8856.

Contains entries for state government offices as well as volunteer and professional organizations offering services. Each entry contains the address, telephone number and name of the director or contact person, as well as information on the services provided. Indexes included are by name of the agency or organization, by service, and by valley location (e.g., Glendale, El Mirage, etc.). A list of abbreviations is also provided.

Appendix E

State Agency Newsletters and Publications Lists

ACCOUNTANCY BOARD

ASBA (Arizona State Board of Accountancy) Update. Twice a year. free. Accountancy Board, 3110 N. 19th Avenue, Suite 140, Phoenix, AZ 85015. (602) 255-3648.

Provides information on Board Activities including rule changes, enforcement actions, policy statements and any relevant proposals before the legislature.

ADMINISTRATION DEPARTMENT

Highlights. bimonthly. free. Personnel Division, Department of Administration, 1831 W. Jefferson, Phoenix, AZ 85007. (602) 542-5482.

Directed at employees of the State, the newsletter reports on activities and policies that impact this employment, including new legislation and executive orders and regulations. New publications of general interest are also announced with order information.

AGRICULTURE DEPARTMENT

ADA Employee News. monthly. free.

Obtain from: Arizona Dept. of Agriculture, Attention: Ladd Harlan, 1688 W. Adams Rm. 421, Phoenix, AZ 85007. (602 542-4373.

Reports on the activities of the offices within ADA as well as interests and concerns of the employees.

AHCCCS [Arizona Health Care Cost Containment System]

Insight AHCCCS. monthly. free.

Obtain from: Public Information Office, Arizona Health Care Cost Containment System, 801 E. Jefferson, Phoenix, AZ 85034. (602) 234-3655.

Includes information for health care providers on the activities of the agency.

ARTS COMMISSION

Bulletin. monthly. free. Arizona Commission on the Arts, 417 West Roosevelt Street, Phoenix, AZ 85003. (602) 255-5882.

Reports on the activities and policies of the Commission and lists grant opportunities, shows and exhibitions, festivals, and job postings in the arts.

BANKING DEPARTMENT

Summary of Actions. monthly. $60/year subscription. Banking Department, Century Plaza, Suite 815, Phoenix, AZ 85012. (602) 255-4421.

Records applications for licenses, renewals of licenses, and other activities for banks and savings and loans.

BAR ASSOCIATION

Arizona Attorney. monthly except August/September issue. $30/year subscription. State Bar of Arizona, 363 N. First Avenue, Phoenix, AZ 85003. (602) 252-4804.

Contains articles of interest to the Bar, also lists continuing education opportunities and meetings for lawyers. "Bar Briefs" records notices of appointments, disciplinary actions, committee activities and publication releases.

CLIMATOLOGIST

Arizona Climate Summary. monthly. $6/year subscription. Office of the State Climatologist, Laboratory of Climatology, Community Services Center Building, Curry Road/Mill Avenue, Department of Geography, Arizona State University, Tempe, AZ 85287-1508. (602) 965-6265.

Provides a narrative summary of the past month's weather data and includes data on air quality for Phoenix and Tucson.

COMMERCE DEPARTMENT

Spirit of Success. irregular. free. Department of Commerce, 3800 N. Central, Suite 1500, Phoenix, AZ 85012. (602) 280-1300.

Includes information on economic development activities in the state and on specific industries. The "International Trade and Investment Calendar of Events" in Arizona and a "Highlights" column give brief summaries of events.

COMMERCE DEPARTMENT, ARIZONA MOTION PICTURE DEVELOPMENT OFFICE

Arizona's Call Sheet. quarterly. free. Arizona Motion Picture Development Office, Department of Commerce, 1700 W. Washington, Fourth Floor, Phoenix, AZ 85007. (602) 542-5011.

Reports the activities of the television and moving picture industry in Arizona, including news of locations for films, videos and advertisements.

COMMERCE DEPARTMENT, STATE CLEARINGHOUSE (ENVIRONMENTAL)

Clearinghouse Biweekly Reviewer. free. Arizona State Clearinghouse, Department of Commerce, 3800 N. Central, Suite 1500, Phoenix, AZ 85012. (602) 280-1315.

Lists state and local government agency and federal area office grant applicants and gives information on the program and the amount of money requested. The project applications can be reviewed at the Clearinghouse. Provides copies of the table of contents in the *Federal Register*[131] dealing with notices and announcements which might be of interest to citizens in Arizona.

COMMERCE DEPARTMENT, SOLAR PROGRAMS

Arizona Solar News. irregular. free. Solar Programs, Energy Office, Department of Commerce, 3800 N. Central, Phoenix, AZ 85012. (602) 280-1402.

Includes state and local information on solar projects and studies.

131 *Federal Register.* U.S. Government Printing Office. daily. 1936 -

CORPORATION COMMISSION

Agenda. bimonthly. free. Corporation Commission, 1200 W. Washington, Phoenix, AZ 85007. (602) 542-3931.

In addition to providing notice of the meetings, the agenda provides a index to the minutes of the Commission meetings. The minutes are available only at the Commission office.

Hearing Calendar. weekly. free. Hearing Division, Corporation Commission, 1200 W. Washington, Phoenix, AZ 85007. (602) 542-4250.

Provides notice of hearings and pre-hearing conferences.

Water News. quarterly. free. Arizona Corporation Commission, 1200 West Washington, Phoenix, AZ 85007. (602) 542-4250.

With general information on water concerns, lists recent Commission decisions dealing with water companies, filing applications, new certificates, transfers, extensions, deletions and revocations, complaints and orders to show cause and rate increase applications.

CORRECTIONS DEPARTMENT

Directions. irregular. free. Directions, Arizona Department of Corrections, 1601 W. Jefferson, Suite 314, Phoenix, AZ 85007. (602) 542-3133.

Contains information on activities of the Department as well as on state and local agency activities and training opportunities.

LaRoca. bimonthly. $12/year. LaRoca, P.O. Box 629, Florence, AZ 85232.

For and by the inmates of the Arizona State Prison Complex in Florence, *LaRoca* reports on issues of interest involving inmates, and administration and acts as a intermediary between the inmates and the Department of Corrections and the prison administration. Includes literary and art pieces as well as articles on crime, alcohol and criminal law.

CRIMINAL JUSTICE COMMISSION

Agenda. irregular. free. Criminal Justice Commission, 1700 N. 7th Avenue, Suite 250, Phoenix, AZ 85007. (602) 255-1925.

Notice of meetings and matters to be considered listed.

ECONOMIC SECURITY DEPARTMENT

DES (Department of Economic Security) Newsletter. monthly. free. Department of Economic Security, Public Information Office, 1717 W. Jefferson, Phoenix, AZ 85007. (602) 542-4296.

ECONOMIC SECURITY DEPARTMENT: RESEARCH ADMINISTRATION

LMI (Labor Market Information) Directory. irregular. free. LMI, Site Code 733A, P.O. Box 6123, Phoenix, AZ 85003. (602) 255-3871.

Lists publications available from the office, their frequency and provides a order form. At the back of the list, cites other organizations that provide data on Arizona's economy and workforce.

LMI [Labor Market Information] Newsletter. monthly. free. Arizona LMI Newsletter, Site Code 733A, P.O. Box 6123, Phoenix, AZ 85005-6123. (602) 542-3871.

Contains data and news on labor and employment as well as on large employers and their activities in Arizona. Addresses alien and migratory workforce as well as local. Also lists other labor market information publications.

Arizona's Workforce, a Newsrelease. monthly. free. Research Administration, Department of Economic Security, 1717 W. Jefferson, Phoenix, AZ 85007. (602) 542-3871.

Reports data on labor force and employment for the state and the counties. Also contains brief statements on labor trends and unemployment rates.

ECONOMIC SECURITY DEPARTMENT: STATE DATA CENTER

State Data Center Newsletter. quarterly. free. Arizona State Data Center, Department of Economic Security, Site Code 045Z, P.O. Box 6123, Phoenix, AZ 85005. (602) 542-5984.

Provides information to data users emphasizing the access of the data resources of the U.S. Bureau of the Census. Lists publications on Arizona from the Bureau as well as from the Center. Narrative focuses on current statistical programs and resources in the state.

EDUCATION DEPARTMENT

Ed.Word. weekly except summers. free. Public Information Office, Department of Education, 1535 W. Jefferson, Phoenix, AZ 85007. (602) 542-5393.

Contains information on local and state conferences and workshops, programs in schools, and news on the State Board's activities.

ENVIRONMENTAL QUALITY DEPARTMENT

Environmental Scene. quarterly. free. Office of External Affairs, Department of Environmental Quality, 2005 N. Central Avenue, Phoenix, AZ 85004. (602) 257-2312.

Reports on environmental problems, federal and state environmental activities, and on the actions of the department. Contains information on proposed and new legislation in Arizona.

GAME AND FISH DEPARTMENT

Wildlife Bulletin. weekly. free. Information Branch, Arizona Game and Fish Department, 2222 West Greenway Road, Phoenix, AZ 85025. (602) 942-3000.

Includes information on hunting and fishing in Arizona. Mainly aimed at sportsmen, contains data on fish catches in Arizona lakes and rivers.

Arizona Wildlife Views. monthly. $6.50/year. Arizona Game and Fish Department, 2221 W. Greenway Road, Phoenix, AZ 85023.

Magazine focusing on use and misuse of Arizona wilderness. Informs public on new books and pamphlets available from the Department and on programs and policies.

GEOLOGICAL SURVEY

Fieldnotes. quarterly. free. Publication Sales, Arizona Geological Survey, 845 N. Park Avenue, Rm. 100, Tucson, AZ 85719. (602) 882-4795.

GOVERNOR'S OFFICE: OFFICE OF TOURISM

Directions, Newsletter of the Arizona Office of Tourism. irregular. free. Arizona Office of Tourism, 1100 W. Washington, Phoenix, AZ 85007. (602) 542-8687.

Presents activities of the Office with regard to marketing Arizona for tourist travel.

GOVERNOR'S OFFICE: OFFICE FOR CHILDREN

Newsletter, Governor's Office for Children. irregular. free. Governor's Office for Children, 1645 W. Jefferson, Suite 420, Phoenix, AZ 85007. (602) 542-3191.

GOVERNOR'S OFFICE: ARIZONA MEXICO COMMISSION

The Cronista of Arizona and Sonora. three times per year. free. The Cronista, Arizona-Mexico Commission, State Capitol Building, 1700 W. Washington, Suite 802, Phoenix, AZ 85002. (602) 542-4331.

Highlights activities on the Arizona-Sonora border. Many of the articles have names and telephone numbers so that more information on a particular item can be obtained.

Boletin Informativo. irregular. free. Arizona-Mexico Commission, State Capitol Building, 1700 W. Washington, #802, Phoenix, AZ 85002. (602) 542-4331.

In Spanish, the publication reports on the activities of the Commission and other events.

HEALTH SERVICES DEPARTMENT

No current newsletter. Planning to start a monthly newsletter in 1992. free. Public Information Office, Department of Health Services, 1740 W. Adams, Phoenix, AZ 85007. (602) 542-1001.

HEALTH SERVICES DEPARTMENT: DIVISION OF DISEASE PREVENTION SERVICES

Prevention Bulletin. quarterly. free. Division of Disease Prevention Services, Health Services Department, 3008 N. 3rd Street, Phoenix, AZ 85012. (602) 230-5808.

Includes updated statistics on selected diseases by county of residence and reports on the policies and activities of the department. Also announces new publications that deal with health and prevention of disease.

Arizona Responds to AIDS. quarterly. free. AR to AIDS, Arizona Department of Health Services, Office of Health Prevention and Education, 3008 N. 3rd Street, Phoenix, AZ 85012. (602) 255-1292.

Provides local, state and national information on AIDS and HIV programs. Statistical data is included. New publications are listed.

HUMANITIES COUNCIL

Arizona Insight: the Arizona Humanities Council Newsletter. 6 times a year. free. Arizona Humanities Council, the Ellis-Shackelford House, 1242 North Central Avenue, Phoenix, AZ 85004. (602) 257-0335.

The Arizona Humanities Council is a nonprofit affiliate of the National Endowment for the Humanities, a federal agency. The newsletter reports activities of the Council, lists events in Arizona, projects recently funded and opportunities for grants and fellowships available. New publications are also listed from the National Endowment as well as from the Council.

INDIAN AFFAIRS COMMISSION

Capitol Drumbeat Newsletter: Legislative and Other Activities. irregular. free. Arizona Commission on Indian Affairs, 1645 W. Jefferson, Rm. 127, Phoenix, AZ 85007. (602) 542-3123.

Includes news on activities and programs of the Commission and also local tribal news and news on proposals in the state which affect Indian populations.

LAND DEPARTMENT

Urban Lands Newsletter. quarterly. free. Land Department, 1616 W. Adams, Rm. 329, Phoenix, AZ 85007. (602) 542-4621.

LIBRARY, ARCHIVES AND PUBLIC RECORDS DEPARTMENT

News-Week, Arizona Libraries. weekly. free. Arizona Department of Library, Archives, and Public Records, State Capitol, Suite 200, Phoenix, AZ 85007. (602) 542-4035.

Reports briefly on activities of the Department and in libraries throughout the state.

PARKS DEPARTMENT

SCORP (Statewide Comprehensive Outdoor Recreation Plan) News. irregular. free. State Liaison Officer, Arizona Outdoor Recreation Coordinating Commission, 800 W. Washington, Suite 415, Phoenix, AZ 85007.

Reports on the activities of the Commission and on programs and projects in the state directed toward implementing SCORP.

PUBLIC SAFETY DEPARTMENT

Communicator. monthly. free. Arizona Department of Public Safety, Central Information Unit, P.O. Box 6638, Phoenix, AZ 85005. (602) 223-2313.

Disseminates information of interest to state officials, law enforcement and corrections officers, judges, and public attorneys.

Digest. monthly. free. Arizona Department of Public Safety, Central Information Unit, P.O. Box 6638, Phoenix, AZ 85005. (602) 223-2313.

Mainly directed at Department employees, does include information on the activities of the Department and notices of publications available.

RADIATION REGULATORY AGENCY

Radiation Review. irregular. free. Radiation Regulatory Agency, 4814 S. 40th Street, Phoenix, AZ 85040.

Provides a digest of radiation regulatory news and other items of interest.

REAL ESTATE DEPARTMENT

Arizona Real Estate Bulletin. irregular. free. Department of Real Estate, 202 E. Earll, Suite 400, Phoenix, AZ 85012. (602) 255-3232.

Reports on news and policies of Department and includes information on new publications. Actions and decisions of the Department with regard to licensed firms or individuals are listed.

REGENTS BOARD

Regent Recap. monthly. free. Arizona Board of Regents, 3030 N. Central Avenue, Suite 1400, Phoenix, AZ 85012. (602) 255-4082.

Reports the Board's policies and decisions and also lists new programs and resources at the three universities.

RESIDENTIAL UTILITY CONSUMER OFFICE

News Release. irregular. free. Residential Utility Consumer Office, 34 W. Monroe, Suite 512, Phoenix, AZ 85003. (602) 255-1431.

Announces meetings of the Residential Utility Consumer Board, the advisory body for the Office and also distributes pages about a particular issue or activity that Office regards of general interest. Meeting announcements include the agenda.

RETIREMENT SYSTEM

Retirement News. irregular. free. Arizona State Retirement System, P.O. Box 33910, Phoenix, AZ 85067. (602) 255-5131.

Reports on policy and law regarding Arizona retirement.

REVENUE DEPARTMENT

Tax News. monthly. $5.50/year. Arizona Tax News, Arizona Department of Revenue, 1600 W. Monroe, 9th Floor, Phoenix, AZ 85007. (602) 542-3062.

Provides information for tax practitioners on policies and policy changes, and reviews the activities of the Department.

SECRETARY OF STATE

Arizona Administrative Register. monthly. $36.00/year. Arizona Secretary of State, Publications Division, 1700 W. Washington, Suite 706, Phoenix, AZ 85007. (602) 542-4086.

Although the *Register's* main function is to print proposed rules and notices, it frequently includes new publications listings, especially handbooks and manuals.

SUPREME COURT

Bench Press. 6 issues/year. free. Editor - Bench Press, Arizona Supreme Court, 1314 N. 3rd Street, Suite 200, Phoenix, AZ 85004. (602) 253-4700.

Reports on programs and policies in the courts or administrative offices of the courts throughout the state. Includes a legislative update and calendar, information on rules and rule changes and the availability of reports.

TRANSPORTATION DEPARTMENT

Urban Freeways and Expressways. quarterly. free. Department of Transportation, 206 S. 17th Avenue, Rm. 100A, Phoenix, AZ 85007. (602) 255-7011.

TREASURER OFFICE

Arizona Treasury Notes. quarterly. free. Office of the Treasurer, State Capitol, West Wing, 1700 W. Washington, 1st Floor, Phoenix, AZ 85007. (602) 542-5817.

Reports articles on topics of interest to the department, and announces policy changes and new statistics on revenues and yields.

WATER INFORMATION CENTER

Arroyo. quarterly. free. Editor/Writer, Water Resources Research Center, Geology Building. Rm. 314, University of Arizona, Tucson, AZ 85721. (602) 621-7607.

Jointly published by the Arizona Department of Environmental Quality, the Water Resources Department, Land Department, Office of Arid Land Studies at the University of Arizona and the Water Resources Research Center at the University of Arizona, the newsletter reports on a wide variety of topics dealing with water, including floodplain management, Indian water rights, pollution.

WATER RESOURCES DEPARTMENT

Water Planning News. quarterly. free. Arizona Department of Water Resources, 15 South 15th Avenue, Phoenix, AZ 85007. (602) 542-1553.

Contains news and information on water issues throughout the state. Includes information on recent publications, on cleanup activities at particular sites and on status reports on management plans.

Chapter 12

Arizona Ethics Opinions and State Bar Publications

Kathy Shimpock-Vieweg

A. Introduction: The State Bar

The first bar association in territorial Arizona began around 1895. It remained an informal organization until the bar's incorporation in 1906.[1] Membership in the bar, however, only became mandatory in 1933.[2]

The state bar is presently a non-profit corporation as organized under Title 10, Chapter 5 of the *Arizona Revised Statutes*.[3] It is under the "direction and control" of the Arizona Supreme Court and exists for the lofty purpose of "advancing the administration of justice, regulating bar admission and lawyer

1 This was changed by Ariz. Const. art. 14, § 2 stating corporations may not be created by special acts. *See also, Bridegroom v. State Bar,* 27 Ariz. App. 47, 550 P.2d 1089 (1976).

2 For more information on early bar activities see *Murphy, Laws, Courts and Lawyers,* 104-122.

3 Ariz. Sup. Ct. R. 31.

discipline, foster[ing] high ideals of integrity ... and ... encourag[ing] practices that will advance and improve the honor and dignity of the legal profession."[4] Therefore, although the Arizona Supreme Court retains control of bar admission and attorney discipline, the state bar has been given the authority to administer this area.[5] The examination and admission process is administered by the Supreme Court's Committee on Examinations and its Committee on Character and Fitness. The process of attorney discipline, disability and reinstatement is administered by the Disciplinary Commission of the Supreme Court. Ethics opinions are issued by the State Bar's Committee on Rules of Professional Conduct.

The State Bar is governed by a Board of Governors, a 21 member body that includes up to two non-attorney "public members." The court has empowered the Board to do the following: fix and collect fees, promote the law, improve the administration of justice, make appropriations and disbursements, formulate rules and regulations, make appointments, prepare an annual statement, maintain the Clients Security Fund, form a non-profit corporation and administer Mandatory Continuing Legal Education.[6] The Board is divided into eight bar districts from which one or more members are elected.[7]

The Officers of the State Bar include a President, President-Elect, First Vice President, Second Vice President, Secretary-Treasurer, and Executive Director.[8] The State Bar of Arizona's Committees are found in these areas: Administrative Law, Appointments, Membership Assistance, Bench and Bar, Civil Practice and Procedure, Continuing Legal Education, Creditor/Debtor Rights, Criminal Code and Rules, Dispute Resolution Committee, Editorial Board, Fee Arbitration, Insurance, Judicial Evaluation Poll, Jury Instructions, Lawyers Professional Liability, Legal Services, Legislative, Long Range Planning, Mandatory Continuing Legal Education, Mental Health and Elder Services, Professionalism, Public Relations, Rules of Professional Conduct, Unauthorized Practice of Law, and Woman and Minorities in the Law.

The State Bar of Arizona Sections include Antitrust; Bankruptcy; Construction Law; Corporation, Banking and Business Law; Criminal Justice; Environmental and Natural Resources; Family Law; Immigration; Intellectual Property; International Law; Labor Law; Law Practice Management; Probate and Trust Law; Public Lawyers; Real Property; Securities Regulation; Sole Practitioners; Tax; Trial Practice; Workers' Compensation; World Peace Through Law; and the Young Lawyers Division.

4 *Ibid.*

5 *Drummond v. Stahl,* 127 Ariz. App. 122, 618 P.2d 616 (1980) *cert. denied,* 450 U.S. 967, 101 S.Ct. 1484, 67 L.Ed.2d 616 (1981). *In re Lewkowitz,* 70 Ariz. 325, 220 P.2d 229 (1950).

6 *See* Ariz. Sup. Ct. R. 45 for Arizona's MCLE requirements.

7 Ariz. Sup. Ct. R. 31.

8 *Ibid.*

B. State Bar Publications

1. *Arizona Attorney. Phoenix, AZ: State Bar of Arizona, 1988- monthly.*

This journal consolidates the *Arizona Bar Journal* and the *Arizona Bar Briefs*. The title change began with volume 25 no. 1, September 1988. The *Arizona Attorney* contains the State Bar's Annual Report, Committee and Section Reports, the Arizona Bar Foundation Annual Report, a digest of Appellate Court decisions, a digest of ethics opinions and MCLE updates. This is all in addition to articles of general legal interest.

2. *Arizona Bar Journal. Phoenix, AZ: State Bar of Arizona. v.1 (June 1965) - v.24, no. 1 (June, 1988).*

This journal was issued quarterly from vol. 1 (1965) - vol. 10 (1976), and bimonthly until vol. 24. There is a three year index in volume 3 (1965-68); and 13 year index in volume 19 (1983). The Bar plans to issue a new index in 1991. The *Arizona Bar Journal* contains some full text ethics opinions and legal articles.

3. *Arizona Bar Briefs. Phoenix, AZ: State Bar of Arizona, 1982-1988.*

This newsletter was published monthly from June 1982 through September 1988. It included digests of ethics opinions and Arizona appellate court decisions.

4. *State Bar of Arizona Membership Directory. Phoenix, AZ: State Bar of Arizona. annual.*

In addition to the attorney listings, the directory includes information on Arizona courts, state bar personnel, state bar committees and sections, the Arizona Bar Foundation, and various government offices.

5. *Miscellaneous Items*

The State Bar sponsors various programs throughout the year for which seminar materials (both written and audio/video tapes) are prepared. These materials can be used to fulfill a portion of the Bar's MCLE requirement. In addition, the State Bar also publishes various books on Arizona practice which are regularly supplemented. The State Bar issues an annual catalog containing its seminar schedule, a listing of satellite programs, and interactive video lessons.[9]

9 Contact the State Bar of Arizona for a catalog of current publications, programs, etc. at: Continuing Legal Education, State Bar of Arizona, 363 North First Avenue, Phoenix, Arizona 85003.

C. Professional Responsibility

1. *Model Rules of Professional Conduct*

The rules regarding the admission and discipline of attorneys can be found in the Rules of the Supreme Court (Rule 31-80). The Arizona Rules of Professional Conduct, Rule 42, is based on the 1983 revision of the ABA's Model Rules and adopted with only some modification. Individual rules are known as "Ethical Rules" or "ERs". These rules provide the basis of the ethics opinions issued by the State Bar's Committee on Rules of Professional Conduct.

2. *Ethics Opinions*

The Committee on Rules of Professional Conduct advises attorneys on ethical issues. Its members provide guidance by issuing advice (either oral or written) to requesting attorneys, but the committee is not involved with lawyer discipline. The Committee began publishing its formal written opinions in 1954. Although these are not binding on the Supreme Court's Disciplinary Commission, they are persuasive.

The Committee has various guidelines on the issuance of opinions. It will only render opinions of ethics, not law. The question must regard future conduct of the inquiring attorney only. It must not be the subject of a pending judgment. No opinions will be given in the area of attorney fees.

Any committee member can give limited oral advice, generally on issues covered by the rules. Written opinions are issued in two formats - formal and informal. Formal opinions are published by the State Bar and constitute the Committee's view as a whole. Ten to 15 formal opinions are issued annually. These are generally issued in areas of importance or general interest. Informal opinions are rendered by individual committee members in areas needing quick resolution or of less importance. They do not represent the views of the whole committee. Informal opinions are not published.[10]

a. Sources:

i. *[State Bar of Arizona] Ethics Opinions*. Phoenix, AZ: State Bar of Arizona, 1952-1982. 5v. looseleaf.

Arizona Ethics Opinions have been issued in two formats. This version is a five volume looseleaf set. Volumes 2 - 5 contain Opinion 1 (June 29, 1954) through Opinion 297 (December 12, 1969), and Opinion 70-1 (January 15, 1970) through Opinion 82-21 (December 30, 1982). Volume 1 contains the Index and Digest. The Key Word Index includes Opinions through 76-29 (December 29, 1976). The Digest, however, includes Opinions through 82-21; with reference to earlier Ethical Considerations (EC), Disciplinary Rules (DR), and Ethical Opinions (EO). There is also an index of provisions of the Code of Professional Responsibility, Code of Judicial Conduct and Canons of Professional and Judicial Ethics which have been cited in Arizona ethics opinions.

10 For more information *see* Colin Campbell, "Committee on the Rules of Professional Responsibility," *Arizona Attorney* 27, no. 3 (Nov. 1990), 23-26.

ii. *[State Bar of Arizona] Ethics Opinions.* Phoenix, AZ: State Bar of Arizona, 1952-

These loose copies of ethics opinions are released as decided by the Committee on Rules of Professional Conduct. (See Illustration A, p.290.)

iii. *[State Bar of Arizona] Ethics Opinions.* Phoenix, AZ: State Bar of Arizona, 1980-90. 1v. looseleaf.

This volume contains only those ethics opinions issued from 1980-90.

iv. *Arizona Attorney.* Phoenix, AZ: State Bar of Arizona, 1988 - monthly.

Digests of recent ethics opinions can be found in the *Arizona Attorney* and previously in the *Arizona Bar Journal* and *Arizona Bar Briefs*. Each opinion digested includes cites to Ethical Considerations (EC), Disciplinary Rules (DR) and Ethical Opinions (EO).

v. *ABA/BNA Lawyers' Manual on Professional Conduct.* Washington, DC: ABA/BNA, 1983- 3v. looseleaf.

Arizona's formal ethics opinions are included in digest form from Opinion 80-16 to current.

b. Current Indices:

i. *Stuart Quick Index: Subject Matter.* Phoenix, AZ: State Bar of Arizona, 1989.

The Committee issues a partial chronological index (from Opinion 70-1) providing major subject headings and a brief synopsis. "See also" references are also provided. (See Illustration B, p.291).

ii. *Key Word Index: State Bar of Arizona Ethics Opinions.*Phoenix, AZ: State Bar of Arizona, 1952-1990.

This index was issued on April 1, 1990. Includes "see" references and broad subject headings through Opinion No. 90-04. This Index should be updated manually with each new release. (See Illustration C, p.292).

The Key Word Index is also available from the State Bar in disk format.

iii. *Lawyers' Manual on Professional Conduct.* Washington, DC: ABA/BNA, 1983 - 3v. looseleaf.

This set contains *the* best professionally produced index available for Arizona ethics opinions.

iv. *Arizona Attorney.* Phoenix, AZ: State Bar of Arizona, 1988- monthly.

The journal occasionally publishes a "key word index to Opinions of the Committee on Rules of Professional Conduct, State Bar of Arizona."

c. Citators:

There are no citators published for Arizona ethic opinions. WESTLAW and LEXIS can, however, be used as a citator to find the most recent cases.

D. Listing Of State, Local And County Bar

For further information on the bar, their publications, and MCLE programs, consult the following list, or contact the Arizona State Bar Association.

State Bar of Arizona
Phoenix Office
Arizona Bar Center
363 North First Avenue
Phoenix, AZ 85003-1580
(602) 252-4804
Telefax: 271-4930

State Bar of Arizona
Tucson Office
117 North Church, Suite 101
Tucson, AZ 85701-1117
(602) 623-8258
Telefax: 623-8102

Maricopa County Bar Association
Nan Wilder, Executive Director
333 W. Roosevelt
Phoenix, AZ 85003

Maricopa County issues annually a pictorial directory.

Pima County Bar Association
Andrea Ibanez, Executive Director
177 N. Church, Suite 101
Tucson, AZ 85701

Pima County also issues an annual directory.

County Bar Associations are also found in Cochise, Coconino, Gila, Graham, Greenlee, Mohave, Navajo-Apache, Pinal, Santa Cruz, Yavapai, and Yuma Counties. Local Bar Associations have been established in Scottsdale, West Maricopa and the East Valley. Addresses vary with the current president.

E. On-Line Resources

1. *Ethics Opinions*

The Arizona State Bar Ethics Opinions are available for viewing through the Bar's Electronic Bulletin Board. The Bulletin Board contains the "Digest of Ethics Opinions" from 1988 and the "Key Word Index." It is irregularly updated.

Neither WESTLAW nor LEXIS contains Arizona ethics opinions. However, WESTLAW's database LS-ABAEO contains all formal and informal ABA Ethics Opinions issued since 1924 by the Standing Committee on Ethics and Professional Responsibility. The ABA Code of Judicial Conduct (LS-CJC) and the Model Rules of Professional Conduct (LS-MRPC) are also included.

LEXIS contains in its (ABA) Library all the ABA formal (FOPN) and informal (INFOP) Ethics Opinions. Their Library also includes the Codes of Professional Responsibility and Judicial Conduct (CODES). The combined file (ETHICS) contains both the above codes and opinions.

2. *Arizona Bar Listings*

West's Legal Directory is available on WESTLAW providing information on attorneys and law firms both nationally (WLD) and in Arizona (AZ-WLD). This directory can be searched full text to retrieve information on attorneys with a specific topical practice or a geographic location, etc. Only those attorneys and firms sending profiles to West Publishing Co., however, are included. As of March 1991, there were approximately 4,000 profiles listed in this database.

Martindale-Hubbell Law Directory is available in full-text on LEXIS (MARHUB). Comprehensive information is available on practically every attorney and firm located in the U.S. and Canada. Search strategy can include many variables including practice area, bar admission, clients, geographic location, etc. Group files are available by geographic region.

In addition, Martindale-Hubbell's seven volume directory is also found in CD-ROM. Numerous criteria can be searched including name, geographic regions (state, county or city) and field of law.

Illustration A

OPINION NO. 89-01
March 10, 1989

FACTS:

The inquiring attorney is presently employed as a hearing officer with a state agency. Her responsibilities as hearing officer are to: preside over hearings; make findings of fact; do legal research; and draft decisions for board approval.

The specialized nature of the matters submitted for hearing usually results in representation of litigants by attorneys from the same seven Arizona law firms. The inquiring attorney wants to enter private practice specializing in the same area of law which she confronts as a hearing officer. Accordingly, she anticipates that it will be difficult to avoid negotiating for employment with a law firm that does not have a case pending before the agency. She points out that it is the responsibility of the agency board to make the final decisions concerning matters that come before her. In view of that, she inquires as to the extent to which Ethical Rule 1.12(b) would apply to her search for employment.

QUESTION:

May an attorney employed as a hearing officer by a state agency, with ethical propriety, negotiate for employment with law firms that concurrently have matters pending before her and/or the agency board?

ETHICAL RULE INVOLVED:

E.R. 1.12. Former Judge or Arbitrator

* * * * *

(b) A lawyer shall not negotiate for employment with any person who is involved as a party or as attorney for a party in a matter in which the lawyer is participating personally and substantially as a judge or other adjudicative officer, or arbitrator. * * *

OPINION:

According to E.R. 1.12(b), an attorney would be prohibited from negotiating for employment with any law firm representing a party in a matter in which the attorney-hearing officer is participating personally and substantially as an adjudicative officer. To determine the scope of E.R. 1.12(b), one must decide the meaning of the expressions "personally and substantially" and "adjudicative officer."

Reprinted from *State Bar of Arizona Ethics Opinions*, 1989.

Illustration B

STUART QUICK INDEX

OPINION NO:	SUBJECT MATTER
70-1	ADVERTISING: Chamber of Commerce professional directory
70-2	ADVERTISING: Newspaper advertisement for estate planning seminars [see also 70-8, 70-26, 71-30, 73-24]
70-3	CONFLICTS: City Attorney acting as criminal defense lawyer
70-4	ADVERTISING: Tucson lawyer listing name in Nogales phone book [see also 70-30, 71-28]
70-5	CONFLICTS: City Councilman-Lawyer--restrictions on Union representation [see also 74-28, 75-8, 75-18, 79-19]
70-6	SOLICITATION: Lawyer's contract with corporation to furnish legal representation to "employer-clients"
70-7	CONFLICTS: City attorney's restrictions on private civil representation of police officers [see also 70-22, 73-31, 73-40]
70-8	ADVERTISING: Participation in "legal seminars"--clarification and reaffirmation of 70-2.
70-9	CONFLICTS: Member of firm represents wife in divorce several years following firm's representation of husband in administration of his deceased father's estate [see also 70-24, 71-36, 72-25]
70-10	ADVERTISING: County Bar Association's publication of professional announcement card [reaffirmed in 71-35]
70-11	ETHICS PRECEDENT: ABA opinions are highly persuasive precedent but are not conclusively binding on this Committee
70-12	SOLICITATION: Lawyer's advice to judge of availability to accept criminal defense appointments
70-13	ADVERTISING: Name, photo or description of lawyer-general counsel of, corporation in corporation's brochure distributed to its customers [see also 70-25]
70-14	CONFLICTS: Restrictions on former Assistant Attorney General now in private practice [see also 71-7, 72-6, 73-1, 73-38, 74-16, 74-22, 76-1 and ABA 134]
70-15	ADVERTISING: Lawyer's name on jacket of book about JP practice [see also 72-29, 73-9]

Reprinted from *Stuart Quick Index [Ethics Opinions]*, 1990.

Illustration C

H (cont'd)	Opinion Nos.
Husband and wife (cont'd) -see, also, "Family relationship" and "Kinship"	
I	
Ill-feeling and personalities between advocates	160, 176A
Impartiality	87-14, 87-17
Immunity -grant of, by prosecutor to one of multiple clients	71-26
Impropriety, avoidance of appearance of -see "Appearance of Professional Impropriety"	
Incorporation of law firms -see "Professional corporations"	
Indians and Indian tribes -representation of	44, 115, 221, 227, 71-37
Indigent clients -representation of in Social Security claims	73-21
-payment of living expenses	89-03
-representation of in unemployment compensation claims	75-19, 76-18
Indigent criminal defendant -fee allowance to appointed attorney	289, 76-01
-duty to represent, on court appointment	70-12, 79-09, 88-03
Indigent farmworkers -Legal Aid Society using radio announcements and public articles to reach	74-07
Indirect solicitation -see, "Solicitation"	
Industrial Commissions practice -see "Workmen's Compensation Practice"	

wp/indx23 (Page 23)

Reprinted from *Keyword Index: State Bar of Arizona Ethics Opinions*, 1990.

Chapter 13

How to Set-up a Law Library:

Hints for the New Lawyer, Solo Practitioner and Paralegal

Marianne Sidorski Alcorn

> "If a man empties his purse into his head no one can take it away from him. An investment in knowledge always pays the best interest."
>
> Ben Franklin in *Poor Richard*[1]

Librarians at a law school adjust to their patrons graduating and leaving every three years. Not all of these patrons sever their ties with the law library. The librarian will occasionally hear from the alumni now in solo practice or in a small firm. Some of these practitioners would like to build a small collection of legal materials. The following are suggestions I have given to former stu-

1 *Respectfully Quoted, a Dictionary of Quotations requested from the Congressional Research Services,* Suzy Platt, ed. (Washington D.C.: Library of Congress, 1989), p. 185.

dents.[2] They are modest and would not cost an extraordinary amount. The suggestions must be adjusted to the location of the law firm. The cost of space for a law firm in a large city will be much higher than a firm in a small town.

To detail all the aspects of building a firm library would take another book. When the law firm reaches the point of needing a more formal approach to planning and building a library, a library consultant should be hired. To locate a consultant contact the Phoenix Area Association of Law Libraries (PAALL), the Southern California Association of Law Libraries (SCALL), or the Southwest Association of Law Libraries (SWALL). These associations and law library associations located in other areas of the country can be contacted through the national office of the American Association of Law Libraries, phone (312)939-4764 or through the librarians at a law school library or law firm.

A. Buying Books

Choose one or two of the best looseleaf services in your practice area. Their selling points are the promptness with which the primary materials are published and sent to the subscriber and that the current cases, laws, regulations and rulings are pulled together in one source (note: looseleaf treatises such as those published by Matthew Bender are generally updated annually and should not be considered looseleaf services for this purpose). The negative side to looseleaf services is that they must be kept up to date (i.e. filed in). When you are planning where to put your looseleafs, leave a small area (even just a desk) adjacent for the filer to work. This may not be possible in locations where space is very expensive.

The three major publishers of looseleafs are Commerce Clearing House, Bureau of National Affairs and Prentice Hall. It might be timesaving and money saving to purchase looseleafs by one publisher. This would result in less confusion for the looseleaf filer and would mean that the user would be more proficient by not having to switch from one format to another. This will only be an advantage, however, if these sets best suit the legal research needs of the user. Looseleafs are expensive so shop carefully. Talk to another lawyer specializing in that area or visit a law library and ask the librarians for their opinion. It may be helpful to purchase the following books when buying looseleafs or newsletters. These may also be used at a local law library.

Eis, Arlene I., comp. and ed. *Legal Looseleafs in Print.* New Jersey:Infosources Publishing. (The more useful of the two.)

Eis, Arlene I., comp. and ed. *Legal Newsletters in Print.* New Jersey:Infosources Publishing.

These two items list hundreds of sources. They can be purchased from Infosources Publishing, 140 Norma Road, Teaneck, New Jersey 07666 for $75 each. Besides being useful for ordering your collection, these books will alert you to what is available by subject. You may not want to buy more than one or two items but when you are researching new areas you can return to these sources,

2 To Gail, one of those few who felt that legal research was an important part of law school.

look under the applicable subject and go to the law library aware of what looseleafs exist on the subject.

It is time saving to be able to research from your office or to locate what you want to use before going to the law library. The entire Arizona State University Libraries' catalog is available through dial-in access with a terminal or microcomputer and a modem. The majority of the materials in the ASU Law Library are also in this catalog. For more technical assistance on dial-in access call Microcomputer & Communication Consultant, Monday-Friday, 9 a.m. to 4 p.m. or leave a message at (602) 965-5677. The University of Arizona also has their catalog available to users from their own personal computers, for more information phone (602) 621-6403. (See also, Chapter 10 on "Online Resources.")

There are numerous ways to cut corners and save on your procurement of legal materials. Each month check the *Arizona Attorney* and *Maricopa Lawyer* classifieds. In recent issues there have been used sets of the *Arizona Revised Statutes* and the *Arizona Reports* for sale. There are also used law book sellers, a list is included at the end of the chapter.

Contact the State Bar for a catalog of books and materials, these include workbooks and materials from past CLE programs (if practicing in Arizona refer to Chapter Nine and call the Arizona State Bar to update, (602) 252-4804). These materials are meant to instruct and they are centered on Arizona law. Check with the county bar associations also to find out what they have available. An example from the Maricopa County Bar Association (phone (602) 257-4200) is the *Domestic Relations Handbook* 1989 edition, which costs three dollars. It includes sections on structure and procedure of the Domestic Relations Division, Conciliation Services, Guidelines for Custody, monetary guidelines for child support and spousal support, and Support Enforcement.

The bookstore in your area that sells law books is also a source of some excellent buys. Here are a few examples of used books from the Varsity Book Exchange in Tempe (phone (602) 967-3253).

Binder, David and Price, Susan, *Legal Interviewing and Counseling: A Client-Centered Approach.* West Publishing Co. 1977. $10.

Block, Gertrude, *Effective Legal Writing* 3rd ed. $6.50

Mauet, Thomas A. *Fundamentals of Trial Techniques* 2d ed. Little, Brown Pub. 1988. $17.95

There are also plenty of other new paperbacks that are fairly cheap listed below:

A Uniform System of Citation 15th ed. Harvard Law Review, 1991, $7.50.

Bankruptcy Code, Rules & Forms. West Pub., approx. $18.

Black's Law Dictionary 6th ed. West Pub., 1990, 24.95

Cohen, Berring & Olsen, *Finding the Law* 9th ed., 1989, $19.95.

Federal Rules of Evidence. West Pub. approx $12.

Federal Rules of Civil Procedure. Foundation Press, approx. $13.

Fisher, Roger and Ury, William, *Getting to Yes; Negotiating Agreement Without Giving In.* Penguin, 1983. $7.95.

Wydick, Richard, *Plain English for Lawyers* 2d ed. Carolina Acad. Press, 1985. $7.95.

Chapter Ten deals with computerized data bases. Be aware of the rates and special discounts available to solo practitioners from WESTLAW and LEXIS before deciding whether to buy books and reporters or subscribe to one of these services. Online databases are wonderful resources for lawyers. It is important to become aware of them and to use them to understand their full value and the time they can save.

1. *Used Book Dealers*

Lawbook Exchange, Ltd., 135 West 29th Street, New York, N.Y. 10001. (800)422-6686.

National Law Resource. 426 S. Clinton, Chicago, IL 60607. (800)279-7799.

Pacific Law Books, 1903 S. Main Street, Santa Ana, CA 92707. (714)549-1187.

Preston Used Law Books, 8751 E. San Pedro Drive, Scottsdale, AZ, 948-7712.

Professional Books Service, Los Angeles Office, (213)256-0833.

Top Value Law Book Exchange, 1120 Radcliffe Avenue, Bakersfield, CA. (800)-873-6657.

Western Law Book Exchange, 1130 Bannock, Denver, CO 80204. (303)825-2772.

William S. Hein Co., 1285 Main Street, Buffalo, N.Y. 14209. (800)828-7571.

B. Core Collection

This is a suggested list of materials, in addition to those selected from section I, for the beginning sole practitioner to start a small personal collection of law books

Title	Publisher	Price	Linear Feet Shelf Space
Arizona Revised Statutes (This set is replaced each year and a new set must be purchased. It is not annotated. If your budget is tight this is the way to go for a few years.)	Michie Co.	$120.00	1
or			

Title	Publisher	Price	Linear Feet Shelf Space
Arizona Revised Statutes Annotated (Pocket parts must be purchased each year at a cost of $425. The advantage would be to have the annotations (cases) that are a part of the set.)	West Pub. Co.	$1869.00	6
Arizona Administrative Code	Arizona Secretary of State	$425.00 set $125.00 annual subscription individual titles available	3
Pacific Reporter 2d (794 vols.) (This set is the regional set for Arizona. The advantage in purchasing this set would be access to appellate cases in the western states.)	West Pub. Co.	$20,735.00 (with two 10% discounts)	148
or			
Arizona Reports (1947-) (covers a much more limited area but less expensive and quicker to access)	West Pub. Co.	$3800. (with 10% discount)	20
Arizona Appeals Reports (1965-76)	West Pub. Co.	$756.00	4
Arizona Advance Reports (Essential updating for *Arizona Reports* and *Pacific Reports.)*	Code Co	$199.00/yr.	under 1
Arizona Index (Subject index for the *Arizona Advance Reports* which updates the *Arizona* and *Pacific Reports*). May not be essential, evaluate it for your collection.	Code Co	$149.00	under 1
Pacific Digest New edition covers from 585 P. 2d and cost $2360. add $3068. for previous edition.	West Pub. Co.	$1560.00	11 (ed. begin 367 P2d) 8 (ed. beginning 585 P2d, with pocket part additions)
or			

Title	**Publisher**	**Price**	**Linear Feet Shelf Space**
Arizona Digest 2d (New edition)*	West Pub. Co.	$1560.00	4
Shepard's Arizona Citations	Shepard's	$679.00	under 1
Shepard's Pacific Citations	McGraw-Hill	$1517.00	under 1
Arizona Legal Forms	West Pub. Co.	$666.00 (In 10 vols. or may buy individual volumes for $87.50) Volume 1 & 2 Civil Procedure Volume 3 Debtor-Creditor Volume 4 Domestic Relations Volume 5 & 6 Commercial Transactions Volume 7 Criminal Procedure Volume 8 & 9 Business Organization (Corporations) Volume 10 Business Organization (Partnerships)	1-1/2

*NOTE: West Publishing Co. has issued a volume, *Arizona Digest 2d Law Finder* with their new edition of the *Arizona Digest*. It is a subject index meant to allow searching of many West publications through just one tool. For example, under the subject "checks" there are the following references;

Checks

Generally

C.J.S. Bills and Notes § 1 et seq.
Bills and Notes key number 1 et seq.

Bad Checks

Generally
A.R.S. § 13-1807 et seq.
Actions
A.R.S. § 12-671
Crimes and offenses
LaFave and Scott, Substantive Criminal Law § 8.9.

Forms

13 West's Legal Forms(Stone) § 37.2.

Payment

C.J.S. Payment § 2.
Payment key number 20 et seq.

The researcher locates key numbers, code cites (A.R.S. and U.S.C.A.), and references to Arizona Legal Forms, Arizona Practice Series, texts and treatises, C.J.S. among other items.

The *Law Finder* can serve as a checklist of locations when researching a topic.

Additional core materials include the following:

Arizona Handbook for Legal Secretaries, Volume I & II. Arizona Association of Legal Secretaries, $135.

Davis, Ann, M.,ed. *Arizona Legal Services Practice Manual* 2d ed. Arizona: State Bar of Arizona, 1989. This is not necessarily just for the legal services attorney. It is divided into the subjects of consumer law, domestic relations, employment, government benefits and guardianship, probate and wills and is useful to attorneys representing individuals.

West has been publishing an Arizona Practice set which includes *Civil Trial Practice* ($71) by Charles Marshall Smith, *Law of Evidence* ($65.75) by Morris Udall and Joseph Livermore, and *Marriage Dissolution Manual* ($71) by Charles Marshall Smith and Irwin Cantor. Chapter Nine on Arizona Practice Materials will be of assistance if choosing Arizona sources. The above list would be a basic collection.

In the beginning of your law career it may not be possible to afford purchasing entire sets of books. There are companies that will sell you just the index volumes or single volumes. Be sure to buy the *CFR Index and Finding Aids*, the 1990 (rev. each Jan.) cost $29. The stock # for the 1990 is 869-011-00053-0; send order to: Superintendent of Documents, U.S. Gov. Printing Office, Washington D.C. 20402-9325. It may be more convenient if you are interested in this or other government publications to contact the U.S. Government Bookstore, World Savings Building, 720 North Main Street, Pueblo, Colorado 81003 (phone (719) 544-3142). You can save yourself trips to the library by checking the index to see if such a regulation is in existence. Individual titles are sold, so for example, if you are primarily going to be working in the area of banking you would purchase title 12.

C. Additions to the Core

For the practitioner starting out there are some wonderful sources that cost very little but can keep you abreast of current law.

Current Index to Legal Periodicals published by the University of Washington, Gallagher Law Library (phone (206) 543-4097) is an inexpensive way to keep up on the latest law review articles for $45 per year in paper copy or $200 for floppy. It is also on WESTLAW, so until you wanted to subscribe to *Index to Legal Periodicals* ($210 per year) or the *Current Law Index* ($425 per year or $209 for just the annual volume) this might provide enough access.

Ninth Circuit Update is a weekly digest of ninth circuit decisions. The cost is $300 per year. The cost is not that much considering the researcher is also able to use the accompanying *Ninth Circuit Online.* This is a computer database having the local rules and full text of Ninth Circuit opinions (these are placed online approximately one hour after they are filed with the court). It can be accessed by any computer with a modem.

A subscription to either B.N.A.'s *U.S Law Week* ($544 for two volumes) and *C.C.H Supreme Court Bulletin* ($475) will furnish the latest U.S. Supreme Court decisions. B.N.A., in addition, reports the abstracts of the latest Federal and State cases and a section on legislative and administrative news.

Two sources that are not as common but are very useful are *Statutes Compared: A U.S., Canadian, Multinational Guide to Statutes by Subject.* 4th ed., (William S. Hein Company, Buffalo, New York, $32.50). They solve the question, "what are the lemon laws in all fifty states?" or other attempts at comparing legal subjects in other states. *Subject Compilations of State Laws 1988-90* ($98.50 from Boast/Nyberg, 716 West Indiana Avenue, Urbana, IL 61801-4836) is now in its fourth edition. Its sources are law reviews, treatises, looseleaf services, federal and state government documents and U.S. Supreme Court opinions. Both of these sources will save you an immense amount of time in comparing state statutes. Certainly LEXIS and WESTLAW are excellent tools of statutory comparisons now that state codes are available on them. However, searching online full-text, state code, data bases can be difficult and very expensive due to the variety of terms used by the different state legislatures to describe the same subject. The three printed sources should be checked first, whether purchased or used at the law library, with the final step being LEXIS or WESTLAW.

Law librarians can recall numerous law clerks and beginning practitioners starting their question with, "I have a case or memo on a topic and I never had that class in law school." Leah Chanin may have heard that once too often. She has edited a book entitled *Specialized Legal Research* (Little, Brown & Co., Boston, 1987, $85 plus annual supplement). The subjects covered are Securities, Uniform Commercial Code, Federal Income Taxation, Copyright Law, Federal Labor and Employment Law, Environmental Law and Land Use Planning, Admiralty and Maritime Law, Immigration Law, Military and Veterans Law,

Banking Law, Patent and Trademark Law and Government Contracts. Each chapter is by an author able to direct researchers to the sources in that area and discuss how to use them. Take advantage of this very practical set.

Another good source when beginning tax research is by Gail Levin Richmond, *Federal Tax Research, 4th ed.* (Foundation Press, 1990, $12.50). This is quick to access when trying to figure out where certain tax memos or treasury decisions are published or various tax questions arise. CCH publishes the annual U.S. Master Tax Guide for $25. It will assist in keeping up with tax legislation and information for filing tax returns.

The Lawyer's Almanac (annual by Prentice Hall, $80) and *Law and Legal Information Directory 6th ed.* (Gale Research Inc., $305) incorporate a tremendous amount of information into their sets. These might be more appropriate to a mid-size law firm rather than an individual practitioner. *The Lawyer's Almanac* lists the nation's 500 largest law firms, lists starting salaries for lawyers, and corporate lawyer's salaries. It has a section on lawyer demographics, legal education, professional publications, bar associations, the judiciary, verdicts, and a government departments and agencies section. *Law and Legal Information Directory* includes legal organizations, bar associations, federal and state courts, federal regulatory agencies, law schools, paralegal schools, law libraries, research centers, legal periodical publications, publishers, legal aid offices, lawyer referral services, law enforcement agencies and other information.

D. Selected Bibliography on Law Firm Libraries

The following books and periodical articles cover various aspects of law libraries. Refer to the beginning of the chapter for information on locating a library consultant.

In addition, the *Library Journal* publishes a "Directory of Products & Services," each October. Everything from where to buy adhesives to book binding services are listed. The *National Law Journal* has a section each June on "Publishers' Directory of Current Law and Law-Related Books."

1. *Books*

Costa, Betty and Mary Costa, Chairpersons. *A Micro Handbook for Small Libraries and Media Centers.* 2d ed. Littleton, CO: Libraries Unlimited, 1986.

Enyingi, Peter. *Cataloging Legal Literature.* Littleton, CO: Fred. B Rothman for AALL, 1988.

Marke, Julius J. and Richard Sloane. *Legal Research and Law Library Management.* New York: Practising Law Institute, 1981.

Strain, Laura M., Chairperson. *The Private Law Library: New Information Functions.* New York: Practising Law Institute, 1981.

Strohofer, Jean and Marie Wallace, Chairpersons. *The Private Law Library in the High-Tech Era.* New York: Practicing Law Institute, 1983.

Voges, Mickie A. *Building Your Law Library, a Step-by-Step Approach.* Chicago: American Bar Association, Section of Economics of Law Practice, 1988. This is a very useful publication for anyone beginning a library.

Practicing Law Institute has a course handbook from its program, "Managing the Private Law Library: Management Challenges, New Technology, and Planning for the 1990s." The cost is $55 plus tax for the course handbook and $125 plus tax for audio cassettes of the program. For further information phone (212)765-5700 or write Practising Law Institute, Dept. NdA1, 810 Seventh Avenue, New York, N.Y. 10019. This is an annual program and some of the handbooks will be more helpful than others.

2. *Periodicals and Newspapers*

Johnston, Janis L. "Training New Law Library Personnel: the Neglected, Essential Activity." Law Library Journal 83 (Winter 1991): 61-71.

Jay, Marjorie, "User Manuals for the Private Law Firm Library: Planning, Design, and Development. Law Library Journal 83 (Winter 1991): 91-108.

Hildebrandt, Bradford W. "Planning the Library Environment." New York Law Journal, p. 3, col. 3, 13 Nov. 1990.

Moyer, Holley M. "Budgeting a Libraries Maintenance Costs." New York Law Journal, p. 42, col. 2, 24 Sept. 1990.

Rogers, James G. "Planning of Law Firm Libraries is in Transition." New York Law Journal, p. 39, col. 2, 24 Sept. 1990.

Reilly, Michael J. "Capitalizing on the Potential of Your Law Library." Law Office Economics and Management 31(Summer 1990):192-196.

Axelroth, Joan L. "Library Space Planning." Legal Management 9 (Jan. 1990):14.

Estes, Mark. "A New Scenario for Research." American Lawyer 11 (Dec. 1989):S7.

Ellenberger, Jack. "The Next Era of Technological Innovation." American Lawyer 11 (Dec. 1989):S22.

Hambleton, Jim. "2000 and Beyond." American Lawyer 11 (Dec. 1989):S15.

Morgan, Barbara D. "Managing the Smaller Law Library for Less." Case & Comment 94 (July 1989):14.

Moyer, Holley M. "New York City: 20 Lawyers (library budgets for start-up firms)." National Law Journal, p. 18, col. 3, 19 June 1989.

Phelps, J.R. "Tampa, Fla.: Sole Practitioner (library budgets for start-up firms)." National Law Journal, p. 18, col. 2, 19 June 1989.

Marke, Julius J. "Planning Library Space; New Technology." New York Law Journal, p. 4, col. 3, 18 April 1989.

Lobenhofer, Louis F. "Tax Law Libraries for Small and Medium-sized Firms." Practical Tax Lawyer 3 (Winter 1989):31-40.

Horne, William. "The Law Firm Library of the Future." Los Angeles Daily Journal, p. S6, 19 Dec. 1988.

Sloane, Richard. "Book v. Computer: Can Library Space Be Saved?" New York Law Journal, p. 4, col. 4, 15 Nov. 1988.

Horne, William. "The Law Firm Library of the Future: Technology Takes Research Beyond the Bookshelves." American Lawyer 10 (Nov. 1988):S6.

Tognazzini, Norman, C. "The Law Library Budget." Legal Economics 14 (Nov. 1988):50-51.

Cottingham, Jennifer. "A New Look for the Law Library." National Law Journal, p. S1, col. 1, 11 July 1988.

Lobenhofer, Louis F. "Tax Law Libraries for Small and Medium-sized Firms." (part 1) Practical Tax Lawyer 3 (Fall 1988):17-32.

Marke, Julius J. "What's New in Law Library Planning?" New York Law Journal, p. 4, col. 3, 19 April 1988.

King, Dwight. "Library Budgeting for Law Librarians: a Selected Bibliography." Law Library Journal 80 (Spring 1988):291-305.

Marke, Julius J. "New Technology in Law Libraries." New York Law Journal, p. 4, col. 3, 1 March 1988.

Hildebrandt, Bradford W. "Ideas for Managing Law Firm's Library Expenses." New York Law Journal, p. 4, col. 2, 5 Jan. 1988.

Sloane, Richard. " Planning a Law Office Library with a Designer." New York Law Journal, p. 4, col. 2, 17 Nov. 1987.

Head, Anita K. "Remodeling and Expanding Space: Library Services during the Construction Period." Law Library Journal 79 (Summer 1987): 535-545.

Fu, Paul S. "Handling Water Damage in a Law Library." Law Library Journal 79 (Fall 1987): 667-687.

Schwarz, Deborah. "Shared Libraries Help Eliminate Overhead." National Law Journal, p. S4, col. 1, 13 July 1987.

Fry, Mary Anne. " Automating the Firm's Library: A Team Project." Legal Administrator 6 (Summer 1987): 46.

Symposium: "Concept through Construction: Mastering the Art of Law Library Design." Law Library Journal 79 (Summer 1987):485-545.

Kaufman, Blair S. "Laser Disks' Future in the Law Library." National Law Journal, p. 15, col. 4, 9 Feb. 1987.

Snyder, Fritz. "The Impact of New Technologies on Law Library Acquisitions." Legal Reference Services Quarterly 6 (Fall-Winter 1986):159-168.

Gasaway, Laura N. "On-line or Buy the Book: A Cost-benefit Analysis." Legal Times, p. 16, col. 1, 7 July 1986.

"Designing the Law Firm Library: the Economics of Space." National Law Journal, p.21, col. 1, 24 February 1986.

Weinberg, Kathie L., Carolyn Ahearn and Susanne Thevenet. "Formation of a Law Library." New York Law Journal, p. 29, col. 4, 25 March 1985.

Sloane, Richard. "How to Choose and Use a Library Consultant." New York Law Journal, p. 23, col. 2, 26 March 1984.

Endres, Heidi. "An Acceleration System for Routing Materials in Law Firm Libraries." Law Library Journal 76 (Winter 1983):121-122.

Chapter 14

Native American Indian Law: A Selected Bibliography

Kathy Shimpock-Vieweg

A. Introduction

"Indian Law" has been described as "that body of law dealing with the status of the Indian tribes and their special relationship to the federal government, with all the attendant consequences for the tribes and their members, the states and their citizens, and the federal government."[1]

Indian law also includes the internal tribal laws that govern the daily life on the reservation. This "tribal law" may vary from oral sources to written codes derived from non-Indian materials. These codes are often ephemeral, amended

1 William C. Canby, Jr., *American Indian Law: In a Nutshell* (St. Paul, MN: West Publishing Co., 1981).

frequently and difficult to locate. Therefore, the tribal council itself should be consulted for all current materials. However, those tribal laws that have been published or microformed can be used as a source of "Indian legal history."

Arizona has a wealth of Native American traditions. The tribes found within this state are many and include Ak-Chin, Yavapai-Apache, Cocopah Colorado River, White Mountain Apache, Mohave-Apache, Fort Mojave, Quechan, Gila River, Havasupai, Hopi, Hualapai, Kaibab-Paiute, Navajo, Pascua-Yaqui, San Juan Southern Paiute, Salt River Pima-Maricopa, San Carlos Apache, Tohono O'odham, Tonto Apache, and Yavapai-Prescott. In addition, many Arizona attorneys find that their practice includes Native American issues: from questions of mineral and water rights to land claims and lease law. This selective bibliography will hopefully serve as an introductory guide to relevant sources in this area. It is by no means all inclusive.

B. Bibliographies

Dupont, Jerry, comp. and ed. *Native American Collection: A Bibliography Describing the Microfiche Collection Assembled and Marketed by the Law Library Microform Consortium.* LLMC Bibliography Services #3. Honolulu, HA: The Consortium, 1990. Entries are arranged by form and include government, state and legal documents, treaties, reference sources,etc. Microfiche copies are available for each title listed. In addition, there is a comprehensive index.

Fausett, Rory SnowArrow, and Judith V. Royster, "Courts and Indians: Sixty-five Years of Legal Analysis: Bibliography of Periodical Articles Relating to Native American Law, 1922-1986." *Legal Reference Services Quarterly* 7 (Summer/Fall/Winter 1987): 107-129.

National Indian Law Association. *A Bibliography of Selected Areas of Federal Indian Law.* Compiled by National Indian Law Library, Native American Rights Fund. Boulder, CO: The Fund, 1986.

National Indian Law Library Catalogue: An Index to Indian Legal Materials and Resources. 1982 Cumulative ed. Boulder, CO: Native American Rights Fund, 1982.

Sabatini, Joseph D., comp. *American Indian Law: A Bibliography of Books, Law Review Articles, and Indian Periodicals.* [Albuquerque,] NM: American Indian Law Center, 1973.

Scott, Cynthia Rixey. "Federal Indian Law: A Selected Bibliography Primarily 1987- Date [1989]. *SWALL Bulletin* 21, no. 1 (September 1989): 18-31.

C. Periodicals And Newsletters

*American Indian Journal.*Vienna, VA: Institute for the Development of Indian Law, 1975 - . quarterly . Formed by the union of the *Education Journal of the Institute for the Development of Indian Law* and *Institute for the Develop-*

ment of Indian Law Legislative Review. Monthly from 1975-82. Quarterly from 1986 to date.

American Indian Law Review. Norman, OK: University of Oklahoma College of Law, 1973 - semi-annual.

American Indian Report. Springfield, VA: Falmouth Institute, 1985 - monthly.

Indian Law Reporter. Washington, D.C.: American Indian Lawyer Training Program, 1974 - monthly.

D. Primary Sources: Tribal Codes And Treaties

Ak-Chin Indian Community, Route 2, Box 27, Maricopa, AZ 85239, (602) 568-2227. In Phoenix: (602) 254-3575. There is no current published code. To request copies of tribal code sections, contact the Secretary-Treasurer.

Ak-Chin Community, *Law and Order Code of the Maricopa Ak-Chin Indian Community, Arizona.* Burton G. Hirsch, preparer. [Phoenix?] AZ: The Community, 1975.

Colorado River Indian Tribes, Route 1, Box 23-B, Parker, AZ 85344. Word Processing: (602) 669-9211 ex. 290. The most recent Law and Order Code can be obtained from the tribe. Send a request on letterhead. The tribe will also photocopy sections of the code.

Colorado River Indian Tribes. *Constitution, By-Laws, and Ordinances of the Colorado River Reservation, Arizona and California.* Lawrence, KS: Haskell, 1947. Includes Indian reorganization act, law and order code, land code and tribal ordinances.

Colorado River Indian Tribes. *Ordinance No. 26 Law and Order Code.* [?]: The Tribe, 1974. Includes Constitution and ByLaws.

Havasupai Tribal Council, P.O. Box 10, Supai, AZ 86435, (602) 448-2731. Their most recent tribal code is not published. Photocopies will generally not be provided.

Havasupai Tribe. *Havasupai: Tribal Code.* Supai, AZ: Havasupai Tribal Council, 1978.

Johnson, Ralph W., ed. *Indian Tribal Codes: A Microfiche Collection of Indian Tribal Codes.* Seattle, WA: Marian Gould Gallager Law Library, University of Washington School of Law, 981. 195 microfiche (with manual). Sixty-nine Tribal Codes are included within this collection.

Johnson, Ralph W., ed. *Indian Tribal Codes: A Microfiche Collection of Indian Tribal Codes,* 2d ed. Seattle, WA:Marian Gould Gallager Law Library, University of Washington School of Law, 1988. 246 microfiche (with manual). Codes of constitutions of 56 American Indian tribes are included within this collection. This edition updates the 1981 version, but is not a replacement. There is an index available.

Kappler, Charles J. *Indian Treaties, 1778-1883.* N.Y., NY:Interland Pub., 1975. Reprint of 1904 edition.

The Navajo Tribe, P.O. Box 308, Window Rock, AZ 86515, (602) 871-6933.

Navajo Tribe: *Navajo Tribal Code.* 3d ed. Edited by the Equity Publishing Corp. Orford, NH: The Corp., 1978. 4 v. (Latest supplement in 1985). This is the most recently published edition of the code. A new edition is forthcoming.

Navajo Tribe. *Navajo Tribal Code.* 2d ed. Orford, NH: The Equity Publishing Corp., 1969.

Navajo Tribe. *Navajo Tribal Code.* Orford, NH: Equity Publishing Corp., 1962. 2v.

Navajo Tribe. *Navajo Court Rules.* 3d ed. [Window Rock,AZ]: Judicial Branch of the Navajo Nation, 1978.

Navajo Tribal Council. *Navajo Uniform Commercial Code.* [Window Rock, AZ]: The Council, 1986.

Pascua-Yaqui Tribe, 7475 S. Camino De Oeste, Tucson, AZ 85746, (602) 883-2838. The current *Law and Order Code* is available from the Secretary. Send a request on letterhead. Photocopying of specific sections is not provided.

Pascua-Yaqui Tribe. *Pascua-Yaqui Tribe Ordinance No.5 (interim): Civil and Criminal Law and Order Code Tucson, Arizona. Enacted 1982.* Edited by James T. Trant. Tucson, AZ: The Tribe, [1984?].

Salt River Pima-Maricopa Indian Community, Route 1, Box 216, Scottsdale, AZ 85256, (602) 941-7277. The most recent code of ordinances is available. Send request on letterhead. Photocopying of specific sections is not provided.

Salt River Pima-Maricopa Indian Community *Code of Ordinances of the Salt River Pima-Maricopa Indian Community.* Tallahassee, FL: Municipal Code Corp.,1981- . (Supp. #4, April 1989).

Salt River Pima-Maricopa Indian Community. *Ordinance No. 1 Revised: Law and Order Code of the Salt River Pima-Maricopa County Arizona.* [?]: [The Tribe?] [1966?].

Salt River Pima-Maricopa Indian Community. *Salt River Pima-Maricopa Indian Community Council Law and Orde Code.* [?, AZ]: The Community, 1976.

White Mountain Apache Tribe, P.O. Box 700, Whiteriver, AZ 85941, (602) 338-4346 ex. 210. The current Law and Order Code can be purchased from the tribe. Send requests on letterhead. Photocopying of specific sections is also available.

Law and Order Code: White Mountain Tribe. Whiteriver, AZ: White Mountain Apache Indian Tribe,1987. 2v. Contents include codes in the following areas: Business, Criminal, Domestic Relations, Education, Game and Fish, Government, Health and Safety, Housing and Construction, Juvenile, Labor, Livestock, Probate and Tax.

White Mountain Apache Indian Tribe. *Law and Order Code of the White Mountain Apache Tribe.* Whiteriver, AZ: The Tribe, [1974?].

White Mountain Apache Indian Tribe. [*White Mountain Apache Tribal Code.*][Whiteriver, AZ: The Tribe, 1988?]. 1v. Contents include codes in the following areas: Housing and Construction, Judicial, Juvenile, Labor, Land, Livestock, Probate, Tax, and Game and Fish. The Rules of Procedure, Formal Rules of Civil Procedure, Rules of Criminal Procedure and Rules of Appellate Procedure are also provided.

E. Reference Sources

Arizona Community Profiles. Phoenix, AZ: Economic Research Division, Arizona Department of Commerce, 1990. looseleaf. annual. Arizona Indian community profiles are included within this volume. The profiles contain a brief description of the community, economic activities, and various statistical information.

Indian Tribes as Sovereign Governments: A Sourcebook on Federal-Tribal History, Law, and Policy. Edited by Charles F. Wilkinson and Christine L. Miklas. Oakland, CA: AIRI Press, 1988.

Ortiz, Alfonso, ed. *Handbook of North American Indians.* Vol. 9, *Southwest.* Washington, D.C.: National Museum of Natural History, Smithsonian Institution, 1979. Includes chapters on the Pueblo peoples.

Ortiz, Alfonso, ed. *Handbook of North American Indians*. Vol. 10, *Southwest.* Washington, D.C.: National Museum of Natural History, Smithsonian Institution, 1983. Chapters are included on non-Pueblo peoples.

Tribal Directory. 19th ed. Phoenix, AZ: Arizona Commission of Indian Affairs, 1990. annual. Address and phone numbers for all Arizona tribes, various federal and state agencies, and Indian associations.

F. Resource Centers

College of Law Library
Arizona State University
Tempe, AZ 85287
(602) 965-6141

The library contains a collection of materials on Southwest Indian law.

College of Law Library
University of Arizona
Tucson, AZ 85721
(602) 621-5455

Information can be found on Federal Indian law, Indian tribal laws and tribal constitutions. The Native American Microfiche Collection is also available.

Hayden Library
Arizona State University
Tempe, AZ 85287
(602) 965-3390

Hayden Library's online catalog (CARL) contains the Labriola National American Indian Data Center (see Chapter 10 for information on dial access). The NIEC (National Indian Clearinghouse Resource) Directory is included providing lists of Native American library collections, and college level courses on Native American Indian issues.

National Indian Rights Fund
National Indian Law Library
1522 Broadway,
Boulder, CO 80302
(303) 447-8760

Scottsdale Community College Library
9000 E. Chaparral Rd.
Scottsdale, AZ 85256
(602) 423-6650

Their collection includes information on tribal government and Indians of the Southwest.

G. Secondary Sources

Canby, William J. *American Indian Law in a Nutshell.* 2d ed. St. Paul, MN: West Pub. Co., 1988.

Cohen, Felix S. *Felix S. Cohen's Handbook of Federal Indian Law.* 1982 ed. Edited by Rennard Strickland and Charles F. Wilkinson. Charlottesville, VA: Michie Bobbs-Merrill, 1982.

Goodman, James Marion. *The Navajo Atlas: Environments, Resources, People, and History of the Dine Bikeyeh.* Norman, OK: University of Oklahoma Press, 1982.

Getches, David H. and Charles F. Wilkinson. *Cases and Materials on Federal Indian Law.* 2d ed. St. Paul, MN: West Publishing Co., 1986.

Navajo Times: The Newspaper of the Navajo People. Window Rock, Navajo Nation, [AZ]: Navajo Tribe, 1987 - weekly. *The Navajo Times* is the only legal publication on the Navajo Reservation qualified to publish legal notices.

Price, Monroe Edwin and Robert N. Clinton. *Law and the American Indian: Readings, Notes, and Cases.* 2d ed. Charlottesville, VA: Michie Co., 1983.

Appendix A

Legal Resource Centers

Kathy Shimpock-Vieweg

It has often been said that the best resource for legal research is a knowledgeable person. With that in mind, the following listing of libraries, courts, governmental offices, information brokers, and organizations has been compiled to bring the researcher closer to the source. This list is by no means all inclusive; it emphasizes, however, the major "resource centers" in the Phoenix and Tucson areas.[1]

1 Many thanks to Shirley Macias, from O'Connor, Cavanagh, Anderson, Westover, Killingsworth & Beshears, who compiled most of this information. See also, the most recent *PAALL* (Phoenix Area Association of Law Libraries) *Directory,* and the *Directory of Special Libraries in Arizona* issued by the Arizona Chapter of the Special Libraries Association.

A. Phoenix Area Centers

1. *Arizona State Libraries*

Research Division of the Arizona Department of Library, Archives and Public Records

1700 W Washington
State Capitol, 3rd Floor
Phoenix, AZ 85007
(602) 542-3701
FAX: (602) 542-4400

Borrowing/Access: Open to the Public. Borrowing limited to members of the Arizona State Bar.

Hours: Monday-Friday: 8 am - 5 pm, Saturday, Sunday: closed

Circulation: Items non-circulating and those on reference or reserve cannot be checked out.

Special Collections: Arizona Collections - 3rd floor; Federal Documents - 3rd floor; State Documents - 3rd floor; Maps - 3rd floor. Law collection has been recently divided between this facility and the State Law Library. Contact the library for further information.

Photocopy Service: Self copy. Pay for copies after they have been made.

Online Services: The library has a public computer terminal and access to various databases including: WESTLAW, VU/TEXT, ALIS (Arizona Legislative Information System), EPIC, Economic Bulletin Board, ELSS, Supreme Court Today, Wilsonline, DIALOG and LEGI-SLATE. The library staff performs all online searches. Charges are set by the database vendors. EPIC searches are free, as are the first 30 pages of LEGI-SLATE. As of this writing, some of these databases may be moved to the State Law Library. Contact the library for further information.

Parking: Parking is free. Visitor parking is available on 18th Avenue between Washington and Jefferson Streets. There is also a parking lot on 17th Avenue between Adams and Jefferson Streets.

Arizona State Law Library

1501 W. Washington
Phoenix, AZ 85007
(602) 542- 5297

Borrowing/Access: Open to the Public. Borrowing limited to members of the Arizona State Bar.

Hours: Monday-Friday: 8 am - 5 pm; Saturday, Sunday - closed

Circulation: Items marked non-circulating and those on reference or reserve cannot be checked out.

Special Collections: Law collection has been recently divided between this facility and the Research Division. Contact the library for further information.

Photocopy Services: Self copy.

Online Services: The library has access to various databases including WESTLAW, LEXIS, VU/TEXT, ALIS (Arizona Legislative Information System), EPIC, Economic Bulletin Board, ELSS, Supreme Court Today, Wilsonline, DIALOG and LEGI-SLATE. The library staff performs all online searches. Charges are set by the database vendors. Contact the library for further information.

Parking: There is a parking lot on 15th Avenue and Washington. Metered parking is also available on Jefferson Street. Park only in visitor lots.

2. *Arizona State and Federal Courts*

Arizona Supreme Court
1501 W. Washington
Phoenix, AZ 85007
(602) 542-4536
Hours: Monday-Friday: 8 am - 5 pm

Arizona Court of Appeals - Division One
1501 W. Washington
Phoenix, AZ 85007
(602) 542-4821
Hours: Monday-Friday: 8 am - 5 pm

Maricopa County Superior Court
101/201 W. Jefferson
Phoenix, AZ 85003
(602) 506-3369
Hours: Monday-Friday: 8 am - 5 pm

Southeast Judicial District
222 E. Javelina Drive
Mesa, AZ 85210
(602) 506-2086

Juvenile Court, Durango Center
3215 W. Durango
Phoenix, AZ 85009
(602) 506-4011

Juvenile Court, Southeast Facility
1810 South Lewis Street
Mesa, AZ 85210
(602) 506-2800

Phoenix Municipal Court
Minor Traffic Division
12 North Fourth Avenue
Phoenix, AZ 85003
(602) 262-6421
Hours: Monday-Friday: 8 am - 4:30 pm
Criminal Division
455 N. Fifth Street
Phoenix, AZ 85003
(602) 262-1834
Hours: Monday-Friday: 8 am - 5 pm

U.S. Bankruptcy Court
230 N. First Avenue
Phoenix, AZ 85025
Clerk: (602) 379-6965
(See Chapter 10 for information regarding electronic access).

U.S. District Court
District of Arizona
230 N. First Avenue
Phoenix, AZ 85025
Clerk: (602) 379-3342
(See Chapter 10 for information regarding electronic access).

U. S. Ninth Circuit Court of Appeals
230 N. First Avenue
Phoenix, AZ 85025
Clerk: P.O. Box 547
San Francisco, CA 94101
(415) 556-6705
(See Chapter 10 for information regarding electronic access).

3. *Bar Associations*

Maricopa County Bar Association
333 W. Roosevelt Street
Phoenix, AZ 85003
(602) 257-4200

State Bar of Arizona
363 N. First Avenue
Phoenix, AZ 85003
(602) 252-4804

There are also an East Valley Bar Association, a Scottsdale Bar Association, and a West Maricopa Bar Association. Contact the State Bar for the name and address of the current president.

4. *Document Retrieval Services*[2]

BNA Plus
The Bureau of National Affairs, Inc.
1231 25th Street, N.W.
Washington, D.C. 20037
(202) 452-4323/1-800-452-7773

State and Federal Court Decisions, Regulations, Administrative Decisions, Studies, Reports, Attorney General Opinions, etc.

Capitol Document Services
826 N. Third Avenue
Phoenix, AZ 85003
(602) 254-4489

UCC Lien Searches, Corporate Document Filings.

Federal Document Retrieval
514 C Street, N.E.
Washington, D.C. 20002
(202) 628-2229

Court documents, state legislative materials, state banking and securities filings, state and local administrative documents, etc. This company is a subsidiary of Disclosure, a retrieval service for SEC filings.
(213) 934-8313 Los Angeles office

LEXDOC
Mead Data Central
234 North Central Avenue, Suite 113
Phoenix, AZ 85004
(602) 256-0454/1-800-634-9738

LEXIS document public record retrieval service, includes corporate documents, UCC liens and name reservation filings.

National Document Retrieval
P.O. Box 25186
Phoenix, AZ 85002
(602) 258-UCC3/1-800-933-UCC3
FAX: (602) 243-1589

UCC information: search and filing

2 This listing is in no way an endorsement of these services, nor represents the quality of work performed.

Search West
Public Records Research
P.O. Box 903
Sacramento, CA 95804
(916) 447-6385/1-800-221-5659
UCC search and filings, corporate filings and retrieval, real property searches, motor vehicle searches.

5. *Federal Libraries*

U.S. Courts Law Library
U.S. Courthouse, Rm 6434
230 N. First Avenue
Phoenix, AZ 85025
(602) 379-3879
FAX: (602) 261-3076

Borrowing/Access: Open to the Public for depository materials.

Hours: Monday-Friday: 7 am - 5 pm;

Circulation: Non-circulating. Interlibrary loan available only for Phoenix area and subject to immediate recall.

Photocopy Services: Self copying.

Parking: Pay public parking is available beneath Pioneer Park on Washington Street and First Avenue.

6. *Information Brokers (contact individual brokers for fees)*[3]

American Information Network
165 E. Southern Avenue, Suite 101
Mesa, AZ 85210
(602) 844-7559
FAX: (602) 869-6445
For profit research, online searches and investigations.

FIRST (Fee-Based Information and Research Service Team)
Arizona State University
Tempe, AZ 85287-1006
(602) 965-4636
FAX: (602) 965-7690
Online searches, custom research, document delivery, current awareness updates, citation verification and translations.

3 See note 2 above.

Specialty Research
425 E. LaJolla Drive
Tempe, AZ 85282-5327
(602) 966-8831
For profit research, online searches.

7. *Maricopa County Libraries*

Maricopa County Law Library
East Court Building, 2nd Floor
101 West Jefferson
Phoenix, AZ 85003
(602) 506-3461
FAX: (602) 506-3677

Borrowing/Access: Open to the Public. Borrowing limited to members of the Arizona State Bar.

Hours: Monday-Friday: 8 am - 6 pm; Saturday: 9 am - 5 pm; Sunday: closed. Note: On Saturdays a building pass is needed to enter the Courthouse. Passes may be obtained at the library during regular hours or acquired through the Security Guard at the County Parking Garage on Madison Avenue (between First and Third Avenues). The guard shack is located at the entrance to the garage. The Guard will hold your driver's license in exchange for a pass. After signing in, you may enter the Courthouse through the Madison Avenue entrance, taking the elevators to the Lower Level. From there, the signs will direct you to the law library.

Circulation: Items marked non-circulating cannot be checked out. These include indexes, digests, city codes, many looseleaf services and books on Reserve or Reference.

Special Collections: Arizona materials including city codes; U.S. and State laws (all 50); and standard legal materials, with an emphasis on law office management, basic medical reference books, and Native American legal materials.

Photocopy Services: Self copy. Change is available at the circulation desk.

Online Services: The library has a public computer terminal and access to three databases: WESTLAW, AUTOCITE and DIALOG. Charges are set by the database vendors. The library staff provides training and research assistance. Call for an appointment.

Maricopa County Law Library
Southeast Branch
222 E. Javelina Drive
Mesa, AZ 85210
(602) 506-2065
FAX: (602) 506-2991

Borrowing/Access: Open to the Public. Borrowing limited to members of the Arizona State Bar.

Hours: Monday-Friday: 8 am - 5 pm; Saturday, Sunday: closed

Circulation: Items marked non-circulating cannot be checked out.

Photocopy/Fax Services: Self copy. Fax charges vary with distance.

8. *Miscellaneous Information Sources*

Phoenix City Government
City Clerk Department
251 W. Washington Street
Phoenix, AZ 85003
Information: (602) 262-6011

The League of Arizona Cities and Towns
1820 W. Washington Street
Phoenix, AZ 85007
(602) 258-5786
FAX: (602) 253-3874

Mesa Chamber of Commerce
120 N. Center Street
Mesa, AZ 85201
(602) 969-1307

Phoenix Chamber of Commerce
34 N. Monroe Street
Phoenix, AZ 85003
(602) 254-5521

Tempe Chamber of Commerce
60 E. Fifth Street
Tempe, AZ 85281
(602) 967-7891

9. *Public Libraries*

Phoenix Public Library

Central Library
12 E. McDowell Road
Phoenix, AZ 85004
(602) 262-4636 (602) 262-4766
FAX: (602) 495-5841

Borrowing/Access: Open to the public. Business cards are available. Send request on letterhead. For an individual card, bring a photo i.d. with current address. There is a charge for non-Maricopa County residents.

Hours: Monday-Wednesday: 9 am - 9 pm; Thursday-Saturday: 9 am - 6 pm; Sunday: 1 pm - 5 pm

Circulation: Primarily monographs. Items marked non-circulating can not be checked out.

Special Collections: Business, Southwest history, federal depository, Arizona.

Photocopy Services: Self copy.

Online Services: DIALOG, VU/TEXT searches are available.

Parking: At facility.

10. State Departments and Agencies

Arizona Commission on Uniform State Laws
2 North Central, Suite 2200
Scottsdale, AZ 85004-2390
James M. Bush, Commissioner (602) 257-5767
Address and message number at Fennemore, Craig

Arizona Criminal Justice Commission
1700 N. 7th Avenue, Suite 250
Phoenix, AZ 85007
(602) 255-1928

Arizona Department of Revenue
1600 W. Monroe
Phoenix, AZ 85007
(602) 542-3572

Banking Department
Century Plaza, Suite 815
3225 N. Central
Phoenix, AZ 85012
(602) 255-4421

Board of Medical Examiners
2001 W. Camelback, Suite 300
Phoenix, AZ 85015
(602) 255-3751
Only written requests are taken for BOMEX transcripts.

Corporation Commission
1200 W. Washington Street
Phoenix, AZ 85007
(602) 542-3935
No phone requests taken.

Department of Building and Fire Safety
701 E. Jefferson Street, Suite 200
Phoenix, AZ 85034
(602) 255-4072

Department of Economic Security
1717 W. Jefferson
Phoenix, AZ 85007
(602) 542-4791
Library: (602) 542-4777

Department of Environmental Quality
2005 N. Central
Phoenix, AZ 85004
(602) 257-2300

Department of Health Services
1740 W. Adams
Phoenix, AZ 85007
Library: (602) 542-1013
Vital Records: (602) 542-1084

Department of Transportation
206 S. 17th Avenue
Phoenix, AZ 85007
(602) 255-7011
Highway Division: (602) 255-7391
MVD: (602) 255-8152
Transportation Planning Div.: (602) 255-7431

Governor, Office of
1700 W. Washington, 9th Floor
Phoenix, AZ 85007
(602) 542-4331

Industrial Commission
800 W. Washington
Phoenix, AZ 85007
Labor Dept.: (602) 542-4515
Safety Dept.: (602) 542-5795
Claims Dept.: (602) 542-4661
Chief Counsel: (602) 542-5781

Insurance Department
3030 N. Third Street, Suite 1100
Phoenix, AZ 85012
(602) 255-5400

Legislative Council
State Capitol
1700 W. Washington, Suite 100
Phoenix, AZ 85007
(602) 542-4236

Legislature (Senate and House)
1700 W. Washington Street
Phoenix, AZ 85007
Senate Info: (602) 542-3559
House Info: (602) 542-4221

Office of Attorney General
1275 W. Washington Street
Phoenix, AZ 85007
Info: (602) 542-5025
Civil Division
Criminal Division
Human Services Division

Real Estate Department
202 E. Earll Drive, 4th Floor
Phoenix, AZ 85012
(602) 255-4345

Secretary of State
State Capitol, West Wing
1700 W. Washington, 7th Floor
Phoenix, AZ 85007
(602) 542-4285
FAX: (602) 542-6172
Publications: (602) 542-6169
Trade Names/Limited Partnerships: (602)542-6187
UCC: (602) 542-6178

11. University Libraries

Arizona State University
College of Law Library
Tempe, AZ 85287-0504
(602) 965-6141
FAX: (602) 965-2427

Borrowing/Access: Open to the Public. Need valid Arizona driver's license to purchase ASU library borrowing card. Must be over 21 years of age.

Hours: Varies somewhat with the academic year. In general, Monday-Wednesday: 7 am - 12 am; Thursday, Friday: 7 am - 10 pm; Saturday: 8 am - 10 pm; Sunday: 10 am -12 am

Circulation: Primarily treatises. Items marked non-circulating cannot be checked out.

Special Collections: Mexican, Native American, technology, selected government depository, Anglo-American law.

Photocopy Service: Self copy. Copy card can be purchased at Hayden Library.

Online Service: No online services are available to the public, with the exception of the ASU Online Catalog. (See entry under ASU First.) Remote access of their "card catalog" is available. (See Chapter 10 for more information.) The Library has the CD-ROM for *Legaltract.*

Parking: Visitor parking is available across from the law school on McAllister Avenue. After 7 p.m. all parking lots are free.

Arizona State University
Government Documents
Hayden Library - 3rd Floor
Tempe, AZ 85237-0706
(602) 965-3390

Borrowing/Access: Open to the public. Need valid Arizona driver's license to purchase ASU library borrowing card.

Hours: Varies somewhat with the academic year. In general, the hours are as follows:

	Reference	*Access*
Monday-Thursday:	8 am - 10 pm	7 am - 12 am
Friday:	8 am - 5 pm	7 am - 5 pm
Saturday:	10 am - 5 pm	9 am - 5 pm
Sunday:	1 pm - 5 pm	12 pm - 12 am

Circulation: Items marked non-circulating cannot be checked out.

Special Collection: Government Depository

Photocopy Services: Self copying. Copy card can be purchased at Hayden Library.

Online Service: No online services are available with the exception of the ASU Online Catalog. (See entry for ASU First.) Remote access of their "card catalog" is available. (See Chapter 10 for more information.)

Parking: Various visitor parking lots are located on the ASU campus. The closest may be at Parking Structure #1, north of Apache Boulevard, or next to the ASU Bookstore off Orange Street. After 7 p.m. all parking lots are free.

Arizona State University
Hayden Library
Arizona State University
Tempe, AZ 85287-0706
(602) 965-6164

Borrowing/Access: Open to the public. Need valid Arizona driver's license to purchase ASU borrowing card.

Hours: Varies somewhat with the academic year. In general, Monday-Thursday: 7 am - 12 am; Friday: 7 am - 5 pm; Saturday: 9 am - 5 pm; Sunday: 12 pm - 12 am

Circulation: Primarily monographs. Items marked non-circulating, reference materials and periodicals can not be checked out.

Special Collections: Arizona and Southwest history, Mexican-Americans in the U.S., humanities, business, social sciences.

Photocopy Service: Copy Center service is located in periodical section. Self copying is also available. There are change machines.

Online Services: There are no online services available to the public with the exception of the ASU Online Catalog. (See entry for ASU First.) These terminals are located throughout Hayden Library. Remote access of their "card catalog" is available. (See Chapter 10 for more information.) However, the Machine-Assisted Reference Service (M.A.R.S.) allows users to access free bibliographic information on CD-ROM. Services include *Newsbank, ABI/Inform On Disc, Periodical Abstracts On Disc, ERIC, PsychLit, CIRR* and *Dissertations on Disc*. Sign up in person to use services. Reference assistance is available Monday - Friday 10 am - 5 pm.

Parking: Various visitor parking lots are located on the ASU campus. The closest may be at Parking Structure #1, north of Apache Boulevard, or next to the ASU Bookstore off Orange Street. After 7 p.m. all parking lots are free.

Arizona State University

Daniel E. Noble Science and Engineering Library
Tempe, AZ 85287-0706
(602) 965-7607

Borrowing/Access: Open to the public. Need valid Arizona driver's license to purchase ASU library borrowing card. Must be over 21 years of age.

Hours: Varies somewhat with the academic year. In general, Monday - Thursday: 7 am - 9 pm; Friday - Saturday: 9 am - 8 pm; Sunday: 10 am - 12 am

Circulation: Primarily monographs. Reference, materials and periodicals are non-circulating.

Special Collections: U.S. Patent Depository, Map Collection, and Solar Energy Collection, engineering, physical and life sciences, mathematics, nursing and health sciences, agriculture and geography.

Photocopy Services: There is a copy service. Self copying is also available. There are change machines.

Online Services: There are no online services available to the public with the exception of the ASU Online Catalog (See entry for ASU First.) Remote access of their "card catalog" is available. (See Chapter 10 for more information.) CD-ROM is available for free bibliographic searches on *Medline, BioAbstracts, Compindex* and *Cassis.*

Arizona State University

Howe Architecture Library, 1st Floor
Tempe, AZ 85287-0504
(Located at University and Forest Streets, one block east of Mill Avenue)
(602) 965-6400

Borrowing/Access: Open to the public. Need valid Arizona driver's license to purchase ASU borrowing card.

Hours: Varies somewhat with the academic year. In general, Monday - Thursday: 8 am - 10 pm; Friday: 8 am - 5 pm; Saturday: 8 am - 5 pm; Sunday: 2 pm - 10 pm

Circulation: Items marked non-circulating, reference, periodicals or over-sized items cannot be checked out.

Special Collections: Architecture, urban design, industrial design, Paolo Soleri Archives, Frank Lloyd Wright.

Photocopy Services: Self copying. There is a dollar bill changer.

Online Services: No online services are available to the public with the exception of the ASU Online Catalog. (See entry under ASU First.) Remote access of their "card catalog" is available. (See Chapter 10 for more information.)

Parking: Meter parking is available on Myrtle Street. The Parking Structure can be used after 7 p.m. and on weekends only. Do not park at the Tempe Center: Cars will be towed.

Arizona State University West Campus

Fletcher Library
4701 W. Thunderbird Rd.
Phoenix, AZ 85069-7100
(602) 543-8501
FAX: (602) 543-8521
(Located at 51st Avenue and Thunderbird)

Borrowing/Access: Open to the public. Need valid Arizona driver's license to purchase ASU borrowing card.

Hours: Varies somewhat with the academic year. In general, Monday - Thursday: 8 am - 10 pm; Friday: 8 am - 5 pm; Saturday: 9 am - 5 pm; Sunday: 11 am - 9 pm

Circulation: Items marked non-circulating, reference, periodicals and some government documents may not be checked out.

Photocopy Services: There is a copy service. Self copying is also available. Copy card can be purchased from copy service.

Online Services: There are no online services available to the public with the exception of the ASU Online Catalog. (See entry for ASU First.) Remote access of their "card catalog" is available. (See Chapter 10 for more information.) CD-ROM is available for free bibliographic searches on *ERIC, PsychLit, Socio/File, ABI/Inform, Newspapers Abstracts, Medline, PAS* and *Wilson* Indexes.

Parking: Visitor Parking is available. Call for location.

B. Tucson Area Centers

1. *Arizona State and Federal Courts*

Pima County Superior Court
110 W. Congress
Tucson, AZ 85701
(602) 740-8351
Hours: Monday-Friday: 8 am - 5 pm

Court of Appeals - Division Two
416 W. Congress
Tucson, AZ 85701-1374
(602) 628-1084
Hours: Monday - Friday: 8 am - 5 pm

U.S. Bankruptcy Court
La Placita Village
110 S. Church Avenue
Tucson, AZ 85701
Clerk: (602) 629-6304
(See Chapter 10 for information regarding electronic access.)

U.S. District Court
District of Arizona
55 E. Broadway Blvd.
Tucson, AZ 85701
Civil: (602) 629-6559
Criminal: (602) 629-6034
(See Chapter 10 for information regarding electronic access.)

Tucson City Court
103 E. Alameda
Tucson, AZ 85701
(602) 791-4581/(602) 791-4216

2. *Bar Associations*

Pima County Bar Association
177 N. Church Avenue
Tucson, AZ 85701
(602) 623-8258

State Bar of Arizona
177 N. Church Avenue, Suite 101
Tucson, AZ 85701-1117
(602) 623-8258
FAX: (602) 623-8102

3. *Federal Libraries*

U.S. Courts Law Library

U.S. Courthouse, Room 220
55 E. Broadway
Tucson, AZ 85701
(602) 670-6552
FAX: (602) 670-6117

Borrowing/Access: All members of the federal bar.

Hours: Monday - Friday: 8 am - 12 pm; 1 pm - 4:30 pm

Circulation: Collection is non-circulating.

Photocopy Services: Special arrangements must be made. The machine is not coin or card operated.

Parking: Parking lots are located across the street from the Courthouse and on Alameda.

4. *Pima County Libraries*

Pima County Law Library

Superior Courts Bldg., Room 256
110 West Congress
Tucson, AZ 85716
(602) 740-8456

Borrowing/Access: All members of the Arizona State Bar.

Hours: Monday - Friday: 8 am - 5 pm

Circulation: Part of the collection circulates to Pima County Bar Association. Items marked non-circulating cannot be checked out.

Photocopy Services: Photocopy machine is available. There is no change machine and the staff does not make change.

Parking: Across from Citibank, Tucson Office.

5. *Miscellaneous Information Sources:*

Tucson Metropolitan Chamber of Commerce
465 W. Saint Mary's Road
Tucson, AZ 85701
(602) 792-1212

6. *Public Libraries*

Tucson Public Library

Main Library
200 S. Sixth Avenue
P.O. Box 27470
Tucson, AZ 85726-7470
(602) 791-4010; (602) 791-4393

Borrowing/Access: Open to the public. Borrowing cards limited to Pima County residents.

Hours: Varies. Call for hours.

Circulation: Items marked reference or non-circulating cannot be checked out.

Special Collections: City of Tucson depository, government documents, Arizona collection.

Photocopy Service: Self copying. Change machines. Can also purchase a copy card.

Online Services: Need to make request in person. It will make up to one week for results. *Infotrac* is available on CD-ROM for free searches.

Parking: There is underground parking. Up to two hours of parking will be validated.

7. *University Libraries*

University of Arizona

Arizona Health Center Library
1501 N. Campbell, Room 3404
Tucson, AZ 85724
(602) 626-6125/(602) 626-3510
FAX: (602) 626-2831

Borrowing/Access: Open to public. Must bring a letter, on letterhead and apply at the Loan Desk for privileges.

Hours: Open 24 hours daily.

Circulation: Journals published within the last ten years do not circulate. Interlibrary loan requests are filled both in-state and out-of-state. Requests made on standard American Library Association ILL (Interlibrary Loan) forms or through E-Mail, DOCLINE, or OCLC.

Special Collections: Medicine, nursing, pharmacy.

Photocopy Services: Self copying. Can purchase a photocopy card.

Online Service: There is an on-line catalog (LS/2000). Remote access of this "card catalog" is available. (See Chapter 10 for more information.) Other online searches can be performed for a fee. Databases include NLM, BRS, and DIALOG. Call ahead to reserve time. Searches are performed on a first-come, first-served basis. CD-ROM searches, however, are free. Services include *Medline,* and *Health Planning and Administration,* etc. Discs go back to 1982. Training classes are held weekly. Sign up to use services for 1/2 hour of time.

Parking: Pay parking lots at the hospital parking garage, and at the parking garage south of the hospital.

University of Arizona
College of Architecture Library
Tucson, AZ 85721
(602) 621-2498

Borrowing/Access: Open to the public. Need valid Arizona driver's license to purchase borrowing card.

Hours: Varies with academic year. In general, Monday - Thursday: 9 am - 9 pm; Friday: 9 am - 5 pm; Saturday - Sunday: 12 pm - 5 pm

Circulation: Only to U of A architecture majors and local registered architects.

Special Collections: Architecture, building technology.

Photocopy Services: Self copying.

Online Services: There is an on-line catalog (GEAC). (See Chapter 10 for information on remote access.)

Parking: There is a visitor parking lot behind the visitor center next to U of A Mall on Cherry Street.

University of Arizona Law Library
College of Law
Tucson, AZ 85721
(602) 621-1413
FAX: (602) 621-3138

Borrowing/Access: Open to the public.

Hours: Varies with the academic year. Reference Assistance: Monday - Friday: 8 am - 5:30 pm

Circulation: Non-circulating.

Special Collections: Community property, Mexican, Native American, Water.

Photocopy Services: Self copying. Coin and card operated.

Online Service: Remote access of their "card catalog" is available. (See Chapter 10 for more information.)

Parking: Paid parking on Park Avenue, west of the law library.

University of Arizona
Government Documents Department
Main Library, 3rd Floor
Tucson, AZ 85721
(602) 621-4871

Borrowing/Access: Open to the public. Need valid Arizona driver's license to purchase borrowing card.

Hours: Varies somewhat with the academic year. In general, Monday - Thursday: 8 am - 5 pm; Friday: 8 am - 5 pm; Saturday: 10 am - 6 pm; Sunday: 1 pm - 5 pm

Circulation: Non-circulating. Reference and unbound periodicals cannot be checked out.

Special Collections: U.S. Government Depository Library, state documents.

Photocopy Services: There is a copy service in the main library. Self copying is also available.

Online Services: There is an on-line catalog (GEAC). (See Chapter 10 for information on remote access.) CD-ROM is available for free bibliographic searches on the *Government Monthly Catalog, City and County Data Book, United Nations Documents* and the *Congressional Record.*

Parking: There is a pay parking lot east of the library on Cherry Street. It is free on Saturdays.

University of Arizona
Main Library
(Located at Cherry and Third Street)
Tucson, AZ 85721
(602) 621-6441

Borrowing/Access: Open to the public. Need valid Arizona driver's license to purchase borrowing card.

Hours: Varies with academic year. In general, Monday - Thursday: 7 am - 2 am; Friday: 7 am - 9 pm; Saturday: 9 am - 9 pm; Sunday: 10 am - 2 am

Circulation: Periodicals are non-circulating.

Special Collections: Rare books, Arizona publications, maps, educational media.

Photocopy Services: Self copying with coin operated machine. Copy center is also available.

Online Services: There is an on-line catalog (GEAC). (See Chapter 10 for information on remote access.) CD-ROM is available for free bibliographic searches on *Infotract, PsychLit, Socio/File, Newsbank,* and *UMI Dissertation.*

Parking: There is a visitor-parking lot behind the Visitor Center next to U of A Mall on Cherry Street.

University of Arizona
Science-Engineering Library
Tucson, AZ 85721
(602) 621-6384
FAX: (602) 621-4619

Borrowing/Access: Open to the public. Need valid Arizona driver's license to purchase borrowing card.

Hours: Varies with the academic year. In general, Monday - Thursday: 7 am - 2 am; Friday: 7 am - 9 pm; Saturday: 9 am - 9 pm; Sunday: 10 am - 2 am

Circulation: Reference materials and periodicals are non-circulating.

Special Collections: Engineering, technology, life and physical sciences, agriculture.

Online Services: There is an on-line catalog (SEL). (See Chapter 10 for information on remote access.) DIALOG searches are performed for a fee. CD-

ROM is available for free bibliographic searches in the areas of mathematics, engineering and water resources. Call ahead to reserve time.

Parking: There is a Visitor Parking lot behind the Visitor Center next to U of A Mall on Cherry Street.